Pearl Harbor

ALSO BY ROLAND H. WORTH, JR.,
AND FROM MCFARLAND

Biblical Studies on the Internet: A Resource Guide, 2d ed. (2008)

*Shapers of Early Christianity: 52 Biographies,
A.D. 100–400* (2007; paperback 2012)

Messiahs and Messianic Movements through 1899 (2005)

Congress Declares War: December 8–11, 1941 (2004)

*Alternative Lives of Jesus: Noncanonical Accounts
through the Early Middle Ages* (2003)

Biblical Studies on the Internet: A Resource Guide (2002)

World War II Resources on the Internet (2002)

*Secret Allies in the Pacific: Covert Intelligence and Code Breaking
Cooperation Between the United States, Great Britain, and
Other Nations Prior to the Attack on Pearl Harbor* (2001)

*Church, Monarch and Bible in Sixteenth Century England:
The Political Context of Biblical Translation* (2000)

*No Choice but War: The United States Embargo Against
Japan and the Eruption of War in the Pacific* (1995)

Bible Translations: A History Through Source Documents (1992)

Pearl Harbor

Selected Testimonies, Fully Indexed, from the Congressional Hearings (1945–1946) and Prior Investigations of the Events Leading Up to the Attack

ROLAND H. WORTH, JR.

McFarland & Company, Inc., Publishers
Jefferson, North Carolina, and London

Dedicated to my parents ROLAND H. WORTH, SR., and RUTH E. WORTH for all their love and kindnesses through these many, many years

---

The present work is a reprint of the library bound edition of Pearl Harbor : Selected Testimonies, Fully Indexed..., *first published in 1993 by McFarland.*

LIBRARY OF CONGRESS CATALOGUING-IN-PUBLICATION DATA

Worth, Roland H., Jr., 1943–
    Pearl Harbor : selected testimonies, fully indexed, from the Congressional Hearings (1945–1946) and prior investigations of the events leading up to the attack / by Roland H. Worth, Jr.
      p.   cm.
    Includes and index.

    ISBN 978-0-7864-7621-3
    softcover : acid free paper ∞

    1. Pearl Harbor (Hawaii), Attack on, 1941— Sources. I. Title.
D767.92W67 2013   940.54'26 — dc20   92-51102

BRITISH LIBRARY CATALOGUING DATA ARE AVAILABLE

© 1993 Roland H. Worth, Jr.. All rights reserved

No part of this book may be reproduced or transmitted in any form or by any means, electronic or mechanical, including photocopying or recording, or by any information storage and retrieval system, without permission in writing from the publisher.

On the cover: Admiral James O. Richardson, USN, takes the oath prior to giving testimony during a Congressional investigation of the Pearl Harbor attack, during World War II. Admiral Richardson was the Commander in Chief, United States Fleet, from January 1940 until February 1941.

Manufactured in the United States of America

McFarland & Company, Inc., Publishers
  Box 611, Jefferson, North Carolina 28640
  www.mcfarlandpub.com

CONTENTS

Introduction ix

Section One • The Final Steps to War

Countdown to Conflict: The View from the War Department 3
Henry L. Stimson, secretary of war / ARMY PEARL HARBOR BOARD

November 1941: The Intragovernmental Discussion of the
War Danger 20
Cordell Hull, secretary of state / JOINT CONGRESSIONAL INVESTIGATION

Was the American Note of November 26 an Ultimatum? 26
Joseph C. Grew, U.S. ambassador to Japan / JOINT CONGRESSIONAL INVESTIGATION

Section Two • Espionage

The Failure of American Espionage in Japan and Her
Possessions 35
Brigadier General Sherman Miles, acting assistant chief of staff (intelligence), War Department / ARMY PEARL HARBOR BOARD via CLARKE INVESTIGATION

The Effective Security Screen in Japan Itself 46
Joseph C. Grew, U.S. ambassador to Japan / JOINT CONGRESSIONAL INVESTIGATION

An Idle Tale That Later Became Reality: The January 1941
Tokyo Rumor of an Attack on Pearl Harbor 48
Joseph C. Grew, U.S. ambassador to Japan / JOINT CONGRESSIONAL INVESTIGATION

The Ease of Japanese Intelligence Gathering in Hawaii 53
George W. Bicknell, assistant G-2, Hawaiian Department, U.S. Army / JOINT CONGRESSIONAL INVESTIGATION

Navy/FBI Hostility Over Rival Hawaiian Wiretaps 62
Henry C. Clausen, member Army Pearl Harbor Board / JOINT CONGRESSIONAL INVESTIGATION

Section Three • *Radar: The Great Missed Opportunity*

Prior American and British Development of Radar 71
William E. G. Taylor, Navy adviser to Interceptor Command, Pearl Harbor / HART INQUIRY

The Problem-Laden Construction of the Hawaiian Radar System 84
Robert J. Fleming, Jr., Army supervisory officer for the planning and erection of the system / via JOINT CONGRESSIONAL INVESTIGATION

The Sighting of the Japanese Planes 93
George E. Elliott, Jr., a trainee on the new radar system / JOINT CONGRESSIONAL INVESTIGATION

The Handling of the Sighting by an Untrained Supervisor 110
Kermit Tyler, momentarily in charge of the Aircraft Information Center / NAVY COURT OF INQUIRY

Section Four • *American Penetration of the Japanese Diplomatic Codes*

The Origin and Work of "Magic" 121
Arthur H. McCollum, chief, Far East Section, Office of Naval Intelligence / JOINT CONGRESSIONAL INVESTIGATION

Work Patterns in "Magic" 129
Alwin D. Kramer, Translation Section, Communications Division, Navy Department / JOINT CONGRESSIONAL INVESTIGATION

The Normal Distribution Pattern for "Magic" 133
Laurence E. Safford, chief, Security Section, Communications Division, Navy Department / JOINT CONGRESSIONAL INVESTIGATION

"Magic": An Exercise in Illegality! 143
General George C. Marshall, chief of staff, U.S. Army / JOINT CONGRESSIONAL INVESTIGATION

The War Warning "Winds" Execute: The One Witness Who Persisted in Asserting It Had Been Received 145
Laurence F. Safford, chief, Security Section, Communications Division, Navy Department / JOINT CONGRESSIONAL INVESTIGATION

Contents vii

Was Kramer Pressured to Alter His Testimony That the Winds
 Message Was Received? 186
 *Alwin D. Kramer, Translation Section, Communications Division,
 Navy Department* / JOINT CONGRESSIONAL INVESTIGATION

FDR on the Final Prewar Diplomatic Intercept: "This
 Means War" 212
 *Lester Robert Schulz, present when the communication was read
 by the president* / JOINT CONGRESSIONAL INVESTIGATION

Did the Japanese Suspect Their Codes Were Broken? 220
 Theodore S. Wilkinson, director of Naval Intelligence / JOINT
 CONGRESSIONAL INVESTIGATION

*Section Five • Evaluating the Pearl Harbor Commanders:
Negligent, Malinformed by Their Superiors, or Just
Plain Unlucky?*

The Impressions, Priorities, and Dangers Implied by the Navy
 Department in Its Communications with Pearl Harbor 229
 *Admiral Husband E. Kimmel, commander-in-chief, U.S. Pacific
 Fleet* / JOINT CONGRESSIONAL INVESTIGATION

Did War Department Communications with the Army
 Commander in Hawaii Imply an Imminent Danger? 255
 *Lieutenant General Walter C. Short, commanding general,
 Hawaiian Department* / JOINT CONGRESSIONAL INVESTIGATION

The Rejected Proposal for an Additional Warning to Kimmel 268
 *Arthur H. McCollum, chief, Far East Section, Office of Naval
 Intelligence* / JOINT CONGRESSIONAL INVESTIGATION

The Scrambler Phone Controversy 275
 *Lieutenant General Walter C. Short, commanding general,
 Hawaiian Department; Walter C. Phillips, chief of staff under
 General Short, Hawaiian Department; Carroll A. Powell, Signal
 Corps, U.S. Army, Washington, D.C.* / ROBERTS COMMISSION /
 General George C. Marshall, chief of staff, U.S. Army / JOINT
 CONGRESSIONAL INVESTIGATION

Shortages of Military Equipment 287
 *Lieutenant General Walter C. Short, commanding general,
 Hawaiian Department* / NAVY COURT OF INQUIRY

Army-Navy Cooperation at Pearl Harbor—and Its
(Severe) Limits 294
*Admiral Husband E. Kimmel, commander-in-chief, U.S.
Pacific Fleet* / JOINT CONGRESSIONAL INVESTIGATION

War Drills Preparing for Conflict 307
*Major General Henry T. Burgin, in charge of Army anti-aircraft
forces, Hawaii* / ARMY PEARL HARBOR BOARD

Why Military Aircraft Were Not Dispersed on the Ground 317
*Lieutenant General Walter C. Short, commanding general,
Hawaiian Department* / ROBERTS COMMISSION

The Lack of Sabotage at Pearl Harbor 326
*I. H. Mayfield, Fourteenth Naval District intelligence officer,
Hawaii* / CLAUSEN INVESTIGATION

The Claim of Alcoholic Impairment of U.S. Service Personnel 328
Melvin L. Craig, provost marshal, Hawaiian Department /
ROBERTS COMMISSION

Submarine Contacts Just Outside Pearl Harbor on December 7 333
Captain William W. Outerbridge, commanding officer / WARD
HEWITT INQUIRY

Why Were There No Torpedo Nets in Pearl Harbor? 339
Admiral Harold R. Stark, chief of naval operations / JOINT
CONGRESSIONAL INVESTIGATION

Section Six • Other Pertinent Data

How the American Fleet Came to Be Permanently Based in
Hawaii 351
*Admiral James O. Richardson, commander-in-chief, U.S.
Fleet (1940)* / JOINT CONGRESSIONAL INVESTIGATION

Wisdom of the Sea Route Chosen by the Japanese 372
*Admiral Richmond Kelly Turner, chief, War Plans Division,
U.S. Navy* / JOINT CONGRESSIONAL INVESTIGATION

The Timing of the Japanese Attacks in the Pacific 376
John Ford Baecher, U.S.N.R. / JOINT CONGRESSIONAL INVESTIGATION

The Effect of the Pearl Harbor Losses on the Course
 of the War   378
  Theodore S. Wilkinson, director of Naval Intelligence / JOINT
    CONGRESSIONAL INVESTIGATION

Rainbow 5: The Role of the Pacific Fleet   381
  *Admiral Richard Kelly Turner, chief, War Plans Division, U.S.
    Navy* / HART INQUIRY

Section Seven • The Index   389

INTRODUCTION

In spite of the various fine works that have been produced concerning the Pearl Harbor assault, the most basic resource document is rarely available and has long been out of print. What can justly be described as the mother lode of data was published in 1946 by the United States Congress under the title *Pearl Harbor Attack*. Because of deep suspicions and bitter accusations about the events leading up to the attack, a joint committee of the House and Senate was appointed and held public hearings during late 1945 and early 1946. The committee members and staff were able to investigate more fully aspects of the controversy that wartime security considerations had made especially sensitive. The committee's 39 lengthy published volumes not only contributed new insights into what had happened, but also reprinted all the prior official investigations (and concluding reports) in unexpurgated form.

No one, unless he or she is determined to become an authority on the event, is likely to take the time to wade through these many thousands of pages. The sheer mass of data discourages even the interested nonspecialist. Nor is the published form "reader friendly": there is no real index and no way to quickly compare testimony on one aspect of the air raid as given by different persons.

Even if one is willing to overlook such inconveniences, the scarcity of the work provides a further discouragement. In most cases it can only be obtained via the sometimes ponderous workings of the interlibrary loan system. Indeed, in one state the editor of this volume used to work in, it would not even have been available from that source because only works currently in print could be obtained, an approach that defeats much of the purpose of having such a system.

For those not wishing to become experts, such difficulties pose yet additional obstacles: If one has the time (or desire) to read only a limited amount of this information, what does one select? Where would one begin? (And end?) Yet it is important to have at least a modest acquaintance with the contents of the key testimony if one is ever adequately to understand the greatest twentieth century military humiliation suffered by the United States. How does one find a way out of this dilemma?

This book attempts to provide a partial solution: It brings together within the confines of one moderately long work a cross-section of the most relevant and interesting testimony. In doing so, it does not overlook the interests of the more advanced student. The printed page numbers of the original volumes have been inserted into the text, and ellipses clearly note where wording has been omitted.

The central problem in compiling such a study as this one is not the lack of good material but in fact its abundance, and the need to prune it to a usable length. The challenge was further intensified by the fact that the majority of those who testified did so before two or three or more investigative bodies. In each case, an attempt has been made to choose the "best" and "most revealing" examples, though sometimes others come in close behind and would be worthy of inclusion if this compendium were substantially longer.

By treating the testimony under key subject headings, the invaluable hard core has been retained while thousands of pages of digression, repetition, and less relevant material have been removed. No effort has been made to limit any speaker's testimony only to that immediately relevant to the theme being discussed. Hence there are places where the speakers wander to other matters of interest which, if isolated under a separate heading, would either lose their context or be inadequately long to justify inclusion.

Upon occasion readers will find an apparent contradiction between the speakers. Such is inevitable in dealing with historical data. Sometimes the difference can be resolved; other times it comes down to whose testimony seems more candid, realistic, and rational. These were men who lived through an extraordinarily traumatic experience, and the inevitable meditation over what "might have been" (and, in some cases, perhaps "should have been") surely must have affected how they shaped and shaded their recollections.

The styles found in this volume differ according to which of the various investigations is being cited. For example, if an investigation numbered the questions asked, the numbering is retained. If it capitalized certain entire words, the capitalization has been retained. If the speaker is not identified each time he speaks, the editor has allowed the initial identification at the head of each extract to suffice. Those cases in which speakers' names are printed in different ways in different investigations have, however, been altered to a uniform style.

In a very real sense, these extracts speak for themselves and require little in the way of interpretive introduction. A brief summary at this point may nevertheless help the reader grasp the central thrust of each of the interrogations.

Section One. The Final Steps to War

Americans remember all too well December 7, 1941. What they less often recall are the events that preceded it, especially when viewed from the perspective of contemporary government officials. To provide this context is the purpose of Section One.

In "Countdown to Conflict: The View from the War Department," Secretary of War Henry L. Stimson recounts various high level meetings held within the executive branch of the government during the final prewar period. Secretary of State Cordell Hull's testimony has been given the title "November 1941: The Intragovernmental Discussion of the War Danger." He makes plain that in the final weeks and months the highest level of government was speaking of a Pacific War in terms of "when" and not "whether." He concisely sums up his underlying attitudes in the negotiations with the Japanese.

United States Ambassador to Japan Joseph C. Grew addresses the question "Was the American Note of November 26 an Ultimatum?" The Japanese so viewed it, just as the American officials viewed the Japanese note of six days earlier in the same light. One congressman leaned heavily on the ambassador to force him to admit the accuracy of the label. Interestingly, he does so not as a means of putting the two sets of proposals on a moral par but because the congressman believed the Japanese fully deserved an ultimatum.

Section Two. Espionage

Assuming that a modern nation has the capacity to penetrate a potential enemy's secrets, there has seemingly been an irresistible temptation to do so even if no current state of war exists. Such a policy can either be the fact-gathering forerunner of naked aggression or (at least primarily) a defensive tool to protect against becoming the victim of such aggression. Either way, powerful nations of the modern era have always assumed there is a need for such foreign information and acted accordingly.

Brigadier General Sherman Miles, acting chief of staff (intelligence), introduces this theme with his discussion of "The Failure of American Espionage in Japan and Her Possessions." American manpower was very limited, and what modest information could be obtained came from personal observation rather than the utilization of native agents. Ambassador Grew discusses "The Effective Security Screen in Japan Itself." So cautious were the Japanese that American travelers would find the train curtains pulled down when passing military installations.

The ambassador also discusses "An Idle Tale That Later Became Reality: The January 1941 Tokyo Rumor of an Attack on Pearl Harbor." The Peruvian embassy passed along the story to the Americans, but no evidence was uncovered at the time to consider it any more than one of the many unsubstantiated rumors that come the way of any diplomatic official working in a hostile environment. In retrospect we can view this as, at the most, a possible security leak at the time the Japanese began their contingency plans for such an operation. The accusation, on the other hand, may have been a mere lucky guess; the United States was an obvious target for a future war and the base at Pearl Harbor sufficiently vital that some kind of raid upon it was a logical possibility.

Colonel George W. Bicknell, assistant G-2 of the Hawaiian Department, discusses "The Ease of Japanese Intelligence Gathering in Hawaii." In contrast to the closed society Japan represented to the outsider, much of the useful information about military activities in Hawaii was easily obtainable. Furthermore, there was no large European community in Japan with the potential to be exploited for intelligence gathering, while the large size of the Japanese population in Hawaii made it likely that at least a modest number could be compromised.

In "Navy/FBI Hostility over Rival Hawaiian Wiretaps," the existence of such interceptions, their contents, and how they resulted in intense bad feelings between the Navy and the Federal Bureau of Investigation are examined. Lieutenant Colonel Henry C. Clausen (who had previously served upon the Army Pearl Harbor Board) sums up what happened and how he uncovered the existence of this previously hidden fact.

Section Three. Radar: The Great Missed Opportunity

In the strict sense, the "sneak" aspect of the assault failed to occur: Radar detected the incoming planes but through a combination of errors (new equipment, inexperienced officers, and a new command structure) this opportunity for response was missed. How this happened is the theme of this section.

William E. G. Taylor, a Navy adviser to the Interceptor Command at Pearl Harbor, discusses "Prior American and British Development of Radar." With a background in British radar as well as American land and naval equivalents, he was in a position to provide a professional evaluation of the training being provided and the quality of equipment currently available.

Robert J. Fleming, Jr., an Army supervisory officer for the planning and erection of the necessary facilities, provides a discussion of "The Problem-Laden Construction of the Hawaiian Radar System." In addition to the expected difficulties posed in erecting stations for a little known technology, what a later generation would call "environmental objections" had to be overcome as well.

George E. Elliott, Jr., a trainee on the new radar system, provides a firsthand account of "The Sighting of the Japanese Planes." Working past the end of their normal shift, Elliott and his supervisor were startled by the radar indication of a large number of incoming planes. Their report was passed on to Kermit Tyler, a young officer who momentarily found himself in charge of the recently established aircraft information center. In "The Handling of the Sighting by an Untrained Supervisor," Tyler explains both his lack of training and the reasons he dismissed the sighting.

Section Four. American Penetration of the Japanese Diplomatic Codes

The chief of the Far Eastern section of the Office of Naval Intelligence, Arthur H. McCollum, provides a useful description of "The Origin and Work of 'Magic,'" the nickname that became the ongoing designation for the successful

Introduction

American deciphering of the Japanese diplomatic codes. Also targeted were the Japanese military ciphers, although success on that front was far more limited and temporary. ("Codes" and "ciphers" are of course distinct methods of secret communication but are nonetheless commonly employed as synonyms.)

Lieutenant Commander Alwin D. Kramer would normally have been functioning in the Far Eastern section of the Office of Naval Intelligence. Because of his foreign language skill, he had been "loaned" to the translation section of the Communications Division of the Navy to assist in its "Magic" project. In "Work Patterns in 'Magic,'" he emphasizes how the endeavor functioned as an organization: the division of the work load, the responsibility of each type of participant, and even the official hours of operation.

Commander Laurence F. Safford, chief of the Security Section, Communications Division, United States Navy, offers a brief on "The Normal Distribution Pattern for 'Magic.'" He discusses this theme of who received the intercepts within the context of emphasizing the handling of the final, 14-point Japanese diplomatic message. He also notes the differing interception and deciphering capacities of the various sites connected with this Joint Army-Navy operation.

In retrospect, it is hard for an American not to take pride in the difficult ongoing effort that broke the Japanese diplomatic cipher—and kept it broken. In Army Chief of Staff George C. Marshall's testimony on "'Magic': An Exercise in Illegality!" we discover the startling fact that this vitally important success was obtained only at the price of explicitly violating existing American law.

Laurence F. Safford plays the central role in the controversy over whether the United States received definite word that war was going to erupt. The Japanese foreign office had warned its diplomatic offices abroad that in the case of a fatal breach in diplomatic relations with normal means of confidential communication unavailable, certain faked weather forecasts would provide advance warning. According to which phony report was used, one could determine against which nation(s) war would occur; one specific wording would forewarn that conflict with the United States was imminent.

Various possible "winds execute" messages (as these are known) were monitored by intercept stations, but closer attention quickly revealed that each had been misunderstood and was a false alarm. So the question was never whether "false" (erroneous) winds executes had been monitored but whether a real one had been intercepted as well. The significance of Safford's testimony can be summed up in the extract title, "The War Warning 'Winds' Execute: The One Witness Who Persisted in Asserting It Had Been Received."

Because of the intense pressures that went with deciphering, the strain could result in physical or emotional consequences. Since the congressional investigation after the war, there has been repeated speculation that Lieutenant Commander Kramer had been threatened with involuntary (and, implicitly, lengthy) hospitalization if he did not recant his earlier testimony. Since he was already in the hospital and desired to get out at the earliest possible moment, even implicit pressure of this type could have been quite unsettling. The extract "Was Kramer Pressured to Alter His Testimony That the Winds Message Was Received?" finds Kramer testifying concerning these accusations and reviewing what he had previously testified.

Regardless of the truth concerning the much contested "winds" issue, what information unquestionably was available to American policymakers in the waning hours of peace left no doubt that war was about to erupt. Lester Robert Schulz was present on the night of December 6 and heard the response of "FDR on the Final Prewar Diplomatic Intercept: 'This Means War.'"

"Did the Japanese Suspect Their Codes Were Broken?" Captain Theodore S. Wilkinson, director of Naval Intelligence, introduces this possibility to a clearly startled group of congressional investigators. He points out that the Japanese had little concern over this danger and that the likelihood of it at least occasionally happening was one of the reasons that their ciphers were regularly changed. As to the key diplomatic codes (which were so important to the "Magic" operation), they entertained little or no worry that these had been penetrated at all; these were considered too "secure" to have been breached.

Section Five. Evaluating the Pearl Harbor Commanders: Negligent, Malinformed by Their Superiors, or Just Plain Unlucky?

That the Japanese were the villains was the unanimous judgment of the American people, but who on the United States' side was responsible for "letting them get away with it"? Since the president was commander-in-chief he was an obvious target for the blame, as were the top men in the Navy and War departments. Except among some long-term Roosevelt foes, the responsibility was, however, quickly assigned to the local commanders at Pearl Harbor itself.

These two officers were Admiral Husband E. Kimmel, commander-in-chief of the U.S. Pacific Fleet, and U.S. Army Lieutenant General Walter C. Short, commanding general of the Hawaiian Department. At first these two men stoically accepted the public odium and rejection, but as the next few years quickly sped by, both became convinced that they had been unjustly turned into scapegoats and that they had been denied vital information by their superiors in Washington. Kimmel reviews the various communications he had received in the extract "The Impressions, Priorities, and Dangers Implied by the Navy Department in Its Communications with Pearl Harbor." Short covers similar ground in the extract "Did War Department Communications with the Army Commander in Hawaii Imply an Imminent Danger?" At least in retrospect, their superiors insisted that more than adequate warnings had been sent ; the two on-the-scene commanders emphatically denied it.

Additional warnings certainly could have been issued by the military bureaucracy in Washington. That these were not sent has resulted in considerable

Introduction xvii

criticism of the military leadership. The head of the Far East section of the Office of Naval Intelligence drafted an additional cautionary telegram for Admiral Kimmel. "The Rejected Proposal for an Additional Warning to Kimmel" explains why he proposed it and how it came to be rejected by his superiors.

When it became amply clear on the morning of December 7 that war was going to explode in the Pacific, General Marshall felt the need to send a last-minute telegram warning the Army command at Pearl Harbor of the grave danger. Because of a breakdown in communications, this was not received until after the attack. In "The Scrambler Phone Controversy," the testimony is presented of four individuals who deal with different aspects of the perplexing question of why Marshall did not cut out all of the delay (and red tape) by utilizing the scrambler phone that was available to him.

Another fault that has been attributed to Washington officialdom has been in regard to the "Shortages of Military Equipment." This involved a number of different types of hardware but had an especially negative repercussion in regard to the aerial reconnaissance that could have provided Pearl Harbor with an advance alert of the approach of attacking carriers. Without an adequate supply of planes of the right type, it was a practical impossibility to mount the kind of ongoing surveillance that would have been desirable. (This does not, however, answer the question of whether the local commanders best utilized what they did have.)

At this point, the emphasis shifts to alleged inadequacies and misjudgments that were within the ability of the local commanders to rectify. Both Admiral Kimmel and General Short insisted that the two services worked together in an efficient and able manner prior to the attack. However, a far less complimentary picture is visible to the alert reader who carefully examines Admiral Kimmel's testimony, which the editor has titled "Army-Navy Cooperation at Pearl Harbor—and Its (Severe) Limits." A dangerous breakdown in communication clearly existed between the two commanders; neither was fully aware of what his opposite number was doing, and an effective structure for interservice cooperation was clearly lacking.

"War Drills Preparing for Conflict" provides the testimony of the general directly in charge of assuring the readiness of Army anti-aircraft forces against surprise attack. Although the effort was made to thoroughly train these units, Major General Henry T. Burgin brings out the difficulties imposed by a peacetime environment and the bureaucratic procedures of other elements in the Army itself.

General Short explains "Why Military Aircraft Were Not Dispersed on the Ground," the reason being the general fear of sabotage assaults rather than aerial ones. "The Lack of Sabotage at Pearl Harbor" is spelled out in a February 1942 memorandum from the Fourteenth Naval District intelligence officer, I. H. Mayfield. Even after the event, this *lack* of sabotage seemed difficult to explain.

Shortly after the assault, there were widespread tales that alcohol had flown

xviii Introduction

so freely the night before the attack that huge numbers of American military personnel were incapacitated the following morning, if they were even back on their bases at all. Lieutenant Colonel Melvin L. Craig, the provost marshal of the Hawaiian Department, provides the statistical data that undermine "The Claim of Alcoholic Impairment of U.S. Service Personnel."

Captain William W. Outerbridge, commanding officer of the *Ward*, discusses "Submarine Contacts Just Outside Pearl Harbor on December 7." That morning his vessel attempted to verify an earlier sub sighting and in the process attacked one itself, all shortly before Japanese planes appeared overhead. If this report had worked its way up the chain of command more quickly it is possible that a higher state of alertness would have been ordered, thereby making the Japanese assault that much more difficult.

Finally, "Why Were There No Torpedo Nets in Pearl Harbor?" These basic protective devices could have saved many of the American vessels from being sunk at all. The chief of naval operations traces the continuing evolution of American thought as to whether such precautions were necessary and the decision to ultimately provide such protection for the Hawaiian naval base.

Section Six. Other Pertinent Data

The final section of testimonies in this compendium deals with assorted pieces of information that deserve inclusion but which do not fit into any of the preceding major sections.

Admiral James O. Richardson, commander-in-chief of the U.S. Fleet in 1940, discusses "How the American Fleet Came to Be Permanently Based in Hawaii." He opposed the decision and, in apparent retaliation, was prematurely moved on to a different position.

Somehow Japan moved a massive five-carrier attack fleet halfway across the Pacific without being detected. The chief of the War Plans Division of the Navy, Admiral Richmond Kelly Turner, elaborates on the "Wisdom of the Sea Route Chosen by the Japanese" and how it was possible for them to accomplish their audacious plan without being detected.

"The Timing of the Japanese Attacks in the Pacific" provides a chart of when the initial assaults occurred. The times are provided in local, Greenwich, and Washington time.

The director of Naval Intelligence ponders "The Effect of the Pearl Harbor Losses on the Course of the War." It was commonly believed that it made the Pacific War longer, but this testimony brings out the fact that even with far fewer naval vessels than desirable, the United States was still able to inflict serious reversals upon the Japanese navy during the following year.

The final extract deals with what would have been the Pacific strategy of the United States if the surprise attack had not occurred. In "Rainbow 5: The

Role of the Pacific Fleet," Admiral Turner explains the war-fighting strategy the United States had planned to adopt.

Section Seven. The Index

Although section seven is, technically, an index to the volume, in all fairness it might better be described as a "reader's guide." In it an individual can find the major themes, a multitude of minor details, and an incredible number of individuals and locations that could easily be missed in a casual reading of the text. One may use this section as a starting point to determine which parts of the text to read first or one may scan it afterwards to find which details of interest may have been missed in the initial reading.

With the information provided in this volume one is ready to tackle the multitude of theories and counter-theories, assertions and denials, that surround the subject of the December 7, 1941, Japanese attack. It will not provide all the answers but it will provide a sound foundation with which to begin one's study. And it will provide an abundance of information that tends to get lost in all the controversies concerning the responsibility for the success of the assault.

If this were a multivolume work, additional testimony would be introduced on the themes in sections one through six. Yet these additions would essentially constitute supplementary evidence. Useful and even desirable as a more exhaustive treatment would be, what is found here is still an enlightening introduction to one of the most bitterly controversial events in American history. It does not provide all the answers, but it does provide the necessary factual foundation with which one can begin to seek out the answers.

NOTE: Only the most minor of corrections have been made to the original *Pearl Harbor Attack* volumes. Oddities that remain (such as an occasional paragraph that begins with no paragraph indention and without capitalization) simply reflect the way the material originally appeared.

SECTION ONE
The Final Steps to War

Countdown to Conflict: The View from the War Department

HENRY L. STIMSON, SECRETARY OF WAR

Army Pearl Harbor Board

7. GENERAL GRUNERT. Has the Secretary prepared a statement that he would rather read or explain, or should we go ahead with the agenda, here?

MR. STIMSON. No; I have prepared what I have to say in the form of proposed answers or notes, really—notes to the questions which you sent me; so I am prepared to take them up in that order.

I had not quite finished what I wanted to say. I wanted to say that in making this statement I do not wish to be in any way interpreted as even suggesting that you should not examine me and ask me [2065] any questions bearing on my own conduct that you may see fit. That is open to you absolutely, but I only do not want to answer questions which might affect adversely the other people who would be afterwards possibly involved.

8. GENERAL GRUNERT. I think the Board thoroughly understands that.

MR. STIMSON. All right.

9. GENERAL GRUNERT. And the Board is not a bit timid!

MR. STIMSON. Well, I should be very sorry if any board that I had appointed in such an important case as this went ahead timidly. That isn't the way to go ahead.

10. GENERAL GRUNERT. I will ask General Russell to lead.

11. GENERAL RUSSELL. Mr. Secretary, the memorandum which we sent you on August 3 was prepared, of course, at the inception of this investigation. Since that time there has been a lot of evidence adduced and much documentary data considered, and all of this has affected our thinking; and it might come to pass that this statement is not so up-to-date now as we thought it was when it was prepared. However, as suggested by you to the President of the Board, I think we can follow it with substantial results.

The first subject that was listed here is that of the "War Councils." By the "War Councils" we meant the meetings that were held by the Secretary of State, possibly the Secretary of War, the Secretary of the Navy, the Chief of Staff, and

Source: Pearl Harbor Attack, *volume 29.*

the Chief of Naval Operations, from time to time, to discuss the relations between the Japanese Empire and the American Government. Did you attend those meetings, Mr. Secretary?

MR. STIMSON. Would you mind my giving a precise definition of what regular organization we had developed here, that would come out in respect to "war councils"?

12. GENERAL RUSSELL. I wish you would.

MR. STIMSON. The name "War Council" is the name of a statutory body which was created in, I think, the National Defense Law of about 1920; but it was purely a War Department board. It did not have any members from the Navy or from any other department in it.

13. GENERAL RUSSELL. I might interject that we borrowed this term, "War Council," from the Secretary of State's book, "Peace and War," and it may not be an appropriate term. For that reason, I was attempting to describe what we were thinking about.

MR. STIMSON. That is the reason I wanted to give you, right now, at the beginning, exactly such organization as we did have.

The War Council was in effect and used to meet, usually on Wednesdays, in the times that we are talking over, but it consisted solely of myself, my assistants, civil assistants, and the Chief of Staff and such other officers as I invited in; and it had nothing to do with the Navy or matters outside of this Department. But we did have two sets of meetings — they can hardly be dignified by the term "organization" — but early, very soon after Mr. Knox and I came into the Government in 1940, we decided that we ought to meet regularly, and we ought to meet with the Secretary of State; we were approaching important matters; and so we went to the Secretary of State and asked him if he had any objection to meeting with us once a week. He agreed cordially, and accordingly we began meeting on Tuesday [2066] mornings at 9:30 every week, whenever we were present in Washington, or able to come, and those series of meetings went on until Mr. Knox died; they lasted right through.

They were perfectly informal and unofficial meetings, but they were very regular, and we met once a week regularly; and during the time at which you are about to inquire, just before Pearl Harbor, we had extra meetings. In fact we were in such a meeting on the Sunday morning that the Japanese attacked. The meetings took place in the State Department, Mr. Hull's office, and during that time the Secretary of State, the Secretary of the Navy, and myself were in constant contact.

The other set of meetings were meetings called by the President, which he usually called with great regularity — the Secretary of State, the Secretary of War, the Secretary of the Navy, the Chief of Staff — that was, of course, General Marshall — the Chief of Naval Operations, who was at that time Admiral Stark; and sometimes, General Arnold. Well, that was also improvised, so to speak; it had no custom before it. It was created in the light of the approaching emergency, and among ourselves, as a nickname we called it the "War

Cabinet," or the "War Council," or something like that; and evidently Mr. Hull, from what you say, used that expression in his White Paper.

There was no regular day set for the meetings of that body. They met on the call of the President, at his office; and during this time about which you particularly ask, the autumn of 1941, they were meeting very frequently, also; and, fortunately, I have records. I have kept records during the time that I am here, in which I have set down very briefly, and without much reference to good English sometimes, what was taking place, including everything that was important, that I deemed to be important, in regard to the crisis that was coming along; and including these meetings; so that I am in a position where I can give you dates of these meetings pretty fully.

14. GENERAL RUSSELL. How frequently were the President's meetings held, would you think?

MR. STIMSON. Well, I can tell you. I will give them all that came within the time that you speak of, but there was no regular day for them, they came at different days; and during the two or three weeks before Pearl Harbor there were a number of those meetings; I cannot give you off-hand how many, but I have got them all enumerated in my answer when you come to that question.

15. GENERAL RUSSELL. Mr. Secretary, as a result of these two sets of meetings that you have referred to, were you kept in touch with the negotiations between the Japanese Empire and the American Government?

MR. STIMSON. Yes; I was.

16. GENERAL RUSSELL. Do you think you were fully advised and that you knew all of the details of those negotiations, and the trend of the negotiations?

MR. STIMSON. I think I knew it as fully as anybody in the Government.

17. GENERAL RUSSELL. Were those negotiations, or the things that transpired at these meetings, communicated to the Chief of Staff of the Army?

MR. STIMSON. They were.

[2067] 18. GENERAL RUSSELL. He was as thoroughly familiar with those details as you were, and with the trend in the negotiation?

MR. STIMSON. I believe so. Now, let me tell you, there, we were then in the old Munition building; and the old Munition building in that respect was built just as our present quarters are. The Chief of Staff had his room right through a door like that, in the old building, and we were in very constant touch every day—every day. We had no intermediaries between us; we went back and forth through that door; and whenever I received any information from the meetings which I attended, and at which he was not present, which was of importance to the conduct of military operations or other things, I talked it over with him and told him. Of course, he was at the head of the staff, and he was my channel to getting things to the military staff of the United States Army.

19. GENERAL RUSSELL. Were any restrictions imposed on you as to the information which you might convey to General Marshall as head of the armed forces?

MR. STIMSON. No. You mean, by whom?

20. GENERAL RUSSELL. By the request of the Secretary of State or the direction of the President of the United States.

MR. STIMSON. Oh, none, whatever! none, whatever!

21. GENERAL RUSSELL. Now, in these meetings that we are discussing, which occurred late in the fall of 1941, did you consider the inevitability of war with Japan and its imminence?

MR. STIMSON. We did; and I am prepared to give you in detail on that question. I suppose that is question 4, that you have, here.

22. GENERAL RUSSELL. As a matter of fact, it is question 5, on a list of subjects. Question 4 related to restrictions, and you have just testified there were no restrictions.

MR. STIMSON. In my order, that was touching question 3. I mean I am taking it from the list that was sent me some time ago.

23. GENERAL RUSSELL. Possibly I missed my number. Well, suppose you answer question 4. That will probably be my question 5.

GENERAL GRUNERT. May I suggest that if the Secretary has anything additional on any question he add it before we go to another subject.

24. GENERAL RUSSELL. Yes.

25. GENERAL GRUNERT. So that we get all that you have.

MR. STIMSON. Well, I think that would be the most advisable way.

26. GENERAL GRUNERT. Unless you wish to submit that statement to us.

MR. STIMSON. I have put it in question-and-answer form.

27. GENERAL GRUNERT. Then if you will see that we get all that you have, there, that will be fine.

MR. STIMSON. And also, as I say, I was prepared to elaborate on certain things.

28. GENERAL GRUNERT. All right.

MR. STIMSON. As an opening, General Russell, to that, I just might remind you—you must have been told by other witnesses—that all through that year 1941 we were engaged in what was literally a desperate effort to reenforce and fortify all our outposts, not only our Pacific outposts but the outposts which we had obtained in the Atlantic. Our production was not yet in full effect at all. It was very scanty. It was just beginning; and of course, there was a tremendous need, beyond what we could give at that time.

[2068] You will also remember that for many years after the treaty of 1921 relating to the Pacific, we were under a treaty obligation not to fortify the Philippines and not to fortify a number of our outposts in the Pacific, and that obligation was carried out loyally by this Government. That did not apply of course to Hawaii, but it did apply to Guam, and I do not remember whether it applied to Midway or Wake. It applied certainly to the Philippines and to Guam and to our outposts in the Far East. Under those conditions, the fortifications of those outposts had fallen very much behind the times; and our attention was directed by trying to keep that out and to bring them up as far as possible, and to also bring up the big, time-honored ring of outposts which has been our Pacific bulwark, beginning to Panama, running up to Hawaii, and then running up to Alaska; and in each case it was always a question of "more beggars than we had alms to give"—very much.

Well, all through that, there was a large number of meetings between Mr. Hull, Mr. Knox, and myself. As I have told you, they were scheduled regularly for Tuesdays; but in October, November, and December there were frequent conversations, in addition to those meetings.

My records show now, to be specific, that I had meetings with Secretary Hull on October 6 and on October 28; and with Secretary Hull and with Secretary Knox, on November 25 and December 7. They also show conferences with the President, the Secretary of State, and the Secretary of the Navy, together with Admiral Stark and General Marshall, on November 25 and November 28; and they show another meeting when Mr. Hull was sick, with Under Secretary Welles and Secretary Knox and the President, on December 2.

In addition to that there were telephone calls on this subject between me and Secretary Hull, on October 28, November 4, 10th, 24th, and 25th; twice on the 26th, November 26th; twice on November 27; on November 28, and on December 6.

It shows that I conferred with Secretary Knox on October 7th, 21st, 23rd, 24th, and on November 18th, 27th, 28th, and 30th. Those were meetings with Mr. Knox.

There were also frequent telephone conversations with him. The reason why there were more meetings with Mr. Knox during that time than with Mr. Hull was that Mr. Hull was ill, as I remember it, a little period during November and possibly October, but Mr. Knox and I went on with our meetings.

Now, during all of this period, the subject of the discussions was very largely concerned with the Japanese situation. I have refreshed my recollection by a study of the contemporaneous memoranda which I made at that time; and when I say "contemporaneous," they were made either in the evening or the early morning of the day following. I had a Dictaphone at my house on which I dictated them, and my secretary used to come to my house, and I can give you in that way perhaps more vividly than I could possibly give you from my unaided memory.

29. GENERAL RUSSELL. It is my suggestion, Mr. Secretary, that you just, since you have a memorandum prepared in question-and-answer [2069] form, go through with it, and we will listen in, and if there is anything to be supplied, we can do that afterwards.

MR. STIMSON. All right; thank you. I agree that that, I think, would be the most satisfactory way of doing it, for you, certainly.

The first one of those records that I have made a note of now—of course, they went back through the whole time ever since I came to Washington, but the first one—you asked for were those in November and December, and I have just confined myself to those. The first one was on November 5, 1941, where I made this entry:

> Matters are crystallizing on both sides of us now, and the Navy is meeting with big losses in the Atlantic—

That was in the convoy work.

> and Japan is sending somebody to us who I think will bring up a proposal impossible of acceptance. I spent part of the morning reading secret reports on the latter matters.

Now, I will say here simply that I had the same information that General Marshall told you, off the record, that he had in regard to such matter. I would rather not make any further record of it.

> November 6th: I had about an hour's talk with the President. We talked about the Far Eastern situation and the approaching conference with the messenger who is coming from Japan. The President outlined what he thought he might say.

The messenger who was coming, you remember, was the one who came to join Nomura.

> November 7, 1941: At cabinet meeting—

Now, it is the general cabinet meeting.

> there was a general discussion of the problem in the Far East.

Of course, we didn't go into the military situation very much, because those were not discussed in the general cabinet, but it was a general discussion of the problem.

> November 10, 1941:—

This was at a statutory war council meeting in the Department, only the members of my own staff present.

> General Marshall read a long letter from General MacArthur in the Philippines telling us of the progress of the reorganization of the Philippine Army and the construction of airports throughout the Islands.
> November 21, 1941: I talked to the President about the danger of poison gas in the Philippines. We have learned that the Japanese have used it on the Chinese at Ichang.

On November 24, 1941, I had a talk with General Olmsted, whom I recently promoted to be the Chief Signal Officer.

That was important on the subject that I will tell later of, in answer to a later question: the use of the air warning service, which, as you know, was a radar operation.

> November 25, 1941:—

This is a long one.

> At 9:30 Knox and I met in Hull's office for our meeting of three. Hull showed us the proposal for a three months' truce which he was going to lay before the Japanese today or tomorrow. It adequately safeguarded all our interests, I thought, as we read it, but I don't think that there is any chance of the Japanese accepting it because it was so drastic.

[2070] Then we had a long talk over the general situation there, which I remember.

> We were an hour and a half with Hull, and then I went back to the Department, and I got hold of Marshall. Then at twelve o'clock I went to the White House where we were until nearly half past one.

That's an hour and a half.

> At the meeting were Hull, Knox, Marshall, Stark, and myself. There the President brought up the relations with the Japanese. He brought up the event that we were likely to be attacked perhaps as soon as—perhaps next Monday, for the Japs are notorious for making an attack without warning, and the quesiton was what we should do. We conferred on the general problem.
> When I got back to the Department I found news from G-2 that a Japanese expedition had started. Five divisions had come down from Shantung and Shansi to Shanghai, and there they had embarked on ships, thirty, forty, or fifty ships, and have been sighted south of Formosa. I at once called up Hull and told him about it and sent copies to him and to the President of the message.

Of this message that I am speaking of from G-2.
That is the end of the notes on November 25th.
The following day, November 26:

> Hull told me over the telephone this morning that he had about made up his mind not to make the proposition that Knox and I passed on the other day—

That means yesterday.

> to the Japanese, but to kick the whole thing over and to tell them that he had no other proposition at all. A few minutes later I talked to the President over the telephone, and I asked him whether he had received the paper which I had

> sent him over last night, about the Japanese having started a new expedition from Shanghai down towards Indo-China. He told me that he had not yet seen it. I told him that it was a fact that had come to me through G-2, and I at once got another copy of the paper which I had sent him last night, and sent it over to him by special messenger.

That was the 26th.

November 27. As you know, this was a very important day.

> November 27, 1941: News is coming in of a concentration and movement south by the Japanese of a large expeditionary force moving south from Shanghai and evidently headed towards Indo-China, with the possibility of going to the Philippines or to Burma or to the Burma Road or to the Dutch East Indies, but probably a concentration to move over into Thailand and to hold a position from which they can attack Singapore when the moment arrives.
>
> The first thing in the morning I called up Hull to find out what his finale—

I put in here, but I mean it was his final decision.

> what his final decision had been with the Japanese—whether he had handed them the new proposal which we passed on two or three days ago or whether, as he suggested yesterday, he had broken the whole matter off. He told me now he had broken the whole matter off. As he put it, "I have washed my hands of it, and it is now in the hands of you and Knox, the Army and Navy." [...] [2071]
>
> I then called up the President and talked with him about it. General Arnold came in—

This is to my office.

> General Arnold came in to present the orders for the movement of two of our biggest planes out from San Francisco and across the Mandated Islands to Manila. There is a concentration going on by the Japanese in the Mandated Islands, and these planes can fly high over them and beyond the reach of their pursuit planes and take photographs.

This is all the 27th.

> Knox and Admiral Stark came over and conferred with me and General Gerow.

He was the Chief of the War Plans Division at that time, corresponding to the present Chief of Operations.

> Marshall is down at the maneuvers today.

That was the maneuvers in North Carolina.

A draft memorandum —

These next three lines are not from my own memorandum, but from what appears from another paper:

> A draft memorandum from General Marshall and Admiral Stark to the President was examined, and the question of the need for further time was discussed.

That appears in the memorandum which is already in evidence, by General Gerow, to General Marshall, the memorandum of November 27.

34. GENERAL RUSSELL. The joint statement is in evidence, not where the Secretary suggested, but General Marshall put it in evidence. We are acquainted with the joint statement.

MR. STIMSON. Are you acquainted with it?

35. GENERAL RUSSELL. Yes.

MR. STIMSON. I just want to be sure.

36. GENERAL RUSSELL. Yes, sir.

MR. STIMSON. Because it governed the — it helped — explains the next sentence. Now I begin with my own record:

> I said that I was glad to have time, but I did not want it at the cost of humility on the part of the United States or of reopening the thing, which would show a weakness on our part.

And I go on:

> But the main question at this meeting —

The meeting of Knox, Stark, Gerow, and myself.

> was over the message that we shall send to MacArthur. We have already sent him a quasi-alert or the first signal for an alert; and now, on talking with the President this morning over the telephone, I suggested and he approved the idea that we should send the final alert, namely, that he —

That was the recipient.

> should be on the qui vive for any attack, and telling him how the situation was.

Now, to understand what I was talking about, an earlier alert, I am not sure which one I meant, but we had sent a message which would [2072] meet with the description, on November 24th, a joint Army and Navy message, but we had also sent warnings back as far as July 7, July 25, October 16, and

October 20, which contained warnings to the members of the—commanders of the outposts as to the situation that was going on with Japan.

Now I go back to my narrative:

> So Gerow and Stark and I went over the proposed message to him—

That is, I was talking about MacArthur especially, but we were sending the messages to four people, not only MacArthur, but Hawaii, Panama, and Alaska.

> So Gerow and Stark and I went over the proposed message to him from Marshall very carefully, finally got it into shape, and with the help of a telephone talk I had with Hull I got the exact statement from him of what the situation was.

That is the situation between him and the Japanese envoys.

Now let me have the message, that message which I have been referring to here.

The thing that I was anxious to do was to be sure that we represented with correctness and accuracy what the situation was between the two governments, and this part I got from Hull, as I said, by telephone, to be sure I was right. You see, that message opens with these sentences:

> Negotiations with Japan appear to be terminated to all practical purposes with only the barest possibilities that the Japanese Government might come back and offer to continue. Japanese future action unpredictable but hostile action possible at any moment.

That was what I was interested in getting out at the time, because that had been a decision what I had heard from the President, as I have just read, and I had gotten the exact details of the situation between the State Department and the envoys from Mr. Hull; and, as I pointed out here, the purpose in my mind, as I quote my talk with the President, was to send a final alert namely, that the man should be on the qui vive for any attack, and telling him how the situation was here.

That was why I was in this matter. Marshall was away. I had had a decision from the President on that subject, and I regarded it as my business to do what I of course normally do: to see that the message as sent was framed in accordance with the facts.

I speak there in the words of the message to MacArthur, but there four messages sent out that are in evidence, and you will see the message to Hawaii carries the annotation on the back of it, which is very extraordinary, "Shown to the Secretary of War," and after they had drafted it. And we were covering the situation in the four great outposts of the Pacific.

37. GENERAL GRUNERT. Has the Secretary finished regarding that message?

MR. STIMSON. No. I have regarding that message, yes. I am just going over to the next, to the following day.

38. GENERAL GRUNERT. I would like to ask whether you saw the rest of that message and whether you prepared the rest of the message or approved what was in that message.

MR. STIMSON. Oh, yes; this message that I have just read a portion of to you, I went over very carefully the whole message. [. . .] [2073]

50. GENERAL RUSSELL. Well, to be perfectly frank about the line of questioning that I am doing at the moment, it appears from the record that the Japanese people did come back on the 1st, 2nd, and 5th of December, following November 27, and did continue to discuss possible adjustments of the situation in the Pacific; and the thinking that I have been doing personally is whether or not the return of the [2074] Japanese, the continuation of the negotiations, and the publicity which was given to those continued negotiations had the effect of weakening the message of November 27th which went to the four commanders.

MR. STIMSON. No message went out relating to those further coming-backs, if they occurred, that I know of.

Is there any message at all in the file there?

(There was colloquy off the record.)

MR. STIMSON. I never heard of any.

51. General Grunert. It was mentioned in the press, though.

MR. STIMSON. Well, we weren't running the war on the press.

52. GENERAL RUSSELL. Well, let us delimit that question a little more: What effect on the thinking of the Chief of Staff—strike that.

What effect on the thinking of the Secretary of War did the Japanese reappearance and re-entering the negotiations have as to the imminence of war?

MR. STIMSON. I can only answer that as to the Secretary of War.

53. GENERAL RUSSELL. I struck the "Chief of Staff" out and substituted "the Secretary of War."

MR. STIMSON. So far as I was concerned it didn't affect me at all. To the best of my recollection, my position remained unchanged in any way by anything that I heard, from the position that I took on the 27th of November.

54. GENERAL RUSSELL. Do you recall discussing those further negotiations with Secretary Hull?

MR. STIMSON. No. The only thing that occurred that came to me about those was on the very morning of December 7th itself, when we were in Mr. Hull's office and he was awaiting the return of the envoys who had asked for that appointment; and, as my record here shows, back—where is that? Oh, yes; here it is. It is a little in advance of my story.

55. GENERAL RUSSELL. I don't want to confuse the story.

MR. STIMSON. Yes.

56. GENERAL RUSSELL. But I was attempting to question you on it.

MR. STIMSON. On December 7, 1941, Knox and I arranged a conference with Hull at ten-thirty, and we talked the whole matter over.

Hull is very certain that the Japs are planning some deviltry, and we are all wondering where the blow will strike.

Now, that was our attitude so far as—it is borne out by the contemporance memorandum from the time that I have been talking about, in November 27th.

54. GENERAL RUSSELL. May I ask a few questions now about these statements that the Secretary has just made relative to your conversations with the Secretary of State on or about the 26th and 27th of November? But first, do you remember when General Marshall first saw this message of November 27th which went out to these four commanders?

MR. STIMSON. Well, he will have to testify to you on that. He was there the following day after that, and I have no doubt, from annotations that I have seen of his on other papers that day, that he saw the message.

58. GENERAL FRANK. This message, Mr. Secretary, in the last part of it, calls for, "Report measures taken." Did you follow through on this message?

[2075] MR. STIMSON. No.

59. GENERAL FRANK. You left that to—

MR. STIMSON.: That was a staff matter that I left to the staff. I did see the message that came back from MacArthur and the message that came back from General Short, as shown simply by my annotation.

60. GENERAL FRANK. Yes.

MR. STIMSON. If it wasn't for that annotation there, I wouldn't have any memory of it at all.

61. GENERAL FRANK. You didn't take the same interest in the reply as you did in the preparation of the original message?

MR. STIMSON. It wasn't my matter, any more than any other message was. It was my duty to get through the President's direction in regard to that first one in accurate form, and in General Marshall's absence I was the messenger, so to speak, from the President.

62. GENERAL GRUNERT. Did you see the replies from General DeWitt and General Andrews, Panama and West Coast?

MR. STIMSON. No, I have no recollection of seeing them at all. I have no recollection of seeing any of them except that on the two that I mentioned there are my initials.

63. GENERAL GRUNERT. It did not occur to you, then, the vast difference between the measures taken by MacArthur and those taken by Short?

MR. STIMSON. It did not. If—well, I don't want to get into "ifs" if I can avoid it; but I am perfectly certain of this: that there was no idea put into my mind that the direct order to make a reconnaissance which was contained in the letter of November 27 had been disobeyed or hadn't been carried out, if it was.

64. GENERAL GRUNERT. You had no means of knowing what he had to obey the order with?

MR. STIMSON. Yes, I have, and I am going to give something on that.

65. GENERAL RUSSELL. There has been evidence to the effect that the statement in the November 27th message that it is desired, in substance—

MR. STIMSON. May I just make myself clear?

In other words, if I were to speculate at all, I would say this: that owing to the fact that there is no record made in any of my daily memoranda that I was making at home of things that were important—there was no record made of having seen either of these return messages, and the only thing that the message that came from Hawaii could have meant to me under those circumstances, as I believe them, would be that sabotage was put on in addition to what we told him directly to do.

66. GENERAL RUSSELL. What did you tell him directly to do, Mr. Secretary?

MR. STIMSON. Make a reconnaissance.

67. GENERAL RUSSELL. Have you the minutes?

MR. STIMSON. Yes, right here:

> Prior to hostile Japanese action you are directed to undertake such reconnaissance and other measures as you deem necessary.

68. GENERAL RUSSELL. Reconnaissance that you might deem necessary. Do you regard that as a direct order to carry out reconnaissance?

[2076] MR. STIMSON. Well, I am not going to go into that. The message speaks for itself. That is what I regarded it. [...] [2078]

79. GENERAL GRUNERT. I would like to develop a few more points about that message that we call the "Chief of Staff's message" of November 27; but I do not want to take it out of your hands, General Russell.

80. GENERAL RUSSELL. Go ahead.

81. GENERAL GRUNERT. Do you want to ask any more questions?

82. GENERAL RUSSELL. No.

[2079] 83. GENERAL GRUNERT. The point is this. The phrase is used—

> Prior to hostile Japanese action, you are directed to undertake such reconnaissance and other measures as you deem necessary, but these measures should be carried out so as not, repeat not, to alarm the civil population or disclose intent.

Was there any idea in the framer's mind, that that curtailed the action that the Commending General might take, or in any way weakened the directive to take action?

MR. STIMSON. There was not, in my mind; but the message speaks for itself, and it must be however considered in the light of the circumstances surrounding that, and also the character of the reconnaissance which could have been made.

You must bear in mind the fact that the reconnaissance by radar—which is altogether now the most important way of getting reconnaissance of coming airplanes—was a thing that was done from either a single hidden outpost or a single mobile wagon that carried the thing around.

84. GENERAL GRUNERT. Then you had in mind more, a reconnaissance, as you call it, by radar, rather than a reconnaissance by air?

MR. STIMSON. I had no limitation.

85. GENERAL GRUNERT. No limitation?

MR. STIMSON. I had no limitation. I didn't know, myself, what the different methods of reconnaissance between the Army and the Navy would be, except I did know that we had given these radar sets for Hawaii's defense. I either had heard or I had assumed that of course the Navy would play a large part in the reconnaisance of Hawaii, because in the first place they were the ships that were being protected, and in the next place they had the mobility to make outer reconnaissance. I have heard a good deal about the difference between inner and outer reconnaissance since; I didn't know it at that time; it was not my job.

86. GENERAL GRUNERT. Have we exhausted this particular subject?

87. GENERAL RUSSELL. Who was the author of the part of the message of November 27 that I will now read:

> Report measures taken. Should hostilities occur, you will carry out tasks assigned in Rainbow Five as far as they pertain to Japan. Limit dissemination of this highly secret information to minimum essential officers.

Do you recall who inserted that language in that message?

MR. STIMSON. Well, I know I did not; but I knew what it meant, and I knew that it was there. I did not draft this. I was present while four gentlemen were discussing what ought to be sent, and when the drafts began to be made I took an active part in the first two opening sentences that I read you, in order to be sure that they corresponded to what I knew, and what they didn't know; but the rest of the message, to me, was merely the carrying out by the staff of a matter which they had been told to do, owing to the President's decision. [. . .] [2082]

110. GENERAL RUSSELL. I want to go back to some statements that you made already. They may be developed a little later in your narrative, though I am not sure.

I was impressed that in your early testimony you stated that when you talked to Secretary Hull on the 27th of November he told you that he was not interested any further in negotiation with the Japanese and had broken off negotiations. Did you know then, Mr. Secretary, that on the 26th of November Secretary Hull had sent a rather lengthy memorandum to the two Japanese Ambassadors here in which he did discuss terms by which an agreement might be reached?

MR. STIMSON. I don't think I have—wait a minute. Let me see. Where is my narrative?

(There was colloquy off the record.)

MR. STIMSON. My memorandum in the case shows that after Mr. Hull had told me that he had broken the whole matter off I learned [2083] that he had broken it off by a restatement of our constant and regular position, which the Japanese had constantly refused to accept. That is the substance of it.

Is that satisfactory? Would that make it clear? or I can come nearer to it. Rather, I feel it is so important that you should get the exact facts here that I am ready to take a moderate amount of chances of—

111. GENERAL RUSSELL. Well, off the record.

(There was colloquy off the record.)

112. GENERAL RUSSELL. Mr. Secretary, did you learn on the day of the 27th of November, 1941, the probable date when the Secretary of State had delivered this statement of policy to the Japanese Ambassador?

MR. STIMSON. I have no present recollection except my notes, but I have the very strong impression from them that it had taken place on the day before, namely November 26th.

113. GENERAL RUSSELL. I think that clears it up, unless there are some other suggestions.

114. GENERAL GRUNERT. If you have cleared it up, suppose we suggest to the Secretary he go ahead with his statement.

MR. STIMSON. Shall I go ahead now?

115. GENERAL GRUNERT. And we will try not to butt in until you have finished, this time.

MR. STIMSON. Well, I think—this is off the record. I think that the last part of my statement was connected with the November 27th.

116. GENERAL GRUNERT. That is right.

MR. STIMSON. I hadn't gotten into November 28th, had I?

117. GENERAL FRANK. No.

MR. STIMSON. Then on November 28th, 1941, according to my records, this is shown: that pursuant to my instructions G-2 had sent me a summary of the information in regard to the movements of the Japanese in the Far East, and it amounted to such a formidable statement of dangerous possibilities that I decided to take it to the President before he got up. That's in the morning. I told him there was an important collection and analysis of facts that I thought he ought to read before his appointment with us for twelve o'clock that morning, when the so-called war cabinet was to meet him, namely: Mr. Hull, Mr. Knox, myself, with Admiral Stark and General Marshall.

I afterwards went to the meeting of the so-called war cabinet, and then the President had read the paper that I had left with him. The main point of the paper was a study of what the expeditionary force which we then knew had left Shanghai and was headed south, was going to do. G-2 appointed out that it might develop into an attack on the Philippines or a landing of further trips in Indo-China or an attack on Thailand or an attack on the Dutch Netherlands or on Singapore. It was the consensus that the fact there was an expeditionary force on the sea of about 25,000 Japanese troops aimed for a landing somewhere—completely changed the situation when we last discussed whether or not we could address an ultimatum to Japan about moving the troops which she already had on land in Indo-China.

Those were discussions which you probably have testimony of in reference to the move of the troops that she already had in Indo-China [2084] and whether there would be a threat to the neighboring countries there.

118. GENERAL RUSSELL. Yes.

MR. STIMSON. It was the opinion of everyone that if this expedition was allowed to get around the southern point of Indo-China and to go off and land in the Gulf of Siam, either at Bangkok or further west, it would be a terrific blow at all of the three powers: Britain at Singapore, the Netherlands, and ourselves in the Philippines.

That's all the record that day.

On December 2nd, the next record, 1941, I left for the White House conference at twelve o'clock, and there were present there just Knox, Sumner Welles, and myself, as Hull is laid up with a cold. The President went step by step over the situation.

Then the last entry that I made up is December 7th, which I think I have already read you, about our meeting. If I haven't, I will restate it to you:

On December 7, 1941, Knox and I arranged a conference with Hull at ten-thirty, and we talked the whole matter over. Hull is very certain that the Japs are planning some deviltry, and we are all wondering where the blow will strike. We three stayed together in conference until lunchtime, going over the plans for what should be said and done.

Just one sentence more, and then I want to go back and say something off the record. This is on the record:

All important information from three meetings and conversations was communicated to the Chief of Staff. The Chief of Staff, as I have said, was present at some of these meetings. In every other case I passed the information on to him verbally.

Now, off the record.

(There was colloquy off the record.)

119. GENERAL GRUNERT. Continue on the record.

120. GENERAL RUSSELL. This is one of the questions I have. Does the Secretary have a further statement?

MR. STIMSON. (5) I was not present at the Atlantic meeting. That is the so-called Atlantic Charter meeting. I never heard of any discussions there on a Japanese air attack. [...] [2086]

13: Do you know of any restrictions placed upon the Commanding General, Hawaiian Department, which limited or prevented him from taking such action in preparation for defense as he deemed necessary under his mission and responsibilities?

Well, so far as messages are concerned, they speak for themselves, and I have nothing further to say; but I think you should remember here that one cardinal policy of the staff in this war has been decentralization. In other words, we pick the best men we can for theater commanders and assign their mission. The manner of accomplishing the mission is their responsibility, and we back them up.

We consider it unsound to attempt to meddle with or make meticulous supervision of theater commanders in the performance of their mission, which they in the field are able better to judge from first-hand contact.

Now, that policy has been hammered into me over and over and over again. Experience has gone on all over the global theaters of the war, and it has always been uppermost in my mind and I have heard it applied by General Marshall so often that I know what is going to come when anybody gets worried or nervous abut what is going on in New Guinea or in France or in somewhere else: "Remember the theater commander. He has the responsibility. Don't joggle his elbow." And that was the policy of the staff at the time of these occurrences. Of course, it has been developed on a very much larger scale ever since, under conditions where the temptation to interfere was much greater, but that has been the policy.

November 1941: The Intragovernment Discussion of the War Danger

CORDELL HULL, SECRETARY OF STATE

Joint Congressional Investigation

[448] MR. GESELL. You had no reason during his time, did you, to feel that the Japanese knew we were intercepting the messages?

MR. HULL. None whatever.

MR. GESELL. Now, is it your understanding, Mr. Hull, that you saw all the messages, or only those that had a diplomatic significance?

MR. HULL. Mainly, so far as I know, it was messages within my sphere of duties, and others, that were not important to me, or to what I was dealing with, were passed on to the Far Eastern Division.

MR. GESELL. But the State Department, one way or another, saw all of them, is your understanding, that were distributed?

MR. HULL. I wouldn't say that we saw all of them. I couldn't say that. Sometimes it would require a little time to decode them and get them to us. We would be late, sometimes, in getting them. But apparently that was unavoidable. There may be, and I am satisfied that there was, a number scattered through this entire list that we didn't see at all.

MR. GESELL. Do you remember at this time whether or not you saw intercepted messages that were really of a nondiplomatic nature, concerned with the ship movements in and out of Pearl Harbor, and the military installations at Pearl Harbor, reconnaissance being conducted, and other matters of what we might call a military espionage nature?

MR. HULL. My impression now is that I was aware of the circulation, but I myself didn't give them any attention, any real attention, so far as I recall.

MR. GESELL. These all came to you from the Army and Navy, did they not?

MR. HULL. They would have come from there.

MR. GESELL. Well, now, during this period, in fact, at any time during this period, did you ever receive any information or any reports or any rumors to the effect that Japan was contemplating a sneak attack on Pearl Harbor?

Source: Pearl Harbor Attack, *volume 2.*

Mr. Hull. I never heard Pearl Harbor mentioned during the later months by anyone. [. . .]

Mr. Gesell. Do you remember Mr. Grew's dispatch of January concerning the rumor that there was to be an attack on Pearl Harbor which was transmitted by the State Department to the Navy Department?

Mr. Hull. I remember his telegrams in the fore part of January and later telegrams. I overlooked whatever there was in reference to Pearl Harbor.

Mr. Gesell. During the latter period that you have referred to, I understood you to say that you had no information.

Mr. Hull. That was January of 1941?

Mr. Gesell. Yes.

Mr. Hull. Oh, yes. I was familiar with that. I misunderstood. I had November on my mind for some strange reason. I was entirely familiar with the one in January.

[449] Mr. Gesell. Now, other than that do you recall any information that came to you in writing or orally from people in our own Government or from representatives of foreign governments or from the President or any source that was to the effect that the Japanese were planning or considering or were likely to make an attack on Pearl Harbor?

Mr. Hull. I saw nothing that came in during that period, the correspondence which I later saw, or knew of, between the Secretary of War and the Secretary of the Navy, which took place in January 1941, that is all I know of, that and the Grew telegram.

Mr. Gesell. You mean the letters of Secretary Knox and Stimson concerning preparations against an attack?

Mr. Hull. Yes.

Mr. Gesell. Well now, you have stated in your statement that was read today that beginning around the latter part of November you were remarking to all your contacts that it was quite likely that the Japanese would strike and strike with boldness and daring in any direction, and we introduced here this morning a memorandum of your conference with Mr. Halifax in which you referred to that subject.

I take it then from what you say that while you were considering and had in mind the possibility of some sort of a surprise action, you at no time had in your mind the possibility of an attack on Pearl Harbor.

Mr. Hull. You may, or may not, recall that for some time we were receiving messages, constantly, almost, about the Japanese movements of men and ships and fleets bound to the lower end of Indochina. We knew that was the jumping-off place for an attack on the south — well, toward Singapore, Burma, Thailand, the Philippines, and other areas, and we were watching that pretty closely, very closely as the days passed by.

So I just, myself, didn't think anything either way about other places in the Pacific that might be attacked, including Pearl Harbor.

Mr. Gesell. Well now, do you recall—

Mr. Hull. Pardon me. Of course, I was in the diplomatic branch of the service.

Mr. Gesell. Do you recall, Mr. Hull, that on November 27 a warning message was sent to the Commanding General, Western Defense Command, at San Francisco and at Pearl Harbor and the Philippines, and to other points, signed by General Marshall, which was apparently sent for the purpose of putting the armed forces at those points on notice of the possibility of some hostilities, do you recall that such messages were sent?

Mr. Hull. I think I do.

Mr. Gesell. Secretary Stimson testified before the Army Board that in connection with that message, which he participated in drafting, he had some conversations with you at the time. Do you recall any conversation with him?

Mr. Hull. I never sat in on the drafting of Army and Navy instructions to their field forces. Sometimes they would call me over the telephone about some particular thing.

Mr. Gesell. Secretary Stimson states just that.

Mr. Hull. He probably called me; if he says he did I am sure he did.

[450] Mr. Gesell. The phrases in the message reading as follows, which he discussed with you on the telephone, I wonder if you recall. The message at the outset reads:

> Negotiations with Japan appear to have terminated to all practical purposes with only the barest possibility that the Japanese Government might come back and offer to continue. Japanese future action unpredictable but hostile action possible at any moment.

Mr. Hull. That first sentence, first line or two there is about the language I was using in talking to high officials during those last days about the situation.

Mr. Gesell. Was the question of sending a warning message to the various theaters in the Pacific, to your recollection, ever discussed at any of the meetings with the President at the White House?

Mr. Hull. I don't recall it. As I say, I didn't participate in the purely military phrases, except as sort of an outsider, and more or less as a layman. That was given attention by the Army and the Navy heads and the President.

For that reason I didn't sit in on the drafting of their orders, which would have contemplated, perhaps, previous conferences. I don't recall having any conferences on those particular orders.

We did always, at these meetings, report to each other everything we knew in our respective lines of activities and sometimes we discussed numbers of questions that were presented.

Mr. Gesell. Well now, at about this time Secretary Stimson reports that there was a meeting at the White House, on the 25th of November, at which you and Secretary Knox and himself were present, and General Marshall and Admiral Stark.

He says there:

> The President brought up the relations with the Japanese. He brought up the event that we were likely to be attacked, as soon as, perhaps, next Monday, for the Japanese are notorious for making an attack without warning, and the question was what we should do. We conferred on the general problem.

Do you remember any conferences at that time or at about that time with the War Council as to what should be done about the general problem?

MR. HULL. The main point I was making during those and subsequent days was the very great improbability that Japan would seriously continue to participate in any conversations. We had learned through the interceptions not only that they had determined on their ultimatum but that they had ordered that conversations cease on the 25th, and then finally they worried me almost sick after the 20th about getting a quick reply.

I couldn't get them, couldn't prevail on them to give me the reason that was rushing them off their feet. I finally said, "Well, I can't make any reply before"—I think it was—"the 26th"—I am not sure but it went beyond the time they wanted me to make it, and I said, "If you can't get on with that situation that confronts me, why, you will have to do the best you can."

I don't recall except they acquiesced in that.

Then, as I say, I felt that first we should keep up these conversations to the last split second, going on and ignoring their ultimatums, ignoring anything that went on, so long as we kept a consistent record, showing an earnest desire for peace and an earnest desire to [451] prevail on Japan finally, by some remote speculative possibility, to change her mind, and also automatically, as well as very desirable, to secure some more time.

For some time, really during much of the summer, whenever I met any of our head military men or high British or Australian or Dutch officials, they would refer to this very great need, each of them had, for more time to prepare for defense.

We proceeded then in an atmosphere of practically grabbing at straws, putting up a development, propositions that we would hope to put up to Japan, and force her to expose her duplicity, that we had overtaken so often.

MR. GESELL. Well, now—

MR. HULL. If you will pardon me, I left this out a while ago.

So we hoped, I hoped that we could, by constant pressure, that if by any hook or crook it should prove possible for the Japanese to decide that they would be willing to wait a month or two it would be a fine thing for us, and I earnestly hoped we could get through with these different arrangements, but when we reached this War College meeting that you talk about, on the 25th, there wasn't much discussion, except the various phases, including my statement that it would be a mistake to assume that this thing is going on. I said, "The Japanese are heavily armed; they have been on this movement for a number of years, this movement of conquest, yoked hard and fast with Hitler most of the time."

And then I said — if I can recall what I wanted to say, what I wanted to get in here — at any rate I said it will not do to trust any phase of that situation because they are in control of this whole movement; we are not in control of it. We can only effect that movement of the Japanese armies of invasion by surrendering to them the principles for which peace-loving nations, including ourselves, stand.

MR. GESELL. Well, now, was there anyone at that meeting who advocated a withdrawal from the principles which we had been taking in the negotiations?

MR. HULL. That never was done, so far as I know, by any high American official in the State, War, Navy, or the White House.

MR. GESELL. When you say it was not done you mean it was not urged upon you by anyone?

MR. HULL. It was not.

MR. GESELL. Do you remember the President making a statement which I quoted from Mr. Stimson's diary, to the effect that at that meeting on the 25th he mentioned that there was a likelihood that we might be attacked as soon as next Monday?

MR. HULL. I do not recall definitely except that there was nothing new, really, if he said that because I was talking along those lines during those strenuous days after we got their ultimatum and other information about their purposes.

MR. GESELL. Yes. Would it be fair to say that that view was the prevailing view among the Cabinet officers and military officers who attended the meetings at the White House of this war council group at this time?

MR. HULL. Well, only the Army and the Navy Cabinet heads attended it.

[452] MR. GESELL. Yes.

MR. HULL. So far as those Cabinet heads were concerned, I do not know really the precise state of mind they were in but I received the definite impression that they felt that the outlook was critical and called for the closest attention.

MR. GESELL. Well, now, you have reviewed in your statement some of the meetings at this time and I do not want to go over it except I wanted to ask you about one specific meeting before taking up the note on the 26th with you in some detail, and that was a Cabinet meeting which the records of the White House indicate was held on December 5th, at which you lunched with the President prior to the Cabinet meeting.

Do you recall any discussion that took place at that meeting or with the President at that luncheon concerning the problems we are concerned with here?

MR. HULL. I might refresh my recollection in some way, somehow, but I do not remember just at the moment.

You will understand that in justice to the Army and Navy, I informed them when I felt that diplomatic efforts to deal with the situation had ended, that the security and safety of the country was then in the hands of the Army and the

Navy, so I did not have so awfully much to talk about, in fact, concerning the difficulties that the Army and Navy were then dealing with, but I was frank to express any comment that I thought would be helpful. [. . .] [455]

MR. GESELL. With respect to the basing of the fleet at Pearl Harbor, Admiral Richardson has testified to conversations that he had with you and has indicated that he felt the State Department was exercising some influence over the disposition of the fleet and I wanted to ask whether you had any information you could give us on that question.

MR. HULL. May I introduce that with what I said almost in my statement, in my written statement? I said soon after I came to the State Department, when I would be talking with the representatives of these thugs at the head of governments abroad, a government of aggression, that they would look at me in the face but I soon discovered that they were looking over my shoulder at our Navy and our Army and that our diplomatic strength in dealing with governments that were not very honest, that were more or less dangerous, that have ulterior purposes, the first thing they throw their ayes on is not you or me or any other official — it is on our Army and Navy.

Now, diplomatic strength goes up or down with their estimate of what that amounts to. It does not mean that they expect to rush in to fight, perhaps, but it is like a desperado who goes around in a suspicious place and he sees somebody who is armed and he is just a little bit more cautious in exploring his plans to explode a safe or commit some other crime than he would be if there was no remote possibility of danger.

[456] That was the feeling that I absorbed during my 10 or 12 years over there as we moved through the awful conditions that finally led into the war.

Now, I do not think our people have time and perhaps the opportunity in this of terrifically critical periods to grasp the full facts and factors that are involved. They did not stop to think.

Some person said, "Why, we were trying to bluff the Japanese." Well, if he was going into that why didn't he say we were trying to bluff Hitler and Tojo, because they were hooked together by links of steel in their plans. Why leave them out if you are going to take up that sort of a thing?

Now, the truth is, I have always said from my experience with them that a bandit government headed by such unmentionable persons as Hitler and Tojo, that such a government recognizes nothing, nobody, unless there is something translated into force, something it is able to rest its attention on. So I said the world is in a state of anarchy.

Was the American Note of November 26 an Ultimatum?

JOSEPH C. GREW, U.S. AMBASSADOR TO JAPAN

Joint Congressional Investigation

[587] MR. GEARHART. Mr. Grew, there has been some discussion of what is and what is not an ultimatum. Would you define what you conceive an ultimatum to be?

MR. GREW. I think, sir, to give a technical definition I would have to look it up in the dictionary, but I would say it was, essentially, a last word.

MR. GEARHART. Now, Mr. Hull has defined the Japanese message which was handed to him on November 20 as an ultimatum.

That agreement would require the United States to abandon all of its time-honored principles, in the event we accepted the agreement the Japanese offered. You have so interpreted it?

MR. GREW. Yes.

[588] MR. GEARHART. It would have required us to consent to the maintenance in China of the Japanese armies and the continuance of the Japanese armies in Indochina; it would have required us to confirm their occupancy of Manchuria; it probably would have required us to abandon the principle of the open door; it would require us to acknowledge the existence of, if not to consent to, the agreement they had made with the Axis; generally speaking that is true, isn't it?

MR. GREW. That is true, I would say.

MR. GEARHART. Therefore, if we had accepted the Japanese agreement of November 20 we would have had to give up everything that Americans call near and dear, pretty near?

MR. GREW. We certainly would have had to abandon principles for which we had stood.

MR. GEARHART. And had stood for for many years?

MR. GREW. Exactly.

MR. GEARHART. Well, we didn't do it. We offered on the 26th a counter-agreement which, if accepted, would have required the Japanese to have

Source: Pearl Harbor Attack, *volume 2.*

withdrawn their armies from Indochina; would have required the Japanese to withdraw their armies from China; would have required the Japanese to withdraw their recognition of the Wei Government; would have required the Japanese to recognize the Chiang Kai-shek Government; would have required them to interpret the Axis agreement so as not to interfere with any of those matters.

Now, if Japan had accepted our agreement she would simply have said, "Excuse, please," and withdrawn all her armies and abandoned her campaign of agression and have gone back to Japan.

MR. GREW. Yes, sir: but that is only a part of the story.

In other words, Mr. Hull, in his proposal of November 26, offered Japan a great many assets. It offered Japan, as I said a few moments ago, eventually a relaxation of our economic measures. It offered access to raw materials, free trade and commerce, financial cooperation and support, and various other things. So that Japan would have had, I would say, not only a great deal to gain but everything to gain by accepting that proposal.

MR. GEARHART. There is no doubt but what there were some very generous inducements offered to the Japanese, but the other issues, the ones that I have named, were absolutely inconsistent with all that Japan had been trying to accomplish during the last several years. She would have had to admit that she was mistaken and would have had to withdraw and go back to Japan, withdraw her armies and admit that she was wrong, which she would have done, but she was not prepared to do it at that time, was she?

MR. GREW. She absolutely was not prepared to, but my feeling was, at that time, and I so stated in my diary, that Japan, since public opinion in Japan is rather easily molded in a comparatively short period, as the Government was able to bring pressure to bear on the people, my feeling was that they could persuade the people that the Japanese Government, in the face of the military, could have persuaded the people that they had achieved by peaceful measures everything that they were ostensibly fighting for.

[589] They were ostensibly fighting for economic, political, and social security. Those things would all have flown from the implementation of Mr. Hull's proposals if they had carried it out. Not at once, but over a period of time. In my opinion, the Japanese Government, if it had really wanted to come to some kind of an agreement, could have persuaded the people that this was all in their interest.

MR. GEARHART. But Japan would have had to abandon her ruthless campaign of aggression and conquest?

MR. GREW. Very definitely. That was fundamental.

MR. GEARHART. And that was what they had been doing. She had been spending millions of yen, whatever they were, she had sacrificed hundreds of thousands of lives, and if she had to give up and abandon her ruthless conquests that would have constituted an ignominious defeat for her statesmen who had led her into her awful position; isn't that true?

MR. GREW. When you speak of Japan you must realize that there is more than one Japan. You have your military extremists.

MR. GEARHART. They were running the show and had been ever since the so-called prosperity scheme of robbery began.

MR. GREW. They had been in control from time to time, but there were periods of relaxation, and there is no question but what some, at least, of their more intelligent statesmen, especially those who had been in our country and knew something about our powers of production, our national spirit, and all the rest of it, realized they would probably, in the case of war with the United States, ultimately be defeated, and must have realized at that time that they were on the brink of an abyss.

If those statesmen had had the courage to take the bull by the horns they might then have shifted the whole situation. I don't say they could have done it, I don't say they would have tried to do it, but there was always that possibility.

MR. GEARHART. Well, statesmen were not running Japan; the militarists were running it at that time, weren't they?

MR. GREW. That is perfectly true.

MR. GEARHART. They were the ones who led the people of Japan into this terrible mistake, and they would be the last to admit it by adopting any suggestion of the United States which would require them to withdraw their troops from China and Indochina and Manchuria.

MR. GREW. True, and that is why the doubt was expressed that this proposal of Mr. Hull would bring satisfactory results.

MR. GEARHART. Did Mr. Hull suggest that that statement was not an ultimatum? Do you mean to say Mr. Hull was willing to negotiate the question as to whether or not Japanese soldiers should stay in Indochina?

MR. GREW. If you read the document—

MR. GEARHART. I have read it.

MR. GREW. I think you will see it is not in itself an ultimatum.

MR. GEARHART. It is a tendered agreement.

MR. GREW. Yes.

MR. GEARHART. It is in the form of a tendered agreement.

[590]   MR. GREW. Yes.

MR. GEARHART. One of the specifications is that Japan should get her troops out of Indochina.

MR. GREW. Correct.

MR. GEARHART. If that wasn't an ultimatum in itself, that they should get their troops out of Indochina, then the United States was willing to compromise on that question and discuss something else.

MR. GREW. No. All I can say is that document contained a very important quid pro quo—

MR. GEARHART. Don't talk about a quid pro quo. Whether the Japs thought there was a quid pro quo in there is one question. The other question is, were we willing to temporize on that question of her getting out of Indochina and China.

MR. GREW. We were not willing to temporize.

MR. GEARHART. Then that was an ultimatum on that question, wasn't it?

MR. GREW. Can you say, Mr. Congressman, because there is a point in a document which definitely must be carried out that the whole document and all the points therein constitute an ultimatum? I would not say so. I would say that was a carefully balanced document. There is a great deal on the other side of the picture.

MR. GEARHART. There is another stipulation in the agreement providing that Japan should get out of China and recognize the Chiang Kai-shek government. Was that a point upon which we were willing to compromise and temporize or consult?

MR. GREW. I think in the long run if we were going to stand on our principles it was essential that Japan should give up all her policy of aggression.

Now, I can't say that we would have demanded on the basis of that document that the Japanese got out of China in a week or in a month. They probably couldn't do it. But I think there was an opening there for an arrangement by which the Japanese could get out of Indochina and China and in the light of the great benefits which they would have received as a result could have done it.

MR. GEARHART. The question I am asking you as an expert in statecraft is this: Were we willing to compromise or temporize or even discuss a change in that particular stipulation, in that contract, which required Japan to get out of China and recognize the nationalist government there headed by Chiang Kai-shek?

MR. GREW. I couldn't answer that. I couldn't answer for what the administration might have done.

MR. GEARHART. I thought we were contending for principles when we tendered that agreement to the Japanese.

MR. GREW. You thought that we were what?

MR. GEARHART. Wasn't it a fundamental principle in our demands upon Japan that Japan should get out of China and Indochina and recognize the nationalist government and respect the territorial integrity of all those eastern countries?

MR. GREW. That had been a fundamental principle with us for years.

MR. GEARHART. Therefore that was not a matter which America would compromise on, was it?

MR. GREW. It was not a matter on which we would have willingly compromised.

[591] MR. GEARHART. Then, insofar as that stipulation was concerned, the Hull tendered agreement constituted an ultimatum, didn't it?

MR. GREW. I would not say so.

MR. GEARHART. Then if it were not an ultimatum, it was an item upon which we, America, were willing to compromise?

MR. GREW. I am sorry, I can't agree. In every document of that kind there are some points which are matters of principle which we do not accept. There are other points which would be open for modification. That doesn't mean that because there are two points in a document such as that, that the whole document is an ultimatum. As I say, there was a great deal on the other side of the picture.

MR. GEARHART. We undoubtedly would have offered greater inducements if she had negotiated further. At least I think we would have, if we could have gotten those other main concessions. If we had been able to induce her to sign an agreement by which she would get out of China and Indochina and would recognize the Chiang Kai-shek government we could give a lot.

MR. GREW. Yes.

MR. GEARHART. Those were the things she would not concede.

MR. GREW. Without question.

MR. GEARHART. Those were the things we would not concede and neither would she.

MR. GREW. There were certain things we couldn't have conceded.

MR. GEARHART. Then the United States raised a stone wall and Japan had a stone wall. They came to an impasse at that moment, didn't they?

MR. GREW. I don't think that that justifies us in calling that proposal an ultimatum, Congressman.

MR. GEARHART. Don't you see what I am trying to do?

MR. GREW. Yes.

MR. GEARHART. I am trying to get you to admit that that document is what every American in his heart wanted it to be. I don't think you should dodte on this ultimatum word. That, in days to come, is going to be one of the most glorious incidents in American history. The time when we took our stand. Why, of course, we told the world that America stood for principles, for good international relationships, for good neighborliness, in that agreement. For some reason a lot of people are quibbling and saying we didn't really mean it; we were willing to discuss and talk further about Japan ending that despicable program of hers called the coprosperity sphere for East Asia.

THE CHAIRMAN. Is that a question?

MR. GREW. Is that a question?

THE CHAIRMAN. I was simply asking whether the Ambassador understood that that was a question.

MR. GREW. No; I did not, Mr. Chairman.

THE CHAIRMAN. I did not expect you to answer.

MR. GREW. Was that in the form of a question, Congressman?

MR. GEARHART. Yes; I will put it in the form of a question. I would like to have your views on this subject.

[592] MR. GREW. In answer to that I can say that through all these years our Government stood on certain fundamental principles of international dealing; at least those were very comprehensively expressed in Mr. Hull's four points which had been put up in the Japanese Government before.

We have never, so far as I know, departed from those principles at any time. Mr. Hull said he supported those principles in every step he took, but at the same time in supporting those principles and in expecting that the Japanese, in order to abide by the principles, would have to get out of Indochina and China, he was offering them something which, as I say, would have completel justified their having accepted those points.

MR. GEARHART. All right. Then will you go this far with me, Mr. Ambassador: Will you admit that that part of that document which would have required Japan if she had accepted it to get out of China and get out of Indochina and get out of Manchuria and quit the aggression, was that part of it an ultimatum?

MR. GREW. Mr. Congressman, I do not think you can take any part of any document and use the term "ultimatum" for it. The term "ultimatum" essentially applies to a complete document. I would not say that that term would apply to any part of that document; no sir.

MR. MURPHY. Mr. Chairman, will the gentleman yield? I have Webster here on the question of "ultimatum."

MR. GEARHART. Mr. Noah Webster, Mr. Daniel Webster, or who? Do you want to read that into the record?

MR. MURPHY. I think it would help the record.

MR. GEARHART. How many definitions are there?

THE CHAIRMAN. The gentleman will read them all.

MR. MURPHY (reading):

> A final proposition, concession or condition; especially, the final propositions, conditions or terms offered by either of the parties in a diplomatic negotiation; the best terms that a negotiator will offer, the rejection of which usually ends the negotiations.

MR. GEARHART. Thank you very much.

MR. MURPHY. Webster's new International Dictionary.

MR. GEARHART. Will you say that the stipulation in that tendered agreement that Japan should get out of China, out of Indochina, out of Manchuria, and to recognize the nationalistic government of China was not final?

MR. GREW. The mere fact that we insisted that those things should be a prerequisite for a building up of relations between the United States and Japan does not, in my mind, characterize that proposal, that whole proposal as an ultimatum because there was another side to it and a very important side and I think you have got to take the thing as a whole. I do not think you can take part of it and apply a definition to it.

MR. GEARHART. But, Ambassador Grew, you are not suggesting to me that we were willing to take those things out of the agreement in order to placate Japan?

MR. GREW. No; we were not going to take them out. They were part and parcel of the whole thing.

Mr. GEARHART. Yes; but I am talking about a part of the whole thing; insofar as those parts of the whole thing are concerned it was an ultimatum, wasn't it?

[593]   Mr. GREW. I would not say so.

Mr. GEARHART. Well, I would like to take the other view of it.

… SECTION TWO

Espionage

The Failure of American Espionage in Japan and Her Possessions

BRIGADIER GENERAL SHERMAN MILES, ACTING ASSISTANT CHIEF OF STAFF (INTELLIGENCE), WAR DEPARTMENT

Army Pearl Harbor Board via Clarke Investigation

[147] WAR DEPARTMENT

WASHINGTON

HEADQUARTERS ARMY PEARL HARBOR BOARD,
Munitions Building, 12 August 1944.

LT. COL. DANIEL L. O'DONNELL, J. A. G. D.
Hqs. First Service Command,
Boston 15, Massachusetts.

DEAR COLONEL O'DONNELL: Pursuant to your request of 10 August 1944, I am enclosing herewith a copy of the transcript of General Miles' testimony. Certain minor inaccuracies such as typographical errors, may appear therein which we haven't yet had an opportunity to correct but will do so at the earliest opportunity. May I suggest that the matter of any possibly "inaccurate statement of fact" be made the subject of a letter to General Grunert.

Please return the transcript when it has served its purpose. With kindest regards, I am.

Sincerely yours,

Charles W. West,
CHARLES W. WEST,
Colonel, J. A. G. D.,
Recorder.

1 Incl: Transcript.

TESTIMONY OF MAJ. GEN. SHERMAN MILES. COMMANDING 1ST SERVICE COMMAND, BOSTON, MASSACHUSETTS

Source: Pearl Harbor Attack, *volume 34.*

(The witness was sworn by the Recorder and advised of his rights under Article of War 24.)

COLONEL WEST. General, will you state to the Board your name, rank, organization and station?

GENERAL MILES. Sherman Miles, Major General, Commanding 1st Service Command, Boston, Massachusetts.

GENERAL GRUNERT. General Miles, the Board, in an attempt to get at the facts, is looking into the War Department background and viewpoint prior to and leading up to the Pearl Harbor attack. It is hoped that, because of your assignment as A. C. of S. G-2, at that time, you can throw some light on the subject. In order to cover so large a field in the limited time available, individual Board members have been assigned objectives or phases for special investigation, although the entire Board will pass upon the objectives and phases. General Russell has this particular phase. So he will lead in propounding the questions and the other members will assist in developing them. So I will turn you over to the mercies of General Russell.

GENERAL RUSSELL. What was your assignment in the year 1941?

GENERAL MILES. I was Acting Assistant Chief of Staff, G-2, War Department.

GENERAL RUSSELL. Can you remember approximately the date on which you entered upon that assignment?

GENERAL MILES. May 1, 1940.

GENERAL RUSSELL. When were you relieved or transferred from that assignment?

GENERAL MILES. The end of January 1942.

GENERAL RUSSELL. During that period of time you were actually the head of what we know as G-2 which embraced the Military Intelligence Division. Was that the name of it?

GENERAL MILES. That was the official name—Military Intelligence Division, War Department General Staff.

GENERAL RUSSELL. Briefly stated, General Miles, what were the functions of the G-2 section, including this Military Intelligence Division?

GENERAL MILES. The Military Intelligence Division, General, was all-inclusive. It was the whole thing, not as it is now, broken and divided between G-2 and Military Intelligence Service. It was all one division, just as the Operations and Training Division, or the Personnel Division, War Plans Division, and so forth. I was head of the entire division, which, in turn, was divided into counterintelligence, positive intelligence, and in turn that was divided geographically to cover the world, or as much as we could cover.

[148] GENERAL RUSSELL. Definitely, General Miles, as to the operations of your department related to the Japanese Government during your period of service there, what were you attempting to learn about the Japanese Government?

GENERAL MILES. We were attempting to learn everything we could about the Japanese Government, and had been doing so, in fact, a great many years. It was only one of the nations which we were attempting to cover, to gather all possible information about. Our system was a running digest.

GENERAL GRUNERT. May I interrupt there? If anything which you put into the record is of such a nature as might be of value to other nations now, I wish you would consider that and, if so, give us that information in closed session, so that it will not be disclosed to anybody who may be able to see this record. Do you see what I am getting at?

GENERAL MILES. Yes, sir; I understand.

This summary digest was maintained on the principal countries of the world. Such a system is no secret. It has been maintained by practically every government. It was a running digest covering the military side, the political side, the economic side, and the psychological side. All the information that ever came in from any country to G-2 was collated and put into this digest and sent out to the various military attaches and G-2s, all the corps areas and overseas departments who were interested in a particular country, in the form of corrected looseleaf, so that you had a running build-up constantly. This had been going on, to my knowledge, for thirty twenty years. In addition to that, of course, we sent out bi-weekly, as I remember, military intelligence summaries, which were short documents of facts that we had gotten in in the last two or three days from all sort of agencies that we had. I say all sorts, because we kept in very close touch with the State Department, the Department of Commerce, the Rockefeller people in South America, and, of course, our own military attaches and observers that we had throughout the world.

That, in general, was our system of getting information and disseminating it.

GENERAL RUSSELL. Did the G-2 section, as such, have personnel available for investigations in foreign fields in the year 1941?

GENERAL MILES. A limited personnel, General. We were building up. When I took over Military Intelligence in May of 1940 I remember there were 36 officers in the entire division. We built up rapidly to something over 400, with an equal proportion of clerical personnel. We built up very rapidly, as the war came nearer and nearer, our agencies in the field, field observers, military attaches. Our personnel was always limited. We did not have unlimited money or unlimited selection, of officers, particularly of officers. That was a time when the Army was building very rapidly. The natural inclination of a soldier is to go with troops and remain with troops. The general officers, in the field of course wanted the best men, naturally, and should have had them. and We did not have a free field for the selection of personnel, and quite rightly. We did the best we could with the personnel and the funds we had available.

GENERAL RUSSELL. About when did this personnel reach its maximum development of 400?

GENERAL MILES. Well, it was increasing all the time I was there. I do not know. I imagine it continued to increase after I left. I am pretty sure it did, I cannot place any date on any maximum reached.

GENERAL RUSSELL. Can you approximate the number of people who were available to you for service in Washington and throughout the country and in foreign fields in October and November 1941?

GENERAL MILES. General, I would not try to answer that question from my memory. The records are certainly available to you. I could not do it.

GENERAL RUSSELL. General, a moment ago you referred to monthly or bimonthly documents of some kind that were sent to the corps commanders and to the overseas departments. Did your office maintain copies of those reports?

GENERAL MILES. Oh, yes.

GENERAL RUSSELL. Are they in the files now?

GENERAL MILES. I imagine they are, sir. They are permanent records of the Military Intelligence Division.

GENERAL RUSSELL. There would be no reason to destroy them at all?

GENERAL MILES. Not that I know of.

GENERAL RUSSELL. I want at this point to say that I have asked for a search of the records over there and have looked at the records, but did not discover copies of such reports, although specifically I have asked for such reports. I am giving you that, because it may be necessary for us to conduct a further search to locate, if possible, these documents.

[149] Now, to discuss for a moment the sources of information which you hae divulged already and to limit it to Japanese information, what sources of information were there in Japan in the fall of 1941 on which you as G-2 could rely as to activities of the Japanese at home and in home waters?

GENERAL MILES. Within the United States?

GENERAL RUSSELL. No. I am now addressing myself to the situation in Japan and have asked what agencies or what sourcies existed in Japan upon which you could rely for information about Japanese activities at home and in Hawaii.

GENERAL MILES. I would say that by far the most important source was our Embassy in Tokyo. We had a very excellent Ambassador who had been there a number of years with a staff that had been there a good deal longer than that. We had, of course, used the military attache and his assistants. The information which we could get on the military side from our military attache and his assistants was of course very limited; the Japanese being extremely close-mouthed. But the Embassy itself was constantly sending in dispatches to the State Department—Mr. Grew, particularly—on the state of mind of the Japanese people and the probability of what they were going to do next, and so forth. We also, of course, had direct access, through our very close connection with the State Department, to what was transpiring in the negotiations in the fall of 1941 here in Washington. Aside from that, I do not think there were any important sources of information in Japan. We were getting a good deal of information from what might be called the borders; in other words, China, and even the part of the Continent occupied by the Japanese. The Koreans would get out once in a while and we would get some information in that way. We exchanged information very freely with the British and, to a certain extent, with the Dutch.

They were a little afraid to give us information, as I remember, but we were getting some.

GENERAL RUSSELL. Did the British have any organization within the homeland of Japan which was watching the movement of their Army and Navy in the fall of 1941?

GENERAL MILES. I believe that they had about the same as we had. As to actually watching the movements of ships and troops, it was necessarily a system that worked sometimes and did not work at other times. You might see the ships move or the troops move, or you might not.

GENERAL RUSSELL. General Miles, is it true or not that from the State Department or from our Ambassador to Japan the information which we obtained related almost exclusively to the state of mind of the Japanese people toward the war and their enmity toward the United States?

GENERAL MILES. Are you putting that in the form of a question, sir?

GENERAL RUSSELL. Yes. Is it true or not that that was the case?

GENERAL MILES. That was the Ambassador's principal concern, naturally. I would not say, from my memory of the information that we got from our Embassy, that that by any means covered the field.

GENERAL RUSSELL. Do you remember a message from our Ambassador along in the fall of 1941, in which he summed up the situation and told the State Department to what extent they could rely upon him for information of troop movements, movements of the Navy, and so forth?

GENERAL MILES. I do not recall that particular message, General.

GENERAL RUSSELL. Maybe I can refresh your memory. May I ask you this as a preliminary? Did you attend the conferences that were held by the Secretary of State, which he refers to as the War Councils, where he had ordinarily the Secretary of War, the Secretary of the Navy, and some of our high-ranking military and naval people in to discuss the Japanese situation?

GENERAL MILES. No, sir. I think only the Chief of Staff attended them.

GENERAL RUSSELL. I refer particularly to this message which is contained in the State Department's book that they call the White Paper, which is a report from our Ambassador to Japan on the 17th day of November, I believe, 1941 (handing a book to the witness).

GENERAL MILES. What is the question, now, sir?

GENERAL RUSSELL. When did you first know about that message?

GENERAL MILES. I don't remember, General; I can't answer that question.

GENERAL FRANK. Did you know about it at all?

GENERAL MILES. I am not sure that I did. I think I did, because we had very close liaison with the State Department. I feel sure that I did; but, frankly, it is so obvious a message that the impression it gives me today is [150] probably the same impression it gave me then: "Yes, of course I know we can't count on it, the Embassy. How can we be sure that any group can tell us the movement of the Japanese fleet or army?" We knew we could not.

GENERAL RUSSELL. In other words, the information which you have testified that you had from Japan about what was going on over there was rather general and indefinite in its nature?

GENERAL GRUNERT. Unless we know about that message the record will not be intelligible. Is it going to be copied into the record?

GENERAL RUSSELL. Yes.

Your information about the activities in Japan in the fall of 1941 was very indefinite and general?

GENERAL MILES. Necessarily so.

GENERAL RUSSELL. The message from Ambassador Grew in Japan to the Secretary of State for purposes of the record will be identified as a paraphrase of a telegram dated November 17, 1941, and it may be copied from page 788 of this White Paper entitled "Peace and War, United States Foreign Policy, 1931–1941."

(Telegram from Ambassador Grew to Secretary of State, dated November 17, 1941, is as follows:)

"The Ambassador in Japan (Grew) to the Secretary of State
"(Telegram: Paraphrase)
"TOKYO, *November 17, 1941 — 1 p.m.*
"(Received November 17 — 2:09 p.m.)

"1814. Referring to Embassy's previous telegram No. 1736 of November 3, 3 p.m., final sentence, and emphasizing the need to guard against sudden Japanese naval or military actions in such areas as are not now involved in the Chinese theater of operations. I take into account the probability of the Japanese exploiting every possible tactical advantage, such as surprise and initiative. Accordingly you are advised of not placing the major responsibility in giving prior warning upon the Embassy staff, the naval and military attaches included, since in Japan there is extremely effective control over both primary and secondary military information. We would not expect to obtain any information in advance either from personal Japanese contacts or through the press; the observation of military movements is not possible by the few Americans remaining in the country, concentrated mostly in three cities (Tokyo, Yokohama, Kobe); and with American and other foreign shipping absent from adjacent waters the Japanese are assured of the ability to send without foreign observation their troop transports in various directions. Japanese troop concentrations were reported recently by American consuls in Manchuria and Formosa, while troop dispositions since last July's general mobilization have, according to all other indications available, been made with a view to enabling the carrying out of new operations on the shortest possible notice either in the Pacific southwest or in Siberia or in both.

"We are fully aware that our present most important duty perhaps is to detect any premonitory signs of naval or military operations likely in areas mentioned above and every precaution is being taken to guard against surprise. The Embassy's field of naval or military observation is restricted almost literally to what could be seen with the naked eye, and this is negligible. Therefore, you are advised, from an abundance of caution, to discount as much as possible the likelihood of our ability to give substantial warning.

"GREW"

GENERAL RUSSELL. General Miles, referring to the statement which is contained in Ambassador Grew's message: "and with American and other foreign shipping absent from adjacent waters the Japanese are assured of the ability to send without foreign observation their troop transports in various directions."

As a matter of information, do you know why at that particular time there was an absence of American and foreign shipping in Japanese waters?

GENERAL MILES. No, sir. I do not remember knowing of any particular absence of American shipping from Japanese waters at that time. Of course we had had information for a great many years which had been considered in all of our war plans in Hawaii that there was a certain part of the Pacific Ocean that we called the "Vacant Sea" in which there are practically no ships and in which large movement of ships could occur without anybody seeing them. It was the part of the ocean between the great southern routes that go from Hawaii to the coast of Japan and China, and the northern great circle routes that go near the Aleutians.

GENERAL RUSSELL. The term which you used intrigues me. What was it you called it?

[151] GENERAL MILES. I used to call it the "Vacant Sea."

GENERAL RUSSELL. As applied to that part of the Pacific adjacent to the mandated islands, would you say that they were in the area of the "Vacant Sea" or not?

GENERAL MILES. No, sir. The southern trade routes, as I remember, from Hawaii to Yokohama, we will say, pass considerably north of most of the mandated islands, such as the Marianas. All the seas surrounding the mandated islands were, as you know, extremely difficult for us to penetrate and get any information on for other reasons.

GENERAL RUSSELL. Why?

GENERAL MILES. Because the Japanese would not allow us in there. You might sail through, but you would not see very much. That had existed for many years.

GENERAL RUSSELL. Was there any restriction on Americans landing on those islands that were mandated to the Japanese?

GENERAL MILES. Absolutely, sir.

GENERAL RUSSELL. Were Americans prohibited from landing in the mandated islands?

GENERAL MILES. Well, they did not say "Americans are prohibited," but Americans did not land. That was well known for years. No American warship went in there.

GENERAL FRANK. Do you know of any American port or any point over which the United States had jurisdiction that excluded Jap vessels or Japanese nationals?

GENERAL MILES. No, sir.

GENERAL RUSSELL. Do you know where there is any documentary evidence of the exclusion of Americans from the Japanese mandated islands?

GENERAL MILES. General, I would not know exactly where to put my hand on documentary evidence. It was one of the things perfectly well known to all of us in the Intelligence. I should think probably the Navy Department could aid you in that respect. I am pretty sure that the Navy Department several times tried to get ships in there.

GENERAL GRUNERT. As far as the so-called mandated islands are concerned, they were sort of a blind spot for our Military Intelligence, were they?

GENERAL MILES. Yes, sir.

GENERAL RUSSELL. That is exactly what I was trying to find out.

How far are the Marshall Islands from Honolulu?

GENERAL MILES. My recollection is, about 1,600 miles. I would not swear to it.

GENERAL RUSSELL. General, were you acquainted with the plans for the defense of Pearl Harbor and the estimates in connection with the Japanese situation as to the probabilities of attack? Were all those things known to you at G-2?

GENERAL MILES. Rather intimately. I was G-3 of the Hawaiian Department from 1929 to 1931. I rewrote the war plan. I wrote the general staff study and estimate of the situation, which was the "bible" at that time and for some years. Then from 1934 to 1938 I was here in War Plans Division and was particularly charged with the three overseas departments, their projects and their plans. So, up to 1938, at least, and between 1929 and 1938, I was intimately acquainted with it.

GENERAL RUSSELL. In our brief study of the plan generally and the evidence just given by you, there was considerable emphasis placed on a probability of an attack on Pearl Harbor by carrier-borne aircraft. During the year 1941 you were, of course, familiar with the estimate and the probabilities?

GENERAL MILES. Yes, sir.

GENERAL RUSSELL. Did it occur to you as G-2 from what port or ports these carriers might depart on a mission of that sort?

GENERAL MILES. They might have departed on a mission from a great many ports. We did not know really what bases they had in the mandated islands, and obviously they could have departed from almost any port in Japan, such as Kobe or Yokohama.

GENERAL RUSSELL. You stated that you did not know what bases they had in the mandated islands?

GENERAL MILES. Very little information on bases in the mandated islands.

GENERAL RUSSELL. As I recall, they acquired jurisdiction, such as they had over the mandated islands, as a result of the settlement at the end of the other war in 1918?

General Miles. That is correct.

General Russell. And in 1941 they had had approximately twenty years to develop their bases in the mandated islands, their ports and so forth. Was [152] there any information in G-2 in preparing ports and bases in any of the mandated islands?

General Miles. Very little, and very general information. We knew that they were developing certain places, such as Palau and Truk particularly, and we suspected Saipan. We relied very largely on information ~~in military and~~ from Naval Intelligence. Taken together it could not have been called any detailed or complete information of possible bases in the mandated islands.

General Frank. Did you have anything on the Island of Jaluit?

General Miles. I do not remember what we had on Jaluit, but it was one of the islands that we used to discuss and suspect that they were developing.

General Russell. General Miles, in the fall of 1941 did you in G-2 have sufficient data on Japanese developments in the mandated islands to predicate an intelligent opinion as to the possibilities of launching convoys from there which might have included aircraft carriers?

General Miles. I would say that positively we knew enough to form an estimate that such a thing was a strong possibility, not a probability; that they had the means. That they would do it is another matter. They had the means to do it. I would say that our estimate at the time was that it was very possible, if not probable, that they did have those means.

General Russell. Do you know whether or not the data on these developments on the mandated islands is a matter of record any place in the G-2 files?

General Miles. Oh, yes; we had files on them. We had maps and whatever we could get. The Office of Naval Intelligence had even more.

General Russell. Did those maps show the developments, or just show where the islands were?

General Miles. So far as possible we made charts of the islands from one source or another and plotted on those charts, both Naval Intelligence and ours, where we thought they were developing, from what information we could get from traveling natives or missionaries or what have you.

General Russell. I was asking you some questions a moment ago about the inhibition as to our going on those mandated islands. Were the inhibitions against going into the mandated islands only those of force or semi-force by the Japanese people who were there?

General Miles. That is what kept us away, General.

General Russell. They just would not let you go in?

General Miles. They just would not let us go in. They had one excuse or another. I don't remember just exactly what they were; but the net result was that mighty few people got into the mandated islands.

General Russell. Did you attempt to send people from G-2 into the mandated islands in 1941?

GENERAL MILES. No, sir. I do not think any attempt had been made by G-2 for ten years. We knew we could not do it and get them out.

GENERAL RUSSELL. Were there any restrictions imposed on G-2 from higher authority about attempting to get in there and develop that situation in the mandated islands?

GENERAL MILES. Not specifically the mandated islands; no, sir.

GENERAL RUSSELL. But you did regard the geographic location of these mandated islands with respect to our naval base at Pearl Harbor as being rather material?

GENERAL MILES. Yes, I did, General; but, on the other hand, we knew perfectly well that Japan could attack the Hawaiian Islands without the use of the mandates. I remember very well writing one plan in which we developed the other side, based on a surprise attack launched from the mainland of Japan, with fast cruisers and carriers, carrying troops on their most rapid liners. We worked it up, just how they would take those liners off their routes for one reason or another—this one to be repaired, and so forth—and suddenly launch ~~this~~ an attack from the "Vacant Sea," ~~and~~ suddenly arrive in Honolulu. So the mandates were always a black shadow, but they were not the only means of attacking Hawaii, and we it as far back as the early 1930's.

GENERAL RUSSELL. In those studies which were made by you, and others with which you may be familiar, did you ever consider steps which might be taken to discover in advance the mission and dispatch of these convoys to carry out that type of attack?

GENERAL MILES. We considered it, General, but, as Ambassador Grew says in that ~~famous~~ dispatch, "Don't rely on us from that point of view." ~~It was much more an~~ we attacked the problem from the other side.

GENERAL FRANK. What do you mean by that?

[153] GENERAL MILES. I mean, from the Hawaiian side, particularly air reconnaissance and submarine reconnaissance [handwritten: by our own people in Hawaii] to detect any force coming in before it could actually attack. I recall particularly during all of General Drum's command out there in the middle 1930's that he was very much interested ~~and~~ in it. He was consistently sending in papers to War Plans, and they were coming to my desk, involving the possibility of a screen of large bombers which would cover the entire enormous perimeter contain~~ed~~ing the ~~in those~~ five big Hawaiian islands. That was a current matter almost. Then, of course, the submarine screen was another matter that was constantly discussed. We had about twenty submarines out there in the middle 1930's.

But, to answer your question more succinctly, I do not think any Intelligence officer ever thought that he could be sure of picking up a convoy or attack force or task force in Japan before it sailed and know where it was going. That was beyond our ~~terms~~ dreams of efficiency.

GENERAL RUSSELL. Or even the mandated islands?

GENERAL MILES. Rather less in the mandated islands.

GENERAL RUSSELL. You had less chance there?

GENERAL MILES. Yes.

GENERAL GRUNERT. Would such a force moving from one of the mandated islands indicate where it was going? Would there be a clear indication that it was bound for Hawaii or elsewhere?

GENERAL MILES. It would be no indication at all where it was going, General.

(There was informal discussion off the record.)

GENERAL RUSSELL. The G-2 people in their studies had to all intents and purposes eliminated investigations in Japan proper and other Japanese territory to determine probable action on the part of the Japanese Army and Navy?

GENERAL MILES. Oh, no, sir. We had not eliminated it. As Mr. Grew says, it was the principal task of the Embassy, particularly of the military and naval part of the Embassy. What I say is just what Mr. Grew says, that we never dreamed that we could rely on getting that information. It would have been almost a military intelligence miracle had we been able to spot a task force in forming and have known before it sailed where it was going.

GENERAL RUSSELL. Now, general, if that be true, then the conclusion has been reached, so far as discovering task forces of any sort moving to the Hawaiian Islands, that the chief if not the sole reliance would have to be placed on reconnaissance agencies based on the islands or on United States possessions contiguous thereto?

GENERAL MILES. Yes, and at sea. I mean, by submarine and air power.

The Effective Security Screen in Japan Itself

JOSEPH C. GREW, U.S. AMBASSADOR TO JAPAN

Joint Congressional Investigation

[577] SENATOR LUCAS. [...] One other question and then I am through. During your stay, Mr. Ambassador, in Japan, did you have any opportunity to discover what [578] the Japanese naval forces or military forces were doing in the way of building up their military or naval machines?

MR. GREW. We had very little opportunity to get really inside information on that. As I say, the Japanese were past masters at secrecy and their secret police were constantly watching all foreigners and all Japanese who were regarded as possibly pro–American or in any way pro-foreign, watching them continually, and if they felt there was any chance of them having imparted information they would generally arrest them immediately.

So it was very difficult to find out exactly what was being done, but those things dripped through from various channels from time to time.

We had a pretty good idea in the Embassy, apart from the statement published in the press, that they were steadily strengthening both their army and navy. While, of course, there were various announcements made from time to time of the building up of both forces.

SENATOR LUCAS. Did you have any military or naval attachés in the Intelligence Department attached to your Embassy?

MR. GREW. Yes, sir.

SENATOR LUCAS. How many did you have at that time?

MR. GREW. I think a military and a naval attaché and several so-called language officers, young officers in the Army and Navy who were there to study the Japanese language.

SENATOR LUCAS. Was that the only intelligence service that you had at that time in Japan that was connected with your department?

MR. GREW. That was the only intelligence service we had, except insofar as we were able to receive information from various sources, our Consuls in the

Source: Pearl Harbor Attack, *volume 2.*

different places, and in some cases friendly foreigners, and in other cases I might say also friendly Japanese.

SENATOR LUCAS. The reason for these questions takes me back to April 1940, when Admiral Stark appeared before the Naval Affairs Committee of the United States Senate, of which I was a member at that time, and he gave the committee the information that it was practically impossible to learn just what Japan was doing at that time in the way of strengthening her military and naval forces.

They knew from past treaties and past information as to the number of battleships, the number of cruisers, and so forth, but after the termination of the treaty in 1936 he advised us it was very difficult to obtain any information at that time as to what the Japanese were doing either in the way of building battleships or other ships.

Incidentally, he thought they were building at that time two battleships, but he was not certain about it. I just call that to your attention, because it seems to me their secrecy must have been of the highest order if our intelligence service was not able to ascertain whether or not they were building a couple of battleships.

MR. GREW. Admiral Stark was quite right about that. They took the utmost precautions to see that information of that kind came into the hands of no foreigner. I know, for instance, on the railway trip from Tokyo down to Shimonoseki at the foot of Honshu Island, very close to one of the Japanese navy yards where they were building ships, they had a big stockade erected around the yard and as the train passed they always pulled down the curtains. [579] Of course, the police were watching all the time to prevent any foreigner from coming into that area. That is just one little instance, but that was the whole system throughout Japan, and it was exceedingly difficult to get accurate information about what they were doing.

An Idle Tale That Later Became Reality: The January 1941 Tokyo Rumor of an Attack on Pearl Harbor

JOSEPH C. GREW, U.S. AMBASSADOR TO JAPAN

Joint Congressional Investigation

[560] MR. GESELL. Mr. Grew, will you state your full name for the record, please.

MR. GREW. Joseph Grew.

MR. GESELL. During what period of time were you our Ambassador to Japan?

MR. GREW. I arrived in Japan on June 6, 1932; left on June 25, 1942.

MR. GESELL. And you were there more or less continuously during that period, particularly during 1941, were you not?

MR. GREW. Yes, sir.

MR. GESELL. Now, if the committee please, before proceeding with Mr. Grew I want to direct specific attention to exhibit 15 in evidence, a series of three dispatches from Mr. Grew to the Department of State dated January 27, November 3, and November 17, 1941, repectively. I would like to read portions of these into the record.

The dispatch of January 27, 1941, states:

> My Peruvian colleague told a member of my staff that he had heard from many sources including a Japanese source that the Japanese military forces planned, in the event of trouble with the United States, to attempt a surprise mass attack on Pearl Harbor using all of their various facilities. He added that although the project seemed fantastic, the fact that he had heard it from many sources prompted him to pass on the information.

The second, the dispatch of November 3, is a lengthy one, and I simply want to call attention to the very last portion thereof, which reads as follows:

> It would be similarly shortsighted to base our policy on the belief that these preparations are merely in the nature of saber rattling the exclusive purpose of

Source: Pearl Harbor Attack, *volume 2.*

The January 1941 Rumor 49

giving moral support to Japan's high-pressure diplomacy. Japan's resort to measures which might make war with the United States inevitably may come with dramatic and dangerous suddenness.

[561] The third dispatch, dated November 17, reads as follows:

In emphasizing need for guarding against sudden military or naval actions by Japan in areas not at present involved in the China conflict, I am taking into account as a probability that the Japanese would exploit all available tactical advantages, including those of initiative and surprise. It is important, however, that our Government not place upon us, including the military and naval attachés, major responsibility for giving prior warning. The control in Japan over military information, both primary and secondary is extremely effective, and we have no expectation that any advance information would be obtained either through the press or from personal contact with Japanese; the few Americans left in Japan are mostly concentrated in Tokyo, Yokohama, and Kobe, and are in no position to observe military movements and the absence of American and other foreign vessels in adjacent waters almost assures to the Japanese the ability to dispatch troop transports in various directions without foreign observation. Recent reports from our Consuls at Taihoku and at Harbin point to Japanese troop concentrations in both Taiwan and Manchuria, and all other available indications are that since the general mobilization of July last, troop dispositions have been made to enable new operations to be carried out on the shortest possible notice in either Siberia or the southwest Pacific or in both.

We fully realize that possibly our most important duty at this time is to watch for premonitory indications of military or naval operations which might be forthcoming against such areas, and we are taking every precaution to guard against surprise. However, our field of military and naval observation is almost literally restricted to what can be seen with our own eyes, which is negligible. We would, therefore, advise that our Government, from abundance of caution, discount as far as possible the likelihood of our being able to give substantial warning.

Now, with those dispatches in mind, Mr. Grew, I want to ask you whether, with the exception of the dispatch of January 27 which I have read referring to the possibility of a surprise attack on Pearl Harbor, you had any information of any nature which indicated the possibility of the Japanese attacking Pearl Harbor?

MR. GREW. No sir; I had no specific information or information of any character.

MR. GESELL. I notice in your book, which I am sure will be referred to from time to time here, your note of that day, for January 27, 1941, in which you say:

There is a lot of talk around town to the effect that the Japanese in case of a break with the United States are planning to go all out in a surprise mass attack on Pearl Harbor. Of course, I informed our Government.

Your reference to "a lot of talk around town" suggests that at that time you had heard the same rumor from sources other than the Peruvian Ambassador; is that correct?

Mr. GREW. Yes, sir.

Mr. GESELL. Could you indicate to what extent there was talk around town at that time?

Mr. GREW. I wouldn't say that talk was widespread, but it came from various sources. I could not now recollect from what sources, because they were not important, but this telegram which I sent on January 27 was based practically entirely on the report which had been brought to me by my Peruvian colleague.

Mr. GESELL. Did that talk persist of a general rumor category or did it prevail only at or about the time of your dispatch?

Mr. GREW. I would say only about the time of your dispatch?

Mr. GESELL. You don't remember any talk about town subsequent to that time concerning a surprise attack on Pearl Harbor?

Mr. GREW. No, sir; I do not.

[562] Mr. GESELL. Was there any talk or gossip or discussion of the possibility of an attack against the United States at any other point other than Pearl Harbor during this period from January on?

Mr. GREW. Well, do you refer to talk by Japanese, from Japanese sources?

Mr. GESELL. Well, I think my question was intended to be as broad as possible, but let's take the Japanese sources first.

Mr. GREW. Well, we were very largely during that last year cut off from our Japanese contacts. The Japanese did not dare to be seen with us and did not dare come to the American Embassy, and most of my contacts had just slipped away, so it was very difficult to keep in touch with what people were thinking. You see, the secret police were constantly watching every Japanese who had contact with any foreigner, and in many cases I am quite sure Japanese—in fact, I know—were arrested and kept in prison for some time as a result of having seen too much of foreigners. So it was very difficult to pick up what the people were thinking at that time apart from what was published in the press.

Mr. GESELL. I suppose you received rumors second-hand, so to speak, through your other diplomatic colleagues who themselves may have been in touch with Japanese; is that correct?

Mr. GREW. Yes, of course I received reports of what was going on from diplomatic colleagues constantly during all that year.

Mr. GESELL. Did you get from any of your diplomatic colleagues any information indicating that Japan was to attack the United States at any point subsequent to January 27, which was of a specific military nature?

Mr. GREW. I couldn't put my finger on any one conversation which would confirm that, but all the evidence which we accumulated during those years intensified as time went on, made it abundantly clear that they were likely to attack.

Mr. GESELL. And, of course, my questions have had to do more with specific military objectives rather than the broad question of likelihood of an attack.

Now we have had here, Mr. Grew, the statement from a Navy officer concerning the Japanese plans for an attack, based upon captured documents and prisoner interviews, and I want to ask you two or three questions based on that.

The reports indicate that the Japanese task force left from Etorofu Jima sometime around the 26th of November, Jap time.

Did you have any information which indicated in any way that there was a Japanese task force at that Island at about that time?

MR. GREW. None whatever.

MR. GESELL. The report also indicates that in August 1941 Admiral Yamamota ordered the fleet commanders and key staff members to Tokyo for war games preliminary to the final formulation of operation plans for a surprise attack on Pearl Harbor and that war conferences were thereafter continuously held at the Naval War College in Tokyo from the 2d of September to the 13th of September.

Did you have any information concerning those war plans or those conferences that were being held which indicated in any way the possibility of a Pearl Harbor attack or an attack on the United States anywhere else?

[563] MR. GREW. Those conferences were generally of a routine nature. They took place from time to time. We knew, of course, that they were going on, but what they were talking about we did not know.

I may say here that we in our Embassy in Tokyo did not have access to any of the secret documents or intercepted telegrams. We didn't even know that they existed. [...]

[571] MR. CLARK. I want to ask you if you inquired from your diplomatic colleague the source of his information in regard to the attack on Pearl Harbor?

[572] MR. GREW. I do not think I did, Mr. Congressman. After all, sometimes when an official, diplomatic official, receives information of that kind or even a rumor report of that kind, it may put him in a rather difficult position to ask him to reveal the source. I do not think I did ask that question.

MR. CLARK. You did not ask him where he learned that there was likely to be an attack on Pearl Harbor?

MR. GREW. What is that?

MR. CLARK. You did not ask him where he learned that there was likely to be an attack on Pearl Harbor?

MR. GREW. I do not recollect hving asked that question.

MR. CLARK. Well, now, I do not mean to insist upon this, but you considered it important enough to make it the subject of a special dispatch to your Government, did you not?

MR. GREW. Definitely.

MR. CLARK. You say now you made no effort to find out the source from which he obtained that information?

MR. GREW. To have gone to my Peruvian colleague and said, "I would like to know the source from which you received that information," would have put him in a very difficult position, because most of those pieces of information were received from Japanese friends who would have been endangered by the knowledge that they had passed that information on. I think in all probability if I had asked my colleague for the source he probably would have felt that he could not give it to me. In any case, it is a rather difficult thing to do, to ask for such a thing as that.

MR. CLARK. Did you know him pretty well?

MR. GREW. I knew him pretty well. He was a man I trusted. I trusted his word and I trusted his judgment.

MR. CLARK. You made some reference in your testimony to some warlike activity by Japan, I think, in 1905 without a declaration of war. Was that against Russia?

MR. GREW. That was against Russia; yes, sir.

MR. CLARK. There is just a hazy recollection in my mind that there was some activity by our fleet about that time. Probably it was headed entirely around the world as a kind of demonstration against Japan. Do you recollect about that?

MR. GREW. I recollect the sending of the fleet around South America and into the Pacific. I do not recollect the date.

MR. CLARK. Well, did it have any connection with the military activity of Japan against Russia?

MR. GREW. I would have to refresh my memory on that.

MR. CLARK. It is not material anyway.

MR. GREW. I am sorry; that is a long time ago. It is a matter of history. I would not like to answer that question without looking it up.

MR. CLARK. I was trying to refresh my own memory through you.

MR. GREW. I am afraid my memory is bad on that.

THE CHAIRMAN. There is one question I omitted to ask, if I may do it now.

MR. GREW. Yes.

THE CHAIRMAN. In regard to this rumor brought to your attention by the Peruvian Minister or Ambassador.

MR. GREW. Minister.

[573] THE CHAIRMAN. The testimony here shows that in January 1941, Admiral Yamamoto, I believe it is, the Japanese Admiral, had formulated some plan by which to attack Pearl Harbor at some indefinite date in the future. Would you be able to know whether the formulation of such plan by the Japanese Admiral might have had any connection with the rumors that the Peruvian Minister passed on to you?

MR. GREW. I think that is very doubtful, Mr. Chairman. The Japanese were pretty effective in their secrecy. I think it is very unlikely that that information would have been allowed to leak out anywhere. It would have been probably retained in a very small group of the highest military and naval officers, so that I would doubt very much if the rumor which I telegraphed the Secretary of State on January 27 had any connection whatever with the elaboration of the plan.

The Ease of Japanese Intelligence Gathering in Hawaii

GEORGE W. BICKNELL, ASSISTANT G-2
OF HAWAIIAN DEPARTMENT, U.S. ARMY

Joint Congressional Investigation

[5089] MR. RICHARDSON. Will you state your full name, Colonel, for the record?

MR. BICKNELL. George W. Bicknell.

MR. RICHARDSON. Colonel, were you in the Army at Hawaii prior to the attack on Pearl Harbor?

MR. BICKNELL. Yes, sir; I went on duty in October 1940.

MR. RICHARDSON. You were there during 1940 and 1941?

MR. BICKNELL. Yes, sir.

MR. RICHARDSON. What was your section?

MR. BICKNELL. I was the Assistant G-2 of the Hawaiian Department, and also the contact officer for the Hawaiian Department.

MR. RICHARDSON. Will you explain to the committee what your general duties were under your assignment?

MR. BICKNELL. My general duties were to keep the department commander thoroughly informed as to activities within the civil population on the Island of Oahu, and the other Hawaiian Islands, and to contact all visiting officials and businessmen coming back from the Orient especially, in order to obtain any information which they might have on the general situation in the Pacific area.

[5090] I also was responsible for the internal security of the islands, and for observations of all measures necessary, counter-intelligence measures necessary, to protect any information from getting into enemy hands, or prevent any espionage that might be conducted in the Hawaiian Islands.

MR. RICHARDSON. Colonel, with what other organizations did you have immediate liaison?

MR. BICKNELL. I had immediate liaison with the Federal Bureau of Investigation, the District Intelligence Officer of the Navy, the Federal

Source: Pearl Harbor Attack, *volume 10*.

Communications Commission and, in fact, all Territorial and Federal departments, such as customs, immigration, and Treasury.

MR. RICHARDSON. Who was your immediate superior?

MR. BICKNELL. My immediate superior was General Fielder, who was at that time Colonel Fielder, of G-2 of the Hawaiian Department.

MR. RICHARDSON. From what source did you seek to get the information that you were supposed to report?

MR. BICKNELL. We used every available source. Our principal source for obtaining economic information and information about the Far East was from businessmen returning on liners or coming in on the clipper ships from the Orient, interviewing them, getting their opinions; interviewing any officials of the British or other national military organizations that came through Hawaii, as well as picking up the intercepts on all Japanese radio stations, reading the Japanese-language papers and obtaining some papers from the Orient and piecing all of that information together. [...]

[5091] MR. RICHARDSON. I will ask you whether you have prepared, as a part of your notes, a statement in relation to your estimate of the espionage situation there in Hawaii?

MR. BICKNELL. Yes, I have, sir.

MR. RICHARDSON. I wonder if you would consult that and read it to us? It is not very long, as I remember it.

MR. BICKNELL. No, sir.

MR. RICHARDSON. I might say, for the information of the committee, that I feel, and have felt that our testimony here, specifically on questions of espionage, was a little vague.

[5092] I went over this statement. It seemed to be a very admirable statement and it would save time if the Colonel was permitted to read it.

THE CHAIRMAN. All right, Colonel, go ahead.

MR. BICKNELL. From the angle of security Hawaii, during the period 1930–1941, was totally unguarded and presented a mecca to agents and observers of any foreign government. This state of affairs, however unwelcome to the Army and Navy, had the full protection of our civil law, a condition which should never be allowed to exist again.

Pearl Harbor, lying low under the surrounding hills, was constantly in view of any and all who cared to look. Japanese training ships, tankers, and auxiliary vessels frequently called in port with all crew members, both officers and men, fully equipped with binoculars and cameras, enjoying shore leave and the hospitality of the local Japanese colony. Invariably, parties of officers were entertained in Japanese homes, on the heights, where the entire installation of Pearl Harbor, Hickam Field, and other airport facilities could be leisurely and minutely observed. At some of these homes, situated on the crown of high ground, elaborate, lattice-work orchid houses had been constructed from which careful observation could be made by large parties of individuals who would remain completely screened from observation by neighbors or others passing on nearby roads.

Photography, in the earlier part of this period, flourished in Hawaii. As late as 1939, after the visit of the United States Fleet, a large photograph showing the entire panoramic view of Pearl Harbor, with each ship clearly defined at its anchorage, was publicly displayed in the show windows of a Japanese photography shop. There were no prohibitions except those placed in effect by the commanding officers of various posts, stations, or cantonments. General prohibition of photos of the crater in Diamond Head as well as certain other specific military and naval areas were adopted and placed in effect by Territorial law which restricted flying over these areas. It was physically impossible to prevent promiscuous photography inasmuch as every road, every hilltop, and many private homes offered the most excellent vantage points for obtaining clear and detailed photographs.

Because of these topographical features, practically all of the islands' protective installations were accessible to photographic recording. In view of this, it was perhaps an exercise of good judgment on the part of the military authorities not to waste much effort in attempting to put an end to this practice.

Another source of complete, detailed, and vital statistics as readily available to enemy agents as to other interested persons, were the many publications issued at frequent intervals by official and semi-official agencies of the Government. Reports of planning commissions, including detailed and accurate drawings, charts, and statistics on all matters such as communications, telephones, electric power plants, distribution lines, transformer stations; public transportation such as railroads, buses, and streetcars; water supply, including sources, reservoirs, distribution mains, gates and shutoffs; and all such data could be purchased for 35 or 50 cents.

In some instances the demands for appeasement and betterment of labor conditions added to the problem. Many of the plantations, uti-[5093]lizing the services of Japanese labor, made every endeavor to improve their morale and contentment. Such a program included the maintenance of homeland culture and practices with the erection of temples, entertaining of visiting Japanese priests, officials or crew members in large parties, sometimes given at company expense.

Personal contacts would thus be established with individuals who often had detailed information relative to maneuvers new gun placements, and other similar matters. In many instances, friends or relatives of these employees lived adjacent to the channel into Pearl Harbor and were intimately acquainted with the movements of naval vessels in and out of the base, their silhouettes, new equipment, and other features viewed from only one or two hundred yards away.

No positive identification was required of seamen leaving and returning to a visiting Japanese vessel. Passes were issued, but not photographic passes. To the average customs guard one Japanese closely resembled another. It was not impossible for an individual to leave the boat and for another, entirely different, person to don the uniform and use the pass to reembark with no suspicion being aroused. Hence, all precautions against illegal entries were frustrated.

In considering such illegal entries, it should be remembered that a great many Japanese ships passed by and entered into Hawaiian waters. Precautions were adopted against smuggling by having each ship closely followed into port by a Coast Guard cutter. However, the ever-present Japanese fishermen, equipped with sampans having cruising ranges of thousands of miles were quite capable of meeting the larger ships many miles away from any possible observation. Indications do exist that such methods were employed to bring in some undesirable individuals who were not discovered prior to the opening of hostilities.

The sampan fleets were divided into three main classes; deep-sea and long-range; offshore and short-range operations; and shallow-water, bait-catching equipment. In the first classification, the boats were large, seaworthy, radio-equipped, and quite capable of prolonged cruising at sea. The second classification included smaller but often equally well equipped craft which cruised around each of the islands in the Hawaiian group, and whose crews were intimately acquainted with reefs, caves, landing places, tides, currents, and local wind and sea conditions. Thirdly, small boats operated within the bays, locks, and harbors, netting small fish to be used as bait for the larger craft.

The operators of these boats knew every detail of these waters, the depths, nature of bottoms and, most important of all, were always present to observe any operations or maneuvers. Through 1938, 1939, and part of 1940 these small boats had access to Pearl Harbor itself, cruised about where naval craft were at anchor, enroached upon landing areas of large seaplanes, and were constantly aware of any change in details of channels, currents, and other features.

The fishermen themselves were a clannish group, having their own "huis" or associations and acting for their own interests in maintaining price levels, demanding special privileges, and so forth. They also made trips back to the homeland and spent periods of time in the Japanese fishing schools in order to become more efficient in their art. [5094] At intervals, officials from these schools visited Hawaii and brought new ideas, methods, or operation, and perhaps, even other thoughts from the Empire. When these fishermen were back in Japan they were "entertained" by various officials, and it is safe to assume that their information was carefully evaluated. In some cases they were royally entertained and visited certain naval establishments in Japan. Every indication points toward a well-planned system of total espionage with perhaps the individuals themselves having little or no knowledge of their own direct contribution.

The Japanese themselves developed a system of such total espionage which perhaps outranks any other similar system in the world. Even at home, in every-day life, it is carried out meticulously. The supervisor of the organization in the Government directs his state or provincial deputies. They, in turn, direct the district or city leader. Under these the territory is broken down into areas or wards, then to neighborhoods and, finally, to blocks. The block leader has in his possession a plan showing each house in his block. He has further data on who lives in the house; how many children; where each is employed; details as to possession of an automobile, electric ice box, telephone, radio receiver, sewing machine, and other information, including a list of visitors who call at regular or irregular intervals, where mail is sent and from whom received. All such data is minutely recorded and reported periodically. Should an individual move to another block, the information on him is passed on to the new block leader and dropped from the records of the first. Such a means of constant surveillance precludes any suspicious acts on the part of the individual from passing unnoticed. Mail and commnications from relatives or friends abroad, and the business and financial affairs of the family, are always under complete observation.

Everyone is familar with the usual depiction of the prewar Japanese tourist or traveler. His field glasses, camera, and sketch pad were always in evidence. He took pictures by the millions and all went back to Japan for examination. As a tourist, member of a trade mission, a minor official, an observer, a priest, or a student, he flooded our country as well as others, always taking photos, collecting picture post cards, vital statistics, trade journals, pamphlets—in fact, everything on which appeared even a scrap of vital information. These, too, always went back to Japan and became available for evaluation, compilation, and file. Japanese banks, business houses, transportation companies, tourists, bureaus, and so forth, were opened in many cities and localities both in Hawaii and on the mainland. Each formed a little collection center of its own and gathered data of a specific nature.

No comparable system either for the collection of world-wide information or to protect the interests of our country existed in the United States prior to the war. The American people have always demonstrated a complete lack of appreciation of such institutions and a simple, naive belief that these practices are not in keeping with the American way of life. Nevertheless, this Nation seems somewhat alone in such ideals. Others carry on intelligence activities in times of peace to prepare for war. Under normal peacetime conditions we rely solely on our military, naval, and commercial attachés for such information and ignore the fact that they are handicapped from the start through their official status and that their movements and [5095] activities are greatly curtailed. No further argument is required when we realize the great wealth of information in the hands of Japan at the start of this war as compared to the meager dribbles of similar information in our possession on Japan and the Japanese.

It can be safely stated that the enemy had complete knowledge of our Hawaiian fortifications, general defenses, armament, naval and air strength, as well as many details of our military, naval, and air facilities. The only thing they lacked was knowledge of our secret military plans, which had been well guarded, resting solely in the hands of military and naval commanders and members of their immediate staffs.

The much-debated question as to whether the attack by Japan could have been foreseen in time to have taken protective action is involved and highly controversial. During the entire year preceding Pearl Harbor, the situation had been developing in steady steps with an absolute certainty of the result.

The Japanese had long been discussing, preaching, and advocating the greater East Asia sphere of coprosperity. Selected representatives of many Asiatic countries convened in Japan to hear discussions of the principles of East Asian coprosperity. In these delegations were many Japanese residents of each area represented. Some Japanese from Hawaii participated.

The war with China gave clear indication of Japanese action and a pattern of the methods adopted by and to be expected from their Government. We had felt the ever-increasing tension with the bombing of the *Panay* and other similar events which took place in the Far East. We had listened to their great volume of radio propaganda directed toward those countries included in their conception of the sphere of prosperity. These programs clearly indicated the working of the master minds and gave every reason to believe that it was their intention to build up an empire in Asia from which would be expelled every influence and semblance of control by the British, Dutch, and Americans. There was no denial of this intention. Japan desired to strengthen her economic and military position. Raw materials needed in her island empire were to be obtained in China, India, Burma, Thailand, and the Dutch East Indies. Strong points for the defense of this empire also were to be located in these countries.

Should it be possible to oust western influence and power from the countries included in the greater East Asia sphere of coprosperity, Japan would be able to control the Asian situation. With the Dutch and British already involved in war with Germany, the opportunity for expansion was present. Should the United States become involved in the war in the Atlantic, her resources and strength might well be diverted from the Pacific. If Japan had assurances from Germany that the attention of our forces could be held in the Atlantic, there seemed to be no logical reason why the Japanese should not strike.

To assure a successful coup, it was only required that what strength the United States and Britain had in the Pacific be neutralized in one great blow. Germany had demonstrated the power of the blitzkrieg—an example for the master minds.

[5096] As a result of the years of gathering information from every conceivable source, Tokyo was well aware of all strongpoints and defenses, as well as the general offensive strength which could be thrown against her in the Pacific. She had been softening up the peoples of Thailand, Burma, and the Dutch East Indies through general fifth-column activities and radio propaganda. Her military and naval machines were fully equipped, well supplied, and ready to move at the moment's notice. All was in readiness. It was only to be determined how and when the strike would be made.

To succeed fully, Japan had to predetermine what counter-action unsympathetic nations would be able to take against this great move to envelop all eastern Asia. American forces in the Philippines, particularly the Air Force, might cause some trouble and delay. Reinforcement of the garrison in these islands must be prevented. To obstruct reinforcement it would be necessary to prevent any American or British naval support from becoming available for convoy and protective service, without which no troop or supply movements could be made into the Philippines in the face of Japan's superior naval strength, submarine, and air support.

The espionage system was working well; information was available daily from Hawaii, reporting ships in port, arrivals, and departures. Other sources kept Tokyo well informed of the location of Dutch naval units and the few British ships then available. The Japanese staff had a complete picture and could readily determine the plan for action.

MR. RICHARDSON. Now, Colonel, let me ask you this question: From your experience in Hawaii, as Assistant G-2, your observation of espionage development there, did you have any doubt at any time during the 2 months prior to Pearl Harbor that Tokyo had complete information as to Pearl Harbor, the location of the ships from time to time in Pearl Harbor, the way in which our fleet was using Pearl Harbor, and all of the details in reference to the military occupation or military use of the harbor as a base?

MR. BICKNELL. I have no doubt whatsoever.

MR. RICHARDSON. Then in estimating your espionage problem in Hawaii, you took it for granted that Tokyo knew all of those details?

MR. BICKNELL. I did.

MR. RICHARDSON. I have no further questions.

THE CHAIRMAN. Did you communicate your information and judgment with respect to that to General Short, or Colonel Phillips?

MR. BICKNELL. Those estimates were submitted, Mr. Senator, through the form of intelligence estimates.

THE CHAIRMAN. Written?

MR. BICKNELL. Written. They were mimeographed, I think some 50 copies were printed.

THE CHAIRMAN. How often were those estimates furnished?

MR. BICKNELL. They came out at least biweekly, and in some cases weekly. [...]

[5098] THE CHAIRMAN. Would you be able to express an opinion as to whether the fullest possible use was made of what was there in the way of equipment, men, and material, on the day of the attack or immediately before it in preparation for it, or in an anticipation of any possible attack?

MR. BICKNELL. Well, I am in a position to say that I could observe the action of the Navy, because I saw the attack from a point 2 miles behind Pearl Harbor, and 900 feet above it.

Within 4 minutes, 3 or 4 minutes after the original torpedo had been dropped, into Pearl Harbor, the entire naval forces opened up with all of their antiaircraft and in fact on the second round of that one plane that was shot down there in Pearl Harbor. So I should say, from what I could observe, a very effective and efficient use was made of all of the equipment which the Navy had on hand.

That was all that was within my immediate line of vision.

I could not say anything as to the Army equipment. [...]

[5102] SENATOR LUCAS. Now here it is:

(J) Hello, is this Mori?

As I read this I would like to have you stop me, if you will, and point out, if necessary, what you consider the significant part of this message which caused you and the FBI man to become somewhat worried about the situation.

(J) Hello, is this Mori?
(H) Hello, this is Mori. [...]
[5103] Japan: I hear there are many sailors there, is that right?
Hawaii: There aren't so many now. There were more in the beginning part of this year and the ending part of last year.
Japan: Is that so?
Hawaii: I do not know why this is so, but it appears that there are very few sailors here at present.
Japan: Are any Japanese people there holding meetings to discuss US-Japanese negotiations being conducted presently?

MR. BICKNELL. That is very significant. I believe there was a great doubt in the minds of the Japanese officials as to what the Japanese in Hawaii would do in case war should break out between the United States and Japan.

They had been subjected to American influences for a long time. Many of the American-Japanese had been back to their mother country and had found that they could not speak that language, that they had lost their taste for Japanese customs of old, and that they did not like Japan, and that they were happier back at home in Hawaii.

I believe the Japanese, in thinking of any possibility of reaction in Hawaii, were especially apprehensive themselves as to what the younger Japanese would do, whether they would support Japan or whether they would support the United States. They had no doubt whatsoever as what the older ones would do, they were bound to be loyal to Japan, but they did have a very great doubt as to the action of the younger generation of Japanese.

As to holding large numbers of meetings, at that time, as you perhaps recall, Japan was beaming propaganda in large degrees to the countries which it was about to attack. They also beamed more innocuous stuff to Hawaii. They were perhaps looking to find out whether or not their propaganda was bearing fruit, and were these ideas which were being broadcast on the radio being taken up, and were the people holding meetings, and was there any indication of activity amongst the local Japanese.

That is a possibility; I do not say it is a probability.

SENATOR LUCAS. Were they holding meetings at that time in Hawaii?

MR. BICKNELL. They were holding meetings, but they were holding meetings at that time in Hawaii at our instigation, where we were trying to Americanize them and cement their loyalty to the United States, so any information they got on that might be misleading.

Navy/FBI Hostility Over Rival Hawaiian Wiretaps

HENRY C. CLAUSEN, MEMBER ARMY PEARL HARBOR BOARD

Joint Congressional Investigation

[4367] COLONEL CLAUSEN. I have here a statement by the Navy, given me at Honolulu by Lieutenant Donald Woodrum, Jr., W-o-o-d-r-u-m, United States Naval Reserve. (Reading)

"This statement has been prepared at the request of Lt. Colonel Henry C. Clausen, JAGD, for the U.S. Army Pearl Harbor Board. The statement is based on a personal recollection of events which occurred over three years ago, and on my personal understanding of what occurred at that time. To my knowledge, there is no documentary evidence available to support this statement.

"The telephone surveillance of local espionage suspects at, or centering around, the Japanese Consulate, Honolulu, was maintained by the District Intelligence Office. The Federal Bureau of Investigation, cognizant of this activity, received almost daily transcripts and translations of conversations monitored.

"About 1 November 1941 the FBI, with the cognizance of the DIO"—that is the District Intelligence Office—"began a telephone surveillance of a suspect in its own office building. To the knowledge of the writer, this was the first such surveillance conducted by the FBI itself in Honolulu. This one surveillance was accidentally uncovered by some employees of the telephone company making routine installations. They reported their discovery to their superior, and subsequently this information was casually passed on to a member of the DIO by the DIO contact at the telephone company. In a spirit of cooperation, the information that their surveillance had been exposed was in turn passed on by the DIO man to an FBI agent. On receipt of the information, the FBI agent in charge apparently went directly to the telephone company and made accusations there that an FBI confidence had been breeched by the DIO's having been given information concerning an FBI tap.

"When Captain Mayfield, then District Intelligence Officer, learned of the FBI protest at the telephone company, he was not only incensed at their failure to consult with him before taking such action, but he considered that action to be a serious breech of security. Cognizant of his instructions from the Chief

Source: Pearl Harbor Attack, *volume 9.*

of Naval Operations to avoid any possibility of international complications, and thoroughly aware of the explosive potentialities of the surveillances being conducted, Captain Mayfield ordered the immediate discontinuance of all telephone surveillances. This was on 2 December 1941. Surveillances were not resumed until the morning of 7 December 1941, following the Japanese attack.

"It should be added that very few of the personnel attached to the District Intelligence Office were in any way aware that such surveillances were being conducted, and considerable pains were taken to prevent that knowledge from gaining any currency in the organization."

[4368] SENATOR LUCAS. Who made that last affidavit?

COLONEL CLAUSEN. That was made by a Navy officer, Donald Woodrum, in the 14th Naval District Office at Honolulu.

SENATOR LUCAS. Was there any question in your mind as a result of your investigation and these affidavits that are in this record that the Office of Naval Intelligence around December the 2nd discontinued the obtaining of information from the Japanese because of the taking away of these phones?

COLONEL CLAUSEN. No, sir, except that I have an affidavit here from, I believe, a Ship's Clerk, a manual, which gives some data around December. That, in my opinion, is erroneous. In other words, I think—

SENATOR LUCAS. Just what do these affidavits disclose as to the reason why they discontinued this surveillance work over there?

COLONEL CLAUSEN. Woodrum gave the reason here. What happened is the telephone company employee found out about the tap and the FBI became incensed at the disclosure. As he says here, "It is one surveillance." In other words, the Navy claimed that the FBI tap was discovered by the phone company man, the phone company man reporting it to his superior reported it in such a manner that it came back to the Navy and the Navy say here:

> In a spirit of cooperation, the information that their surveillance had been exposed was in turn passed on by the DIO man to an FBI agent.

In other words, the Navy found out from the phone company that the FBI tap had been uncovered, so the affidavit told me, and then the FBI got peeved because that exposed their position and then the Navy got scared and took out their taps. That is what it amounts to.

SENATOR LUCAS. But the FBI continued on?

COLONEL CLAUSEN. The FBI continued the one they had on and, as I read you this morning, Mr. Shivers said had they told him this he would have covered all the taps and I have here, sir, in my documents photostats of the last day's work by Navy, where the Navy man said he had been doint it for twenty-two months and he bids good-bye, after twenty-two months, and 2 December was this date, from which we knew they quit on December 2nd.

SENATOR LUCAS. They quit on December 2nd after having done this surveillance work for twenty-two straight months?

Colonel Clausen. Yes, sir.

Senator Ferguson. You mean there was surveillance for twenty-two months at the Hawaiian Department?

Colonel Clausen. Yes.

The Vice Chairman. Why did they say they quit it?

Colonel Clausen. Just what the affidavit says here. Mayfield got peeved.

The Vice Chairman. They quit it because somebody else did not like it that they were doing it?

Colonel Clausen. He says right here:

> When Captain Mayfield, then District Intelligence Officer, learned of the FBI protest at the telephone company, he was not only incensed at their failure to consult with him before taking such action, but he considered that action to be a serious breech of security. Cognizant of his instructions from the Chief of Naval Operations to avoid any possibility of international complications, and thoroughly aware of the explosive potentialities of the surveillances being [4369] conducted, Captain Mayfield ordered the immediate discontinuance of all telephone surveillances. This was on 2 December 1941.

The Vice Chairman. All right.

Senator Lucas. So the Navy just turned the work over to the FBI?

Colonel Clausen. No, they did not turn it over. They just quit.

Senator Lucas. They just quit and let the FBI handle it alone?

Colonel Clausen. No, they didn't do that. They did not tell the FBI. They just quit and said nothing.

The Vice Chairman. They just quit, period, then?

Colonel Clausen. Period.

Mr. Gearhart. The FBI continued their taps of the kitchens or cook's quarters?

Colonel Clausen. That is right.

Me. Gearhart. And if the FBI had known that the Navy had withdrawn they would have extended their taps to cover the other parts of the consulates?

Colonel Clausen. Yes, sir.

Mr. Gearhart. I have heard of that. ...

[4464] Senator Lucas. ... [4465] One of the things that intrigued me was your testimony on yesterday that for 22 months, as I recall, the Navy had been tapping Japanese communication lines.

Colonel Clausen. Yes, sir; telephone lines running to the Consul, and then they had some taps on lines running to the Japanese Consul's home, and some taps running to the line of the Jap Steamship company. ...

[4465] Senator Lucas. ... [4466] Now I want to read Captain Mayfield's testimony that was given in the Hewitt Report, page 570:

> Mr. Sonnett. Admiral, did any information come to you prior to December 7, 1941, of military significance which had been obtained from tapping a telephone line to the Japanese Consul?

REAR ADMIRAL MAYFIELD. None that I recollect and I do not believe that any information received by this method was considered of military or naval importance by me or my assistants.

MR. SONNETT. You have, Admiral, examined at my request, have you not, Exhibit 38-A and 38-B, the transcripts from October 1, 1941, to December 2, 1941? Can you state whether having examined those transcripts, there appears to be anything of military or naval significance contained therein?

REAR ADMIRAL MAYFIELD. I do not believe there is anything of military or naval significance contained therein.

MR. SONNETT. Will you state, Admiral, why there are no transcripts after December 2, 1941, and up to December 7, 1941?

REAR ADMIRAL MAYFIELD. On or about December 2nd, it was reported to me by one of my assistants that employees of the telephone company had discovered a jumper put across the connections in a junction box by a member of the FBI organization, and that an employee of the telephone company had reported this discovery to one of my assistants. It was further reported to me that one of my assistants reported this matter to one of the agents of the FBI. It was further reported to me that a member of the FBI organization, name unknown to me, had taken the matter up with the telephone company. What representative of the telephone company I do not know. To the best of my recollection, I discussed the matter with Mr. Shivers and the report made to me did not agree with the report made to him by his assistants. My organization long before my arrival had worked up a contact with an employee of the telephone company and through this contact was able to obtain any telephone interception desired by my office. Because of the highly explosive nature of such practice, I did not desire to enter into an argument or controversy as to the merits or demerits of the case since I was afraid that by doing so, the fact that such interceptions were being made might be discovered and thereby jeopardize the future of any further interceptions. Furthermore, since the interceptions to that date had revealed nothing of particular value, I considered the wisest thing to do was to cease all interceptions of whatever kind and so instructed my assistants.

MR. SONNETT. Admiral, I show you Exhibit 39 of this investigation.

REAR ADMIRAL MAYFIELD. I would like to add that later along—the exact date I do not remember, but I believe after December 7 the whole matter was satisfactorily straightened out and we were again able to resume interceptions.

MR. SONNETT. Admiral, I show you Exhibit 39 of this investigation which has been previously identified as a transcript of the so-called Mori conversation. Will you state whether that conversation and transcript came to your attention and fully circumstances surrounding that?

REAR ADMIRAL MAYFIELD. To the best of my recollection a transcript of this exhibit was brought to me by Mr. Shivers on the morning of December 6. I believe it was very late in the afternoon. We discussed the transcript and were unable to determine that it did have any definite or particular significance. It was thought desirable to have Lieutenant Commander Carr listen to the recording and give us his further opinion as to the value of the contents of the transcription before decision was arrived at as to whether or not it should be reported to the Commandant of the District.

MR. SONNETT. Was it brought to the attention of the Commandant, or to any other superior officer prior to the attack?

REAR ADMIRAL MAYFIELD. To the best of my recollection it was not.

MR. SONNETT. Do you know whether or not it was brought to the attention of General Short prior to the attack?

REAR ADMIRAL MAYFIELD. I have no knowledge of that.

Now, is that the same message that we are talking about now, that was delivered by Captain Bicknell?

COLONEL CLAUSEN. That is Colonel Bicknell—brought the Mori message out to General Short.

[4467] SENATOR LUCAS. That is the message we are talking about that Colonel Bicknell telephoned General Short about on Saturday evening, December 6, 1941.

COLONEL CLAUSEN. Yes, sir.

SENATOR LUCAS. And Short told him that he was going out to dinner, that if he could get out there in 10 minutes he would hear him?

COLONEL CLAUSEN. General Fielder, I think, said that, relaying it for General Short.

SENATOR LUCAS. All right. He finally got there and this was the one in which General Short told us he could not see anything wrong in?

COLONEL CLAUSEN. He could not see anything wrong with it.

SENATOR LUCAS. Later on, General Short admitted that this fellow was right, and he was wrong?

COLONEL CLAUSEN. Yes, sir.

MR. KAUFMAN. That message, Senator, is Exhibit 84 in this proceeding.

SENATOR LUCAS. Thank you.

Now, continuing:

> MR. SONNETT. Referring, Admiral, to the transcript of the telephone conversation between Mori and a person in Japan which you have before you, it appears, does it not, that after a question from Japan concerning the United States Fleet and the number of ships present, the person in Japan inquired what flowers or whether the flowers were in bloom, and that that question was answered by Mori, who pointed out that poinsettias and some other flowers were in bloom?
>
> REAR ADMIRAL MAYFIELD. It does. The question from Japan asks "What kind of flowers are in bloom in Hawaii at present?" The reply from Honolulu was to the effect that flowers in bloom were the fewest out of the whole year, but that hibiscus and poinsettias were in bloom.
>
> MR. SONNETT. When you studied that transcript on December 6, 1941, Admiral, did that particular portion of it come to your attention?
>
> REAR ADMIRAL MAYFIELD. It did.
>
> MR. SONNETT. What were your thoughts concerning it at the time?
>
> REAR ADMIRAL MAYFIELD. Our thoughts at the time were that it was somewhat curious but that it was a disconnected conversation in which Mori seemed to be somewhat at a loss, and, according to my recollection, that was the reason for our desire to study it further and have Dr. Carr listen to the recording itself.
>
> MR. SONNETT. Did you have any knowledge at that time, or have you now any knowledge, as to the establishment by the Japanese of a code in which by

the broadcast of trans-Pacific radio telephone conversation references to flowers would signify movement of United States ships from Pearl Harbor?

REAR ADMIRAL MAYFIELD. I think that is rather a complicated question to answer, did I have then or do I have now.

MR. SONNETT. Would the answer be different?

REAR ADMIRAL MAYFIELD. Yes.

MR. SONNETT. Let's make it, did you have then? Then we will ask you the other.

REAR ADMIRAL MAYFIELD. I did not have knowledge of any such code at that time.

MR. SONNETT. Have you knowledge of any such code at this time?

REAR ADMIRAL MAYFIELD. Of my own personal knowledge of the existence of such code, I have none. I mean I have heard or read something about it, but then—

MR. SONNETT. Well, I think you might just state that.

REAR ADMIRAL MAYFIELD. I have heard or read something to the effect that such a code may have been in existence. I have no personal knowledge of the existence of such a code.

Upon that point, had any of your inquiries been as to whether anybody in Hawaii, either in the Navy or Army, did have knowledge of the existence of such code?

[4468] COLONEL CLAUSEN. No, sir. The point was in Colonel Bicknell's mind that these words to him, as G-2 officer, might be code words. That was his thought on the night of December 6.

You remember in his affidavit, Senator, he said he had been trained under General Knowland; General Knowland was in charge of that G-2 in the European war, and he had always instructed his men no matter how insignificantly the detail might appear, the information might have some important bearing.

Colonel Bicknell was especially alarmed because of the use of these two words, poinsettias and hibiscus, and he testified before the Grunert Board that the next morning when the attack was going on, he stood on the veranda of his home, repeating automatically to himself, as the Japs were dropping bombs on the ships, "poinsettias and hibiscus."

He sais these two words stood in his mind. He was almost automatically doing this at the time the attack was going on.

THE VICE CHAIRMAN. Who was doing that?

COLONEL CLAUSEN. Colonel Bicknell, sir, George Bicknell.

THE VICE CHAIRMAN. He is the man who took the message to General Short?

COLONEL CLAUSEN. Yes, sir, the preceding night.

THE VICE CHAIRMAN. All right. . . .

[4469] COLONEL CLAUSEN. . . . I always had a hunch that in Hawaii they must have tapped phone lines. When I got over there to Hawaii I went first to a man who was a ship's clerk. I had been given his name by Colonel Bicknell. Well, when the man sat down and said that he was a Navy agent I, of course, said, "What do you do?" I had no knowledge of phone taps. He said, "I am a technician."

Well, you know, Mr. Gearhart, when a fellow is secretive and says he is a technician, and a private detective, we, as lawyers, immediately think of dictaphones, et cetera. When I found out he was a technician, why, then that was very interesting. And the more I talked to him the less he wanted to talk. When he finally did say that his technique extended to phone taps, when I put the question to him direct, he didn't even want to sign the paper.

[4470]   Now, that is an example of some of the things that were brand new.

MR. GEARHART. That is the point I wanted to make. That is, to bring out that you were under an injunction to bring out new evidence as well as to eliminate the uncertainties of old evidence. Isn't that correct?

COLONEL CLAUSEN. Yes, but, Mr. Gearhart, I was just as free as the wind as to what I could do so far as uncovering evidence was concerned. I mean by that, Mr. Gearhart, and I want you to believe this, there was no compulsion, no restraint, nothing put upon me except that in which I agreed. I agreed it didn't seem to me to be my province to go into the Navy to find out whether Admiral Kimmel should be court-martialed by the Navy. My functions resolved around, Mr. Gearhart, as I read your Public Law 339, I agreed with that scope of my investigation completely.

SECTION THREE

Radar: The Great Missed Opportunity

Prior American and British Development of Radar

WILLIAM E. G. TAYLOR, NAVY ADVISER
TO INTERCEPTOR COMMAND, PEARL HARBOR

Hart Inquiry

[368]   1. Q. What is your name, rank, and present station?
A. William E. G. Taylor, Commander, A-V(T), U.S.N.R., attached to Commander, Fleet Air, Quonset, Quonset Point, Rhode Island.

2. Q. Were you born and brought up in a family of the armed Services?
A. Yes, sir. I was born in Fort Leavenworth, Kansas. My father is Colonel James G. Taylor, U.S. Army, Retired.

3. Q. What was your college education?
A. My college education consisted of two years of aeronautical engineering at New York University.

4. Q. State, briefly, the circumstances surrounding your first connection with the naval service.
A. During the second year of my college, I had a particular desire to get into the flying end of aviation rather than the technical end, and applied for flight training, was accepted, went through flight training in 1926 at Hampton Roads, Virginia; completed flight training and was commissioned an Ensign AF, U.S.N.R., in March, 1927.

5. Q. Did that course of training make you a full-fledged naval aviator?
A. Yes, sir, I was designated a naval aviator on the completion of the course.

6. Q. State, briefly, your duties and experiences in naval aviation subsequent to that acceptance.
A. On July 1, 1927, I was ordered to active duty as a pilot in the Fifth Fighting Squadron, later attached to the *U.S.S. Lexington,* and I served one year's active duty with the Fleet. On the completion of the year's duty, at the end of the year, I was ordered to inactive duty, was then asked to transfer to the Marine Corps Reserve as an instructor, during the period when the Marine Corps Reserve was building up an aviation reserve.

Source: Pearl Harbor Attack, *volume 26.*

7. Q. When was that?

A. I resigned my commission as an Ensign in July, 1928, and was commissioned a Second Lieutenant in the Marine Corps Reserve the same month. I served as instructor at Pensacola as an officer in charge of the Marine Corps Reserve Aviation Unit at Squantum, Grosse Isle Field; served a period of duty at Quantico. Most of this period of active duty was as an aviation instructor. In 1934, I was ordered to inactive duty.

8. Q. During these years in the Navy and the Marine Corps, which I understand totaled about seven years, were you specialized in any particular type of aircraft?

A. Yes, I specialized in fighter aircraft.

9. Q. What was your rank when you were placed on inactive status in 1934?

A. Captain, U.S. Marine Corps Reserve, sir.

10. Q. Do you know why you were transferred to the inactive list at that time?

[369] A. No, sir, I do not. I was given to understand that the Marine Corps Reserve, which was limited in its funds for training, wanted to increase the number of officer instructors by ordering senior officers to inactive duty and taking on new Second Lieutenants.

11. Q. Following your placement upon inactive status, in what pursuit or occupation did you engage?

A. After I was ordered to inactive duty, the first occupation that I took up was as manager and flight instructor at the Aviation Country Club in Hicksville, Long Island. I remained at this work for approximately two years and left to take a job as pilot with United Air Lines. I was with United Air Lines about nine months. I next became a pilot for an oil processing company in New York. I remained at this job until 1938 when I left the job and went to England.

12. Q. While in the employ of the United Air Lines, what were your actual duties?

A. I was employed as a co-pilot.

13. Q. On what run?

A. On the run between Chicago and New York, sir.

14. Q. What were the circumstances and reasons for your going to England in 1938 and what was the approximate date?

A. I sailed for England in mid–July for the purpose of attempting to get into the Royal Air Force if war were declared. As it appeared that war would not be declared by mid–August, I returned to the United States.

15. Q. How long did you remain in the United States?

A. I remained in the United States until August, 1939, when I again went to England to join the Royal Air Force. I was put in touch with Royal Air Force officers and British Naval Air Officers by the Naval Attache, London. The Royal Air Force was non-committal or would not commit themselves to accepting me until war was declared. The British Navy signified their willingness to accept me as a Sub-Lieutenant, R.N.V.R., even before war was declared. I sent my resignation as a Captain of the Marine Corps Reserve back to the United States via the American Naval Attache, London, on 1 September 1939. I was commissioned a Sub-Lieutenant in the R.N.V.R. about 4 September 1939.

16. Q. Upon accepting that commission, what became your employment in the British Navy?

A. I was first sent to the Fleet Air Fighter Training School at Donibristle, Scotland, following which I was sent to the Mediterranean in *H.M.S. Argus* for carrier qualifications. Upon completion of carrier qualifications, I was ordered to Scapa Flow to a Fleet Fighter Squadron whose function was the defense of the Fleet in Scapa Flow.

17. Q. About what date was that?

A. That was about November or December, 1939. My squadron remained at Scapa Flow until the beginning of the Norwegian Campaign, which, I believe, was March, 1940, when we were attached to *H.M.S. Glorious* and *H.M.S. Furious;* we made four trips between Scapa Flow and the Norwegian Coast. We returned to Scapa Flow at the end of the Norwegian Campaign in June, 1940. [...]

[372] The Air Ministry and Admiralty reached an agreement and I was transferred to the Royal Air Force. This transfer was effected on 2 October 1940. I was sent to a Royal Air Force Fighter Operational Training unit for three weeks, at the end of which time I was ordered, at my own request, to 242 Fighter Squadron, stationed at the Royal Air Force Station at Duxford. I asked to be sent to 242 Squadron before taking over 71 Eagle Squadron because I wanted to get some operational experience in an active air force squadron before forming my own.

31. Q. Give a brief summary of your operational experience while attached to R.A.F. Fighter Squadron No. 242.

A. During the four month period I was attached to 242 Squadron, I participated in four or five actual interceptions against hostile aircraft, flying wing on the Squadron Commander. Although we saw numerous hostile aircraft during these operations, we were never ordered to attack. The actual attacks were to be made by other squadrons which were also in the air. The greater part of my time in the 242 Squadron was spent learning current tactical information and learning the organization of R.A.F. squadrons. [...]

[373] 38. Q. Did you, yourself, become acquainted with the British radar apparatus and with its technical operation?

A. I was given a very good basic understanding of the function and limitations of the radar equipment, but I had never actually seen a British radar system until after I had resigned from the Royal Air Force.

39. Q. In addition to the representatives of the United States Army Air Corps, were similar bodies of naval aviators also given opportunities to learn the British fighter direction system?

A. I did not hear of any naval observers studying either the Royal Air Force or British Navy Fighter Direction System until late Spring of 1941.

40. Q. Did you, during 1940, make any reports, formal or otherwise, which may have reached the Navy Department and particularly describing the British radar apparatus and its operation?

A. Yes, sir, I made a full report of all of the operations that I had been engaged in and of all the information that I had picked up in England to several groups of officers in the Bureau of Aeronautics. I particularly sought out the officer who was, at that time, in charge of radar development in the Bureau of Aeronautics to give him what in [374] formation I had on the British Fighter Direction System. I was told that the U.S. Navy had radar either in our ships or being developed for shipboard use. I could arouse no interest in the use of this radar for fighter direction.

41. Q. At about what date did you complete the assembling and training of your own squadron and where did it then become stationed?

A. 71 Eagle Squadron completed its training and became operational in January, 1941, at Kirton Lindsey, Lincolnshire, on the East Coast of England, and we were immediately ordered to Martelsham Heath where our main function was the defense of convoys going to and from the Thames and Humber Rivers.

42. Q. What kind of planes did you have?

A. We were originally equipped with Hurricane fighters and, later, were re-equipped with Spitfires.

43. Q. Give a brief resume of your experiences while in command of the Eagle Squadron, operating under the R.A.F.

A. From the time that we became operational, in January of 1941, until July of 1941, our squadron stood a regular fighter watches on the Southeast Coast of England. Our combat work was mainly the protection of convoys off the Coast and making interceptions on any hostile aircraft which came over. During this period, there was very little German activity except at night. During the moonlight periods, we sent up four planes of our squadron to join the night fighter defense. Having no radar, our night work was ineffective. Up until this time, the only type of radar that was functioning in England was the seaward-looking radar. All overland direction of fighters was done by radio direction finding on the fighters. All of the hostile aircraft positions were reported by visual observers. Radar interceptions overland were, therefore, almost impossible except with the aid of searchlights or airborne radar. This was approximately the period during which the R.A.F. was building up an improved system for interception of enemy planes overland and at night.

44. Q. What were the circumstances of the termination of your services in the Royal Air Force?

A. In July, 1941, I was called to Group Headquarters and told that because of my age, I was going to be made a Wing Commander and put in command of a fighter operational training unit. I was disappointed in losing my squadron and asked to be allowed to go back either to the British Navy or to return to the American Navy. The American Naval Attache had been, for the past year, asking me to return to the American Navy for the purpose of working on fighter direction. I was allowed to go to London to talk to the American Naval Attache, who sent a dispatch to the Navy Department, Washington, advising them that my services were available. In approximately two weeks' time, my commission and orders to duty to the Bureau of Aeronautics in Washington were received in London. I was commissioned Lieutenant Commander, A-V(S), U.S.N.R., in London in the month of July, 1941. However, as there was no immediate transportation back to the United States and as the Naval Attache wanted me to collect more information on radar equipment, I was given a special assignment to visit several radar stations. I was given every opportunity to thoroughly inspect the most modern [375] radar stations in the South of England and all of my questions were answered willingly. In August, in about 15 August 1941, I was returned to the United States by Clipper and reported to the Chief of Bureau of Aeronautics.

45. Q. Upon your arrival in the Navy Department, did it occur to you that you were being looked upon as an expert in the utilization of radar for purposes of command and direction of airborne aircraft?

A. Only by a very few officers. The vast majority of officers in the Bureau of Aeronautics seemed to consider fighter direction of very little importance.

46. Q. Did those who seemed to realize its importance appear to look upon you as expert in that specialty?

A. Yes, sir.

47. Q. From your experiences, soon after you returned to Washington, did you find anyone else whom you considered, at the time, as equally expert as yourself?

A. There were several officers in this country who had been in England studying both the Royal Air Force and the British Navy method of fighter direction who were, at that time, setting up fighter direction schools at Norfolk and at San Diego. However, it was apparent that their brief period of observing in England did not give them nearly the full picture of what fighter direction involved.

48. Q. Then you found no one who had the breadth of experience in that line which you had enjoyed?

A. No, sir.

49. Q. Please state, briefly, the duties which you came to perform upon your return to the United States.

A. I was sent out on temporary duty in the *Yorktown, Ranger,* and *Wasp* in September, 1941, to lecture to the fighter squadrons on combat tactics and fighter direction to pass on to the ships' officers what information I had on the use of search radar for fighter direction purposes, and to learn what I could of what each ship contemplated as a fighter direction organization. I completed this duty in approximately one month's time and returned to Washington.

50. Q. Did that brief assignment with the carriers in our Atlantic Fleet acquaint you with the capabilities of the radar installations which you found on board those ships?

A. Yes, sir. There was radar only aboard the *Yorktown* at that time.

51. Q. At the time, what was your judgment as to the performance of that radar as compared with those which you had recently seen in Britain?

A. It was my impression that the radar equipment aboard the *Yorktown* was superior to any radar equipment used in the British Navy and at least as good as the Royal Air Force shore-based search radar.

52. Q. What did you find as to the comparative ability of the radar operators?

A. The radar operators were largely under training, but the main radar enlisted man and the main radar officer aboard ship were both very well trained and versed in the operation of the equipment.

53. Q. Next, following that detail, what became your duties?

[376] A. I was given temporary duty orders to report to Commander Aircraft, Battle Force, for temporary duty. My duties were to be the same as they had been on the East Coast carriers. I joined the *U.S.S. Lexington* at San Diego and lectured the fighter squadrons and spoke to the ship's officers en route to Pearl Harbor in early October, 1941. On my arrival at Pearl Harbor, I found the *Enterprise* was at sea. I, therefore, reported to the Air Officer on CinCPac's Staff. When the *Enterprise* returned in early October, approximately three days later, I reported to Admiral Halsey. Admiral Halsey instructed me to report to Admiral Kimmel for such use as he wanted to make of me. Admiral Kimmel questioned me while I was at Pearl Harbor. He also instructed me to lecture to the fighter squadrons of the Army Air Force. Admiral Kimmel's Staff made arrangements for my lectures at Wheeler Field. I made a series of four lectures to all of the fighter squadrons at Wheeler Field.

54. Q. Upon completing those lectures, what became your duties?

A. On completion of the lectures to the Army Fighter Squadrons, I lectured to the pilots and ship's officers of the *U.S.S. Saratoga* and I then reported to the *U.S.S. Enterprise*. I went to sea in the *U.S.S. Enterprise*, lectured to the squadrons attached to her, also had an opportunity to observe their method of fighter direction. The *Enterprise*'s fighter direction had gone much further than any other ship. The *Enterprise*'s fighter direction was considerably behind the British methods. This was so because the fighter system had been improvised by the Staff Communications Officer with little information to work on.

55. Q. Then you found the *Enterprise* considerably advanced over the other carriers in the utilization of radar?

A. Yes, sir.

56. Q. As regards the radar equipment and its actual operation, will you state the conditions which you found on the various carriers of the Pacific Fleet?

A. The *Enterprise* had had their radar aboard a considerable time and had been able to calibrate the radar equipment and train to a certain extent one or two fighter director officers. The *Saratoga* had no radar. The *Lexington*, on which I came out from San Diego, had just had her radar installed and was just learning to use it. In all ships equipped with radar, the radar installation had been very recent and all hands were going through a training period in the operation and utilization of the equipment for fighter direction.

57. Q. Was it the same variety of equipment which you found in the carriers in the Atlantic and which you have stated was very good for its kind?

A. Yes, sir.

58. Q. Following that period at sea in the *Enterprise*, what was your next duty?

A. While I was at sea in the *Enterprise*, a dispatch was received from the Commander-in-Chief, Pacific Fleet, stating that my services were requested by the Commanding General, Hawaiian Air Force, for technical purposes. Upon our return to Pearl Harbor, I was instructed to report to the Acting Commanding Officer, Interceptor Command, to assist in an advisory capacity in setting up the Army Information Center at Fort Shafter.

[377] 59. Q. Did you have reason to believe that either the Navy or the Army, or both, in the Hawaiian Area, were looking upon you as expert in that specialty?

A. Yes, sir. A very few officers in both the Army and Navy seemed to feel that I was an expert on fighter direction and the utilization of radar.

60. Q. Was that because the installations and the use of it was so new that very few officers knew anything about it?

A. Yes, sir. That was true generally in both the Army and Navy. [...]

[379] 61. Q. Please give a resume of your experiences while thus loaned to the United States Army, Hawaiian Department, including your relations with Army officials, and with Navy officials as well if such occurred, covering also radar apparatus, ability to use same, communications from the radar stations, and so on.

A. I was instructed to report to the Interceptor Command at Wheeler Field and reported to find the Commanding General of the Interceptor Command was in the United States. The Acting Commanding Officer requested me to work in an advisory capacity with his Operations Officer and assist him in expediting the completion of the air warning system. During the first week in November, we inspected all of the installations and plans for the air warning system and I found these facts to be true: (1) Construction and maintenance of the air warning system was a Signal Corps function directly under the cognizance of the Chief Signal Officer, Staff of the Commanding General, Hawaiian Department. This Command appeared to have little conception of the vast function of the air warning system and exhibited very little interest in expediting its installation. At no time before December 7, 1941, did this Command furnish either the authority or impetus badly needed to get the work or organization properly started. (2) The actual operation of the air warning system — that is, the evaluation and dissemination of radar information and the control of fighter defense — was under the Interceptor Command. The [380] Interceptor Command fully realized the importance of the air warning system. Although the officers concerned were not fully informed of its complicated functions, they were willing and eager to take advice and lend all assistance in their power to help complete its installations. They seemed relatively impotent, however, in getting assistance needed from the Commanding General's Staff. (3) One Captain of the Air Corps and one Captain of the Signal Corps had been through the Air Warning School at Mitchell Field, New York. It was with these two officers that I worked. Both were capable and energetic. They worked twelve to fifteen hours a day, seven days a week, in an attempt to speed up completion of the air warning system. (4) The air warning equipment and communications system were largely field or mobile equipment and the entire system was temporary. However, with the exception of the ground-to-air and air-to-ground radio equipment, the system was adequate to serve its purpose as was later proved. (5) There were only five Army mobile radar equipments in the Hawaiian area. These equipments had bee in Oahu about three months. The five sets were installed and, in my opinion, as well sited as terrain would permit and were the absolute minimum needed to cover the entire seaward search for the Island. The radar equipment itself was inferior to any I had seen before. The deficiency in the equipment, however, was due to crude mechanical construction rather than to any electronic fault. This made the operation of the equipment difficult and slow, with the result that the reported azimuth readings were frequently very inaccurate and the reports were slow in coming in. The equipment had a reliable range of eighty to one hundred miles. A "dead" area existed through a fifteen mile radius from the equipment. It was, therefore, impossible to pick up aircraft plots within the first fifteen miles off shore. At each radar station, there was at least one officer or sergeant well trained to operate and maintain the equipment. In addition, there were seven or eight other enlisted operators under instruction at each station. All stations were under-manned for twenty-four hour operation. At the time of my inspection, either commercial or Signal Corps field telephone lines had been installed between the radar stations and the Information Center. (6) The Information Center itself had been planned on an Area Command scale similar to the Boston or New York Information Centers and was too large in scope to effectively handle raids on the small Island of Oahu. The building was a temporary, wooden building and had just been completed at the time of my inspection. The communications equipment was mostly field telephone equipment of the type developed during the last war. Positions had been provided for controllers and liaison officers, but liaison command lines had not been installed. These were not installed, primarily, because the activities at which the liaison command lines were to terminate were uninformed as to the purpose concerning the air warning system and because the Commanding General had not taken the steps to coordinate these activities with the air warning system. The Signal Corps had furnished sufficient plotters to man two watches only. These were just starting their training at the time of my inspection. There were no controllers or liaison officers available at this time and no provisions had been made to provide them. (7) The anti-aircraft battalion had installed a command post but no liaison had been established   [381]   between the anti-aircraft command and the Information Center. (8) No attempt had been made to secure control of the anti-aircraft guns of ships in harbor. (9) No liaison had been established between the searchlights and the Information Center. (10) No attempt had been made to disperse the fighter squadrons at Wheeler Field. (11) No automatic aircraft recognition system was installed which would identify all types of aircraft. (12) No aircraft approach lane system had been planned. (13) No system for identifying aircraft approaching Oahu by reports from parent aviation activities had been organized. (14) No visual observers reporting system had been organized. The foregoing is a summation of conditions found at Oahu during my inspection about 1 November 1941. These were reported by myself and the Inspector Command Operations Officer to the Staffs of Commander-in-Chief, Pacific Fleet; Commandant, Fourteenth Naval District; Commander, Patrol Wing Two; Commanding General, Hawaiian Department; Commanding General, Hawaiian Air Force and Bomber Command, prior to November 15, 1941. By December 7, 1941, all telephone communication lines had been installed with the exception of the Civilian Air Raid Precaution Command lines, and the command lines from the Information Center to five fighter squadron dispersal points at Wheeler Field. Direct command lines were installed from Liaison position in the Information Center to the various Army and Navy commands and activities. The civilian line had not been completed due to the fact no air raid center had been set up in Honolulu. The command lines to the fighter dispersal points were not completed, due to switchboard complications at Wheeler Field. Two fighter squadrons were dispersed, one at Bellows Field and one at Haliena Field. The dispersal of the remaining fighter squadrons was awaiting installation of command lines. An excellent liaison had been established between the Army anti-aircraft batteries (three and five inch) and searchlights. About 15 November, I was instructed by CinCPac's Staff to request control of anti-aircraft guns of ships in harbor from Com 14. This request was refused by Com 14 on the grounds that "No Army organization would control guns on any naval vessel. If anything comes over, we will shoot it down." However, this control was voluntarily turned over to the Information Center on December 9, after ships' guns had shot down *U.S.S. Enterprise* aircraft. At the same time, I was also instructed by CinCPac to request naval liaison officers for the Information Center from Com 14. His Chief of Staff informed me that these liaison officers should come from the Fleet. I was referred to Commander, Patrol Wing Two. I was told by Commander, Patrol Wing Two, that no liaison officers were available in that Command. I returned to CinCPac and reported my failure to obtain naval liaison officers. CinCPac's Operations Officer informed me that he would take steps to find some. These officers did not report to the Information Center until December 8. I was further instructed by CinCPac to confer with Commander, Patrol Wing Two, in order to establish an aircraft identification system and aircraft approach lanes to Oahu. A conference was held at the Information Center, between November 15 and 20, at which officers from all flying activities were present to discuss these matters. It was decided by the aviation activities concerned that these systems would not be put into effect until war was [382] declared, because it was felt that activating these systems prior to that time would complicate crowded flying conditions and hinder flying training. The Army stated that movements of aircraft from the United States to the Southwest Pacific were secret, and it was, therefore, not desirable to report those movements at that time. It should be noted that without an aircraft movement reporting system to the Information Center, it was impossible for the Information Center to determine whether radar reports were of friendly or of hostile aircraft. CinCPac's Operations Officer stated, however, that their Operations Office was prepared to report the movements of aircraft under their cognizance at any time this information was requested. Some doubt existed as to whether the Signal Corps' (Hawaiian Department) or Interceptor Command should furnish controllers. As no controllers seemed to be forthcoming from the Hawaiian Department, Interceptor Command decided to use Squadron Commanders as controllers at the Information Center. These officers were heavily occupied with training their squadrons and were seldom available for controller training. However, no other source of controllers seemed to exist. Bomber Command, G.H.Q., and G-2 liaison officers were not made available until several days after December 7, when their importance at the Information Center was finally realized. Interceptor Command had taken the initiative in the training of Information Center plotters. This training was progressing satisfactorily when, during the last week in November, the Commanding General, Hawaiian Department, ordered that the radar stations would operate only between 0400 and 0700. I was informed that the decision to limit the operating hours was made to prevent breakdown of the radar equipment from prolonged operation. Training which had been conducted from 0800 to 1700 daily only, due to the shortage of radar operators and plotters, was necessarily limited to the hours of 0400–0700 by the order. The Information Center, therefore, virtually ceased to function except during those hours. I informed CinCPac's Operations Officer of the situation as it existed on or about 1 December and was told that in view of the failure of the responsible commanders to take action to provide necessary personnel and to activate the Information Center on a twenty-four hour basis, he would initiate a letter requesting the Commanding General, Hawaiian Department, to take action immediately. I do not know whether this letter was ever written, or not. However, no action was taken up to December 7. On the morning of December 7, I was informed, by the telephone operator of the hotel in which I was staying, that all naval officers were instructed to report to their ships immediately. I reported to the Information Center between 0800 and 0830 to find considerable confusion in progress. The duty controller was a Squadron Commander who had stood his first training watch during the 0400–0700 period that day. Through no fault of his own, he was almost totally unable to cope with the situation. The Interception Command Operations Officer had reported before my arrival, and was doing his utmost to get the Information Center organized. Sentries, mess cooks, and telephone linesmen were pressed into the liaison positions to man the telephones. As they were untrained, it was impossible for them to interpret and report the current situation to the activities requesting information. Someone had removed the large scale overlay chart of [383] the Islands from the plotting table. The scale of the plotting table chart was too small for plotting, with the result that the plotting table was covered with a confusion of plots too numerous and large to evaluate properly. The Operations Officer was doing the best job possible under the circumstances to control the few fighters which were air-borne. During this time, I was occupied in an attempt to keep all of the interested activities as well informed as possible over the many liaison command lines. I should like to state here that several traced records were kept of the many plots which appeared on the plotting board. After the raids on December 7, their tracings were studied in an attempt to determine exactly where the raids had come from, and in what direction they had returned. As a flight of Army B-17 bombers had arrived almost simultaneously with the first raid, and as there were a considerable number of friendly aircraft in all areas, it was only possible to reconstruct an estimated plot of what had occurred. This plot was not completed until nearly forty-eight hours after the raids. However, it is my understanding that this plot was shown to the Secretary of the Navy during his visit as evidence that all information was received in an orderly manner by the Information Center during the raids.

62. Q. Referring to your statement concerning the fifteen mile "dead area" around Oahu, was there any visual system to supplement that weakness in the radar coverage?

A. After December 7 only, sir.

63. Q. Will you please elaborate your statement concerning what seems to have been a dual responsibility as between the Army Signal Corps and the Army Air Corps covering the installation of the complete warning system?

A. Where it was the Signal Corps' job to expedite the completion of the Information Center, the full initiative for expediting this work was taken on by Inspector Command. The Chief Signal Officer, Hawaiian Department, seemed to attach very secondary importance to the completion of the Information Center, both as regards providing materiel and trained personnel.

64. Q. Which organization had the responsibility for the supply of personnel in the first place?

A. It was my impression that the Signal Corps had the job of furnishing all personnel for the Information Center.

65. Q. What, as regards the installations and operators of the remainder of the system outside of the Combat Information Center?

A. The Signal Corps equipment was field equipment but satisfactory; personnel for installing communication lines were well trained, capable, and in sufficient numbers; the radar operators and maintenance men at the radar stations were too few in numbers and were not fully trained even up to December 7.

66. Q. Was all that a responsibility of the Army Signal Corps?

A. Yes, sir.

67. Q. You have stated that you obtained no liaison officers for the Information Center from the Navy. How many did you ask for?

A. I asked for six. On December 8, I received ten who were survivors from the *California*.

[384] 68. Q. Other than the failure of the Naval District to supply liaison officers, did you experience other lack of cooperation from that organization?

A. I can not remember receiving any active cooperation from Fourteenth Naval District, at any time, prior to December 7.

69. Q. In your estimation, at the time, what additional cooperation or measures were required of the Naval District?

A. The Commander-in-Chief's Staff pointed out to me that according to the war plans, the Commandant, Fourteenth Naval District, had the responsibility of the defense of Oahu, and I was, therefore, instructed to report to him for any assistance needed to activate the Information Center.

70. Q. What assistance did you ask for?

A. Other than to ask for liaison officers, I requested that control of the antiaircraft guns in naval vessels in the harbor, which were directly under his control, should be held by the Information Center. I asked that some action be taken to identify aircraft approaching Oahu. At the Commander-in-Chief's Operations Officer's suggestion, I asked him to initiate a letter to the Commanding General, Hawaiian Department, to expedite putting the Information Center on a twenty-four hour basis.

71. Q. Did you, at any time during the period during which you were loaned to the Army, report to the Comamnder-in-Chief, or his representatives, of the unreadiness of the warning system in general or of the Information Center in particular?

A. Yes, sir. A full report concerning the readiness of the Army Air Warning System was made to the Commander-in-Chief's Staff immediately after my initial inspection. On about 1 December, I reported to CinCPac's Operations Officer that Information Center personnel were still not forthcoming, and that the operating hours had been limited to 0400–0700 daily. During the entire period of my duty at the Information Center, I made frequent visits to CinCPac's Office and conferred with his Chief of Staff, Operations Officer, Air Officer or Communications Officer.

72. Q. Did you make those reports in such form and with such emphasis as to convey the thought that little could be expected in the way of information concerning a surprise air attack?

A. Yes, sir, I did. I feel quite sure that the Commander-in-Chief, Pacific Fleet's Staff fully realized the situation.

73. Q. During your association with the Army, what did you gather was in the minds of the Army fighter command as constituting their primary mission while based on Oahu?

A. It is my distinct impression that the Interceptor Command believed that they were charged with operating the air warning system, once it was completed, and furnishing the fighter defense for the Hawaiian Islands.

74. Q. Do you mean that the conception of that part of the Army Air Force, Oahu, was that their primary mission and purpose was repelling air attacks upon the installations on that Island?

A. No, sir, I do not. The Army Air Force was broken up into two commands. The Army Interceptor Command which had their fighters, I believe they considered their primary mission to repel enemy air attacks.

[385] 75. Q. Based upon your experiences in England, what was your estimate in those days as to the ability of the number of fighter planes based on Oahu to repel a heavy air raid if they had been properly handled in the air?

A. I believe there were sufficient numbers of fighters at Oahu to repel the number of aircraft that actually attacked Pearl Harbor on December 7.

76. Q. Was the quality of those fighter planes good enough for the purpose?

A. The quality of the P-40 fighter plane was not sufficient to out-perform the Japanese fighter aircraft, but the performance was sufficient, I believe, to break up, to a large extent, a raid of the sort that came in on December 7.

77. Q. If you had any opportunity to estimate the quality and state of training of the fighter pilots, please give the conclusions which you reached at the time.

A. As I remember, at least fifty per cent of the fighter pilots in Interceptor Command were well trained; the other fifty per cent were green pilots who had just been received from the United States.

78. Q. Does that answer mean that only half of the Army fighter aircraft could have been ready to combat the attack of 7 December?

A. No, sir. All aircraft in commission could be ready, as far as the pilots were concerned. I meant that approximately half of the pilots were well trained fighter pilots. The other half had not had sufficient squadron tactical training to be "experienced" fighter pilots. Pilot training was being pressed.

79. In your recollection, what actual opposition did the Army fighters bring to bear upon the Japanese air attack?

A. I was never told the actual number of Army fighters that took the air, but I was under the impression that between ten and twenty Army fighters were airborne and engaging the Japanese more or less on their own.

80. Q. Did that number get into the air in time to effectively oppose the attack?

A. No, sir.

81. Q. About how many did?

A. I have no idea how many actually got into the air, sir.

82. Q. Were the ones which were in the air in any way directed by the Interceptor Command officer on the ground?

A. They were not actually directed. The Operations Officer informed the fighters in the air by radio of the situation, as well as he could interpret it. In discussions with Army pilots who did engage the Japanese, I learned that there were so many Japanese aircraft in the air that they did not need fighter direction from the ground to find them.

The Problem-Laden Construction of the Hawaiian Radar System

ROBERT J. FLEMING, JR., ARMY SUPERVISORY OFFICER FOR THE PLANNING AND ERECTION OF THE SYSTEM

via *Joint Congressional Investigation*

[653] 1. COLONEL WEST. Will you please state to the Board your name, rank, organization, and station?

COLONEL FLEMING. Robert J. Fleming, Jr., Colonel, Corps of Engineers, Serial 01795, Headquarters 22, Fort DuPont, Delaware.

2. GENERAL GRUNERT. Colonel, the Board is after facts, both as to what happened before and what happened at the attack on Pearl Harbor in 1941, on December 7. Through the testimony that the Board has had, your name came up as having occupied a position and as having been liaison officer for General Short in connection with certain construction work, and so forth. So we want you to throw some light on this subject; and General Frank will propound the questions and the other members of the Board will later question you.

3. GENERAL FRANK. On what duty were you in November and December, 1941?

COLONEL FLEMING. I was on the General Staff at that time, sir. I was placed on the General Staff in August 1941, ostensibly in the G-4 section. Actually I did very, very little formal G-4 work, but, under then Colonel Hayes, who was Chief of Staff, I was given more or less of a special section on all Army construction work, the planning phase of it and the supervision of the execution. [. . .]

[654] 8. GENERAL FRANK. Were you a member of the group that selected the sites for the permanent Aircraft Warning Service?

COLONEL FLEMING. Yes, sir. That started, I think, about February of 1940, and the first board on that consisted of Colonel Van Deusen, now General Van Deusen, of the Signal Corps, who was Hawaiian Department Signal Officer. General Lynn of the Air Force, I think [655] was the Air Force member. I was the Engineer member. I do not know whether there were any other members or not.

Source: Pearl Harbor Attack, *volume 17.*

9. GENERAL FRANK. Will you tell us the sites that were selected at that time?

COLONEL FLEMING. Yes, sir. We had very little information; no one had any information about the technical aspects of this A.W.S. equipment, and the only information we had from the War Department was that Hawaii would be allotted, depending on what the board finally recommended, about eight of these sets. That was their tentative study on the matter. We were also told that the characteristics of this device were that it was more or less a beam line of sight proposition. It went out the same way that light did, but not the same wave lengths, and therefore the range that it would be effective would depend entirely upon the height of the station. Of course you know that horizon distance is the function of the height above sea level. The range at that time was supposed to be 90 miles, and the Signal Corps had promised that it would be developed up to a range of about 120 to 140 miles. So our instructions were to locate feasible locations for it and, of course, since the range depended upon altitude, to pick those places as high up as we could get them.

The only site on the Island of Oahu which met those considerations was on top of Mt. Kaala; and we got into a terrific argument with various people around there because they said it was feasibly uneconomical to get up on top of that mountain. But we finally got that through in the board.

The next primary one would have been on top of Haleakala. On the Island of Hawaii there were to be two stations, and we recommended one at Mauna Loa, on the upper slopes of the military camp on Pahoa; one at a place called Kokee, and another one on Oahu at Pali; another one on Maui on the road leading up to Haleakala.

10. GENERAL FRANK. That finally resolved itself down, in 1941, into how many main stations?

COLONEL FLEMING. Three. They had another board. They came in and reviewed it. They learned more about this thing. It resolved itself into the main stations being at Kokee, Kaála, and Haleakala, on on Hawaii at a place called Pahoa, and another one about 20 miles north of Morse Field. In addition, they had mobile stations put in at various other places to cover the spread. [...]

[656] 18. GENERAL FRANK. Do you remember about contracts having been let for the construction of base camp facilities for Kokee, Kaála, and Haleakala? If so, will you discuss the accessory work that had to be done, such as roads leading into the sites, cableways, who received the contracts, and any changes that were made in the contracts, and the necessity therefor? Do you have sufficient memory of the situation to discuss that?

COLONEL FLEMING. Yes, sir; I think I have.

At Kaála, in order to get on top of the mountain, it was necessary to build a cableway which was about 7,000 feet long. This (indicating on map) is the Kolekole Pass Road, and right here (indicating) the road took off at Firebreak. The top of Mt. Kaála is here (indicating), and from a point about here on the map—this is about an inch and a half on the map—we had to build a cableway, and the only place was about 1,500 feet. It was probably about 1,900 feet from this point up to the top. That cableway had to be designed to carry a ton per hour, and we had to build a road from this point (indicating) all the way around in through there (indicating). It was a rather difficult range. The trail wound around, and over here (indicating) we improved that Firebreak trail. One of the points that delayed it a little bit was the fact that this take-off point of the cableway was right at Schofield Barracks artillery range, and there was much discussion about where we would locate this take-off point and whether it would interfere with artillery fire. So, finally we had to guarantee to them that we would put this in beyond their target limit and then splinter-proof the installation so that there would be no damage. The cableway having been selected and designed, had to be procured, and about that time steel was critical, and it took some time to get it over there. This material started arriving for the cableway sometime in October 1941. To the best of my knowledge the thing was not finished before the war, although it was well under construction. I base that statement on the fact that there was a very bad accident that occurred on this cableway, killing about three or four men at the upper terminus, and I think that happened along about in February or March, 1942. At that time it was in operation. It took a considerable amount of time to build it, so I would say it was about half or 75 percent completed at the time the war started.

[657] 19. GENERAL FRANK. Aside from the delay in procuring the material, in your argument with the Artillery about its interfering with their range, was there any other delay? Was there any delay in building the road along the Firebreak road?

COLONEL FLEMING. Yes, sir. This is entirely a matter of opinion, but I think that the people who executed this went in built a much more elaborate road than would have been necessary.

20. GENERAL FRANK. Do you remember who had the contract for that particular installation?

COLONEL FLEMING. I do not believe there was a special contract for that, sir. I would like to go into the contract if I may, sir.

The Engineers took over this work and it was decided to open up a cost-plus-a-fixed-fee contract. The reason for having a cost-plus-a-fixed-fee contract at that time was that the restrictions on Government procurement were so rigid that we could not get anything done in a hurry. That was the experience all over the country. In buying equipment, for example, the contractor could buy the equipment, just exactly what we needed, and have it delivered to the Engineers somewhere in about ten or fifteen days, and we could get it on a rental-purchase agreement. If we had to do it otherwise, we would have been restricted to certain kinds of equipment and surrounded with a lot of red tape. So the Engineers and the Constructing Quartermasters went into these contracts all over the country. To the best of my knowledge I think that the contract that the Engineers had over there was a blanket contract; that the cost-plus-a-fixed-fee contract entered into by the District Engineer's Office and approved directly by the Chief of

Engineer's Office was: blanket contract which covered not only this aircraft warning project but all other engineering work that we had to do over there.

21. GENERAL FRANK. We have had a history of that and an explanation of it before the Board. It was a blanket contract, and then specific contracts were covered by job orders?

COLONEL FLEMING. Yes, sir; job orders under this contract. [...]

[658] 30. GENERAL FRANK. Do you know when this station was finished?

COLONEL FLEMING. It was never finished, sir, to the best of my knowledge. I left Hawaii in September 1943, and up to that time it had never been used as an aircraft warning station. That was not due to the incompleteness of the facilities, but after we got this station in operation we found out that the preliminary information we had had from the Signal Corps technical people that the range depended on the height was in error, apparently. It would get out to the horizon the higher we got it, but when you got up into higher altitudes there was too much interference. When we put it up on one of these high mountains, instead of picking up an airplane or ship at sea, it would pick up to many reflections from secondary waves from the surrounding terrain. The station at Haleakala was completed first, and they took a mobile station up there, one of these Army portable units.

31. GENERAL FRANK. The 270s?

COLONEL FLEMING. Yes, sir. They tried that for a while, and that did not work well. So they then installed all of the fixed equipment. There was a great argument about that fixed equipment on Mt. Haleakala, by the way. The board never wanted it. We wanted a mobile set there. When they got that over there the Signal Corps worked and worked and worked; they had special radar people over. They would come back from England; and then they had some people called electronics experts who came out and talked very wisely about this thing, but they could never get the station to work. The reason for that was that the station at Haleakala was right up on Kolekole Peak.

32. GENERAL FRANK. There was already a road up there, wasn't there?

COLONEL FLEMING. There was a road up to the observation tower, sir, and then we had to build a road that was about a mile long up on top of that one little knob that stuck up. The elevation on this knob was ten twenty-five, and there was another one over here ten fourteen or something like that. But anyway, this station, you could ac-[659]tually see the horizon from this point all the way around except for being blanketed by the high ground on the Island of Molokai; so the only dead space theoretically on the station was a little core that came out along through there (indicating) and went up the windward side of Oahu.

Theoretically, then, this station up here (indicating) was ideal. You could go up there and you could use this in any direction, almost 360 degrees traverse on that thing. But it never worked out, because — I am not an expert on radar, but what the Signal Corps explained to me was that when your main beam that went out this way there was an auxiliary beam that went out of this thing;

another node went out of this thing, and that one went out to the rear from this antenna, and as this thing swung around in trying to pick up a plane, say in this direction (indicating), these auxiliary beans would pick up these high mountains on the Island of Hawaii, and there was so much difference in the terrain between this one little bump up here on Haleakala and these high mountains out in here (indicating) that as that thing swung around and the secondary beams picked up these, what the Signal Corps call echoes, they could never chart them into the oscilloscope on this device: they could never get them entered in there as standard interferences and eliminate them.

So as a result of that they finally decided to abandon the station on Haleakala; and just on a guess that they would find the same condition on Mt. Kaala, they never put the aircraft warning station up there. The decision on Kaala and also on Haleakala to abandon those was also based upon the fact that they had developed a supplemental communications equipment which was a direct-talking telephone system to pursuit planes, and also a very ultrahigh-frequency telephone communication between the various islands, and both of these places became key points in the communications network; and, as the Signal Corps and the authorities apparently wanted them for that purpose, why, neither of them was ever used as an aircraft warning station.

33. GENERAL FRANK. So that the money expended to develop them did bear fruit because, while they were not used as radar stations, they were used as communication centers?

COLONEL FLEMING. Yes, sir. In fact, the people told me that the development of those as communication center, as far as fighter control and also talking back and forth for permanent use, was probably much more valuable than radar; that the radar could pick the stuff up by duplicating a station down below, but you wouldn't be able to duplicate them for communications. [...]

[660] 39. GENERAL FRANK. Do you feel that there were delays that in normal times could have been eliminated?

COLONEL FLEMING. Yes, sir.

40. GENERAL FRANK. Will you make a list of those?

COLONEL FLEMING. Well, one I think was the procurement—

41. GENERAL FRANK. Take your time there and enumerate them, and then we will put them in the record.

COLONEL FLEMING. One was the procurement of labor; two was procurement of materials; three were transportation.

42. GENERAL FRANK. From the mainland?

COLONEL FLEMING. Yes, sir; transportation trans–Pacific. Four I think was this question of priorities back on the mainland, and five was the question of approvals.

43. GENERAL FRANK. Where and by whom?

COLONEL FLEMING. By the War Department, sir.

44. GENERAL FRANK. Were there delays in those approvals?

COLONEL FLEMING. To those of us sitting out there, we thought there were, yes, sir.

45. GENERAL FRANK. Were complaints made to the headquarters who had those approvals in hand?

COLONEL FLEMING. Yes, sir.

46. GENERAL FRANK. Complaints were made?

COLONEL FLEMING. Yes, sir.

47. GENERAL FRANK. When you made complaints did you get action?

COLONEL FLEMING. In the majority of cases, yes, sir.

48. GENERAL FRANK. Well, then the delays in approvals were not so serious? Or were they?

COLONEL FLEMING. I think they were, sir, some of them. I mean that is just a worm's-eye opinion, sir. For one thing, let us take the case of Haleakala. That station was located in a national park. We had to get on top of this mountain, which unfortunately was the most visible thing in the national park, and there was a long delay in there about getting the right of entry.

49. GENERAL FRANK. From whom?

COLONEL FLEMING. From the National Park Service, sir.

50. GENERAL FRANK. Department of Parks?

COLONEL FLEMING. Department of the Interior.

51. GENERAL FRANK. Who was Secretary of the Interior? Do you remember?

COLONEL FLEMING. Mr. Ickes, sir. The local man out there in charge of that park was a man named Wingate. Mr. Wingate.

52. GENERAL FRANK. He was in charge of all national parks in the Hawaiian Islands?

[661] COLONEL FLEMING. Yes, sir; the one on Haleakala and then the one down in—

53. GENERAL FRANK. At Hawaii?

COLONEL FLEMING. The one down at Hawaii. There had been a considerable amount of contacts back and forth with Mr. Wingate by the Army. For instance, the Air Corps wanted a bombing range down at what is known as the Kau Desert down in the Island of Hawaii, right in through here (indicating on map). I think that all this area is just absolutely worthless as far as anything except scenery is concerned. It wasn't very good for scenery because there were no roads into it.

54. GENERAL FRANK. They were all old lava beds?

COLONEL FLEMING. All old lava beds. You couldn't go through there. I think you could walk through there. And I remember before the war we were trying to get that bombing range in there from the National Park Service and had a tremendous amount of difficulty on that. I don't think we ever did get it, unless we got it with so many restrictions that we couldn't use it.

But when we wanted to get in Haleakala, when we wanted to start work up there, the question immediately came up as to what damage this installation was going to do to the scenery in view of the Hawaii National Park. And that started before General Herron left the Islands, and he left in February 1941, I think; February or early March; and we wrote letters back and forth about this thing and tried to get Mr. Wingate to agree, and every time we would write Mr. Wingate a letter he would apparently refer it back to his people in Washington, and it dragged on and on, and the only commitment we could get was that we would have to design this station completely and submit all plans, architectural drawings of the buildings, and everything like that to Mr. Wingate, who would then forward them to the National Park Service people so they could pass on them from an architectural standpoint.

Well, obviously, if we were trying to build something in a hurry we couldn't wait around until the National Park Service approved these plans from an architectural standpoint. So we finally resolved that argument: I remember General Short sent a special telegram (it was one of these "eyes alone" telegrams) to General Marshall asking him to please secure the necessary permits to proceed with the construction of that station; and as a result of that appeal, why, we got authority to go into Haleakala and start work building the road and constructing buildings and submit the plans later on; that we would guarantee to make the buildings look like what the Park Service wanted us to, provided we could put the buildings where we wanted to.

55. GENERAL GRUNERT. When did you get that permission?

COLONEL FLEMING. I don't remember, General. I think to the best of my knowledge it was sometime after General Short got there, and he arrived in February. I think that exchange of radios probably took place about in, oh, I would say in May of 1941, because I remember I had to explain this thing in great detail to General Short, to give him all the background and show to him that we had exhausted the local possibility of getting the thing done, before he would sign the radio.

56. GENERAL FRANK. What about Kokee?

[662] COLONEL FLEMING. Kokee we didn't have any trouble with, sir. That is on the Island of Kauai, and it was located, fortunately, in territorial land. We had excellent relationships with the Territorial Department of Forestry, I think it was, controlled it.

57. GENERAL FRANK. Was there any delay in the construction of that once the job order was let?

COLONEL FLEMING. Yes, sir.

58. GENERAL FRANK. What was it?

COLONEL FLEMING. The delay on that was that originally the fixed stations — and this is the reason we didn't like the fixed stations, sir — the fixed stations were supposed to be built with the detector building and the detector tower, the antenna gadget, all in the same building. In other words, the framework for the building was made sufficiently strong to hold this tower up on the top. Well, in furnishing the first people in this board we had no idea — we suspect that nobody else had any idea — how this thing was going to work. We thought we might have to move it maybe a hundred feet or a couple of hundred

The Hawaiian Radar System

feet in various directions to get the best place to locate it. Also we had no detailed plans for the footings of the supports for this tower. The buildings sort of stuck up like this, of course, with the tower coming out where my pencil does (indicating), and that building and the tower were supported by heavy steel members inside of the building.

The only thing we had was the location of where the tower was, on the top of the building, and where the concrete foundations would have to go to support this structure. Of course, in building construction we have to have a lot more detailed information than that. You have got to either have your detail design of the footings of that tower so you can cast your bolts in the concrete when you pour it, or else you have got to have a template accompanying this thing.

Right in the middle of that one they found out that this gadget would not measure height or something on approaching planes, as I recall it, with the tower which was only 35 feet high, so they increased—

59. GENERAL FRANK. What do you mean by "this gadget"? What gadget? The tower?

COLONEL FLEMING. The radar, sir.

60. GENERAL FRANK. The radar?

COLONEL FLEMING. The radar.

61. GENERAL FRANK. The oscilloscope?

COLONEL FLEMING. Yes, sir.

So they increased the height of the antenna to a hundred-foot tower at this one particular station. And I don't know how long it took us to get the actual detailed design of the footings of that tower so we could start pouring that concrete. I remember that there was a lot of correspondence back and forth about that, trying to find out just exactly how that tower should be poured and what the relationship between the tower and the buildings was going to be after the hundred-foot tower was decided on.

62. GENERAL FRANK. Who determined those details that you needed to make this change in construction that was causing the delay?

[663]   COLONEL FLEMING. That was done somewhere in this country, sir.

63. GENERAL FRANK. What branch of the service? Signal Corps?

COLONEL FLEMING. Signal Corps; yes, sir.

64. GENERAL FRANK. It was the Signal Corps' responsibility to prepare the plans and specifications on which you should proceed with the construction?

COLONEL FLEMING. It was our responsibility, sir, for preparing the—rather, the Engineers'. I was the General Staff Officer, but it was the Engineers' responsibility for designing the buildings in the thing and making all the layout except for this one building, the detector building.

65. GENERAL FRANK. Yes.

COLONEL FLEMING. That was a specially screened building. The Signal Corps furnished the tower and all the equipment that is in it, furnished everything complete for it.

66. GENERAL FRANK. Well, who was responsible for the plans that caused the delay?

COLONEL FLEMING. I think the Signal Corps was, sir.

67. GENERAL FRANK. All right. Now, you have told us about the delays at Kokee and the delays at Kaála and the delays at Haleakala. In any of these delays were the contractors in any way responsible for those or any other delays?

COLONEL FLEMING. I don't think so, sir. There may have been inefficiencies in management which would decrease the speed at which the work was going on, but I don't think there were any particular delays that the contractor had to do with. For example, the contractor couldn't proceed with that Kaála cableway until the thing had been designed and he was told where to put it.

The Sighting of the Japanese Planes

GEORGE E. ELLIOTT, JR., A TRAINEE ON THE NEW RADAR SYSTEM
Joint Congressional Investigation

MR. RICHARDSON. Sergeant Elliott, will you state your name for the record?
MR. ELLIOTT. George E. Elliott, Jr.
MR. RICHARDSON. How old are you?
MR. ELLIOTT. Twenty-eight, sir.
MR. RICHARDSON. You are not in the service at present?
MR. ELLIOTT. No, sir; I am lucky enough to have been discharged 4 months ago.
MR. RICHARDSON. You were on duty in Hawaii at the time of the Japanese attack on Pearl Harbor?
MR. ELLIOTT. That is right, sir.
MR. RICHARDSON. In what division of the Army?
MR. ELLIOTT. I was in the Signal Corps, Aircraft Warning.
MR. RICHARDSON. And that brought you in contact with the radar sets that the Army had on Oahu?
[5028] MR. ELLIOTT. Yes, sir.
MR. RICHARDSON. You were present at one of those mobile radar sets on the morning of the attack?
MR. ELLIOTT. Yes, sir.
MR. RICHARDSON. Can you indicate on this map, Sergeant, where the mobile station was located, and where you were on the morning of the attack?
MR. ELLIOTT. Yes, sir.
MR. RICHARDSON. Indicate on this map where the station is located where you were on the morning of the attack.
MR. ELLIOTT. The station was located at the top of the mountain, I believe they call it Opana, at the northernmost point of the island of Oahu, as I indicate here [indicating].
MR. RICHARDSON. Now, coming to this map, Sergeant, this colored chart of what is supposed to be a radar chart of approaching Japanese planes prior to the attack, you were at this point [indicating]?

Source: Pearl Harbor Attack, *volume 10.*

Mr. ELLIOTT. That is correct.

Mr. RICHARDSON. Will you indicate with the pointer where you saw any indication of approaching planes, where it would be on this map?

Mr. ELLIOTT. At this point up here [indicating] 3° northeast at the azimuth that they came in on.

We picked them up at the mileage of 136 or 137 miles. That was the very first indication of the flight that we had picked up.

Mr. RICHARDSON. Now, follow with your pinter, just generally how the planes came down toward your station.

SENATOR BREWSTER. Will you place the time so it will be identified?

Mr. RICHARDSON. What was the time when you first found any information of planes?

Mr. ELLIOTT. That was 7:02.

Mr. RICHARDSON. All right; now, follow with your pointer the course, as nearly as you can recall it, that the planes followed as you watched them on the radar.

Mr. ELLIOTT. I believe that they came in on a very straight line. I do not recall of their being any differences, as indicated here. It was fairly straight.

Mr. RICHARDSON. Now, when they approached your station, did they disappear finally from your radar?

Mr. ELLIOTT. Yes, sir; they disappeared at approximately 15 to 20 miles away from the island. We lost them due to distortion from a back wave from the mountains, and it was impossible to follow them further than we had.

Mr. RICHARDSON. Up to the time they disappeared, had there been any diversion of the planes? Were they still all in the main group which you had seen at 7:02?

Mr. ELLIOTT. Yes, sir; they were all in the same group, so far as I know.

Mr. RICHARDSON. That is the last you saw of them?

Mr. ELLIOTT. Yes, sir.

Mr. RICHARDSON. Who was with you, Sergeant, at the time these planes were sighted?

Mr. ELLIOTT. Another private, Joseph L. Lockard.

[5029]   Mr. RICHARDSON. Who first saw these planes? You or Lockhard?

Mr. ELLIOTT. We actually both saw them together.

Mr. RICHARDSON. What discussion was there between you with reference to the matter when you saw them?

Mr. ELLIOTT. At the time I was receiving instructions on the operation of the scope. Lockard looking over my shoulder noticed that there was a target, so he, knowing more about the operation of the scope, actually took over the control there. I went over to the plotting board, and we got an azimuth and mileage and figured out a reading as to the location where the flight was, where the target was.

Mr. RICHARDSON. How long did that take you, would you say?

Mr. ELLIOTT. Well, just a very short time.

Mr. RICHARDSON. A minute or two?
Mr. ELLIOTT. Less than a minute.
Mr. RICHARDSON. All right, go ahead.
Mr. ELLIOTT. At the time I suggested to Private Lockard that we send it in to the Information Center. Private Lockard, figuring that our problem was over at 7 o'clock, disagreed as to sending the reading.
Mr. RICHARDSON. What do you mean by your problem was over at 7?
Mr. ELLIOTT. The normal operating period at that time was from 4 in the morning until 7 in the morning.
Mr. RICHARDSON. Was that true of weekdays as well as on Sundays?
Mr. ELLIOTT. Yes, sir, I believe it was.
Mr. RICHARDSON. For how long a period prior to the morning of the 7th had you been on the 4 to 7 status?
Mr. ELLIOTT. Well, our particular station at that time had only been set up, it was only in operation about 2 weeks before December 7th.
Mr. RICHARDSON. And during that whole 2 weeks, were you on the 4 to 7 schedule?
Mr. ELLIOTT. Yes, sir, I believe we were.
Mr. RICHARDSON. Had there been other men in the station up to 7 o'clock that morning?
Mr. ELLIOTT. No, sir; the only ones present at the station were Private Lockard and myself.
Mr. RICHARDSON. Now, before that, during the 4 to 7 period that morning, had there been other men on this station?
Mr. ELLIOTT. Oh, yes, sir.
Mr. RICHARDSON. And what had become of them?
Mr. ELLIOTT. I do not quite understand.
Mr. RICHARDSON. What became of them? How did it happen that only you and Lockhart were left there?
Mr. ELLIOTT. I will have to go back to December 6. It was a standing rule that we would keep two men at the unit at all times.
Mr. RICHARDSON. Twenty-four hours of the day?
Mr. ELLIOTT. Yes, sir.
Mr. RICHARDSON. All right.
Mr. ELLIOTT. That was for protection of the unit. They were armed with .45 guns.
[5030] Mr. RICHARDSON. That was to protect the unit? It was not to operate the unit as a radar system?
Mr. ELLIOTT. Well, they were there to protect the unit but they did not operate.
When the men that operated came to the station, the two men that guarded the unit were there at the same time, although they did not do any operation.
Mr. RICHARDSON. All right; go ahead now.
You got back to the 6th? What were your hours on the morning of the 6th?

MR. ELLIOTT. Well, we went out to the station at Opana to relieve the two men that had been on the unit, guarding it all the week. We went out there to give them a break, more or less, to come in and get a pass to go to town.

MR. RICHARDSON. Did you go out as guards?

MR. ELLIOTT. Yes, sir; we went out as guards. The idea was we would stay there all night and be there at 4 o'clock in the morning, to start working on our problem.

MR. RICHARDSON. This was the night of the 6th?

MR. ELLIOTT. Yes, sir.

MR. RICHARDSON. Go ahead. When did the other men that had been on the station during the night leave?

MR. ELLIOTT. Well, there had been no other men there since 12 o'clock on December 6, when we relieved them, when Private Lockard and I relieved them.

MR. RICHARDSON. Then, as a matter of fact, from 4 until 7 on the morning of the 7th you two were the only men at that station?

MR. ELLIOTT. Yes, sir. We were the only two at that station from noon of December 6 through 8 o'clock on the morning of December 7.

MR. RICHARDSON. And that was the station at Opana?

MR. ELLIOTT. Yes, sir.

MR. RICHARDSON. At the farthest north station?

MR. ELLIOTT. Yes, sir.

MR. RICHARDSON. The station most immediately adjacent to the whole northwest sector north of Oahu?

MR. ELLIOTT. Yes, sir.

MR. RICHARDSON. All right.

Now, at 7:02 you two men discovered planes on your target?

MR. ELLIOTT. Yes, sir.

MR. RICHARDSON. You suggested that you contact the information center?

MR. ELLIOTT. Yes, sir.

MR. RICHARDSON. At first Lockard did not approve of that?

MR. ELLIOTT. Yes, sir. That was after we had figured out the reading from the azimuth and mileage. At that time I spoke to Private Lockard. I even recall saying to him since he did not want to send it in, even if we sent it in and the Army and Navy would work together, they may not know just whose planes they are, but if we worked out through the information center and had it not on any scheduled problem, that it would be more effective as to actually going out there and intercepting like, say, the Army go out and intercept planes, or vice versa.

[5031] Finally, after mentioning a few of those things to Private Lockard, he finally told me to go ahead and send it in if I liked.

MR. RICHARDSON. How long from the time you discovered the planes was it until you concluded to phone the information center? How many minutes?

MR. ELLIOTT. I would say offhand 7 or 8.

MR. RICHARDSON. During that time, you could still see the target on your charts, these planes coming from the north?

The Sighting of the Planes

Mr. ELLIOTT. Yes, sir.

Mr. RICHARDSON. You called up the information center?

Mr. ELLIOTT. Yes, sir. We had two phones in the mobile unit: One was a direct line, a tactical line, as it was called. That was from the plotting board directly to the information center which was located at Fort Shafter.

Mr. RICHARDSON. Which phone did you use?

Mr. ELLIOTT. I picked up the tactical phone on the plotting board and I found nobody on the other end at the information center.

After that, I went to the administrative line and called the information center.

After getting the information center—

Mr. RICHARDSON. Who answered?

Mr. ELLIOTT. A corporal or Private McDonald answered the phone. He was a switchboard operator at the information center.

Mr. RICHARDSON. All right.

What conversation occurred?

Mr. ELLIOTT. At that time, I explained to Private McDonald what we had seen, and he told me that there was nobody around there, and he did not know what to do about it.

I asked him if he would get somebody that would know what to do and pass on the information, and have him take care of it.

Well, a few minutes later—

Mr. RICHARDSON. How many minutes? Just make a guess.

Mr. ELLIOTT. Two or three, I would say.

Mr. RICHARDSON. Two or three, All right.

Mr. ELLIOTT. Two or three minutes later, this lieutenant that is referred to, or was first referred to in the Roberts report, called back to the station, and Private Lockard picked up the phone and spoke to the lieutenant.

It was at this time that the lieutenant told us to forget about the flight.

Mr. RICHARDSON. Well, now, you, of course, did not hear what the lieutenant said over the telephone.

Mr. ELLIOTT. No, sir; I did not.

Mr. RICHARDSON. What did you hear Lockard say over the telephone, to whomever he was talking?

Mr. ELLIOTT. Well, he only acknowledged that we were to forget it, that we were to forget the flight.

Mr. RICHARDSON. Did Lockard say anything to the lieutenant about having discovered planes coming on the chart?

Mr. ELLIOTT. Yes, sir; I believe he did. He again repeated the distance that we had picked up the planes.

[5032] Mr. RICHARDSON. When Lockard had finished his telephone conversation, what did he tell you the lieutenant on the other end said?

Mr. ELLIOTT. He told me that the lieutenant said to forget it.

Mr. RICHARDSON. Did he say anything about the lieutenant mentioning what these planes might be, or from where the planes might be coming? Did he make any statement that the lieutenant had mentioned that subject to him over the telephone?

Mr. Elliott. I do not recall whether or not he did.

Mr. Richardson. I am referring to the question of whether the lieutenant mentioned the fact that a flight of B-17's from San Francisco was expected in that morning, and that these planes were probably those planes.

Was there any discussion on that subject by Lockard in reporting the telpephone conversation to you?

Mr. Elliott. That is what I do not quite remember. I cannot place it together, whether we received that information then, or whether that came out after the publicity of the Roberts Commission.

I cannot say for sure.

Mr. Richardson. Now, what did you continue to do after the end of the conversation over the telephone with the lieutenant at the information center? What did you and Lockard continue to do, if anything?

Mr. Elliott. Private Lockard at that time wanted to shut down the unit and just go off the air, and the original intention was that I was to have gotten further training on the unit. I insisted again, and we continued to operate.

Mr. Richardson. You could still see the plane target?

Mr. Elliott. Yes, sir.

Mr. Richardson. And you followed it in until it got within about 20 miles of your station?

Mr. Elliott. That is right, sir.

Mr. Richardson. Now, then, did you make any chart of the course of those planes?

Mr. Elliott. Yes, sir. We had an overlaid chart; that is, a transparent paper that is put over the map itself, of the island, with true north on the overlay. That is, the grid lines on the overlay were true north on the map, and in the center is a radius, a mileage radius rule.

From your azimuth and your mileage you can plot exactly where your location is on the map. That is used so that you could have a record of all the flights that you had.

In other words, as you posted your target on this overlay, you could take it off of there and put it on a new sheet of transparent paper and continue on again.

Mr. Richardson. Now, you did complete a chart following the course of those planes as they approached your station?

Mr. Elliott. Yes, sir.

Mr. Richardson. Did you make any readings?

Mr. Elliott. Yes, sir; we had a running log, a record of reading sheets that covered the time, mileage, azimuth, and coordinate readings.

Mr. Richardson. And you filled that out?

Mr. Elliott. Yes, sir.

The Sighting of the Planes

[5033] MR. RICHARDSON. When did you leave the station that morning?
MR. ELLIOTT. It was approximately 15 minutes of 8.
MR. RICHARDSON. Where did you go?
MR. ELLIOTT. Our station at Opana was 9 miles away to our camp where he billeted and of course coming down the mountain to the highway took some time, and then the 9 miles was from the highway.
MR. RICHARDSON. How did you go?
MR. ELLIOTT. At approximately just shortly before 15 minutes of 8, a private—
MR. RICHARDSON (interposing). How did you go, by shank's mare or in a car?
MR. ELLIOTT. That is just what I am going to explain.
MR. RICHARDSON. All right.
MR. ELLIOTT. Just a few minutes before a quarter of 8, Private Farnback came out in a truck to pick us up, and take our bedding and ourselves back to the camp.
MR. RICHARDSON. He took you back to the camp?
MR. ELLIOTT. Yes, sir.
MR. RICHARDSON. What time did you get back to the camp, do you think?
MR. ELLIOTT. It was very close to 8 o'clock.
MR. RICHARDSON. Did you have with you either your chart or your readings?
MR. ELLIOTT. We only had the record of readings, the log.
MR. RICHARDSON. Did your record or reading log show the direction from which these planes were coming?
MR. ELLIOTT. It could have been replotted on the map with the information given to get the exact location of the flight.
MR. RICHARDSON. What did you do with that log?
MR. ELLIOTT. That log was turned over to a Lieutenant Upson, the commanding officer of the two platoons that were out in that particular camp.
MR. RICHARDSON. Was it turned over immediately upon your return to the camp?
MR. ELLIOTT. Yes, sir. We were very proud of the reading that we had gotten; that is, the distance out, and we brought it along, not knowing what was taking place, but it was just the fact that the reading was a very good reading. We brought it back to show it off, so to speak. [...]
[5035] MR. RICHARDSON. [...] When did you first know of the attack?
MR. ELLIOTT. At the time that we arrived at our camp. However, as we were going to the camp, and just, oh, about a quarter way away from the camp, we noticed from our truck all of the men from the camp driving very fast in the opposite direction in which we were going. They were going to the unit.
They had their field packs, and helmets, and what not.
We still had no indication as to what had happened until we arrived at the camp, when we were told that we had been attacked by the Japanese.
MR. RICHARDSON. I have no further questions.

THE CHAIRMAN. Sergeant, if I understand you, this unit up there on this mountain at the tip of the island, was under guard 24 hours of the day by somebody.

[5036] MR. ELLIOTT. Yes.

THE CHAIRMAN. What were they guarding against?

MR. ELLIOTT. Well, the only thing they were guarding against was to see that no one came around to interfere with the equipment we had.

THE CHAIRMAN. Now, during 4 hours of that 24, or 3 hours, from 4 to 7 in the morning, the radar station was in operation?

MR. ELLIOTT. Yes, sir.

THE CHAIRMAN. Why was it in operation during those particular hours?

MR. ELLIOTT. Well, those were the instructions that we had from our company commander, and, as I imagine, they came from—

THE CHAIRMAN. Headquarters.

MR. ELLIOTT. He had taken the orders from higher headquarters.

THE CHAIRMAN. Did the selection of those 3 hours from 4 to 7 have any relationship, as far as you know? Was it generally understood that those hours were selected because they might have some relationship to a possible air attack?

MR. ELLIOTT. As a matter of opinion, as I would have looked at it at the time, I would say we were not operating under those conditions. I mean, it was more practice than anything else.

THE CHAIRMAN. As far as you were concerned, and Private Lockard, you were students, in a sense, you were practicing to become more proficient in the operation of the radar station?

MR. ELLIOTT. Yes, sir. [...]

[5039] THE VICE CHAIRMAN. And then at 7:02, why, you picked up this flight of planes coming in?

MR. ELLIOTT. Yes, sir. I wonder if I could make mention of the fact that at the time that we reported off the air to the information center by our clock at the unit I am very sure that time was 6 minutes of 7 and I can't recall just whether or not we had made a time check with the information center. But I know very definitely that the time [5040] on the clock when we actually closed down the unit, that is, went off the air with the information center, was approximately 6 minutes of 7.

THE VICE CHAIRMAN. Six minutes before 7 o'clock?

MR. ELLIOTT. Yes, sir.

THE VICE CHAIRMAN. You notified the information center?

MR. ELLIOTT. We were told at that time that the problem was over and that we were to go off the air. In other words, we wouldn't forward then to the information center.

THE VICE CHAIRMAN. Anything you received after 6 minutes to 7 o'clock you would not send on to the information center?

MR. ELLIOTT. Yes, sir. The point I am trying to bring out there is that it was

6 minutes before 7 and I don't recall whether or not we had made a time check to verify the time with the information center.

THE CHAIRMAN. That is, your clock showed 6 minutes to 7 and you don't know whether you synchronized your time with the information center?

MR. ELLIOTT. That is right.

THE VICE CHAIRMAN. So that from the time you were told by the information center at 6 minutes before 7 o'clock that you could go off, the remaining time then was just on a voluntary basis by you and Lockhart?

MR. ELLIOTT. Yes, sir.

THE VICE CHAIRMAN. And you picked up this flight of planes coming in at 2 minutes after 7 o'clock?

MR. ELLIOTT. Yes, sir.

THE VICE CHAIRMAN. And within 5 or 6 minutes after you first sighted them, why, you undertook to contact the information center to tell them about it?

MR. ELLIOTT. Yes, sir. It was between 6 and 8 minutes, offhand. I can't recall just what it was.

THE VICE CHAIRMAN. Between 6 and 8 minutes after 7 o'clock?

MR. ELLIOTT. Somewhere between there.

THE VICE CHAIRMAN. And when you used the first phone there was nobody that responded at the information center?

MR. ELLIOTT. No, sir. That was the actual phone that went through to the actual plotting table in the information center.

THE VICE CHAIRMAN. That was the phone you were supposed to use to give that information?

MR. ELLIOTT. Yes, sir.

THE VICE CHAIRMAN. And there was nobody that responded at the other end?

MR. ELLIOTT. That is right.

THE VICE CHAIRMAN. Or, at the information center?

MR. ELLIOTT. That is right.

THE VICE CHAIRMAN. Then you used the other phone which you say was the administration phone?

MR. ELLIOTT. Yes, sir.

THE VICE CHAIRMAN. And Private McDonald answered that switchboard?

MR. ELLIOTT. Yes, sir.

THE VICE CHAIRMAN. And you gave him the information and he told you that there was nobody there to tell him what to do about it?

MR. ELLIOTT. Yes, sir.

[5041] THE VICE CHAIRMAN. And you asked him to please get word as quickly as he could to somebody who would know what to do?

MR. ELLIOTT. Yes, sir. I might mention that as I was explaining it to McDonald on the switchboard I spoke in a very nervous voice and from the time that I spoke that way Lockard seemed to take more note of what I was trying to do in sending in the reading, although I didn't know at the time that they were enemy planes. It was just that I did talk over the phone in a very nervous tone of voice.

THE VICE CHAIRMAN. That was probably your first experience of that type, was it?

MR. ELLIOTT. Yes, sir, it was.

THE VICE CHAIRMAN. I see.

MR. ELLIOTT. It probably was the idea of getting such a large flight of planes at such a distance, because ordinarily before then we hadn't picked up anything really over 100 to 110 miles, I would say. But this was very big and it was very noticeable and it was just something out of the ordinary.

THE VICE CHAIRMAN. It was out of the ordinary to the extent that you were a little bit excited about it?

MR. ELLIOTT. Yes, sir.

THE VICE CHAIRMAN. And also proud of your achievement?

MR. ELLIOTT. Well, yes, sir. I only wish that it could have been followed through. It could have saved any number of lives.

THE VICE CHAIRMAN. Well, you really did do a good job in the work you did there.

MR. ELLIOTT. I hope I did, sir.

THE VICE CHAIRMAN. How many men were there at that time that operated this radar?

MR. ELLIOTT. In our platoon we had, I believe it was, 18 men. Out of that 18 men there were three drivers, I believe, truck drivers, and I believe there were two cooks.

THE VICE CHAIRMAN. That would leave—

MR. ELLIOTT. That would leave—

THE VICE CHAIRMAN. Thirteen.

MR. ELLIOTT. Thirteen.

THE VICE CHAIRMAN. Operators.

MR. ELLIOTT. Operators; yes, sir.

THE VICE CHAIRMAN. Now, although you were still in training and had not had the experience that Lockard had, why, the events of that occasion showed that you had become rather efficient in that line of work.

MR. ELLIOTT. Yes, sir.

THE VICE CHAIRMAN. Now, just how did you conduct this type of work Sergeant? Was there a platoon or squad or definite number of men assigned to each of these radar units?

MR. ELLIOTT. We had the men assigned, we had what we called the crew chiefs, and I believe with the assigned strength that we had they only had two men under them, and the three men together each operated the unit in shifts of, as I recall it on December 7 especially, very close to that time, we operated 4 hours on duty on the radar, 4 hours on guard on the unit, and then 4 hours off, and then repeating 4 hours on the unit and so forth; and I believe at that time we had four different crews.

[5042] THE VICE CHAIRMAN. Four different crews of two men each?

MR. ELLIOTT. Yes, sir. There were three men, actually three men, on each crew.

THE VICE CHAIRMAN. Three men on each crew and you had four crews?

MR. ELLIOTT. Yes, sir. I believe that is the way it was set up; yes, sir.

THE VICE CHAIRMAN. And you had four crews?

MR. ELLIOTT. Yes, sir.

THE VICE CHAIRMAN. Well, of course, then you spent as much time on guard duty as you did in operating the unit?

MR. ELLIOTT. Yes, sir. The number of men we had at that time was not a sufficient number to operate 24 hours a day.

THE VICE CHAIRMAN. Well, now, if all the operators had been used for operational purposes and ordinary infantry soldiers had been used for guard duty, you could have done that, couldn't you?

MR. ELLIOTT. Oh, yes.

THE VICE CHAIRMAN. And ordinary infantry soldiers could have been used for guard duty, and were used for guard duty at all other places around the island, weren't they?

MR. ELLIOTT. Yes, sir; but there were none assigned to us at that time.

THE VICE CHAIRMAN. I know, but that could have been done, for the guard duty?

MR. ELLIOTT. Yes, sir.

THE VICE CHAIRMAN. And then that would have left all of you operators to work in shifts just in operational work?

MR. ELLIOTT. Well, yes, although in the Army they sort of put you to work to the best advantage. In other words, they wouldn't have considered us working 4 hours on the unit and 8 hours' rest, whereas they probably would have fixed it up 8 hours' work and 4 hours' rest.

THE VICE CHAIRMAN. Yes; that could have been done.

MR. ELLIOTT. Yes, sir. I mean that is the general practice, so to speak.

THE VICE CHAIRMAN. What was done in that respect after the attack, after December 7, how did they do it?

MR. ELLIOTT. Well, at the time I believe we received a few more men from the company. I would say offhand four or five to help out in the operations. We operated under those conditions for approximately 3 weeks.

THE VICE CHAIRMAN. After December 7?

MR. ELLIOTT. Yes, sir. And at that time our company was enlarged to a regiment and we had some men transferred there from the Infantry to enlarge our company and the infantrymen were to be trained in the operation of the unit.

THE VICE CHAIRMAN. They assigned other men there on the island to train in radar work?

MR. ELLIOTT. Yes, sir.

The Vice Chairman. That was done after December 7?

Mr. Elliott. Yes, sir; approximately, I am not sure whether it was 2 or 3 weeks. It was somewhere in between that time.

The Vice Chairman. The forces were greatly enlarged then?

[5043] Mr. Elliott. Yes, sir. Instead of 18 men, as we had on December 7, we had approximately 40 men. That was 2 or 3 weeks after December 7.

The Vice Chairman. I see.

Mr. Elliott. But they had to be trained.

The Vice Chairman. But those same men had been on the island before December 7?

Mr. Elliott. Yes, sir.

The Vice Chairman. Now, what hours did you operate the unit after December 7?

Mr. Elliott. Twenty-four hours a day, sir.

The Vice Chairman. Twenty-four hours a day?

Mr. Elliott. Yes, sir.

The Vice Chairman. After December 7?

Mr. Elliott. Yes, sir.

The Vice Chairman. You increased it from 3 hours to 24 hours a day?

Mr. Elliott. Yes, sir.

The Vice Chairman. Well, didn't anybody have to go to the hospital as a result of that, did they?

Mr. Elliott. Well, none that I recall, sir. They were probably afraid to go to the hospital.

The Vice Chairman. All right. Thank you.

The Chairman. I would like to ask one other question.

You say that you called this information center about 7 or 8 minutes after 7?

Mr. Elliott. Yes, sir.

The Chairman. How long was it after that before Tyler came back and talked to Lockard?

Mr. Elliott. Between 1 or 2 or 3 minutes, I don't recall. It was fairly shortly.

The Chairman. From the time of that conversation between Tyler and Lockard until you went into the information center did they call back any more to seek any information about these planes?

Mr. Elliott. No, sir. The last time that we talked to the information center during the flight that we had plotted, the plane flight, there was no other conversation about it. Now then, when the flight was finished and we took the record of the reading sheets back to the platoon commander, he passed that on, I imagine, to the company commander.

The Chairman. That was about a quarter to 8?

Mr. Elliott. At the time that we went.

The Chairman. Now, the attack was on right away pretty soon after that?

Mr. Elliott. Yes, sir. As I understand it was on about 5 minutes of 8.

The Chairman. That is all.

The Sighting of the Planes

THE VICE CHAIRMAN. There is one question I overlooked.

[5044] You told us that after December 7, why, the hours of operating the station were increased from 3 hours to a full 24-hour basis.

MR. ELLIOTT. Yes, sir.

THE VICE CHAIRMAN. And the men held up all right under that. Did this wear out the sets, radar sets, did they operate all right?

MR. ELLIOTT. Well, our particular set was somewhat of a good set. I mean, we continued operating, I don't know just whether we were lucky or what, but we didn't have very much trouble. Another thing I might mention is that the different units on the islands could overlap each other and where one went off for servicing, and incidentally we did go off an hour a day for servicing and repair, they would cover the particular unit that went out.

But so far as having any serious trouble with the unit I don't recall any.

THE VICE CHAIRMAN. You don't recall any?

MR. ELLIOTT. No, sir. [...]

[5045] SENATOR GEORGE. Could you tell anything about the number of planes in the flight?

MR. ELLIOTT. No, sir; not definitely. You could just tell that there was a large number.

SENATOR GEORGE. Now, on that very point, Sergeant, I think the committee would like to have full information. Did you judge it to be a large number of planes?

MR. ELLIOTT. Yes, sir; by the size of the echo we judged it to be a fairly large number of planes.

SENATOR GEORGE. And not merely one or two or three or four planes?

MR. ELLIOTT. We knew that it was not one or two or three or four since at that distance the echo would have shown up very much smaller. This was very definitely very big.

SENATOR GEORGE. And you picked up this flight actually at a distance of about 137 miles?

MR. ELLIOTT. Yes, sir. [...]

[5046] SENATOR GEORGE. Were any other radar stations on the island in operation that morning?

MR. ELLIOTT. Yes, sir; there were. Offhand, I don't know how many. One that I do know definitely of was on until 7 o'clock.

SENATOR GEORGE. Until 7 o'clock?

MR. ELLIOTT. I believe they continued on a little after 7 also, and they had a partial record of the flight that we had picked up. It wasn't quite out as far as the one we had picked up because the station itself was right on the coast—it wasn't up higher in the air.

SENATOR GEORGE. It didn't have the elevation?

MR. ELLIOTT. The efficiency wasn't as great, but that is the only station that I know of that actually picked up any portion of the flight that we recorded that morning.

Senator George. I believe that is all.
The Chairman. Mr. Clark.
Mr. Clark. No questions.
The Chairman. Senator Lucas.
Senator Lucas. Sergeant, what do you mean by the technical term "echo"?
Mr. Elliott. The screen goes about a circle—about a 5-inch circle. On this screen you see a horizontal line, and that horizontal line was broken up from zero to 150 miles of scale. At the point that the target is hit by the transmission being sent out and referred back to the unit it will come up and there is a break in that line and there extends a vertical line up. Then, by the mechanism on the scope, we bring the air line over to the echo, and that is where you get your mileage. But the echo looks like a straight line, and at a right angle a vertical line up, which is the particular target that you see.
Senator Lucas. When you first discovered these planes, did you find more than one?
Mr. Elliott. As I recall it, there were a couple of other flights, but we only followed the main flight because we had all we could do to follow that one.
Senator Lucas. Would you care to give the committee an estimate of the number of planes you thought, from radar, was in that flight?
Mr. Elliott. Any figure that I would say, or that we did have in mind would be only a guess.
Senator Lucas. I understand that, but it would be interesting to the committee to get the guess, from your experience out there with this radar.
Mr. Elliott. I really don't recall even guessing that there were any particular number. We knew that there were probably more than 50, but, of course, we didn't know. I mean, it all enters into the picture just how high the plane is flying and just where you strike it, as to the size of the echo you might get.
Senator Lucas. Now, do you recall when you talked to Private McDonald over the phone, whether you indicated as to the number of planes you thought might be in this flight?
[5047] Mr. Elliott. There was no definite number stated. It was just that there were many, very many. [...]
Senator Lucas. Where was the information center on the island located with reference to Opana?
Mr. Elliott. Well, that was down in Fort Shafter. Fort Shafter itself was about, I believe 8 miles from Honolulu.
Senator Lucas. And Fort Shafter is where General Short and his staff were located?
Mr. Elliott. Yes, sir. That was the Hawaiian Department headquarters.
Senator Lucas. You had a direct communication from the radar station to the information center?
Mr. Elliott. We had two lines. One, a tactical line was connected directly to the information desk where the individuals would place their targets in respect to the map.

The Sighting of the Planes

SENATOR LUCAS. What was your understanding as to what the information center was supposed to do with the information that you sent day after day while you were in that training program?

MR. ELLIOTT. By plotting the different targets that we sent in, the plotters on the end of the information center would plot the targets on the table with the map.

Directly overhead in a balcony would be the liaison officers and signal officers and they would determine as they saw the target going up in that locality, each unit, each liaison officer would decide whether it was his flight or not, and if nobody could identify that flight, of course, they had prearranged routes that their planes would be taking, and if no one could identify that flight it was considered an enemy flight.

SENATOR LUCAS. Did you ever learn, Sergeant, whether or not those men who were charged with this responsibility were on duty that morning, December 7, 1941?

MR. ELLIOTT. No, sir. I had no contact with them. I mean, I assume that they were there. That is all I can say. I didn't have any direct conversation with any of them, to know.

SENATOR LUCAS. I understand.

Now, how long had this training program been going on from 4 to 7 in Hawaii?

MR. ELLIOTT. As I recall it, it was going on all the time that we were in operation which was 2 weeks prior to December 7.

SENATOR LUCAS. Two weeks prior to December 7?

[5048] MR. ELLIOTT. Yes, sir.

As to the other units and the time for duty, 4 to 7, I would not be able to state.

SENATOR LUCAS. Did you get any different information or orders after November 27, 1941?

MR. ELLIOTT. No, sir; none that I can recall. [. . .]

[5058] MR. GEARHART. Mr. Elliott, I was called out of the room for a short time.

MR. ELLIOTT. Yes, sir.

MR. GEARHART. Some of the questions that I want to ask you might have been asked heretofore.

First of all I want to know about your tour of duty on this machine on the 6th and on the 7th.

MR. ELLIOTT. How do you mean that? You mean to explain it to you?

MR. GEARHART. Well, what I mean is what hours did you go on duty with the machine and what hour did you leave it on the 6th?

MR. ELLIOTT. I see. On the 6th of December we were sent out there to relieve two men, to so to speak, guard the unit. We were armed with .45 pistols.

MR. GEARHART. You mean to guard the unit or operate the unit?

MR. ELLIOTT. Yes, sir, to guard the unit.

Mr. Gearhart. All right; what time of the day did you arrive there on the 6th?

Mr. Elliott. It was around 12 noon. We relieved the two men and in sending us out there we were to remain there and at 4 o'clock the next morning we were to operate our scheduled operating period, 4 to 7 a.m.

Mr. Gearhart. Do I understand you correctly, you arrived out there at noon on the 6th with instructions to guard the machines until 4 the next morning and at 4 the next morning you were with Lockard to operate the machine; is that correct?

Mr. Elliott. That is right, sir. I might explain about this guarding the unit. It was no walking guard post; it was not considered as such. That is the impression that we had. The impression that we had was that there were just to be men there in case anything came up, any prowlers around or anything like that and that is the reason [5059] we had the gun there, but so far as any walking guard, or patrolling around there was brought up, there was nothing like that. It was just that somebody should be there and we got arms in case any prowler came around.

Mr. Gearhart. And you and Lockard were there from noon on the 6th day of December 1941 until 4 a.m. on the 7th day of December 1941 and during that time the machine was not operated at all?

Mr. Elliott. The machine between 12 noon and 4 a.m.; the machine was not operated; no, sir.

Mr. Gearhart. Was it warmed up?

Mr. Elliott. No, sir; not that I recall.

Mr. Gearhart. Did you enter the compartment in which the machine was contained between those hours that I have just mentioned?

Mr. Elliott. Yes, sir; we had trouble with the oil pump on the generator motor in the power plant.

Mr. Gearhart. You spent some of that time repairing those particular items?

Mr. Elliott. Yes, sir; we repaired the oil pump.

Mr. Gearhart. How long did it take you to repair the oil pump on Saturday?

Mr. Elliott. It took a good part of the afternoon.

Mr. Gearhart. Is that the reason why the machine was not operating for the entire day, or was it because you were not supposed to operate it that day?

Mr. Elliott. I don't believe there were any direct orders not to operate it. It just was not operated.

Mr. Gearhart. Now, there was an officer's tent, war tent, near the mobile instrument, wasn't there, and that is where you slept that night?

Mr. Elliott. That is right, sir.

Mr. Gearhart. Lieutenant Lockard slept there that night, too?

Mr. Elliott. Private Lockard at that time, yes, sir.

Mr. Gearhart. Private at that time?

The Sighting of the Planes 109

Mr. Elliott. Yes, sir.

Mr. Gearhart. How were you awakened? By an alarm clock?

Mr. Elliott. Yes, sir.

Mr. Gearhart. When was that set for?

Mr. Elliott. Off-hand I do not recall. I imagine around a quarter of 4.

Mr. Gearhart. And when you got up did you have to do anything to the radar instrument to prepare it for service beginning at 4 o'clock?

Mr. Elliott. Yes, sir; as I recall, we had some small work to finish up on the oil pump. I believe we had worked through until it was dark and we stopped work on it, and all there was left was just to make the connections, and we planned to do that in the morning.

Mr. Gearhart. It was still dark at a quarter of 4, wasn't it.

Mr. Elliott. Yes, sir.

Mr. Gearhart. As soon as you were awake did you start to work on your oil pump?

Mr. Elliott. Yes, sir.

Mr. Gearhart. Before 4 o'clock?

Mr. Elliott. Yes, sir.

[5060] Mr. Gearhart. Did you have the machine ready to operate at 4 o'clock in the morning?

Mr. Elliott. We went on the air at 4:15, sir.

Mr. Gearhart. You went on the air before you had completed the oil pump repair?

Mr. Elliott. No, sir; we finished our oil pump repair and reported on the air approximately 4:15.

The Vice Chairman. What time?

Mr. Elliott. 4:15.

Mr. Gearhart. Then these repairs delayed you?

Mr. Elliott. Yes, sir.

Mr. Gearhart. Fifteen minutes?

Mr. Elliott. Yes, sir.

Mr. Gearhart. Then you went on the air?

Mr. Elliott. Yes, sir. [...]

Mr. Gearhart. Now, how many days had you been with Lockard assigned to that machine prior to the 7th day of December?

Mr. Elliott. For actual operation, 2 weeks, and for setting up the unit another 2 weeks. We moved out there just about a month before December 7.

The Handling of the Sighting by an Untrained Supervisor

KERMIT TYLER, MOMENTARILY IN CHARGE OF THE AIRCRAFT INFORMATION CENTER

Navy Court of Inquiry

[341] 1. Q. Will you state your name, rank, and present station.
A. Kermit A. Tyler.
2. Q. Rank?
A. Lieutenant Colonel, Air Corps, Army Air Force Board, Orlando, Florida.
3. Q. What was your rank and duty on 7 December 1941?
A. I was assigned as Executive Officer in the 8th Pursuit Squadron. I was a first lieutenant in the air corps at that time.
4. Q. What particular duties were you performing at about 0755 on the morning of 7 December 1941?
A. I was assigned as pursuit officer with a duty as Assistant to the Controller, at the information center at Fort Shafter.
5. Q. Fort Shafter, Territory of Hawaii?
[342] A. Yes.
6. Q. Will you tell the court in a brief way what these duties consisted of that you were performing on this particular morning?
A. The duties of a pursuit officer was to assist the Controller in ordering planes to intercept enemy planes or supposed enemy planes, after the planes got in the air.
7. Q. Your duty, then, was in connection with a pursuit squadron, and not in some capacity such as the aircraft warning center?
A. That is correct. I was sent down there for training. Inasmuch as this was just beng started, it was necessary to detail certain officers who had some background in order to get the thing going.
8. Q. This duty was actually performed in the, shall we say in the Command Post of your pursuit squadron? I am not familiar with your terminology, and I would ask you to explain just exactly the nature of the post of duty at which you were stationed.

Source: Pearl Harbor Attack, *volume 32.*

Handling of the Sighting   111

A. The information center was a post from which fighter squadrons on the alert would be ordered to take to the air; in fact, my task at this information center had involved a small switchboard which would reach fighter squadrons.

9. Q. What I am trying to get at now, were you in a branch of an information center, or at an information center, or what?

A. I was at the one information center for all of the islands.

10. Q. At the one information center of all the islands. Now you were in contact at such station with all radar stations?

A. Yes, sir, they had direct lines.

11. Q. Now how long had you been assigned these duties that you were performing that morning?

A. I had one previous tour on the preceding Wednesday, at which time there was only myself and the telephone operator at the information center. This was my second assignment of that nature.

12. Q. Now this particular station or post at which you were then stationed was in what locality in the island of Oahu?

A. It was at Fort Shafter.

13. Q. Fort Shafter is where with reference to Pearl Harbor?

A. I would say it is about eight miles east of Pearl Harbor.

14. Q. How many officers and men were on duty with you in this particular post or station on this morning of 7 December, 1941?

A. Approximately seven or eight enlisted men, and I was the only officer present.

15. Q. Now what duties in general did they perform? Were they assistants to you, or what were they doing?

A. There were five or six spotters whose duty was to display arrows on the information center board, to indicate radar plots of aircraft. There was one man on the telephone exchange, and one man on the historical record—which keep a historical record of all plots that are made by the radar.

16. Q. Now these plots that you were making—the information upon when they were based, where did you get that?

A. They came by direct lines to each plotter from one radar station which gave him the information.

17. Q. Could you give an example as to about what sort of data would come in from a telephone from one radar station when a plane or group of planes were sighted?

[343] A. Simply be a bearing of so many degrees and range, certain number of miles.

18. Q. And then as I understand it, somebody plotting in the center where you were located put that down in the form of a record, a graphic record?

A. It was plotted with a replaceable arrow on the table, and also there was a system of recording it on this sheet of paper which was an overlay of the Hawaiian Islands and surrounding waters. I might say probably they included in the report of the radar station the number of planes expected in the plot, but that wasn't at the time conveyed in each plot.

19. Q. In other words, that was not always done?
A. No.

20. Q. Now, were you the Senior Officer Present in this central station where you were on post?
A. I was the only officer present.

21. Q. And it is my understanding that you were the officer in charge of this particular station or post?
A. Yes, sir.

22. Q. Was there a Naval officer present at this post on the morning of 7 December 1941?
A. There was after the attack started, sir.

23. Q. Was there an officer present before the attack?
A. No, sir.

24. Q. Did you receive, while you were on duty on the morning of the 7th December 1941, any report of interest?
A. How do you mean by that sir,?

25. Q. DId you receive any information or any report that you considered of any importance?
A. Well, I received a call from one of the radar stations, I believe it is called Opana, which indicated that they had a larger number of planes than he had seen before on his scope; that is, the original report.

26. Q. Can you recall at about what time this report was received in the station?
A. I would estimate it was around 7:15.

27. Q. Now where is Opana station located from where you say you got this report?
A. It was the north side of the island.

28. Q. And it was about how many miles from Fort Shafter, where you were?
A. I would say thirty-five miles in a direct line, perhaps.

29. Q. Now is this station on top of a mountain, on seashore, or can you tell how it was located?
A. I had never been there, and I don't know.

30. Q. Can you remember the language of the report?
A. I can't remember the exact language. As I said before, the radar operator reported that he had a larger plot than he had previously seen; that is about all there was to it.

31. Q. Did you have any abnormal reaction to this report at that time?
A. No, sir. I thought about it for a minute, and then told him, "Thanks for calling in the report."

[344] 32. Q. Had you any information during your tour of duty on this morning of 7 December 1941, as to the movements of any friendly planes in the Hawaiian area?

Handling of the Sighting 113

A. I had no official information. However, I had very good reason to believe that there was a flight of B-17's en route to the Islands from the mainland. I had a friend who was in the bomber command who told me that any time the radio stations were playing this Hawaiian music all night, I could be certain that a flight of our bombers was coming over, and when I had gotten up at 4:00 a.m., to report for duty, I listened to this music all the way to the station, so I was looking for a flight of B-17's.

33. Q. Now when you went on watch, or duty shall I say, that morning, were you given any information by the officer stationing you or the officer whom you relieved, if you did relieve anybody — were you given any special instructions as to what to be on the lookout for?

A. No, sir.

34. Q. Did you actually relieve anybody that morning?

A. No, sir.

35. W. How did you happen to come to go on duty? Was that in response to a detail that went on duty at that time every morning?

A. Yes, sir. There was a roster of various fighter pilots. My tour of duty was from 4:00 to 8:00 a.m. on that morning, sir.

36. Q. Did you have any instructions for your post?

A. No, sir.

37. Q. And you say the only previous experience you had had with that post of duty was the time, several days before, when you did a tour of duty there?

A. Yes, sir.

38. Q. Did you have any familiarity with the mechanics of radar interceptors? That is, how they functioned mechanically or electrically?

A. I understood the principle of radar, yes, sir. [...]

[345] 45. Q. Did you know whether or not the particular type of radar that was then in use, had any means of distinguishing a friendly plane from an unfriendly one?

A. Oh, I knew that there was no way of distinguishing by radar.

46. Q. And the only information of friendly planes that you had on this morning was the deduction you made when you heard a Honolulu radio station playing Hawaiian music at a very early hour; is that correct?

A. That is the only definite indication I had. I think I was equally divided between the thought that it could be the B-17's, or a carrier force.

47. Q. You mean, by "carrier force," U.S. Naval carrier force, or enemy?

A. Friendly force, U.S. Naval airplanes.

48. Q. Had it occurred to you to identify with the Navy whether or not they had any planes in flight at this time?

A. No, sir.

49. Q. I don't suppose, from the information you had, that you had any idea at that time of the course on which these B-17's would approach Oahu?

A. Only the rough idea, sir.

50. Q. What was this rough idea?

A. Well, somewhere from the northeast.

51. Q. And why do you say somewhere from the northeast?

A. Well, that would be the course from San Francisco.

52. Q. Did you have any special information on the morning of 7 December 1941, as to international developments, especially those between the Japanese and the United States, which would indicate any imminence of war?

A. The only special information was what I read in the papers, and that was that a friendly relations—or that some agreement—had been reached approximately a week before, or thereabouts.

53. Q. Well, had you or had you not been put in some sort of a frame of mind of being on the alert against any possible enemy action when you went on duty that morning?

A. No, sir; in fact, just the opposite, because we had been on alert about a week before, and the alert had been called off.

54. Q. Now do you know whether or not there was actually an airplane attack on the Pearl Harbor Naval Base that morning by Japanese planes?

A. Yes, sir.

55. Q. When did you first become aware of this attack?

A. It was about five minutes after 8:00 when the telephone operator received a call from some source, which I don't know right now, that there was an attack on.

56. Q. You don't recall the language of the report that you heard?

A. No, sir, the operator was very excited; and so I told him to call in all information center personnel who had gone off duty at 7:00 o'clock. There was ust the operator and myself there at the time.

[346] 57. Q. Did he tell you the kind of attack, whether it was a naval surface ship attack, aircraft attack, or what?

A. He didn't say, but, however, I knew that it was an air attack, because at 8:00 o'clock I had just stepped outside for a breath of air and I saw the attack in progress, but at that time I thought it was the Navy practicing dive bombing.

58. Q. Do you recall what action you took when you received this report?

A. I called in the information center personnel, who had all gone off duty at 7:00 o'clock, except the operator and myself, and in a very few minutes, Major Tindall, who was one of the controllers, arrived from Hickam Field, and took charge of operations.

59. Q. Did you go off duty then, or what was your status after Major Tindall arrived?

A. I remained on duty as assistant to him and to Major Berquist, who also arrived soon thereafter, for approximately thirty-six hours. [...]

[347] 69. Q. What were your duties, Colonel, when you reported at 4:00 o'clock on that Sunday morning.

A. My duties, I believe, were chiefly for training, inasmuch as it was the first morning I had ever been there on such duty when the information center was even manned in any degree at all. I had no specified duties, either written or oral—just to report there for duty.

70. Q. Well, did you have any instructions to report information that came from different radars to any superior officer?

A. No, sir.

71. Q. Would you have reported it to a superior officer, if you had information that alarmed you?

A. Certainly, if I had been warned that there was any possibility of attack I would have. However, at that time, there being no means of identifying plots, there was not much that one man could do, without having a liaison officer from both the Navy, bombers, and civilian airways, to give you identification between friendly and enemy plots.

72. Q. Did you get any reports between 4:00 and 7:00 a.m. that morning?

A. There were a number of plots in and around the Islands. I believe they started sometime before 7:00 o'clock; the actual time I am not certain of.

73. Q. At 7:00 o'clock, did you get a report of a plot northerly? I mean as distinguished from 7:15.

A. At around very close on 7:00 o'clock, it might have been a little after — I don't know — I walked over to where the boy was working on his historical record, and didn't know what he was doing, so I asked him what his duties were, and so forth. [...]

80. Q. Well, now what happened at 7:15?

A. That was when I received a call from this radar operator. You see, at 7:00 o'clock, all the plotters folded up their equipment and left the information center.

81. Q. What did you do after 7:00 o'clock, then?

A. There was nothing. I didn't do anything. I was just waiting for my tour to be finished.

82. Q. What did your tour consist of between 7:00 and 8:00? What were you supposed to do after 7:00 until your tour was completed?

[348] A. I had no particular duties to perform, except to learn all I could at the information center. [...]

[349] 105. Q. Colonel, when you went on duty at this post at 4:00 a.m., on 7 December, had you ever had any instructions whatsoever as to what you were to do or why you were there?

A. On the previous Wednesday when I went on duty, there was just myself and the telephone operator there, and not having any instructions, I called the operations officer, then Major Berquist.

106. Q. You heard my question, didn't you?

A. Yes, sir. And I asked him why I was there and what my duties were. He told me that they were trying to get the information center set up and that we were leading off by furnishing personnel to man it. I got the idea that I was there for training, and he said if any ships went down, if any of our planes went down we might, by radar reports, be able to tell where they went down and I would be able to assist in that.

107. Q. But prior to 4:00 o'clock when you went on duty, you had no

instructions as to what you were to do in reporting in any large number of planes or anything else in the air?

A. That is right, sir.

108. Q. You had no instructions?

A. I had no instructions.

109. Q. And was this the first time you were on duty there, or the second?

A. That was the second time.

110. Q. And there were no further instructions given you as to what you were to do while you were on duty from 4:00 to 7:00 a.m., of that morning?

A. That is right, sir.

111. Q. Do you know how many radar stations were in operation on that morning?

A. Because I had about 5 plotters, I gathered there were about 5 in operation.

112. Q. Did you know their locations?

A. I knew the exact location of just one radar, sir.

[350] 113. Q. You had no information from anyone to look out for a large plot of planes, did you, or did you have?

A. I had no warning, sir.

114. Q. You spoke of Hawaiian music playing all night. Will you please explain that?

A. Well, the conventional Hawaiian music, guitars and so forth.

115. Q. But you mentioned that as an indication of planes coming in.

A. Because they would play this music without interruption and even without announcement, and it had been standard practice to do so for homing for the planes coming in.

116. Q. Did anyone tell them to play this music for homing for planes to come in, to your knowledge?

A. From the information I had from this bomber pilot friend of mine, it was that someone, probably in the Air Force or the Bomber Command, apparently had arranged for such homing, you see, because it didn't play on other nights.

117. Q. But you don't know what arrangement they had?

A. No, I don't know, definitely.

118. Q. The instant you saw or became aware of enemy planes over Oahu, what did you do?

A. I instructed the operator to call the information center plotters back in. They arrived very shortly and Major Tindal also arrived almost simultaneously.

119. Q. Did it ever occur to you at that time to report immediately to your senior, or the officer who would like to have that information?

A. Yes, sir. I'm not certain whether I called Major Berquist, or whether I told the operator to call Wheeler Field and tell them of the events, or just what happened then. It was really quite confusing for a while, sir.

120. Q. About what time was this?

A. About 8:10, I would say, sir. As a matter of fact, Major Tindal arrived so soon and took over that there was hardly time to do anything there. He apparently started on the way as soon as the first bombs hit Hickam Field.

SECTION FOUR

American Penetration of the Japanese Diplomatic Codes

The Origin and Work of "Magic"

ARTHUR H. McCOLLUM, CHIEF, FAR EASTERN
SECTION, OFFICE OF NAVAL INTELLIGENCE

Joint Congressional Investigation

[3394] [...] An examination of Exhibits 1 and 2, and some of the other intercepts, indicates delays in transmission. Will you tell us whether anything was done about that?

CAPTAIN MCCOLLUM. As to that part of it, there are officers of the technical service that are probably better qualified to answer that than I am. However, I would venture this general explanation:

These dispatches were intercepted at a great many intercept or pick-up stations located in various parts of the world.

One they were picked up, the pick-up station had no personnel qualified to either decode or translate any of this material. They only had operators who were skilled in taking the Japanese equivalent of our Morse code. Those dispatches, therefore, from any given pick-up station, when received, were sent to a center, depending on who was the control center—either Washington, Pearl Harbor, or Corregidor.

They might have sent it either by radio, teletype, or by mail.

Radio and teletype facilities were not always available.

When sent by mail to one of the decryption and translational centers, as soon as they arrived, there was an office procedure for taking through the dispatch, and an attempt was made to decrypt the code.

[3395] It is my understanding that priorities were first given on the basis of the code classification. In other words, the higher the code classification, probably the more important the information was.

There was also the precedence of the dispatch, that is the urgency with which it was sent. Those were obtained from the normal procedure signs at the head of the dispatch.

Then an attempt was made to decrypt them together, if we had the particular code table in which that code was sent.

We did not always have it. Sometimes these codes would be received and

Source: Pearl Harbor Attack, *volume 8.*

we did not have the method or means or decrypting them until sometime afterwards.

Once it was decrypted, or sufficiently decrypted to indicate some importance, it was handed to one of the translators who took a look at it to determine whether he thought it should be completely broken down for further decryption. That had to be done because of the limited number of people capable of translating the language, and to make the very best use of the people we had.

When we were working full blast, the way we were, oh, for the month immediately preceding the attack on our fleet, great effort was made to get the stuff out of these negotiations right away, just as quickly as we possibly could.

Now, that was dependent on the time of arrival at the decoding center, which was not of necessity directly related to the time of transmission from Tokyo, whether the code to decode it was available or not, and dependent upon the relative importance of it as determined prior to reading any of the contents.

Now, when you come then to a slack period, that is, when we weren't getting so many messages, they would go back and work on the old ones. The effort was to decode everything but to try to decode the most important ones first.

MR. KAUFMAN. Captain, you said a moment ago that Pearl Harbor was a central point for decryption. What type messages were decrypted at Pearl Harbor, if you know?

CAPTAIN MCCOLLUM. Going back somewhat here, sir, the Navy Communications Intelligence organization was set up first with headquarters in Washington. Then we put an organization out in the Asiatic sphere with headquarters in Cavite first, and later at Corregidor. We originally had pick-up stations in Pekin, Shanghai, Guam, and I think at one time one almost in Japan, some years ago.

Until the early 30's very little had been done so far as Honolulu was concerned. We didn't have very many people. The first idea was that they would be a mobile movement, that would move with the commander in chief of the fleet. I had such a movement when I was Fleet Intelligence Officer. That was found unworkable. They couldn't get the sets. As a result of that, a route of entry was set up in Honolulu with the hope that that could be built up.

Until about early 1941, we had only, it is my understanding, a very rudimentary organization in Honolulu. At that time we were very fortunate in having become available the services of Captain Rochefort, who is the only officer in our Navy who is a top-flight cryptographer and radio man, and who also has a thorough knowledge of the Japanese language. He was obtained from the staff of [3396] Vice Admiral Andrews, and put in charge at Honolulu with instructions to build up his organization as rapidly as he could.

He did not get very much help, I believe, from Washington. We didn't have the people, and he was in the process of building up that organization with the primary job of making an effort to break Japanese naval codes and ciphers when the war occurred.

It is my understanding that they did not have the complete codes to enable them to read the Japanese diplomatic messages, nor is it my understanding that they were expected to; that their principal effort was to be directed on an attack on Japanese naval codes.

MR. KAUFMAN. Do you know whether Admiral Turner thought that the organization in Hawaii could decode Japanese diplomatic codes?

CAPTAIN MCCOLLUM. This is hearsay, Mr. Counsellor. I heard him say before this committee that he thought so, sir.

I wish to clarify one point. This organization at Honolulu, by dropping everything else that they were doing and using some of the standard books that they had, and by exercising cryptographic efforts, in other words, a direct attack with some of the very clever officers they then had out there, were able to read the gist of some of the low-grade stuff in the Japanese diplomatic ciphers.

In other words, it was a major cryptographic effort on each code; that was my understanding, but they couldn't read it right straight through. [...]

[3399] THE VICE CHAIRMAN. Captain, why was not priority given to the decoding, decrypting, and translating of these Japanese messages?

In other words, what I am trying to ascertain is this, I got the impression that these intercepted Japanese messages were handled more or less in a routine manner. I was wondering why the highest type of priority was not given for the immediate decoding, decrypting, and translating of these messages intercepted from Japanese sources.

CAPTAIN MCCOLLUM. Oh, but they were, sir. If the impression was given that the thing was routine, that is a wrong impression, sir. Everyone was working tooth and nail to get these things out as quickly as they possibly could, sir.

THE VICE CHAIRMAN. To the exclusion of others?

CAPTAIN MCCOLLUM. That is correct, sir. In other words, the people working on the Japanese, the major effort was put on the Japanese and all other things that had relations to it were dropped completely out of the picture. Every effort of that organization was bent on this thing, the decrypting of these dispatches.

THE VICE CHAIRMAN. My recollection is that the evidence presented here during the appearance of General Miles, who was G-2 of the General Staff of the Army, as you know, it was called to his attention that all the way from two to twenty-odd days of time elapsed from the time the Japanese message was sent before it was decoded and translated.

Now, did anything of that kind happen with the Navy?

CAPTAIN MCCOLLUM. Yes, sir; I have tried to explain that, sir. In other words, if I may take a hypothetical case, assume that a Japanese diplomatic dispatch was picked up in one of the pick-up stations in Alaska. I, again, do not know the physical means they had but there were such stations that the only communication they had was by mail. Assume, again, that that was the only station that picked up that particular dispatch. That would come in to us here in Washington we will say by mail. As much as a week might elapse from the time it was actually received at the pick-up station until it was received in the decoding center in Washington. The minute that thing then came in it would be looked at to see if we had the code that would permit us to decode it, sir. If we had that code it would be decoded in part, handed to a translator, who would translate part of it to ascertain whether, as far as he had gone, whether it merited complete breakdown, particularly if there was more code work to be done on it.

Then if it didn't look important it would be set aside in favor of things that looked to be more important and pressing, sir.

Those things were done first. Then when you came to a slack time everything that you hadn't done before would be decoded. The set-up was to try to decode what appeared to be the most important things first and get them out just as quickly as we could, sir. [...]

[3400] THE VICE CHAIRMAN. Of course, there is a definite physical problem involved in this type of work.

CAPTAIN MCCOLLUM. Yes, sir. Not only that, I might add, Mr. Congressman, but there is a mental problem involved.

SENATOR LUCAS. A what?

CAPTAIN MCCOLLUM. A mental problem. This type of work is one of the most trying mental exercises that you have.

THE VICE CHAIRMAN. I can appreciate that.

CAPTAIN MCCOLLUM. We have had a number of our officers and a number of our civil people break down rather badly under continual punching on this sort of thing and it is a continual concern of officers who handle those peole to keep them from coming to a mental breakdown on this type of work.

THE VICE CHAIRMAN. I can readily appreciate that it is a difficult task. That would certainly be my idea about it.

I want to see if you can clear me up on this point. The records presented here, these exhibits of the messages, rather indicate that some relatively unimportant messages were decoded and translated more promptly than some other messages here which were much more important. Now, can you help me some on that?

CAPTAIN MCCOLLUM. That may be because on the more important messages they weren't able to break them at the time they arrived. They might not have arrived until after the unimportant ones were here. On the more important messages we couldn't use all of our translators. We had to use only the few top-flight ones. We only had six or seven. We had increased our number 100 percent, sir, but it was still six or seven when we got through with that in 1941.

And, if I may be pardoned for going back to this, the so-called translator in this type of stuff almost has to be a cryptographer himself. You understand that these things come out in the form of syllables, and it is how you group your syllables that you make your words. There is no punctuation.

Now, without the Chinese ideograph to read from, it is most difficult to group these things together. That is, any two sounds grouped together to make a word may mean a variety of things. For instance, "Ba," may mean horses or fields, old women, or my hand, all depending on the ideographs with which it is written. On the so-called translator is forced the job of taking from unrelated syllables and grouping them into what looks to him to be intelligible words, substituting then such of the Chinese ideographs necessary to pin it down, and then going ahead with the translation, which is a much more difficult job than simple translation, sir.

[3401] For that reason all of the people, however qualified they might be in the Japanese language, had to have considerable experience in this particular field before they could be trusted to come through with a correct interpretation of the dispatch.

THE VICE CHAIRMAN. I can understand those difficulties. Is it true that many words in the Japanese language can be given a variety of meanings, as you have indicated by this one word you have used here?

CAPTAIN MCCOLLUM. It depends on the Chinese ideograph. The reason is this: The Japanese language is an uninflected language. It is straight out. They borrowed and applied to the Japanese the Chinese characters. The Chinese indicate a difference between the characters by a difference of inflection. Therefore the Chinese, when he talks, sounds like he is singing. The Japanese, not being able to sing, when he says "Ba," we will say, he doesn't know whether it is one of a half a dozen different things that he means. It is not uncommon to see two Japanese in discussion who get out of tune and one of them has to write the character down to show the other what he is talking about.

THE VICE CHAIRMAN. In ordinary conversation?

CAPTAIN MCCOLLUM. Yes, sir.

THE VICE CHAIRMAN. Well, I might take a second to state that I had the experience one time when I was in school of meeting a Chinese student, and he said, "So many words in your language mean such a different thing." He said, "You talk about a horse running fast and then you talk about a man being tied hard and fast." He said, "One is going, and the other can't move at all. What do you mean?"

I can understand some of the difficulties. Let me ask, if I may—assume that one of our stations somewhere picked up a Japanese message. It is then rushed by the fastest available means of communication to a center where the decoding, decrypting, and translating is done. Is that correct?

CAPTAIN MCCOLLUM. That is correct, sir.

THE VICE CHAIRMAN. Then there is somebody there who has to make an appraisal on the value of the information contained in that message?

CAPTAIN MCCOLLUM. Yes, sir; that is correct, but that appraisal in the first instance is done without the benefit of reading any of it.

THE VICE CHAIRMAN. Just by looking at it?

CAPTAIN MCCOLLUM. By judging from the—as I say, I may be contradicted later on because I am not exact on this, but you have at least two methods of judgment of that. One is the urgency of the dispatch, in other words, whether it is priority, triple priority, or so on.

THE VICE CHAIRMAN. The Japanese—do they use terms for that?

Captain McCollum. Not those terms, but I mean they use a similar system. They have to in practically all of these systems.

The Vice Chairman. I see.

Captain McCollum. Then by looking at it they could tell whether it was in one of the highest security codes or a code of less security or what kind of code, and the presumption was that the higher the security of the code the more important was the information contained in that, sir. [. . .]

[3403] Then, after that, you would look to see where it came from, whether it was the Embassy in Washington, the Foreign Office in Tokyo talking, or something that concerned us more directly.

The Vice Chairman. And after that appraisal was made, why, then—

Captain McCollum. After that they would then see whether it was a code they could read themselves or whether some cryptographic work was required, how much of it we had, how much could be decrypted of that, if it could all be decrypted or not. It would be decrypted, or parts of it would be, and then handed to a translator if it looked urgent. All these factors were considered in there; and it was then sent to a man who then said—from virtually looking at the Japanese syllables—said: "I think that they ought to work full blast on this one or spend more time on that one and get it out."

The Vice Chairman. Then your explanation of the details of getting at these messages is to explain, apparently, the delay in the decoding, decrypting, and translating of some of them?

Captain McCollum. Yes, sir. We tried to run time after time what we called, technically, time studies in there; that is, to see how fast we could get them out.

The Vice Chairman. As I recall, we also received information that one difficulty was the lack of trained, qualified personnel.

Captain McCollum. Oh, yes, sir; that was all the way through. I might add on that, sir, that from 1907 until the outbreak of the war in 1941 the Navy had exposed to Japanese language instruction a total of about 50 officers. By 1941 about 43 of those were available, either active or retired. All but 8 of those people were on specialty jobs when the war commenced.

In October of 1941 the Navy started schools for the instruction of college men in the Japanese language, and those schools opened on October 1, 1941, I think, with about 40 selected students, one at Harvard and the other at the University of California out in Berkeley. They were subsequently combined at Boulder in Colorado, sir. [. . .]

[3403] The Vice Chairman. Now, Captain, did you state that the best decoding, decrypting, and translating officer in the United States Navy was at Pearl Harbor? You gave the name of some man.

Captain McCollum. That was my impression, Mr. Cooper. I have known Rochefort a good many years.

The Vice Chairman. What is the name?

Captain McCollum. Rochefort, sir; R-o-c-h-e-f-o-r-t.

THE VICE CHAIRMAN. What was his rank?

CAPTAIN MCCOLLUM. He was then a commander, sir.

THE VICE CHAIRMAN. Commander Rochefort?

CAPTAIN MCCOLLUM. Yes, sir. As early as 1925, Mr. Cooper, he was looked on as being one of the outstanding cryptographers and radio officers in the service, and because of those special qualifications he was sent to Japan to acquire a knowledge of the Japanese language, which he did, and to my mind he is the only officer in the entire naval service that in this particular field is preeminent because of his training in both the language and the decryption, together with my evaluation of his ability. I rate him as one of the ablest officers in the service, sir.

THE VICE CHAIRMAN. And he was on duty there in Hawaii on December 7?

CAPTAIN MCCOLLUM. That is correct, sir.

THE VICE CHAIRMAN. And had been for some time prior thereto?

CAPTAIN MCCOLLUM. In May, I believe it was, of 1941 he took over that job.

THE VICE CHAIRMAN. He went to Hawaii in May 1941 and continued there until after December 7, 1941?

CAPTAIN MCCOLLUM. And he stayed there until the Battle of Midway, sir. [...]

[3404] THE VICE CHAIRMAN. Now, did you state that these intercepted Japanese messages were sent to Pearl Harbor by the stations that picked up the message?

CAPTAIN MCCOLLUM. Yes, sir; they had a pick-up method. Whether Pearl Harbor merely passed them on to the decryption center here or not, I do not know, sir. I think each one of these centers—the idea was that each one of these centers controlled a certain pick-up station. Those pick-up stations flowed—the information went from the pick-up station to the center, and then anything that center could not do they sent on to another center that could handle it.

For instance, these diplomatic messages of the Pearl Harbor net—or the Hawaii net—might well be flown into the—might well have moved first into the center at Hawaii and then been transmitted by radio or cable direct to Washington, because they were not working on this particular type of stuff out there, sir. [...]

[3421] SENATOR FERGUSON. On page 204 of Exhibit 1 there is a message from Tokyo to Berlin, November 30, 1941, in three parts, that indicates part 1 of 3. It is:

Re my circular #2387.

Have you got that?

CAPTAIN MCCOLLUM. Yes, sir.

SENATOR FERGUSON. Now I want to ask you whether you noticed, when you got that message, that you did not get part 2, whether you recall that. Have you read those?

CAPTAIN MCCOLLUM. Those are the messages, Senator, starting towards the top of page 204 and running over to page 205, sir?

SENATOR FERGUSON. Yes, No. 985, and No. 985 at the bottom of the page.

CAPTAIN MCCOLLUM. Yes, sir; I saw those, sir.

SENATOR FERGUSON. When those came through your hands did you notice that part 2 was not there?

CAPTAIN MCCOLLUM. Yes, sir.

SENATOR FERGUSON. Was not that a very significant thing?

CAPTAIN MCCOLLUM. No, sir; not necessarily, sir.

SENATOR FERGUSON. Not necessarily?

CAPTAIN MCCOLLUM. No, sir. Part 2 might have been received. [...]

SENATOR FERGUSON. Now, did you get in touch with the British to see whether or not they got that No. 2?

[3422] CAPTAIN MCCOLLUM. No, sir. That exchange was run between the Communications and Intelligence Service, as to the check-up of these things, sir; not by me, sir. [...] Yes, we frequently would pick up one part of a dispatch. In other words, this was one transmission and then the other part would be sent in another transmission, and not infrequently you would pick up one part sent as one transmission and not get the other part sent as another transmission, sir.

SENATOR FERGUSON. We had the same kind of station in the Philippines that we had in Washington, to get the secret messages?

CAPTAIN MCCOLLUM. Not precisely the same, sir, but they were merely technical differences. They were substantially the same, sir.

SENATOR FERGUSON. Do you know whether you ever took it up, to try to find this second part?

CAPTAIN MCCOLLUM. There was a regular exchange between all of the stations and Washington, and vice versa, sir. Everything that we got, they had a system of checking up on, to see whether they got it, and possibly they did have the fill-in, sir.

Work Patterns in "Magic"

ALWIN D. KRAMER, TRANSLATION SECTION,
COMMUNICATIONS DIVISION, NAVY DEPARTMENT

Joint Congressional Investigation

[3895] MR. RICHARDSON. Do you speak Japanese?
CAPTAIN KRAMER. I do, sir.
MR. RICHARDSON. Fluently?
CAPTAIN KRAMER. I will leave that to my betters to judge.
MR. RICHARDSON. Were you supposed to be a fluent Japanese linguist?
CAPTAIN KRAMER. I presume I was supposed to be.
MR. RICHARDSON. What were your duties, Captain, during the months of November and December 1941 in a detailed way, if you will describe them to us?
CAPTAIN KRAMER. I was in charge of a section in the Division of Naval Communications which was a subsection under then Commander Safford, known as OP-20-GZ, OP-20 being the designation of the then Commander Safford, known as the Communications Security Group.

GZ was the subsection concerned with the translation of decrypted ciphers and the recovery of Japanese codes. My permanent assignment was to the Far East section of the Division of Naval Intelligence. My status was a loan status to OP-20-GZ.

As a subordinate of the Director of Naval Intelligence I was given the further duty of disseminating at the direction of the Director of Naval Intelligence or my immediate superior, the head of the Far East section, translations produced in my section.

MR. RICHARDSON. What were your customary office hours at that period?
CAPTAIN KRAMER. That is a difficult question to answer, counselor. The regular working hours in those days was from 8 o'clock in the morning until 4:30 in the afternoon, except Saturday, when closing hours were, I believe, at a quarter of 1. However, not only myself but translators and yeomen were all considered on duty, especially during the latter part of 1941, on a 24-hour basis. There were numerous occasions when we worked until 9, 10, or 11 in the evening. There were a number of occasions when I was called down to the office during

Source: Pearl Harbor Attack, *volume 8.*

the course of the night and when I phoned for certain translators to come down to help out.

Does that answer your question?

MR. RICHARDSON. If messages came into your unit by whom were they received?

CAPTAIN KRAMER. By "my unit" you refer to Section GZ, I take it.

MR. RICHARDSON. That is right.

CAPTAIN KRAMER. Normally they went to then Chief Yeoman Bryant, who passed them to translators.

MR. RICHARDSON. Right at that point, how did they come in mechanically?

CAPTAIN KRAMER. By hand from the GY watch officer.

MR. RICHARDSON. And where were those watch officers located and how many were there?

[3896] CAPTAIN KRAMER. I believe there were four, with the most experienced one, a fifth one, in general charge, keeping the office hours which he saw fit or which was required by the situation at the time.

MR. RICHARDSON. Well, my recollection is that at this particular time Ramsay, Linn, Pering and Brotherhood were the watch officers.

CAPTAIN KRAMER. Linn, Pering, and Brotherhood I recall. I do not recollect Ramsay. There was one other whom I distinctly recall, named Murray.

MR. RICHARDSON. That is right. They, as I understand it, Captain, would take the messages mechanically in the first instance. Is that correct?

CAPTAIN KRAMER. Yes, sir.

MR. RICHARDSON. And what would they take it from?

CAPTAIN KRAMER. From whatever source it arrived in Section GY from. There were many sources.

MR. RICHARDSON. Illustrate the sources that would bring a message into GY?

CAPTAIN KRAMER. In 1940 and early 1941 the primary source was mail, air mail from the intercept stations. At some date during 1941, I am uncertain as to the exact date, teletype transmission of that traffic was instituted from shore stations within the United States proper. Furthermore, I know that some time during 1941 stations in outlying possessions were directed to encode in United States naval systems traffic on certain channels we were intercepting. One I recall distinctly is the Tokyo-Berlin channel. We had other sources than I have given.

MR. RICHARDSON. Yes. When these messages would come in they would be in the precise language of the message as it was delivered to GY?

CAPTAIN KRAMER. Do you mean when they came into GZ?

MR. RICHARDSON. Into GZ, yes.

CAPTAIN KRAMER. No, sir.

MR. RICHARDSON. What change would occur in the message after it was received in process of handling it?

CAPTAIN KRAMER. GY was a subsection of this Communications Security Group, responsible for the attack on, the break-down, and the decryption or decoding of recovered systems.

MR. RICHARDSON. Including translation?

CAPTAIN KRAMER. No, sir; by "break-down" I mean cryptanalytical break-down.

MR. RICHARDSON. After that stage had been passed through what was the next stage into which a message would pass?

CAPTAIN KRAMER. The text broken down into the Japanese text which we had recovered was sent to my section from that point. That applies primarily to ciphers, of course. In the case of codes most of the recovery work, at least after the initial breaks into a new code were made, were done by my section. It was primarily a language problem.

MR. RICHARDSON. And about how many people did you have there in late November and early December assisting in the translation of such messages?

CAPTAIN KRAMER. We had three linguists whom I would characterize as the most highly skilled occidentals in the Japanese language [3897] in the world. We had three others that we had acquired, I believe the first one in 1940 and the second two in the fall of 1941, who were less skilled in the work of our office. The two last ones I mentioned above were in more or less of a training status at that time.

MR. RICHARDSON. Well, now, when the message had been put into the Japanese language was there anyone that assigned a particular message to a particular linguist?

CAPTAIN KRAMER. Not a particular message, no, sir. However, I made general assignments of what translators would handle what type of traffic. I will amplify that, if you desire, by stating that the most important circuits, two of which at that time were the Tokyo-Washington circuit and the Tokyo-Berlin circuit, were for the most part in a system which was the best the Japanese had, namely, the so-called purple machine.

The Berlin circuit, of course, was concerned with the war in Europe and negotiations with reference to the Tri-Partite Pact. The Washington circuit primarily was concerned with the Japanese-American negotiations.

Certain minor circuits, for example, what we termed the "China net," I assigned to one of the less skilled translators who did most of the work on that traffic. That was not an ironclad assignment by any means. If a translator finished important traffic he was handling he dug into whatever remaining traffic was untranslated in the section.

MR. RICHARDSON. Well, then, Captain, until someone in your immediate section translated the message that came in, no one in the Navy Department beyond you would know what that message meant?

CAPTAIN KRAMER. In general that is correct, sir. However, it should be modified to this extent. It is of some assistance to crypt-analysts to have at least a slight knowledge of the language with which they are working, the language in the crypts they are working with. For that reason there had been periodic lecture courses given to the crypt-analysts, not only the top crypt-analysts but those in training, by my predecessor Captain Mason, I believe by my immediate predecessor now Captain Carlson, and by myself, so that the GY watch officers and a number of the crypt-analytical clerks had a certain familiarity with the Japanese language.

MR. RICHARDSON. But the information which they might get, be it little or be it much, would not pass out for use by the Navy Department except out of your section after the message had been adequately interpreted?

CAPTAIN KRAMER. With one exception which I have in mind that is precisely correct.

MR. RICHARDSON. What is the one exception you mean?

CAPTAIN KRAMER. The one exception is this winds message, sir.

The Normal Distribution Pattern for "Magic"

LAURENCE F. SAFFORD, CHIEF, SECURITY SECTION, COMMUNICATIONS DIVISION, NAVY DEPARTMENT

Joint Congressional Investigation

[3555] MR. RICHARDSON. Captain Safford, will give your full name and your age to the reporter?

CAPTAIN SAFFORD. Laurence Frye Safford. Age 53 years.

MR. RICHARDSON. How long have you been in the Navy?

CAPTAIN SAFFORD. Thirty-four years this June.

MR. RICHARDSON. Will you detail in a general way to the committee, Captain, just what your naval experience has been, the general work that you have done and the present position which you occupy?

CAPTAIN SAFFORD. After graduation from the Naval Academy I served in battleships, destroyers, submarines, mine craft, cruisers, and battleships. I have had a total of 14 years' sea duty, the last 3 [3556] of which being spent as gunnery officer on the battleship *New Mexico*.

I was in charge of the Antiaircraft Gunnery School in the summer of 1935, which was fairly successful.

All my shore duty has been spent in my specialty as a cipher expert and radio intelligence expert. I came ashore to assume this duty in charge of the Navy Department Communications Intelligence Unit in May 1936, and remained on that duty until February 15, 1942, at which time I was removed by the orders of Admiral Horne.

In 1938 I was assigned to engineering duty only by the Secretary of the Navy and ordered to remain on shore duty at my post at that time in order to get ready for the war which everybody could see was coming.

MR. RICHARDSON. Are you on active service in the Navy now?

CAPTAIN SAFFORD. At the present time I am on active service in the Navy and am called the Assistant Director of Naval Communications for cryptographic research.

MR. RICHARDSON. Will you detail a little more what you mean by the work

Source: Pearl Harbor Attack, *volume 8.*

that you did in cryptology and in intelligence, what the scope of those activities was, what the general field was that you were working in when you were doing that work?

CAPTAIN SAFFORD. I was ordered to duty in the Navy Department in January 1924, to establish a radio intelligence system for the United States Navy. At that time, and previous to that time, I was given some reports and told to study them and to see what I could accomplish.

MR. RICHARDSON. What do you mean by "radio intelligence"?

CAPTAIN SAFFORD. By "radio intelligence" I mean the interception of the radio messages of enemy foreign nations and agents, their solution by cryptanalytic processes.

MR. RICHARDSON. You recall in a general way that it was a message which came into this country from Japan in 13 — first a pilot message that was followed by a 13-part message.

Now, will you tell me when you first heard of anything with reference to what turned out to be the 14th part message?

CAPTAIN SAFFORD. I probably heard of the pilot message in the early afternoon of Saturday, December 6, 1941, although I cannot recall it.

MR. RICHARDSON. Would it have been the regular procedure or custom there to have acquainted you with such a pilot message?

CAPTAIN SAFFORD. It was the regular procedure to immediately acquaint me with anything of particular importance and this was of particular importance.

MR. RICHARDSON. Why would you think that would be a particularly important message?

CAPTAIN SAFFORD. Because it gave information that the long-awaited reply to the Secretary of State note of the 26th of November was about to be transmitted.

MR. RICHARDSON. Now, you were acquainted, were you not, with the fact that the Secretary of State had submitted such a note about the 26th?

[3557] CAPTAIN SAFFORD. We had read the text of his note from the Japanese intercept. We also knew the Japanese reaction to it.

MR. RICHARDSON. And your knowledge and that reaction made you very much interested in when the answer would come in?

CAPTAIN SAFFORD. That was extremely important to me, both for information and to perform my duty, in getting this information to higher authority with the least possible delay.

MR. RICHARDSON. Now, would there be any duty on your part when the pilot message came in to take any steps to circulate the pilot message as an independent message of itself?

CAPTAIN SAFFORD. That was the duty of Naval Intelligence and was normally performed by Lieutenant Commander Kramer who was attached to that office but working under me in space of my section.

MR. RICHARDSON. Would it have been the regular practice where the first message that came in was a pilot message for Lieutenant Kramer to proceed to deliver that message without waiting for any further message in confirmation thereof?

CAPTAIN SAFFORD. That is correct, it would be, and this pilot message indicated that the next message would probably not be received until the following day.

MR. RICHARDSON. Have you any recollection that the pilot message as a separate message was delivered by Lieutenant Kramer?

CAPTAIN SAFFORD. Lieutenant Commander Kramer was absent from the office from noon until about 3:00 p.m. I do not know where he was. I doubt if he can recall, but he was probably delivering this message. We know now from information which has become available to me in the last 2 weeks that there was a time stamp on the War Department copy of this message which said, "Received 12:05 p.m. December 6." I think that is the time. That is a matter of record. It was about 12:05.

MR. RICHARDSON. That would refer to the pilot message?

CAPTAIN SAFFORD. That refers to the pilot message.

MR. MURPHY. Mr. Chairman, there was an answer of the witness to the question just before that indicated there was something that said the 14th part would come in the next day. May I have that?

MR. RICHARDSON. Let me ask him.

Captain, was there anything in connection with the pilot message that would inform you that there was another message to come?

CAPTAIN SAFFORD. Yes. It says in the second paragraph, "This separate message is a very long one. I will send it in 14 parts and imagine that you will receive it tomorrow. However, I am not sure."

MR. RICHARDSON. And it was that language which informed you that there would be more to follow?

CAPTAIN SAFFORD. It was that language which informed me there was more to follow.

MR. RICHARDSON. Now, if this message was delivered and how it was delivered would be the responsibility and act of someone other than yourself?

[3558] CAPTAIN SAFFORD. That is correct. That message was translated by the Army and the time of delibery in the Navy Department all depended upon what time the Army sent our copies of the translation over to the Navy Department. That is not a matter of record and we can only guess.

MR. RICHARDSON. Can you tell me how long it was after your attention was called to the pilot message that any execute appeared on the long 14-part message to which it referred?

CAPTAIN SAFFORD. The long 14-part message actually was received in the Navy Department and our men on watch began what we call processing it before I could have seen the translation of the pilot message.

MR. RICHARDSON. What do you mean by, before your men were processing it, what do you mean by that, what is "processing"?

CAPTAIN SAFFORD. The first five or six parts of the long 14-part message were

Four. American Penetration of Codes

received in the Navy Department I believe about 10 minutes of 12, just before noon. The officer on watch telephoned over to the War Department and found out that the War Department unit was securing it at 1 o'clock because they were observing the normal working hours prescribed by the Civil Service Commission at that time and therefore he held it and worked on it himself although it was an Army responsibility under a joint agreement under date of 1941 whereby the Army processed the messages on the even days of the month and the Navy on the odd days. Processing means decoding or decrypting where it had to be done, exclusion of the code where that had to be done, recovering of the key where that had to be done, translation and finally smoothing up and typing the smooth copies for distribution to higher authority.

A number of copies were typed; early in the year I think we were limited to 4; by December 1941 I think there were 12 or 14 copies prepared, half of which went to the Navy and half to the Army for distribution.

Mr. Richardson. Would they go to anyone else than the Army and the Navy?

Captain Safford. By agreement which was made and approved on the 12th of November 1941 the Navy made all deliveries to the White House via the Naval Aide to the President, who at that time was Rear Admiral Beardall and the Army made all deliveries to the Secretary of State.

Mr. Richardson. Well, would those deliveries be made out of the number of copies that had been furnished to the Navy and to the Army?

Captain Safford. They were made out of the total number of copies and their copy was identical with the ones of the Army and Navy.

Mr. Richardson. Would there be new copies or simply one of the multifold copies that had been delivered to them?

Captain Safford. They were one of the multifold number of copies.

Mr. Richardson. Well, then, when that message was delivered in that way a copy of what was delivered, in the ordinary course of recording, would appear in the files of the particular department that got the copy?

[3559] Captain Safford. There was a file copy kept in the Navy Department in my section. There was a file copy kept in the War Department. I think it was originally kept by the SIS and later taken over by G-2 after there had been an unfortunate leak and name calling in connection with it which was followed by a controversy as to who was responsible for the leak.

Mr. Richardson. And the Navy assumed the responsibility for sending one of these copies to the White House?

Captain Safford. That is correct, sir.

Mr. Richardson. And the Army would have the responsibility of sending a copy to the Secretary of State?

Captain Safford. That is correct, sir.

Mr. Richardson. And when those copies were delivered they would become a part of the files of the office or person to whom they were delivered?

Captain Safford. No, sir. They were collected afterwards. Sometimes they were allowed to keep them 24 hours. We wanted them back as soon as we could get them. And they were destroyed. I believe the Army destroyed everything but the file copy. The Navy kept one file copy and also another copy so that we would have a loose copy to work with and not have to remove a copy from the file.

MR. RICHARDSON. Then there would be one copy remaining in the files of the Navy and one copy remaining in the files of the Army?

CAPTAIN SAFFORD. At all times.

MR. RICHARDSON. How many copies would come to rest and remain in your files?

CAPTAIN SAFFORD. Always one; generally a second.

MR. RICHARDSON. How many communications units, where messages were being intercepted and brought in, were we maintaining at that time?

CAPTAIN SAFFORD. Do you mean the intercept stations where we were intercepting?

MR. RICHARDSON. I want the intercept stations first.

CAPTAIN SAFFORD. We had major intercept stations at Winter Harbor, Me.; Cheltenham, Md.; Bainbridge Island, Wash.; Heeia on the island of Oahu, and at Corregidor.

We had a small intercept direction-finding station at Guam, a small one at Imperial Beach, Calif. We had a small intercepting direction-finding station at Amagansett, Long Island; and Jupiter, Fla.

In addition a number of direction-finder stations which did not attempt any intercepting.

MR. RICHARDSON. If anyone made an intercept that would be transferred by them where?

CAPTAIN SAFFORD. Normally to their primary control station or office, or CI unit, as we called it.

Occasionally it would come direct to Washington, depending upon what type of message it was, and what the instructions were in the case.

MR. RICHARDSON. It is a fact, is it not, Captain, that the Washington office had the most experienced personnel and was   [3560]   the most extensive office of that kind that we had in the world, was it not?

CAPTAIN SAFFORD. It had a few of the most experienced personnel, but 90 percent of them had been in service less than a year. It was a training ground, as well as a working place.

MR. RICHARDSON. But it was the best we had?

CAPTAIN SAFFORD. It was the largest we had. I would say that the best we had, as far as experience and all-around skill was up at Pearl Harbor.

MR. RICHARDSON. Was there any division of activity assigned to these various stations, for instance, Washington, Pearl Harbor, and Corregidor, as to what character of work they should do, or were they all doing the same thing?

CAPTAIN SAFFORD. That was highly specialized. The Navy Department was responsible exclusively for the handling of anything which originated in the Atlantic Ocean, I mean from the European Continent. It was responsible for

Japanese diplomatic communications; it was responsible for backing up our other two stations on their particular problems, and was responsible for the training of personnel to send out to the outlying stations, because we did not believe in sending untrained personnel into the field.

MR. RICHARDSON. Then this 14th part message we are talking about came into the station here in Washington in the regular course of the kind of intercepting that that station was supposed to do?

CAPTAIN SAFFORD. That is correct.

MR. RICHARDSON. Now, I think you testified that around 12 o'clock the first four or five sections of this 14-part message came in.

Does that mean when they came in in code?

CAPTAIN SAFFORD. That is when they came in, in code in teletype from Bainbridge Island, Wash., or other stations which had intercepted the message.

MR. RICHARDSON. Now, how long did it take before those various sections of the message that came in were translated into English?

CAPTAIN SAFFORD. Bainbridge Island copied a whole what we call schedule of radio transmissions from Tokyo to San Francisco. They transcribed all of the Government messages and ignored the commercial messages. The Government messages included in other systems on other points, and a lot of messages which had no connection with the 14-part. There was no external way to differentiate. Everything of interest to Washington was punched on a teletype tape and when the tape was completely prepared it was sent into the Navy Department by TWX through the teletype wire exchange by mechanical transmission at a rate of 60 words a minute, and received by the Navy Department.

This high speed transmission cut our tolls to a third, and we got faster service.

Then it was taken by the watch officer and decoded into the basic form as rapidly as possible. Then we knew what we had to do with it next. In many cases the Japanese would use another code underneath this so-called purple machine. In this case they did not. Therefore we saved time. Usually these messages came in Japanese   [3561]   and had to be translated into English. In this case it came in English.

MR. RICHARDSON. Let me be sure that I understand. This message, 14-part, as I understand it, came in in ordinary code which, when translated in the ordinary way, gave you the English translation?

CAPTAIN SAFFORD. Not translated in the ordinary way. We were in possession of the Japanese diplomatic cipher machine known as purple to conceal its real nature. The Army got that for us. We helped build the machines.

MR. MURPHY. Mr. Chairman, I am wondering if it is necessary to go into technicalities. We have gone far enough in attacking national security without going into details on this.

MR. RICHARDSON. Since this is the first time anybody has raised that point I am perfectly willing to stop.

MR. MURPHY. It was raised before by me and I want to again protest the necessity of the Captain revealing the mechanics and the details of how we broke the code. I do not see how it could help national security or help national defense or add anything to the inquiry. . . .

THE VICE CHAIRMAN. Well, have you said anything so far that would endanger the element of security?

CAPTAIN SAFFORD. No, sir; nothing that has not been brought out in the papers. . . .

[3562] MR. RICHARDSON. When this message began to come in was there any attempt made to make any delivery of any portion of it prior to the reception of the first 13 parts?

CAPTAIN SAFFORD. No, sir; not to my knowledge, except that Commander McCollum, who was the head of the Japanese section of Naval Intelligence, knew that the message was in and coming in and being worked on when it was partially in. I think he knew that around 3 or 4 o'clock in the afternoon.

MR. RICHARDSON. But there was no delivery outside of your office of this message so that anyone could read it or see it or know of it or act on it or deliver it until the first 13 parts had come in, was there?

CAPTAIN SAFFORD. The message was not ready for delivery until about 9 o'clock in the evening. It might have been ready for delivery a little earlier on a limited scale.

MR. RICHARDSON. Now, by "the message" you refer to the first 13 parts?

CAPTAIN SAFFORD. I mean the first 13 parts.

MR. RICHARDSON. Did you consider the first 13 parts as a complete message for the purpose of delivery?

CAPTAIN SAFFORD. I never saw the first 13 parts until Monday morning.

MR. RICHARDSON. When did you last see or hear anything of this message of Saturday, December 6th?

CAPTAIN SAFFORD. I left the office at the close of working hours, at 4:30 p.m. on Saturday, December 6th. It was the first time in 2 weeks that I had observed normal working hours.

At that time Commander Linn had come on and was re-working the message. There had been a mistake in the key which was set up on the machine which decoded the message and the whole entire part we had in that was badly garbled and because of its importance Linn thought it was better to check the key first and find out the mistake and produce perfect copy rather than to clear the garble by guess and maybe make mistakes at critical points in the message. This would take quite a little bit of time and we simply had to throw away all the work that had been done before.

Linn was my best man on the watch side. Normally I do not expect watches from a man in charge of a section. He was taking the place of a man whom we had let go on Christmas eve and we were hoping that we would be able to get somebody else to take his place.

Kramer was standing by to deliver the message. As soon as it was completed McCollum knew about it.

MR. RICHARDSON. Were you there?

CAPTAIN SAFFORD. I was there until 4:30. I checked it and said:

> There is nothing I can do but get in your way and make you nervous. I am going home.

MR. RICHARDSON. Then after 4:30 you knew nothing of your own knowledge as to what happened to the 13-part message?

[3563] CAPTAIN SAFFORD. Until Monday morning, when I got the reports from Linn and Kramer on it. ...

MR. RICHARDSON. Did you see the 13 parts before you left at 4:30 that afternoon?

CAPTAIN SAFFORD. No. I saw all 13 parts in their original code form but you could not identify them until they had been decoded.

SENATOR LUCAS. That is what I say. You could not identify them.

CAPTAIN SAFFORD. They had probably 20 or 25 messages on hand, 13 of which were the various parts of this and the rest were other messages. They could not be identified until they had all been decoded.

MR. RICHARDSON. Then you left your office at 4:30?

CAPTAIN SAFFORD. That is correct.

MR. RICHARDSON. And you did not again see any part of this message until Monday?

CAPTAIN SAFFORD. Until Monday.

MR. RICHARDSON. And all of the transactions that occurred after 4:30 on Saturday—on Saturday evening and Sunday morning came after you left?

CAPTAIN SAFFORD. That is correct.

MR. RICHARDSON. And you had no independent knowledge of this?

CAPTAIN SAFFORD. That is correct. ...

[3564] MR. RICHARDSON. At what time did you return to your office on Monday?

CAPTAIN SAFFORD. At the beginning of working hours, which I believe was 8 a.m. at that time.

[3565] MR. RICHARDSON. And was your attention then called to anything relating to this 14-part message?

CAPTAIN SAFFORD. I immediately called all of my heads of subsections under me into conference.

SENATOR LUCAS. Who was it that you called?

MR. RICHARDSON. Whom did you call into conference?

CAPTAIN SAFFORD. Commander Kramer, Commander Linn, particularly, and Commander Parke. I believe they were all lieutenants at the time. I called them in to find out what had gone wrong and how the people had been surprised the way they had; first, to see if our section had been to blame in any other way and the second, to immediately start writing out a full report of the circumstances, as required by Navy regulations, I believe, and certainly by Navy custom.

Now, I have been in other accidents and collisions, and so forth, and that was always done. In view of so many people being involved it seemed better to prepare such a statement or report of those in my section and let those who were in agreement with that report sign with me and those who held counterviews submit their own views.

Sometime within the week following Pearl Harbor I and the other officers were called into conference in the office of the Director of Naval Communications; I am not certain whether Admiral Noyes presided and he was called away suddenly and Captain Redmond, the Assistant Director of Naval Communications, presided.

MR. RICHARDSON. When was this?

CAPTAIN SAFFORD. This was in the week following the attack on Pearl Harbor; some time prior to the 15th I remember, probably Thursday or Friday.

MR. RICHARDSON. And where did it take place?

CAPTAIN SAFFORD. In the office of the Director of Naval Communications.

MR. RICHARDSON. The meeting was called for what purpose?

CAPTAIN SAFFORD. The meeting was called of all of the section heads to discuss the attack on Pearl Harbor and the whispering campaign against Admiral Kimmel and Admiral Bloch which was then getting into full swing.

MR. RICHARDSON. Now, we are concentrating here at this moment on the 14-part message.

CAPTAIN SAFFORD. Yes, sir. May I finish my statement?

MR. RICHARDSON. Will you bring your testimony to that point?

CAPTAIN SAFFORD. The discussion in that meeting was that all section heads were asked to tell all the people not to talk, there was too much loose talk going around, that there would undoubtedly be an investigation later and that anybody who had anything to say would be called before that investigation and permitted to say all they had to say, if they had anything to say, and if we had written out anything to destroy it immediately. I considered it a perfectly logical order from my superior.

MR. RICHARDSON. Who gave you the order that you were to destroy anything, name these people?

CAPTAIN SAFFORD. It was either Admiral Noyes or Captain Redmond, the director or assistant director, on the instructions of Admiral Stark. . . .

[3566] MR. RICHARDSON. Well, then, you understood that it became your duty to go to your office, accumulate all of the files of your office that had to do with the events leading up to Pearl Harbor, and destroy them?

CAPTAIN SAFFORD. No, sir; only notes which we had made ourselves.

MR. RICHARDSON. Oh. Was there any reason given why those should be destroyed?

CAPTAIN SAFFORD. Yes; that this was an emergency situation, we had just suffered a terrible defeat, the morale was low, that all kinds of rumors were going out from the Navy Department and we had to put a stop to this whispering campaign. It seemed perfectly logical at the time.

Mr. Richardson. Well, how would you stop the whispering campaign by destroying the notes you made as to the facts?

Captain Safford. At that time I did not question my orders any more than Admiral Wilkinson questioned his verbal orders. We carried them out.

Mr. Richardson. What did you destroy yourself?

Captain Safford. I destroyed considerable notes concerning statements given to me by Lieutenant Linn and Lieutenant Commander Kramer and other people who were intimately associated with them. . . .

"Magic": An Exercise in Illegality!

GENERAL GEORGE C. MARSHALL, CHIEF OF STAFF, U.S. ARMY
Joint Congressional Investigation

[1100] MR. MITCHELL. Did you also see these decoded intercepts of Jap messages relating to military installations and ship movements?

GENERAL MARSHALL. I would assume I would, yes, the same as the diplomatic.

MR. MITCHELL. I think the record shows, I think General Miles said that at a certain date about that time, in the summer or early fall of 1941, you ordered not only the G-2 evaluations of those messages but the raw material or original copies of dispatches should be shown to you.

GENERAL MARSHALL. Yes, sir.

MR. MITCHELL. Do you remember that at that time?

GENERAL MARSHALL. I have a recollection of that.

MR. MITCHELL. He said it was commencing August 5, 1941.

GENERAL MARSHALL. Yes, sir.

MR. MITCHELL. How did they come to you? Were copies delivered and kept in your files?

GENERAL MARSHALL. I beg pardon, sir?

MR. MITCHELL. Were copies delivered and kept in your files?

GENERAL MARSHALL. At first they came in somewhat of a loose-leaf arrangement and they were all returned and I stopped that and required that they be put in a locked pouch because I found in the various offices there was inevitable carelessness and also I felt inevitably the fact that we were doing this would leak out.

I had been told when I became Chief of Staff that my predecessor, General Craig, was very guarded in the matter, primarily because he thought it was illegal and that, therefore, if we were to continue we would have to be exceedingly careful. That factor, of course, more or less vanished from consideration and was replaced entirely by the urgent necessity, from our point of view, of guarding the secret.

MR. KEEFE. Mr. Chairman, I am not sure that I understood that last state-

Source: Pearl Harbor Attack, volume 3.

ment of General Marshall. You mentioned the fact that your predecessor, General Craig, considered the practice, some practice, as being illegal?

GENERAL MARSHALL. The intercepting of these messages.

MR. KEEFE. The intercepting of these foreign messages?

GENERAL MARSHALL. Yes, sir.

MR. KEEFE. As being illegal?

GENERAL MARSHALL. Yes, sir; contrary to the Espionage Act, I believe.

MR. KEEFE. I wanted to be sure that I understood you.

GENERAL MARSHALL. Yes, sir.

MR. MITCHELL. Did you happen to know at that time of the provision in the Federal Communications Act which forbids the interception of communications?

GENERAL MARSHALL. What is that?

MR. MITCHELL. Did you know anything about it then?

GENERAL MARSHALL. I think that is the act I should have referred to. When I said the Espionage Act I should have said the Federal Communications Act.

[1101] MR. MITCHELL. And that the Supreme Court held before December 1941 some time that that applied to Government Intelligence or police authorities as well as to private persons?

GENERAL MARSHALL. I think I knew that, sir.

MR. MITCHELL. Were you aware of the fact that at Hawaii, for instance, there wasn't any legal way up to December 7, when the attack occurred, of obtaining copies of the Jap messages that the Japs sent from Hawaii to Tokyo or that Tokyo sent back to their spies in Hawaii that came over commercial cables?

GENERAL MARSHALL. Yes, sir; I was aware of that, particularly because, as I recall, Mr. Stimson was very much concerned in his desire to obtain that information.

MR. MITCHELL. But afterwards you were concerned with the question of security?

GENERAL MARSHALL. When you say "afterwards," I am not referring to December 7. I am referring to about a year back before that.

MR. MITCHELL. Prior to that day.

GENERAL MARSHALL. Prior to that day.

MR. MITCHELL. I mean after the remark had first been made to you about the matter.

GENERAL MARSHALL. Yes, sir.

MR. MITCHELL. And the fear of war became apparent.

GENERAL MARSHALL. The minute the danger of war to America became apparent our intense concern was the secrecy of the source because its value was quite evident.

The War Warning "Winds" Execute: The One Witness Who Persisted in Asserting It Had Been Received

LAURENCE F. SAFFORD, CHIEF, SECURITY SECTION, COMMUNICATIONS DIVISION, NAVY DEPARTMENT

Joint Congressional Investigation

[3598] MR. RICHARDSON. Now, that is a copy of our message from the commander in chief of the Asiatic Fleet, isn't it?

CAPTAIN SAFFORD. That is correct, sir.

MR. RICHARDSON. And that is the one that in your statement to the committee you relied on for your interpretation of the message that you got on the morning of December 4?

CAPTAIN SAFFORD. At the time the winds message was intercepted and translated by Kramer and sent up to higher authority; that is correct.

MR. RICHARDSON. All right. Now, will you tell me what there is in that message that says that the language that was to be used meant war? Read it to me from the message.

CAPTAIN SAFFORD (reading):

> NISHI NISHI England including occupation of Thai or invasion of Malaya and NEI—

which is an abbreviation for Netherlands East Indies.

MR. RICHARDSON. Now, stop right there. We had been getting messages, had we not, for 10 days with reference to the movements of the Japanese toward the Thai Peninsula and the occupation of Malasia, hadn't we?

CAPTAIN SAFFORD. We had numerous signs indicating that they were possibly contemplating an act of war; correct.

MR. RICHARDSON. Toward those places; toward the Thai Peninsula and Malasia?

CAPTAIN SAFFORD. That is correct.

Source: Pearl Harbor Attack, *volume 8.*

MR. RICHARDSON. So there wasn't anything in that language with reference to "NISHI NISHI" that was either new or particularly startling to us, was there, at that time?

CAPTAIN SAFFORD. Nothing except the confirmation of our suspicions or deductions.

MR. RICHARDSON. And the only thing you could draw—the only deduction you could draw from it fairly, Captain, would be that if the execute message came in that said "NISHI NISH" it would mean that the Japs were going after England by going upon that occupation, did it not, or invasion of Malaya?

CAPTAIN SAFFORD. And the Netherlands East Indies; that is correct.

MR. RICHARDSON. Now, proceed and show me what there is in that dispach that shows war on the United States?

[3599] CAPTAIN SAFFORD. There is nothing in the literal translation of that dispatch which says war on the United States.

MR. RICHARDSON. Now, when you turn back, Captain, to 1-A, which is 2353, you find the phrase "HIGASHI NO KAZEAME," with the definition, "Japan-U.S. relations in danger."

Do you find anything in the dispatch from the commander in chief of the Asiatic Fleet that changes that interpretation of "HIGASHI NO KAZEAME," or whatever it is?

CAPTAIN SAFFORD. There is nothing that changes the translation of that phrase.

MR. RICHARDSON. All right. This dispatch that you say was the execute, which you say was what you had been looking for, which was the great triumph of the Navy over the Army, you say come in on the morning of December 4 about 8 o'clock?

CAPTAIN SAFFORD. After 8:30; shortly before 9.

MR. RICHARDSON. Well, now, you testified at least twice before, didn't you, Captain, that it came in on the evening of December 3?

CAPTAIN SAFFORD. I was testifying from memory and doing the best I could without the aid of the written notes which I had unfortunately destroyed in December 1941.

MR. RICHARDSON. Well, they were still destroyed when you made your statement here to the committee, weren't they? They still remained destroyed, didn't they?

CAPTAIN SAFFORD. Those notes remained destroyed; yes.

MR. RICHARDSON. Well, what you mean is after you testified in these earlier hearings you sat down with yourself and your pencil and you made some new notes, is that true?

CAPTAIN SAFFORD. I got new written evidence about 2 weeks ago which up till that time had not been in my possession. It helped me tremendously in reconstructing what had happened as well as refreshing my memory.

MR. RICHARDSON. Well, now, Captain, let us go into this question.

MR. MURPHY. Mr. Chairman, may I request that the written evidence be now produced so that we may examine it? I ask that his written evidence that was produced 2 weeks ago be submitted to the committee.

THE VICE CHAIRMAN. He said he obtained written evidence about 2 weeks ago that refreshed his memory. Mr. Murphy asks that that written evidence be produced.

MR. MURPHY. And that it be spread on the record.

MR. RICHARDSON. What was that written evidence, Captain—what is the nature of it?

CAPTAIN SAFFORD. Monthly reports from the interceptor stations at Winter Harbor, Maine, and at Cheltenham, Md., which I had requested 2 years ago and had been informed could not be discovered. We made one more attempt about 2 weeks ago, and those particular reports were located, and my assistant read them and got pertinent parts for me, and I have his penciled copies of that stuff. I have quoted those parts in my testimony, in these extracts from the logs—rather, the monthly reports of Winter Harbor, Maine, and Cheltenham, Md.

MR. RICHARDSON. But it is true, Captain, is it not, that at least twice before under oath you placed the date of the receipt of this [3600] execute message that you testified concerning on the evening of December 3?

CAPTAIN SAFFORD. I believe I said "December 3 or 4." I think I made it broader than that.

MR. RICHARDSON. I don't think you did. Let me call your attention to your testimony at page 361 of the Hart investigation. Didn't you testify there as follows:

> The winds message was actually broadcast during the evening of December 3, 1941 Washington time, which was December 4th by Greenwich time and Tokyo time.

CAPTAIN SAFFORD. That is correct. [...]

MR. RICHARDSON. Well, now, Captain, you do not know myself of your own knowledge, when the message was received, do you?

CAPTAIN SAFFORD. I do not know from first-hand knowledge exactly what time it was received.

MR. RICHARDSON. All you know, Captain, is that Kramer came to you with a piece of paper in his hand that had a message on it?

CAPTAIN SAFFORD. It was a piece of paper which I recognized as the yellow paper from a roll on a teletype machine.

MR. RICHARDSON. All right. Now, before we go into that, let me inquire, Captain, along this line: Now, after all of this episode had transpired and you had destroyed your notes—by the way, do you now contend that you made notes of what occurred at the time this message came in?

CAPTAIN SAFFORD. I made notes while events were fresh in my memory as to the things which were not matters of official record and were important to know, such as such things as times of deliveries of certain messages, and so forth.

The winds message was then in existence. I could have referred to it for nothing that I wanted, and there would be no occasion to try to check the exact time at which it was intercepted.

MR. RICHARDSON. You testified before the Army board, didn't you?

CAPTAIN SAFFORD. Correct.

MR. RICHARDSON. And I refer now to page 160 of the Army board. Didn't you testify as follows there, Captain:

> CAPTAIN SAFFORD. Kramer made his statements of 8th and 9th of December immediately after the event when I discussed it fully with him. I called for statements. I talked to everybody concerned to see if my people had been negligent in any way, that this thing had been our fault. I made a very careful investigation.
> GENERAL RUSSELL. Did you make any records of that investigation?
> CAPTAIN SAFFORD. No, sir.

Was that true?

CAPTAIN SAFFORD. There was no written record made. All the notes I had in the rough form were destroyed when I got the orders.

MR. RICHARDSON. All right. Now, Captain—

[3601] MR. MURPHY. Mr. Chairman, may I—well, I don't want to interrupt. He testified yesterday the meeting was on the 15th and now he says there were notes made on the 8th and now he says that on the 14th or 15th they were destroyed.

MR. RICHARDSON. Captain, after all of this episode and at the time of this episode you had been a very busy man, hadn't you?

CAPTAIN SAFFORD. That is correct; yes, sir.

MR. RICHARDSON. You might almost say that you worked day and night.

CAPTAIN SAFFORD. Not quite that much, but I was working long hours.

MR. RICHARDSON. And your staff was working hard?

CAPTAIN SAFFORD. That is correct.

MR. RICHARDSON. And your office had never been as busy as it was during this week before the Pearl Harbor attack, had it?

CAPTAIN SAFFORD. That is correct.

MR. RICHARDSON. And after this episode with reference to this so-called winds execute, you never turned your attention to that matter until prior to the summer or fall of 1943, did you, approximately 2 years?

CAPTAIN SAFFORD. Approximately 2 years; a few months less.

MR. RICHARDSON. And the fact is, is is not, Captain, that in the fall of 1943, you concluded that you might be a witness, and then you undertook, by inquiry, by investigation, by conversation, by letters, to try and remember what occurred during that period before the attack in December 1941?

CAPTAIN SAFFORD. I was doing more than that at that time. I was engaged in writing up a history of radio intelligence from 1924 to 1941 by the direction and instruction of the Director of Naval Intelligence. That was carried for

7 months in my monthly report of progress, in addition to doing that work.

MR. RICHARDSON. It was the official work you had to do. You were very deeply exercised in trying to make up your mind as to what you might testify to, if you were called as a witness?

CAPTAIN SAFFORD. I was trying to do double duty with the same set of data.

MR. RICHARDSON. And the other duty, I repeat again, was to get your mind made up as to what the facts were, so if you were called as a witness you could testify?

CAPTAIN SAFFORD. So I could testify and not be confused on the witness stand by counsel.

MR. RICHARDSON. Now, Captain, I want you to know that I do not care a tinker's damn whether the winds execute message came in or whether it did not. I am only interested in whether there should be reviewed by the committee all of the reliable facts that can be adduced so they can reach a conclusion.

I do not want to mislead you or browbeat you, if I talk rather loudly. It is because I am a rather loud talking individual.

I just want to make it clear that when you started, in the fall of 1943 to prepare yourself as a witness, your whole recollection was exceedingly hazy as to what had happened 2 years before, wasn't it?

CAPTAIN SAFFORD. There were a few outstanding facts and the details linking them together were very hazy.

[3602] MR. RICHARDSON. Now, let me read you what you testified to on that point in the Hewitt investigation, at page 112:

> CAPTAIN SAFFORD. In the fall of 1943, it appeared there was going to be a trial, a court martial of Admiral Kimmel. It was hinted in the newspapers and various people in the Navy Department were getting testimony ready for it. I realized I would be one of the important witnesses, that my memory was very vague, and I began looking around to get everything that I could to prepare a written statement which I could follow as testimony.
>
> That was the time when I studied the Roberts report carefully for the first time, and noted no reference to the winds message, or to the message which McCollum had written, and which I had seen, and which I thought had been sent, and then I began talking to everybody who had been around at the time and who knew I had been mixed up in it, to see what they could remember to straighten me out on the thing, and give me leads to follow down to where I got my hands on official messages, and things so it would be a matter of fact and not a matter of memory.
>
> I also talked the thing over with whatever Army people were still around at the time, and had anything in this line, and bit by bit these facts appeared to come together.
>
> The investigation was conducted, if you call it that, for the purpose of preparing myself to take the stand as a witness in a prospective court martial of Admiral Kimmel.

Now, you regard that today, do you not, Captain, as a fair statement of how you brought your mind to a factual conclusion as to what happened during that period, that week prior to Pearl Harbor, in the fall of 1943?

CAPTAIN SAFFORD. That is correct.

SENATOR LUCAS. 1941?

MR. RICHARDSON. 1943.

Now, Captain—

CAPTAIN SAFFORD. May I add something to that statement?

MR. RICHARDSON. Yes.

CAPTAIN SAFFORD. At the time I did this, I expected to be called as a witness for the prosecution, to represent the Navy Department, in the charges which I thought would be preferred against Admiral Kimmell.

MR. RICHARDSON. Well, that made it all the more important, did it not, Captain, that you should testify as to what you knew and not what you found out from what somebody told you, because you were then dealing with the guilt or innocence of a human being?

CAPTAIN SAFFORD. That is correct.

MR. RICHARDSON. Now, Captain, you were exceedingly anxious to get hold of an execute message to the winds code, were you not?

CAPTAIN SAFFORD. I first looked for the—

MR. RICHARDSON (interposing). No, no. I am asking you as to your mental condition. You were very anxious, while you waited to see what the monitoring stations would send in to see when an execute code would come in?

CAPTAIN SAFFORD. That is correct.

MR. RICHARDSON. All right. Now the first time you ever saw the message that you say in your statement was an execute message, was when Kramer brought it to you, sometime after 8 o'clock on the morning of December 4?

CAPTAIN SAFFORD. That is correct.

MR. RICHARDSON. You were not a Japanese linguist?

CAPTAIN SAFFORD. No.

MR. RICHARDSON. You did not decode the message?

[3603] CAPTAIN SAFFORD. No.

MR. RICHARDSON. Do you know under whose watch station the message came in?

CAPTAIN SAFFORD. Lieutenant Murray was on watch at the time.

MR. RICHARDSON. Did not you specifically testify in the former hearing that it came in to Lieutenant Brotherhood?

CAPTAIN SAFFORD. I did on the first hearing, when I was under the belief that it had come in on Brotherhood's watch, because he told me it had.

MR. RICHARDSON. Well, I will take up the Brotherhood matter with you a little later.

I want to pursue this matter just a moment.

Now, Kramer brought you this message, is that correct?

CAPTAIN SAFFORD. That is correct.

MR. RICHARDSON. Now, there was some writing on the message when he brought it to you?

CAPTAIN SAFFORD. There was writing on the message.

MR. RICHARDSON. Now, outside of that writing, what was on that message when he brought it to you?

CAPTAIN SAFFORD. He had understood the code words in the middle of the message, so they stood out very plainly.

MR. RICHARDSON. Just tell me Captain, in what form was this message? Was it in English?

CAPTAIN SAFFORD. The message was in Japanese.

MR. RICHARDSON. All of it?

CAPTAIN SAFFORD. All of it.

MR. RICHARDSON. And you could not read Japanese?

CAPTAIN SAFFORD. I can read a few words in Japanese, if they point it out by underscoring, and I compared them with the original words of the two winds codes.

MR. RICHARDSON. Now, let us not go quite so fast on that, Captain. When the message was brought to you by Kramer, was it typewritten?

CAPTAIN SAFFORD. It was the teletype message as it came in the machine.

MR. RICHARDSON. In Japanese?

CAPTAIN SAFFORD. In Japanese.

MR. RICHARDSON. And with the exception of these specific words that you were watching for, you did not attempt to read it in Japanese?

CAPTAIN SAFFORD. I did not attempt to read it.

MR. RICHARDSON. Now, there was some writing on that message, was there not?

CAPTAIN SAFFORD. That is correct.

MR. RICHARDSON. In handwriting?

CAPTAIN SAFFORD. In handwriting.

MR. RICHARDSON. In English?

CAPTAIN SAFFORD. In English.

MR. RICHARDSON. What was written in longhand on that message?

CAPTAIN SAFFORD. "War with England including NEI," and so forth. "War with the U.S.," or possibly United States, and "Peace with Russia."

That is to the best of my recollection after 4 years.

[3604] MR. RICHARDSON. Well, it is not quite 4 years, in view of the fact that this is the fifth time you are testifying on it, is it, Captain?

CAPTAIN SAFFORD. That is correct.

MR. RICHARDSON. Was there anything else written in longhand on this message in Japanese, except those three phrases?

CAPTAIN SAFFORD. There was nothing in Kramer's handwriting.

MR. RICHARDSON. Well, there was no other handwriting on it but Kramer's?

CAPTAIN SAFFORD. No.

Mr. Richardson. The only other writing there was on the paper was the teletype message in Japanese?

Captain Safford. And the identifying data, such as the frequency, time of intercept, station which sent it, which I glanced at, but promptly forgot.

Mr. Richardson. Well, that is not unreasonable.

Now then Captain, that message that you got, with respect to the Japanese words that were underlined, which you say Kramer interpreted in longhand on the message, was a dead ringer execute for the original code message 2353 that had been sent out, was it not?

Captain Safford. That is correct, except that it reversed it in the case of Russia, because we thought no war would be no mention, but they gave a positive, specific mention as to Russia, but in a negative sense, which we concluded meant peace, or not war as yet.

Mr. Richardson. Well, then, Captain, we can dismiss from our attention in connection with any examination of you, or any contention of you as to the winds execute circular 2354, cannot we?

Captain Safford. Let me see that.

Mr. Richardson. Because this execute could not have been in completion of circular 2354, could it?

Captain Safford. 2354 is out completely, except for the fact that is what we expected to find in a Morse code message, and it did not turn out that way.

Mr. Richardson. So that the only code message, winds code message, so far as your testimony is concerned, that the committee need pay any attention to is 2353?

Captain Safford. That is correct.

Mr. Richardson. All right.

Now, were the words "HIGASHI NO KAZEAME" in the middle of the broadcast?

Captain Safford. That is the place they were underscored.

Mr. Richardson. Were they also at the end?

Captain Safford. I do not know now. The were not underscored at the end if they were there.

Mr. Richardson. That would be a very important item in order to ascertain whether this was intended to be an execute of 2353, would it not?

Captain Safford. Not necessarily. They would be repeated at the end only as a precaution so that if they missed the early part of the broadcast, they could pick it up at the last and not lose it.

Mr. Richardson. Just a minute, Captain. Don't you think you are extending you authority a little when you interpret what the Japanese [3605] meant in a code direction? Did not you tell me a few minutes ago that every one of those directions that were contained in 2353 were important to be considered in determining whether or not a given message was an execute message?

Captain Safford. I said they were important, that is correct.

Mr. Richardson. Well, you did not even look to find out whether these three sets of words that had been translated were also at the end of the message, did you?

CAPTAIN SAFFORD. I never made such a statement.

MR. RICHARDSON. Well, you did not?

CAPTAIN SAFFORD. I said I cannot remember whether they were repeated at the end or not. I was well satisfied that that message was authentic, an authentic signal of the execute given by the Japanese Government.

MR. RICHARDSON. Captain, I am not the least interested in whether you are satisfied or not. I am only interested in ascertaining whether, when you saw the message, you endeavored to ascertain, as a careful, trained Intelligence man, whether it was an execute of the winds code message 2353, and consequently I asked you, first, was it in the middle and you said "yes"; and I then asked you, was it at the end, you said you did not look.

Now, third, was each sentence repeated twice?

CAPTAIN SAFFORD. I did not say I did not look. I said I could not tell you from present memory.

MR. RICHARDSON. Well, then, you cannot give us any help as to whether it was at the end, can you?

CAPTAIN SAFFORD. I can give you no help at the present time.

MR. RICHARDSON. But the fact that it was in the message just impressed you, so that to this day you can remember just those words that were underlined, cannot you?

CAPTAIN SAFFORD. I can remember them because we had the words preserved in the written record in circular 2353. I cannot remember the words in my mind. I can only leave them to this which had been preserved in the written record, and I knew it was this form, and not the other form.

MR. RICHARDSON. And when you looked at 2353, right in front of your nose was the phrase that all three of these phrases had also to appear at the end of the broadcast message, but that did not seem to impress you as being important.

Have you any reaction on that now? Does your mind give any reaction on that now?

CAPTAIN SAFFORD. I have no doubt that I checked through the rest of the message, and found everything in due form and technically correct, according to 2353, but I cannot swear from memory to it at this late date. [. . .]

[3606] MR. RICHARDSON. Was this message, Captain, a short-wave news broadcast?

CAPTAIN SAFFORD. It was a short-wave news broadcast.

MR. RICHARDSON. How do you know?

CAPTAIN SAFFORD. Because the frequency was recorded on the message, and we could not hear the long wave or low-power stuff, anyhow; the only thing we could hear in Washington from Tokyo was on short wave.

MR. RICHARDSON. How did you know it was news if you could not read Japanese?

CAPTAIN SAFFORD. I counted on Kramer to do that.

MR. RICHARDSON. Well, you could have counted on Kramer to do it, but now you have not testified that you asked him anything about it.

CAPTAIN SAFFORD. Kramer told me when he gave me the paper, he said, "This is it." There is no question in my mind or the mind of anybody else what he meant by it.

MR. RICHARDSON. Now, let us just temporarily, because I am going to question you about it again, Captain, probe that question.

You know, do you not, Captain, now that Kramer has three times in his sworn testimony heretofore, denied that he saw anything in this message with reference to Japanese words relating to the United States, and says that the only thing there was in the message he saw had reference to Russia. You know that, don't you?

CAPTAIN SAFFORD. I did not know that.

MR. RICHARDSON. He told you that, didn't he?

CAPTAIN SAFFORD. Kramer never told me anything about Russia.

MR. RICHARDSON. Did not he tell you that he was completely uncertain as to what the Japanese words were in this message?

CAPTAIN SAFFORD. I think that Kramer had been pretty well befuddled by the middle of 1945.

MR. RICHARDSON. Had been pretty well what?

CAPTAIN SAFFORD. Well, befuddled.

MR. RICHARDSON. Well, did the befuddling, Captain apply only to Kramer? Were you befuddled at all in 1945?

CAPTAIN SAFFORD. In 1945 there was a determined effort made to have me reverse my testimony before previous investigations and to say I had never seen the winds message.

MR. RICHARDSON. All right.

Now, explain to the committee in detail just who started to exercise influence on you to make you change your testimony. Give name and dates, and the full conversations.

MR. MURPHY. May I request, Mr. Chairman, that we also have him produce the original memorandum he made 2 weeks ago?

MR. RICHARDSON. I did not hear that.

MR. MURPHY. I would like to request that we have presented the written memorandum of 2 weeks ago. He said he had a written memorandum of 2 weeks ago that he just got for the first time.

MR. KEEFE. He already identified it.

MR. MURPHY. I would like to have that produced.

MR. RICHARDSON. Go ahead and read it in detail. Give us now all of the evidence that you have to indicate that anybody tried to get [3607] you to change your testimony in just as much detail as you can, Captain. [...]

THE VICE CHAIRMAN. Read your paper completely, and distinctly, so we may all hear it, and then when you have finished reading it, why you may supplement it by any other statement you desire to make on this subject, in response to the question counsel has asked you.

SENATOR FERGUSON. Might I suggest that he read it not so fast.

CAPTAIN SAFFORD. All right.

SENATOR FERGUSON. I have difficulty at times hearing you.

CAPTAIN SAFFORD. This paper is dated July 14, 1945: "Memorandum of Conversations in Connection With Admiral Hewitt's Investigation of the Pearl Harbor Disaster."

MR. RICHARDSON. This was after you had testified before Admiral Hewitt?

CAPTAIN SAFFORD. This was after I had testified before Admiral Hewitt.

MR. RICHARDSON. All right, go ahead.

CAPTAIN SAFFORD. I believe—I am not certain on the dates.

MR. MURPHY. The Hewitt testimony was taken between May 14 and July 12, 1945, and this memorandum is July 14, 2 days after Admiral Hewitt concluded taking testimony.

[3608]   CAPTAIN SAFFORD (reading):

> 1. This memorandum is prepared, while events are still fresh in my mind, for possible use in connection with future Investigation of the Pearl Harbor Disaster, or Court-martials in connection with Pearl Harbor. It includes certain acts which strike me as irregular or unusual, and probably illegal.
>
> 2. On or about Friday, 11 May 1945, I was called to an unofficial conference (or meeting) conducted by Lieutenant Commander John Sonnett, U.S.N.R., in room 1083A, Navy Building. [...]
>
> He was in civilian clothes, as he has been on every occasion on which I have seen him. Sonnet told me that he had been assigned as a legal assistant to Admiral Hewitt in an investigation of the responsibility for the Pearl Harbor Disaster, that he was also a special representative for Secretary Forrestal in this investigation and that he was authorized to handle Top-Secret and Secret information and documents. He showed me papers signed by Secretary Forrestal and Fleet Admiral King verifying these statements.
>
> At my request he let me read the Precept which directed Admiral Hewitt to conduct the investigation. It was my understanding that Admiral Hewitt had not yet returned to Washington and that Sonnett was getting things lined up to expedite matters after the Admiral's arrival.
>
> 3. I answered many questions pertaining to my testimony before previous investigations, and discussed discrepancies between my testimony and the testimony of other witnesses.

MR. RICHARDSON. Let me stop you right there, Captain.

Does not it commence to dawn on you that this statement of yours was made before you testified in the Hewitt examination?

CAPTAIN SAFFORD. Some of the notes were made before, but it was written up and typed and dated afterward.

MR. RICHARDSON. I see. But this conversation that you had with Sonnett took place before you testified in the Hewitt investigation?

CAPTAIN SAFFORD. That is correct.

Mr. Richardson. All right.
Captain Safford (continuing reading):

Sonnett requested that I give him, by the end of the next week, written memoranda to be used as a basis of study and examination (under oath) on the subjects listed below. This was done and the memoranda submitted. [...]

[3609] On Sonnett's request, I prepared and furnished him copies of certain U.S. Naval messages, the Station "H" Chronology for 1–6 December, 1941, and Com 14 Daily CI Summaries for 1 Nov.–6 Dec. 1941.

4. It was apparent to me on my very first meeting with Lieutenant Commander Sonnett that he was acting as a "counsel for the defense" for the late Secretary Knox, and Admiral Stark rather than as the legal assistant to the investigating officer. His purpose seemed to be to refute testimony (before earlier investigations) that was unfavorable to anyone in Washington, to beguile "hostile" witnesses into changing their stories and to introduce an element of doubt where he could not effect a reversal of testimony. Above all, he attempted to make me reverse my testimony regarding the "Winds Execute" Message and to make me believe I was suffering from hallucinations.

5. I talked to Sonnett the second time on 18 May 1945, and the third time a day or two later. On these latter occasions, like the first, Sonnett tried to persuade me that there had been no "Winds Execute" Message, that my memory had been playing me tricks, that I had confused the "False Winds Message" with what I had been expecting, and that I ought to change my testimony to permit reconciling all previous discrepancies and thereby wind up the affair. In some cases the idea was stated outright, in some cases it was implied, and in other cases it was unexpressed but obviously the end in view. [...]

6. I distinctly recall Lieutenant Commander John Sonnett, U.S.N.R., making the following statements to me during the course of the above-mentioned conferences:

"You are the only one who seems to have ever seen the 'Winds Execute' Message."

"How could the 'Winds Execute' be heard on the east coast of the U.S. and not at any of the places nearer Japan?"

"It is very doubtful that there ever was a 'Winds Execute' Message."

"It is no reflection on your veracity to change your testimony."

"It is no reflection on your mentality to have your memory play you tricks — after such a long period."

"Numerous witnesses that you have named have denied all knowledge of a 'Winds Execute' Message."

"You do not have to carry the torch for Admiral Kimmel."

[3610] 7. I testified before Admiral Hewitt the first time on or about 24 May 1945, before he went to Pearl Harbor. I testified before Admiral Hewitt a second time on 22 June, 1945, after his return from examining witnesses at Pearl Harbor. Upon completion of my testimony (in which the "Winds Execute" Message had figured), I asked him, "off-the-record" if there was still any doubts in his mind as to the "Winds Message" having been sent by Japan and disseminated in the War and Navy Departments. The Admiral looked startled, and before he could reply Sonnett said

"Of course, I am not conducting the case, and I do not know what Admiral Hewitt has decided, but to me it is very doubtful that the so-called 'Winds Execute' Message was ever sent."

Admiral Hewitt thought a minute or two more, and then said:

"You are not entitled to my opinion, but I will answer your question. There is no evidence of a 'Winds Execute' Message beyond your unsupported testimony. I do not doubt your sincerity, but I believe that you have confused one of the other messages containing the name of a wind with th message you were expecting to receive."

Maybe I ought to go on with paragraph 9.

8. For my part, I do not doubt Admiral Hewitt's integrity—

THE VICE CHAIRMAN. Just a minute. You are reading everything that is on that paper?
CAPTAIN SAFFORD. I am reading everything that is on this paper.
THE VICE CHAIRMAN. All right. Go ahead.
CAPTAIN SAFFORD (reading):

For my part, I do not doubt Admiral Hewitt's integrity, but I do believe that Sonnett has succeeded in pulling the wool over his eyes.
9. I also believe that Sonnett employed similar tactics on other witnesses whose testimony had favored Admiral Kimmel, particularly Rochefort and Kramer.
10. Copies of the Memorandum described in paragraph 3 are appended hereto. Also appended is a memorandum to Admiral Hewitt dated 22 June, 1945, clarifying my testimony regarding the "Winds Execute" Message and indicating that Sonnett had attempted to trick me into stating the opposite of what I intended to say.
Signed, "L. F. Safford, Captain, U.S.N."

MR. MURPHY. There are more pages?
THE VICE CHAIRMAN. Does that complete your statement?
CAPTAIN SAFFORD. That completes my statement. The other pages appended are copies of the memoranda which were referred to in paragraph 2. [...]
[3616] MR. RICHARDSON. Let me ask you this: You prefaced this reading with a statement that efforts had been made to silence you and influence you. Have you any other record of any kind, manner of description, that shows or tends to show or relates to any pressure or influence exerted upon you or towards you to get you to change your testimony or give no testimony?
CAPTAIN SAFFORD. This has been the only time and it was before the investigation. Not during the investigation. I want to make that very distinct.
MR. RICHARDSON. Then you have no more to add to what you have read?
CAPTAIN SAFFORD. That is correct. [...]
[3622] MR. RICHARDSON. Now, Captain, in circular 2353 the emergency which gave birth to the desire for the new code, winds code, is recited as "the danger of cutting off of our diplomatic relations and the cutting off of international communications," is it not?

CAPTAIN SAFFORD. That is correct.

MR. RICHARDSON. That would mean, would it not, that the Japanese felt that there might come a time when because of the status of their diplomatic relations and their international communications that they would have to have some new way ot communicating and to furnish that new way they invented this so-called winds code?

CAPTAIN SAFFORD. This so-called winds code which was to be used there by their broadcasts and not by the commercial telegraph companies.

MR. RICHARDSON. Well, now, it is a fact, is it not, Captain, that on the 4th of December all of the methods of communication were open to the Japanese that had been open at any time since the 1st of January 1941, were they not?

CAPTAIN SAFFORD. That is correct.

MR. RICHARDSON. So there wasn't any reason on the basis of a loss of other methods of communication on December 4th to use this winds code at all, was there?

CAPTAIN SAFFORD. There was no reason that you could account for but we had been listening for it from the 28th of November and we had made every effort to get it.

MR. RICHARDSON. Now, keeping in mind your testimony that the message which Lieutenant Kramer brought to you was in Japanese and in that message, in the middle of that message were the phrases in Japanese which are used as 1, 2, and 3 and mentioned in circular 2353, keeping that in mind can you point to any record then in existence of which either you or Kramer had any knowledge that interpreted or translated those words as meaning war?

CAPTAIN SAFFORD. War was the meaning that we gave it and war was what appeared in the translation, whether justified or not.

[3623] MR. RICHARDSON. All right. Except for the written words that Lieutenant Commander Kramer put on this dis-atch there is no known writing emanating from Japan or any other source at that time that puts the interpretation on the language "HIGASHI NA KAZEAME" as meaning war with the United States, is there?

CAPTAIN SAFFORD. If that word had appeared alone it might have merely meant the breaking off of diplomatic relations, they might have meant nothing else.

MR. RICHARDSON. Now, Captain, you pay attention to my question. I want to find out whether you can put your finger on any existing authority that up to the time you saw the message interpreted the phrase "HIGASHI NO KAZEAME" to mean war with the United States?

Now, let me carry it further. The message from the Commander of the Asiatic Fleet does not so say, does it?

CAPTAIN SAFFORD. Not for "Higashi," and so forth.

MR. RICHARDSON. And the message 2353 does not so say, does it?

CAPTAIN SAFFORD. No.

Mr. RICHARDSON. And you did not have the Foote or Thorpe messages available at 8 o'clock on the morning of December 4, did you?

CAPTAIN SAFFORD. That is correct.

Mr. RICHARDSON. So that so far as you know the definition of those words that appeared on that message that morning was the invention of Lieutenant Commander Kramer?

CAPTAIN SAFFORD. I would not call it that.

Mr. RICHARDSON. Well, it was the act of Lieutenant Commander Kramer.

CAPTAIN SAFFORD. I would say that all the higher authority—

Mr. RICHARDSON. Now, wait a minute, I am speaking about this specific message when it was brought to you by Lieutenant Commander Kramer and I want to know what authority he had, if you know, for translating the phrase "HIGASHI NO KAZEAME" as meaning war with the United States?

CAPTAIN SAFFORD. I do not know now what authority he had for using those words.

Mr. RICHARDSON. All right. And it was the first time in your whole life up to that point that you had ever seen the word "War" used as a part of the definition of the words "HIGASHI NO KAZEAME"?

CAPTAIN SAFFORD. In written form, correct. [...]

[3624] Mr. RICHARDSON. But you remembered the word "war"?

CAPTAIN SAFFORD. Rather than merely the weaker form, "Relations in danger."

Mr. RICHARDSON. Well, the form "Relations in danger" would be a good deal weaker, wouldn't it, Captain?

CAPTAIN SAFFORD. It would be very much weaker.

Mr. RICHARDSON. It would be right along the line of the various messages that had been going back and forth for several days, wouldn't it?

CAPTAIN SAFFORD. That is correct, as far as the wording is concerned.

Mr. RICHARDSON. You knew that the Japanese-United States relations were in danger?

CAPTAIN SAFFORD. We had known that for 3 months. [...]

[3625] Mr. RICHARDSON. Now, as a matter of fact, Captain, before this message was received there had been a series of messages sent out by Japanese by other methods of communication all over the world directing the destruction of codes?

CAPTAIN SAFFORD. That is correct.

Mr. RICHARDSON. So there wasn't any reason to use this message on December 4 for that purpose either, was there?

CAPTAIN SAFFORD. Not for just the destruction of codes.

Mr. RICHARDSON. I see.

Mr. GEARHART. But there was a purpose indicated by you in your original statement, was there not?

CAPTAIN SAFFORD. That is correct.

Mr. GEARHART. The British had destroyed their codes. There were no

Japanese codes in London. This is the only way they had of informing the Japanese at London that something was imminent?

CAPTAIN SAFFORD. That is correct, and the same situation existed at Singapore and Hong Kong.

MR. RICHARDSON. I would like at this point, in view of the interrogation of the Congressman, to advise the committee that under date of January 31, 1946, we have a memorandum from the War Department reading as follows:

> Pursuant to your request the War Department has made inquiry of the British concerning the number of coded messages sent by the Japanese representatives in London subsequent to December 2, 1941.
>
> The War Department has been informed that two coded messages were sent by the Japanese representatives in London on the 3rd of December 1941 and one coded message on the 5th of December 1941 and one coded message sent on the 6th of December 1941 and all four messages were sent on the code system known as PA-K2—

indicating that coded messages were proceeding to England both before and after December 4.

MR. MURPHY. Mr. Chairman, may we request that we have produced the memorandum which the witness acquired 2 weeks ago? If there was information made available to him 2 weeks, I think it should be produced at this time.

MR. GEARHART. May I inquire of counsel? I am interested in it very, very much. If that is true, as reported by the British, it merely means the British Ambassador had violated the instructions and had not destroyed his codes; isn't that right?

MR. RICHARDSON. I am not going into the implication.

[3626] CAPTAIN SAFFORD. May I explain that?

There were two systems that were exempt from destruction. One was PA-K2, and the other was LA, neither of which were considered by ourselves as secret, and we presumed the Japanese did not consider them secret.

MR. RICHARDSON. The only point, Captain, involved in it would be there was still a method open to the Japanese to communicate with the British outside of the winds code.

CAPTAIN SAFFORD. Yes, but not to communicate secretly. I used that word "secretly" in my statement.

MR. GEARHART. That is the point.

SENATOR LUCAS. Does the counsel now know what messages went from Japan?

MR. RICHARDSON. I read everything that the War Department gave us. What is the system known as PA-K2?

CAPTAIN SAFFORD. That is a minor system which had been in effect for a very long time, and was used for matters of negligible importance, but they presumably wanted to keep up with the newspapers, minor money matters, visas, things like that.

War Warning "Winds"   161

I believe there were only three or four PA-K2 messages that had ever been submitted in evidence before this investigation and that were sent by Pearl Harbor after Pearl Harbor had destroyed its J-19 system, and I do not—I won't go into that.

MR. RICHARDSON. Are you sure, Captain, that you are correct when you say that important messages were not sent in this code PA-K2?

CAPTAIN SAFFORD. Until after Pearl Harbor had destroyed its J-19 system, which really had some security.

MR. RICHARDSON. Let me read you from Exhibit 2, page 29, which is a message that went from Honolulu to Tokyo on December 6, 1941. It is No. 254.

> 1. On the evening of the 5th, among the battleships which entered port were _____ and one submarine tender. The following ships were observed at anchor on the 6th:
> 9 battleships, 3 light cruisers, 3 submarine tenders, 17 destroyers, and in addition there were 4 light cruisers, 2 destroyers lying at docks (the heavy cruisers and air plane carriers have all left).
> 2. It appears that no air reconnaissance is being conducted by the Fleet air arm.

That would be a rather important message, would it not, Captain?

CAPTAIN SAFFORD. That is correct, and that message was sent after the Japanese Consulate had destroyed its J-19 system. [...]

[3634] MR. RICHARDSON. Captain, after you handed this message which Kramer gave to you to an officer whose name you can't be sure of, and which is understandable, to take to Admiral Noyes, you never saw that message again, did you?

CAPTAIN SAFFORD. I never saw that particular message in that particular form.

MR. RICHARDSON. All right.

Now, did you—well, wait a minute. What do you mean, you never saw that message in that particular form? Did you see that message in some other form?

CAPTAIN SAFFORD. I saw that message in the smooth write-up as a translation with the Japanese eliminated and merely the translation of the code part.

MR. RICHARDSON. Now, then, the message that you gave to Kramer—that you gave to this officer to take up to Admiral Noyes, was an approximately 200-word message?

CAPTAIN SAFFORD. That is correct.

MR. RICHARDSON. All in Japanese?

CAPTAIN SAFFORD. That is correct.

MR. RICHARDSON. Do you know whether Admiral Noyes could read Japanese?

CAPTAIN SAFFORD. Admiral Noyes could not read Japanese.

MR. RICHARDSON. Then all he had to go on was what you had to go on, the presence in the dispatch of these words that were set forth in 2353?

CAPTAIN SAFFORD. That is correct.

MR. RICHARDSON. And the writing of Kramer on the bottom?

CAPTAIN SAFFORD. That is correct, plus—

MR. RICHARDSON. And—

CAPTAIN SAFFORD. May I finish my answer?

MR. RICHARDSON. Yes.

CAPTAIN SAFFORD. Admiral Noyes also had a card on his person on which was written the Japanese expressions and their meaning, their translation.

MR. RICHARDSON. And that translation that he had on the card was the translation taken from the original winds code message 2353?

[3635] CAPTAIN SAFFORD. I presume so. I believe that Kramer prepared the card. I didn't—[...]

MR. RICHARDSON. And you never saw that precise paper again?

CAPTAIN SAFFORD. No, sir.

MR. RICHARDSON. What did you make your copies from then?

CAPTAIN SAFFORD. Everything that came in by the teletype was in duplicate. There was a whole paper in duplicate with a carbon behind it. The original remained in the role.

MR. RICHARDSON. But the duplicate wouldn't have Kramer's writing on it, would it?

CAPTAIN SAFFORD. That is correct.

MR. RICHARDSON. When you made up your smooth copies, did you put on the bottom that Kramer translation?

CAPTAIN SAFFORD. Kramer made up those smooth copies, not me.

MR. RICHARDSON. Did you make up any copies of it?

CAPTAIN SAFFORD. No, sir. I made up no copies.

MR. RICHARDSON. Do you know of your own knowledge when Kramer made up the copies? Did you see him make them up?

CAPTAIN SAFFORD. I did not.

MR. RICHARDSON. Did he deliver them to you or expose them to you after he had made them up?

CAPTAIN SAFFORD. I saw one copy about noon between 11 and 12 o'clock on the morning of the 4th of December 1941.

I took it for granted—

MR. RICHARDSON. Now, wait a minute. Don't let's take anything for granted. You saw a copy?

CAPTAIN SAFFORD. Yes, sir.

MR. RICHARDSON. Now, that copy that you saw, was it in Japanese?

CAPTAIN SAFFORD. That was in English.

MR. RICHARDSON. Then the copy that you saw was a translation of the whole message?

CAPTAIN SAFFORD. It was a translation of only the part that contained the warning, the hidden warning.

MR. RICHARDSON. Did the rest of the 200 words, outside of these three set Japanese phrases, remain in Japanese?

CAPTAIN SAFFORD. They were disregarded.

MR. RICHARDSON. They didn't appear in the message you saw?

CAPTAIN SAFFORD. They did not appear in the message I saw at noon.

MR. RICHARDSON. Then all you saw in these copies that were circulated with the three code phrases HIGASHI NO KAZEAME—what is the rest of it?

CAPTAIN SAFFORD. I will have to look.

[3636] MR. RICHARDSON. I will get it. HIGASHI NO KAZEAME, KITANOKAZE KUMORI, and NISHI NO KAZE HARE.

CAPTAIN SAFFORD. Yes.

MR. RICHARDSON. Were those three Japanese phrases all there was on the one message that you saw around noon on that day?

CAPTAIN SAFFORD. It was the translation—

MR. RICHARDSON. Just answer my question, please. Was there anything on the message that you saw around noon except those three phrases in Japanese?

CAPTAIN SAFFORD. Yes; there was.

MR. RICHARDSON. What else was there?

CAPTAIN SAFFORD. There was the identification date of the intercepting station at the time and other things that were customarily put on messages.

MR. RICHARDSON. I realize that. What, with reference to the substance of the message?

CAPTAIN SAFFORD. The translation as to what it meant.

MR. RICHARDSON. Well, now, that translation was in type?

CAPTAIN SAFFORD. That was typed.

MR. RICHARDSON. You don't know of your own knowledge who typed it?

CAPTAIN SAFFORD. No; I didn't see it typed.

MR. RICHARDSON. What did that typed translation say?

CAPTAIN SAFFORD. It said the same thing as was said in pencil at the bottom of the other message.

MR. RICHARDSON. And it said that the words HIGASHI NO KAZEAME meant war with the United States?

CAPTAIN SAFFORD. I do not believe that the words HIGASHI NO KAZEAME appeared. I believe only the translation of what it meant in English. Its meaning. Not the literal translation. The meaning was there.

MR. RICHARDSON. Let me reform our recollection. You just told me in detail that on the copy you saw were the three Japanese phrases to which we refer. Now am I to understand you were in error and that all there was on the copy that you saw were the three English phrases which you said were an interpretation of these Japanese phrases?

CAPTAIN SAFFORD. I am sorry, I did not understand your question.

MR. RICHARDSON. That is all right.

CAPTAIN SAFFORD. The Japanese did not appear there. It merely would have had the expression in the upper left-hand corner in plain language, possibly the winds code, and then would have mention of these three code words; and it was the same wording that had been written in pencil on the bottom of the sheet that was sent up to Admiral Noyes.

MR. RICHARDSON. Then it is perfectly clear in your mind, is it, that there were no Japanese words on the message that you saw around noon?

CAPTAIN SAFFORD. That is correct.

MR. RICHARDSON. And the English words that were there were simply the definition of these Japanese phrases; and that definition was given, was it, the same as that written by Kramer on the bottom of the original message you saw?

[3637] CAPTAIN SAFFORD. That is correct.

MR. RICHARDSON. Then there was no part on this message in type with the phrase "War with the United States"?

CAPTAIN SAFFORD. That is correct.

MR. RICHARDSON. That copy that you had was one of a number of copies that had been made for circulation?

CAPTAIN SAFFORD. It was a flimsy copy and presumably one of a book which had been typed at the same time.

MR. RICHARDSON. That is, you mean, at the same time that the copies were prepared for distribution?

CAPTAIN SAFFORD. For distribution. We prepared 12 or 14 at one time.

MR. RICHARDSON. Now, when they were distributed, where would they go in the ordinary practice?

CAPTAIN SAFFORD. Half would be sent over to the War Department and in the case of important messages they were sent immediately by special courier and the less important messages were sent over in a routine delivery trip which were two or three a day.

MR. RICHARDSON. Where would they go to in the War Department, what division?

CAPTAIN SAFFORD. I believe they were sent over to the Japanese section of the Signal Intelligence Service and they took off the file copy.

MR. RICHARDSON. Don't say what they did. They went to that office.

CAPTAIN SAFFORD. And they made subsequent delivery to Military Intelligence, who were responsible for the detailed distribution.

MR. RICHARDSON. You are getting into the realm of supposition. I only asked you where they would send the message. You said, it would go to the War Department. Now, I asked you what division of the War Department it would be; and that would be the Japanese section?

CAPTAIN SAFFORD. Of the Signal Intelligence Service. Office of the Signal Intelligence Service.

MR. RICHARDSON. Who was in charge of that office at that time, if you know?

CAPTAIN SAFFORD. Major Doud was in charge of that office. D-o-u-d.

MR. RICHARDSON. Now, the other copies would be sent to the Navy Department?

CAPTAIN SAFFORD. Were sent to the Navy Department. One copy was retained in Commander Kramer's own files, never left there; one copy was given to the naval aide to the President; one copy was given to the naval aide to the Secretary of the Navy; one copy was given to the Director of Naval Intelligence; one copy given or shown to the Director of War Plans, Admiral Turner; and one copy was given to the aide to the Chief of Naval Operations who showed it to both Admiral Ingersoll and Admiral Stark. That is the best distribution that I can give you at the present time from memory. There are written notes to that effect.

MR. RICHARDSON. Well, now, Captain, all of those officers, how many or few they were, would simply get a sheet of paper [3638] that had on it the phrase, "War with the United States, War with Britain, No War with Russia," in English?

CAPTAIN SAFFORD. In English, that is correct.

MR. RICHARDSON. There would be no Japanese words on that copy?

CAPTAIN SAFFORD. No. [...]

[3639] MR. RICHARDSON. Let us start again. Was there more than one sheet of paper with the so-called winds execute English words on it sent to Beardall under the regular practice? That can be answered "Yes" or "No."

CAPTAIN SAFFORD. Under the regular practice, there would be.

MR. RICHARDSON. And what would the extra paper be? Would it be a translation?

CAPTAIN SAFFORD. It would be our own copy of Tokyo's circular 2353 which had been previously distributed, or we might merely have a summary or a condensation of that as a footnote on the bottom of the original translation of the message and from my own personal memory I do not know which form Kramer used on that occasion.

MR. RICHARDSON. Well, then the idea would be that with this group of English words which would be Kramer's translation, something of 2353, either in form or substance, would be sent with that message?

CAPTAIN SAFFORD. That is correct.

MR. RICHARDSON. That would be so that the man who got the message, the message of Kramer's language, could refer back to the original winds code?

CAPTAIN SAFFORD. That is correct and he would know where he stood.

MR. RICHARDSON. Well, then I ask you again how could Beardall find out from the message that went to him with Kramer's language on it that it meant that it was an execute of circular 2353 which did not say one single word about war?

CAPTAIN SAFFORD. We were listening for the execute with the expectation of finding in it the Japanese Government's decision as to peace or war with the United States as well as with England and with Russia.

MR. RICHARDSON. Wait a minute.

CAPTAIN SAFFORD. That was thoroughly understood.

MR. RICHARDSON. Now, wait a minute, Captain. Will you turn your attention to circular 2353 again? It is in Exhibit 142.

Mr. Murphy. On page 154 of Exhibit 1.

Mr. Richardson. Will you tell me what there is in that dispatch which fixed the winds code, which you have testified with the dispatch and the code under which your winds execute message came—will you tell me what there is in that dispatch that entitles you to say you were waiting for a message that reported war with the United States?

Captain Safford. There is nothing in the dispatch as written which specifically states "War with the United States."

Mr. Richardson. Is there anything in it that implies war with the United States?

Captain Safford. There certainly is.

Mr. Richardson. What? What is it? What language implies war with the United States?

[3640] Captain Safford. For one thing there is instruction to destroy all code papers. If that is regarded as synonymous with the outbreak of war, as I have heard testified before in this room, that by itself means something more than the wording in these three paragraphs above.

Mr. Richardson. And you had had a number of dispatches with reference to burning of codes and this Government, your own Government, had sent out a number of dispatches with reference to burning of codes before the morning of the 4th, hadn't they?

Captain Safford. The warnings from—

Mr. Richardson. Now you can answer my question "Yes" or "No."

Captain Safford. That question cannot be answered by a plain "Yes" or "No."

Mr. Richardson. All right, go ahead. I think it can; but I will take your explanation.

Captain Safford. Tokyo had sent out instructions to various people telling them to burn their most important codes but to leave two codes open. One was the so-called PA-K2 code and the other was the LA code. Now, with those two exceptions all codes had been burnt, but this said, "Please destroy all code papers," and so forth. In other words, there were no exceptions in this one.

Mr. Richardson. And it is that phrase which led you to believe that when you got an execute message that said "HIGASHI NO KAZEAME" you could safely interpret it as meaning "war with the United States"?

Captain Safford. There was much beyond what appears in this paper that led to our interpretation of it in that way.

Mr. Richardson. Well, the men who were getting a copy of that dispatch with this dispatch wouldn't have your imagination as to what it meant. How would he find out what it meant?

Captain Safford. The Navy Department had been very jittery about whether by any chance this winds execute might have been sent out before the 28th, when we began listening for it. I have been questioned on that repeatedly. They were also very much worried about the fear that with all the stations which were known to be listening for it, by some freak chance we might fail to catch it and the reason for that was everyone in authority from the President down believed that this would be the Japanese Government's decision as to peace or war announced to their own officials overseas and that was our chance of a tip-off, to gain the necessary time to prevent a surprise attack on our fleet.

MR. RICHARDSON. Captain, did it ever occur to you that you are taking in an elastic authority when you quote what the President understood and every other important official down? Was there any official in the Government, from the President down, that had any basis, sir, for the interpretation of this message 2353 except what the message 2353 said?

CAPTAIN SAFFORD. I do not know the basis on which they made their evaluation.

MR. RICHARDSON. Now, Captain, will you take a look again at Exhibit 142 and turn over to the dispatch from the commander in chief of the Army forces in the Pacific under date of November 13, 1945? There seems to be no page number. It is under 4—A. Have you the one of November 13th?

[3641] CAPTAIN SAFFORD. I have BSG 196. Is that the one?

MR. RICHARDSON. That is right. Now, from your experience in this message and intelligence work wouldn't you construe that message from MacArthur as indicating that the Japanese never sent out an implementing message?

CAPTAIN SAFFORD. I would not.

MR. RICHARDSON. Why not?

CAPTAIN SAFFORD. It says here:

> Interrogation of authorities so far has resulted in absolute denial of transmission of such an implementing message and existence of any prearranged instructions which would permit transmission of such an implementing signal.

In other words, the Japanese authorities denied ever having sent Tokyo circular 2353 and 2354.

MR. RICHARDSON. All right. You find from that, do you, evidence that they did send out the execute?

CAPTAIN SAFFORD. I find evidence from that that they had denied everything.

MR. RICHARDSON. All right.

CAPTAIN SAFFORD. And also that they burned all pertinent records prior to August 14, 1945.

MR. RICHARDSON. All right; we will take the Japanese at any sort of an estimate you want, but insofar as that message refers to an execute winds message they deny having sent it, don't they?

CAPTAIN SAFFORD. The Japanese deny having sent it. [...]

MR. RICHARDSON. Now, turn over to the dispatch of the 24th [from MacArthur, RW], the next following, the language reading:

> Only use of Winds code (either voice or radio telegraph) shown here by available contemporaneous records is voice broadcast from Tokyo between 0902 and 0935 on 8 December.

That also indicates that the response from the Japanese records further was negative on this execute, doesn't it?

CAPTAIN SAFFORD. I do not agree with that, sir.

MR. RICHARDSON. All right. What does it indicate?

CAPTAIN SAFFORD. That was from the War Department to General MacArthur.

MR. RICHARDSON. That does not spoil it, does it?

[3642] CAPTAIN SAFFORD. And they were referring to the FCC monitoring records and the FCC were only monitoring voice, and the winds message intercepted by the Navy came in Morse code.

MR. RICHARDSON. Well, it shows that there was a message, however, that was sent on December 8.

CAPTAIN SAFFORD. That is correct.

MR. RICHARDSON. All right. Now, go on over to the one of the 27th from MacArthur where he says that:

> Persons who conducted interrogation had no knowledge that prior to interrogation United States had information establishing use of Winds code on 8 December Tokyo time.

Making it certain that the people who were doing the interrogating did not know what they did it for would be important, wouldn't it?

CAPTAIN SAFFORD. That is correct.

MR. RICHARDSON. Well, turn over now to the document entitled, "U.S. Naval Technical Mission to Japan," one or two pages following the one I just read from. Do you have that before you?

CAPTAIN SAFFORD. I have that before me.

MR. RICHARDSON. Now, look at the last paragraph on that page, where the person making the document says:

> He stated that he would have known of it if a message such as that described as being broadcast December 4 had been transmitted and that he had no recollection at all of any "east wind rain" report or any similar phrase being broadcast prior to December 8.

That would also indicate that they did not know out there if this man was telling the truth that there had been any winds execute message until December 8, doesn't it?

CAPTAIN SAFFORD. I would not consider that conclusive.

MR. RICHARDSON. It is quite pertinently suggestive, though, isn't it, Captain?

CAPTAIN SAFFORD. From one point of view; yes. [...]

MR. RICHARDSON. Now Brotherhood was one of your watch officers?

CAPTAIN SAFFORD. That is correct.

MR. RICHARDSON. If there was an execute message that came in on the morning of December 4, Brotherhood would naturally know about it, would not he?

CAPTAIN SAFFORD. Not in the morning.

MR. RICHARDSON. Beg pardon?

CAPTAIN SAFFORD. Not in the morning of December 4.

MR. RICHARDSON. Would he naturally know about it during the day?

[3643] CAPTAIN SAFFORD. If it came in on his watch he would have known about it.

MR. RICHARDSON. Well, what was his watch?

CAPTAIN SAFFORD. He was on watch from 4 p.m. to midnight on the 3d and from 4 p.m. to midnight on the 4th of December 1941. That is established from an official record.

MR. RICHARDSON. Now all of those watch officers were on edge to pick up this winds execute, weren't they?

CAPTAIN SAFFORD. That is correct.

MR. RICHARDSON. And that message coming in, as it did, at 8 o'clock, Captain, on the morning of December 4, was the most important piece of business transacted in that office that morning, wasn't it?

CAPTAIN SAFFORD. I will go further and say it was the most important piece of business transacted up to the time of the attack on Pearl Harbor in 1941.

MR. RICHARDSON. All right. Then don't you think it quite reasonable that as soon as Brotherhood came into the office at 4 o'clock for his watch, that someone there would tell him that the great day had come, that the execute was there and they all knew about it?

CAPTAIN SAFFORD. It has been my impression all along that Brotherhood did know it.

MR. RICHARDSON. All right. You know now, don't you, that he, under oath, testified that he never heard anything about the winds execute message in the office there on December 4?

CAPTAIN SAFFORD. That is correct.

MR. RICHARDSON. And you know also that on the evening of December 4 he, as one of your watch officers, was telephoning to the Federal Communications Commission to find out if they had located any piece of an execute message?

CAPTAIN SAFFORD. No, it was just the reverse.

MR. RICHARDSON. All right. They phoned him?

CAPTAIN SAFFORD. And said they had one.

MR. RICHARDSON. They knew that he was looking for one?

CAPTAIN SAFFORD. They had been requested if anything came in to call up certain telephone numbers, including the GY watch officer.

Mr. RICHARDSON. Captain, he certainly told them just as soon as they phoned him that the stuff was all off and you had the message?

CAPTAIN SAFFORD. We were telling the FCC nothing.

MR. RICHARDSON. That was not because nothing had happened, was it, Captain?

CAPTAIN SAFFORD. We did not tell the station at Cheltenham that we had intercepted anything we wanted.

MR. RICHARDSON. I have before me, Captain, under Exhibit 142-A, a copy of the log, if you may call it that, of the FCC on the 4th day of December. Under item 6 —

CAPTAIN SAFFORD. I haven't gotten to it yet.

MR. RICHARDSON. Have you got a copy that you can lay in front of the captain?

CAPTAIN SAFFORD. I have got it. What was that date?

MR. RICHARDSON. I will get it for you.

CAPTAIN SAFFORD. December 6?

[3644] MR. RICHARDSON. December 4. Item 6, reading as follows:

> 9:05 p.m. Lieutenant Brotherhood 20-G Watch Officer, Navy Department, telephoned to state that he was authorized to accept message in question. Gave Lieutenant Brotherhood the message from Mr. Carter.

Going back to No. 2 is a notation:

> 8:12 p.m. received a message from Mr. Carter at Portland, Oregon.

Now you know, don't you, Captain, that the message that was received from Carter was one of these false winds messages?

CAPTAIN SAFFORD. Yes, a true weather report.

MR. RICHARDSON. So Brotherhood was telephoning the Communications Commission about that message, wasn't he?

CAPTAIN SAFFORD. No, they told him.

MR. RICHARDSON. Now just let us look —

CAPTAIN SAFFORD (interposing). Let me read 5 first, please.

MR. RICHARDSON. All right.

CAPTAIN SAFFORD (reading):

> 8:45 p.m. called ONI Watch Officer at Navy Department to ascertain if he was permitted to accept messages of interest to Colonel Bratton's office. The officer in charge stated that he was not certain, but that he would inquire and call back.

MR. RICHARDSON. Read the next one.

CAPTAIN SAFFORD. That was standard practice, to check up to be certain we did not get pulled in by some unauthorized person.

War Warning "Winds"

MR. RICHARDSON. All right, read the next one.
CAPTAIN SAFFORD (reading):

> 9:05 p.m. Lieutenant Brotherhood 20-G Watch Officer, Navy Department, telephoned to state—

MR. RICHARDSON. Telephoned whom?
CAPTAIN SAFFORD. He telephoned the FCC.
MR. RICHARDSON. All right.
CAPTAIN SAFFORD (reading):

> —to state that he was authorized to accept message in question. Gave Lieutenant Brotherhood the message from Mr. Carter.

MR. RICHARDSON. Now read No. 7.
CAPTAIN SAFFORD (reading):

> 9:32 p.m. Lieutenant Brotherhood called to inquire if any other reference to weather was made previously in program intercepted by Portland. Informed him no other reference was made.

MR. RICHARDSON. That would rather throw some light on your suggestion that Brotherhood did not telephone the FCC, wouldn't it, Captain?
CAPTAIN SAFFORD. Brotherhood called back for a verification and check-up to see if he had the whole story; that is correct.
MR. RICHARDSON. Now if a copy of this alleged winds execute message that you said came in went to the War Department, you would expect that Colonel Bratton would see it, wouldn't you?
CAPTAIN SAFFORD. I would expect they would all see it.
MR. RICHARDSON. You would expect Colonel Bratton, from his position as Chief of Staff, to see it, wouldn't you?
CAPTAIN SAFFORD. I would.
[3645] MR. RICHARDSON. Then would it be a matter of surprise to you that Colonel Bratton was telephoning the FCC at 7:50 p.m. on the 5th day of December trying to find out if there had been any receipt of any winds execute message?
CAPTAIN SAFFORD. I would not expect such a thing as that.
MR. RICHARDSON. And the only inference that you, with your experience, could draw from such a telephone, Captain, would be that Bratton did not know there had been any winds execute message received 56 hours before, or 36 hours before? That would be your inference, wouldn't it?
Let me turn it around. I don't want to confuse you. There would be no reason for Bratton telephoning to find out something that he already knew, would there?
CAPTAIN SAFFORD. That is correct. [...]

[3647] MR. RICHARDSON. Well now, Captain, let us orient this just a little. You did have a talk with Brotherhood about what had become of these copies, did you not?

CAPTAIN SAFFORD. No; I wrote to him. He was out in—

MR. RICHARDSON (interposing). Wait a minute. Before you wrote to him, you had a talk with him, did you not?

CAPTAIN SAFFORD. Not about the copies.

MR. RICHARDSON. What did you write to him about the copies?

CAPTAIN SAFFORD. Brotherhood had told me it had come in on his watch. He verified that. Then I wrote him, "Do you know what became of the copies?" [...]

[3648] MR. RICHARDSON. And he told you, as I recall the testimony—I can find it, but I haven't been able to just this minute—he told you that he knew but would not tell you?

CAPTAIN SAFFORD. That he would not tell me now.

MR. RICHARDSON. All right.

MR. MURPHY. Page 113 of the Hewitt report is what you are looking for.

MR. RICHARDSON. Let me see it.

MR. MURPHY. That is right in the middle of the page.

MR. RICHARDSON. Oh, yes.

Now, let us take the exact language here on page 113 of the Hewitt report. You are right, Captain, when you say this:

> I wrote him a letter about the thing because that was looked for throughout a period of six months repeatedly. Various people looked for it in the Army and finally couldn't find it, and I asked him if he knew anything about it. He said yes, but he did not care to tell me about it then; but when he came back to the States, I asked him about it and found out he hadn't understood. We were working at cross-purposes. I found out that he was referring to the false "winds" message, which we had thrown in the wastebasket.

MR. RICHARDSON. So it was the false winds message that Brotherhood was talking about when he mentioned the winds execute message that came in on his watch?

CAPTAIN SAFFORD. Yes; but we only called it the winds message.

MR. RICHARDSON. All right.

Now this story that you told in secret—and, Captain, I am not criticizing you for telling it in secret, because all of those hearings were secret and had to be—but the story you told here that Friedman had told you that the messages had been destroyed by Colonel Bissell under the direction of General Marshall—

CAPTAIN SAFFORD (interposing). That is the way I got the story and remembered it. I did not write it down.

MR. RICHARDSON. And you said you thought it was true?

CAPTAIN SAFFORD. That is correct.

MR. RICHARDSON. All right. Now, you know, later, do you not, Captain, that Mr. Friedman denied having made any such statement to either you or anybody else—you know that, don't you?

CAPTAIN SAFFORD. I did not know that he denied it.

MR. RICHARDSON. And you know that Colonel Bissell also, in sworn testimony, before Admiral Hewitt, or before Colonel Clarke in the Clarke investigation, denied having destroyed any records?

CAPTAIN SAFFORD. I did not know that until this movement.

[3649] MR. RICHARDSON. Are you, Captain, familiar with the testimony of Lieutenant Kramer, or Commander Kramer, in the naval court of inquiry?

CAPTAIN SAFFORD. Only in a general way.

MR. RICHARDSON. You know, do you not, Captain, that Kramer testified that he never would have gathered the winds execute message, if received, to mean war?

CAPTAIN SAFFORD. You were quoting from that?

MR. RICHARDSON. Yes.

CAPTAIN SAFFORD. All right. [...]

[3650] MR. RICHARDSON. I give you pages 968 and 969 in Kramer's testimony before the naval court, and I am wondering whether you were familiar with the fact that Kramer took the position that the winds message, under code 2353, would not mean war, the winds execute message?

CAPTAIN SAFFORD. Kramer left the United States, I believe, in the spring of 1943, and did not return until, I believe, the spring of 1945, or possibly late in 1944; I am not certain. I had no idea what Kramer's answer had been, and I am giving the translation of the winds message from my memory, and nobody else's. [...]

MR. RICHARDSON. Now, Captain, you have no doubt, have you, that all of these copies that were sent out to be distributed were distributed in the regular order to the people who should have received them?

CAPTAIN SAFFORD. I have not, or I had no reason for doubting it.

MR. RICHARDSON. And there should be in the files of those respective departments the one copy of that message which they are supposed to keep?

CAPTAIN SAFFORD. That is correct.

MR. RICHARDSON. And when you investigated you found that none of the files had any copy?

CAPTAIN SAFFORD. That is correct.

MR. RICHARDSON. Including your own files in your own office?

CAPTAIN SAFFORD. There was only one other file in which it could be expected and that was in the War Department.

MR. RICHARDSON. All right. Now, then, in order to completely erase that order from the entire Military Establishment in Washing-[3651]ton, there would first have to be deleted from the file the copy that went to Beardall in the White House, would not there?

CAPTAIN SAFFORD. No, because that was taken back and destroyed as a matter of routine within probably 24 hours.

Mr. Richardson. And nothing was left with him?

Captain Safford. Nothing was left with him.

Mr. Richardson. All right. You would expect him to remember the message, would not you?

Captain Safford. I would expect him to remember the message; yes.

Mr. Richardson. So that if the message was destroyed he should remember that he saw it regardless of the destruction, should not he? Keep in mind, Captain, that this message, according to you, meant war. Can you think of anything that would fix a man's mind more than such a message as that?

Captain Safford. He should have remembered it.

Mr. Richardson. And the President should have been very interested in it, should not he?

Captain Safford. He should have been. I think he was.

Mr. Richardson. All right. Now, then, someone would have had to have gone into the office in the War Department and filched the copy there and destroyed it, would not he?

Captain Safford. That is correct.

Mr. Richardson. And someone would have to go in the Navy Department office where a file copy was kept and destroy the copy there?

Captain Safford. That is correct.

Mr. Richardson. And somebody must have gone into your office and destroyed the copy there?

Captain Safford. I had no personal copy.

Mr. Richardson. Was not there a copy kept in your section?

Captain Safford. Kramer was the sole custodian.

Mr. Richardson. Where would he keep it? In his pocket?

Captain Safford. In his safe.

Mr. Richardson. Then somebody would have to get into Kramer's safe to destroy his copy?

Captain Safford. That is correct.

Mr. Richardson. Well, who was in charge of the files in the Navy Department?

Captain Safford. These magic or intercepts, Kramer was in charge of them. I was indirectly responsible up to the 15th of February 1942. The actual custodian was Lieutenant Commander Harrison, U.S. Naval Reserve.

Mr. Richardson. What was that last statement?

Captain Safford. The actual custodian was Lieutenant Commander Harrison, U.S. Naval Reserve. He had the physical custody.

Mr. Richardson. Well, do you think that there was a general conspiracy running from the White House through the War Department and Navy Department and through Kramer's section to destroy these copies?

Captain Safford. I have never indicated the White House at any time in my testimony.

[3652] Mr. Richardson. Well, do you think there was a conspiracy between the Navy Department and War Department to destroy these copies?

CAPTAIN SAFFORD. There is an appearance of it.

MR. RICHARDSON. And whom do you suspect as individuals who took part in that conspiracy?

CAPTAIN SAFFORD. I have no first-hand knowledge.

MR. RICHARDSON. All you have is a suspicion?

CAPTAIN SAFFORD. I have more than that.

MR. RICHARDSON. Well, let us have your knowledge, let us have you tell this committee in words of one syllable what evidence you have that any human being in Washington sought to destroy official copies in the military department.

CAPTAIN SAFFORD. Messages have been known to be mislaid, but we always, as a matter of policy from the very beginning, kept a file copy of the original incoming message, we kept a copy of all our codes and we could prepare a new message at will. When I began working on the winds message I was much more interested in the intercept form of it than I was in its translation. We were requested first and I think finally we were permitted to search ourselves through the files of intercepted messages in the custody of OP-20-GX, that is the intercepting direction finder station of the Navy Department, and not only was there no copy of the winds message but there was no copy of any intercepted messages from any of our east coast stations for the month of December 1941, and possibly other times. That search was made repeatedly. The men in charge did not know that these were missing, they had no record of it being missing, they had no authority for destruction and no record of destruction.

When that became known Capt. E.E. Stone, who was in charge of the Navy Department Communications Intelligence Unit at that time and is now Rear Admiral Stone and Director of Naval Communications, immediately called for written statements from everybody concerned, to see what could be found out about it, and nothing showed up.

They had simply evaporated from the face of the earth. They were gone, and no records of them.

It was an unwritten law in that section that we retain the original intercept forever, because we could never tell when it would be useful or how many years we might want to go back to verify something. At the time I turned over the section some of our logs were running back, without missing, as far as 1925. Then we tried to find the orders which had gone out, and there was no trace of the original teletype orders to either Cheltenham or to Bainbridge Island, that we had ever told them to do anything about trying to monitor for the winds message.

They did find the reports as well as the intercepted messages from Bainbridge Island and that told us the whole story. They were intact and the monthly report acknowledged the orders to monitor the message and told exactly what they had done toward it, as appears in my written statement.

MR. RICHARDSON. But they didn't report at Bainbridge that they had any winds execute message, did they?

CAPTAIN SAFFORD. Because they did not know what they were looking for but their message reports, when we finally checked them over [3653] in January 1946—I don't mean the messages—not only the messages but also in their reports it showed specifically that they had monitored every one of those schedules given them and had not been able to hear the message on December 4, or practically on any other day. They were listening for them but did not hear them. We got that distinct negative information. They attempted to hear the message but didn't get anything. [...]

MR. RICHARDSON. Now, it is a fact, isn't it, Captain, that every single witness who has testified on the winds code, on the subject of having received or seen a wind execute message, testifies that they never saw one; isn't that a fact? Every single one of them.

CAPTAIN SAFFORD. Do you mean before this committee or other investigations?

MR. RICHARDSON. I mean before any investigating committee, including this one.

CAPTAIN SAFFORD. I don't think it is as complete as "everyone."

MR. RICHARDSON. Can you think of one individual today that has not under oath testified that he never saw a wind execute message with [3654] the exception of the one that came in on the 7th or 8th which all agree upon?

CAPTAIN SAFFORD. I think that Admiral Ingersoll for one has testified that he saw the wind message and it meant war with the United States. I think he gave that testimony before the Navy Court of Inquiry.

MR. RICHARDSON. Doesn't Admiral Ingersoll's testimony specifically say that he doesn't remember whether he saw a written execute message before December 7 or after; isn't that what he testified to?

CAPTAIN SAFFORD. He also testified to that. He wasn't certain as to the date but he saw it and it was in writing.

MR. RICHARDSON. Now, there was a wind execute message came in on the 8th?

CAPTAIN SAFFORD. Yes; but it was not in writing in the Navy Department.

MR. RICHARDSON. It eventually was in writing, wasn't it?

CAPTAIN SAFFORD. Yes, sir; in the summer of 1944.

MR. RICHARDSON. We have it here in the exhibit in writing, don't we?

CAPTAIN SAFFORD. May I see it, please?

MR. RICHARDSON. Yes. I read it to you this morning and showed it to you. I refer to the message 3 (d) which I read this morning and which you identified this morning as having been the message of December 8 out of Tokyo.

CAPTAIN SAFFORD. That is correct.

Have I been asked a question, or what?

MR. RICHARDSON. I asked you this morning to look at 3 (d) and called your attention to the form of that message.

CAPTAIN SAFFORD. That is correct.

MR. RICHARDSON. To point out to you that that was a very different looking message from the one you described of December 4.

CAPTAIN SAFFORD. That is correct.

MR. RICHARDSON. Now, the admonition at the bottom discloses that was a message of December 8, 1941?

CAPTAIN SAFFORD. Correct.

MR. RICHARDSON. It meant war with England?

CAPTAIN SAFFORD. Correct.

MR. RICHARDSON. Now, the point that I make with reference to it is that there was, and everybody admits there was and almost every station took it as it came in, an execute message on the 8th of December, so that when you say that Admiral Ingersoll admitted that he saw a wind execute message, I ask you whether he didn't testify that he didn't remember whether he saw one before or after December 7, so it may have been this message that he saw.

CAPTAIN SAFFORD. Admiral Ingersoll could not possibly have seen that message on, before, or shortly after December 7, 1941.

MR. RICHARDSON. Why not?

CAPTAIN SAFFORD. This page 3 which precedes—sheet 3 which precedes 3 (d), the certificate from the Federal Communications Commission dated August 18, 1944, and signed by T.J. Slowie, secretary, states in part:

> Document No. 4 is a true copy of two weather messages intercepted by Commission monitors from Tokyo stations JLG-4 and JZJ between 0002 and 0035 [3655] GMT, December 8, 1941, and telephoned to Lieutenant Colonel C. C. Dusenbury, U.S. Army Service Corps, at the request of Colonel Bratton's office at approximately 8:00 p.m. EST, December 7, 1941. Document No. 4 also contains the Romaji version of these messages.
> on file in this Commission and I am the proper custodian of the same.

That was a telephoned message to the War Department and no written copy of this was received in the Navy Department prior to August 18, 1944.

MR. MURPHY. Mr. Chairman, in Exhibit 1 at page 251 it is shown dated December 7, translated by the Navy December 7:

> Relations between Japan and England are not in accordance with expectation.

CAPTAIN SAFFORD. That is a different one.

MR. MURPHY. There is an execute on the 7th.

MR. RICHARDSON. Were there two executes on December—

CAPTAIN SAFFORD. That was in the so-called hidden word code.

MR. RICHARDSON. That is right.

Now, Captain, let me ask you this question: Why do you think anybody wanted to destroy the wind execute message that came in as you say on December 4?

Four. American Penetration of Codes

CAPTAIN SAFFORD. Because that was the unheeded warning of war.

MR. RICHARDSON. Well, everybody in the Military Establishment in Washington was looking for war, weren't they?

CAPTAIN SAFFORD. That question cannot be given a simple answer.

MR. RICHARDSON. If you can't answer it simply, was there any doubt generally in the minds of the people, the heads, the high command and the Military Establishment, that we were heading for a war with Japan?

CAPTAIN SAFFORD. There was considerable doubt in the high command of the Navy Department, at least, that war with Japan would commence in early December 1941. Eventually, yes; but not at that particular time.

MR. RICHARDSON. All right. And nothing on earth was of more interest to them than to try and find out when that would be?

CAPTAIN SAFFORD. That is correct. That is the reason we had all the pressure put on us to monitor, to intercept that wind message if it were humanly possible to get it.

MR. RICHARDSON. And you believe, do you not, that everyone of the officers in a subordinate capacity and in the high command were anxious to find out when and where war would begin?

CAPTAIN SAFFORD. And also against whom.

MR. RICHARDSON. All right.

Now, why would anyone want to fail to make use of a wind execute message that meant war, just the minute it came in? What motive would they have in doing it?

CAPTAIN SAFFORD. That is a question that has puzzled me for 4 years. I have no logical answer to it.

MR. RICHARDSON. The reason that it wasn't used is because it is diametrically contrary to the theory you have got in your head that there was a winds execute message on December 4, isn't it?

CAPTAIN SAFFORD. By no means.

MR. RICHARDSON. Don't you think, Captain, with your long experience in the Navy, that there were a hundred officers in the military [3656] establishments that would be anxious to get their hands on a winds execute message that meant war on December 4?

CAPTAIN SAFFORD. I would doubt if more than 20 officers in both the Army and Navy ever knew about the winds message at the time it was sent or immediately thereafter.

MR. RICHARDSON. Do you think seriously, Captain, that any of those 20 would secrete, delete, purloin, destroy, cover up that message so that our people here and our people on the Pacific front wouldn't know that Japan was about to commence war; is that your belief?

CAPTAIN SAFFORD. No.

MR. RICHARDSON. Well, then, why would anybody want to press the veil of secrecy, destruction, on this wind execute message that you say came on the 4th of December, why would they?

CAPTAIN SAFFORD. It is human to try to cover up mistakes.

MR. RICHARDSON. Well, what was the mistake that was made with reference to that message?

CAPTAIN SAFFORD. The fact that no war warning was ever sent. The fact that an attempted war warning in the Navy Department was suppressed by higher authority and that the War Department didn't even attempt to get a war warning out.

MR. RICHARDSON. Then it is your idea that, with a message in the hands of the officers of the Navy, the officers of the Army, and the President of the United States, that everybody forgot that they were interestd in the war and forgot to make use of this message?

CAPTAIN SAFFORD. I do not know why the warning did not go out.

MR. RICHARDSON. I suggest, Captain, that the reason the warning didn't go out was because there never was a winds execute message on the 4th day of December. You disagree with that?

CAPTAIN SAFFORD. I disagree with that. [...]

[3807] MR. KEEFE. And you had reason to believe that you would not be coming before this committee standing alone, did you not?

CAPTAIN SAFFORD. That is right, sir.

MR. KEEFE. I shall not take the time to read at this time the testimony of Colonel Bratton or Colonel Sadtler. Those witnesses will be here to testify. But from the whole picture as you had it from the testimony that these people gave under oath and from the information which they gave you in the talks you had with them subsequently, were you of the opinion that your position would be corroborated by these witnesses when they came here to testify?

CAPTAIN SAFFORD. I believed that they would support me in general.

MR. KEEFE. Now, the thing that has puzzled me, and I assume that it must be puzzling to other members of this com-[3808]mittee, and I speak with utter and complete frankness, Captain Safford, I am unable to understand any possible interest, personal interest, that you might have in this controversy, and if you have any such personal interest, I would like to have you state it.

CAPTAIN SAFFORD. I have no personal interest, except I started it and I have got to see it through.

THE CHAIRMAN. The guests of the committee will be in order.

MR. KEEFE. You realize, of course, that in view of the implications that have been stated in the cross-examination of you, especially by the gentleman from Pennsylvania, that you have made some rather strong charges?

CAPTAIN SAFFORD. Yes, sir.

MR. KEEFE. That may well militate against your career as a naval officer. Did you realize that when you came here as a witness?

CAPTAIN SAFFORD. I realized that every time I have testified.

MR. KEEFE. And despite the fact that you have nothing personally to gain, and everything to lose, you have persisted in this story every time you have testified?

CAPTAIN SAFFORD. I have. [...]

[3810] MR. KEEFE. Now, you have testified and Kramer testified before the Naval Court of Inquiry that this winds execute message that was received on the 4th was sent right up to Admiral Noyes?

CAPTAIN SAFFORD. Yes, sir.

MR. KEEFE. After Admiral Noyes got that message and the same afternoon were messages prepared and sent out to Guam and our outlying possessions to destroy their codes and confidential papers?

CAPTAIN SAFFORD. Yes, sir, they were.

MR. KEEFE. Who drew those messages?

CAPTAIN SAFFORD. I did myself personally.

MR. KEEFE. And were they sent out?

CAPTAIN SAFFORD. They were all sent out.

MR. KEEFE. And did those messages follow in immediate sequence to the receipt of this so-called winds execute message?

CAPTAIN SAFFORD. I began working on them, checking up to see what we had to go, immediately after the receipt of the message.

MR. KEEFE. And were those messages prompted entirely by the receipt of this winds execute message, so far as you were concerned?

CAPTAIN SAFFORD. So far as I was concerned, they were.

MR. KEEFE. And did Admiral Noyes approve the sending of those messages for the destruction of codes and confidential papers?

CAPTAIN SAFFORD. Admiral Noyes did. [...]

[3843] SENATOR LUCAS. Captain, in the statement you furnished to the committee, on page 1, you state, "The broadcast was probably in Japanese Morse code."

You were there speaking about the winds execute message?

CAPTAIN SAFFORD. The winds execute message.

SENATOR LUCAS. Now, as you go through your statement, and as I have understood the testimony from time to time, you have almost taken a clear position that it was broadcast in the Morse code, and I would like to have you explain what you mean by "probably" because it seems to me to be somewhat important.

CAPTAIN SAFFORD. There are two forms of Morse code. The International Morse code, which has an alphabet of 26 characters, and the Japanese Morse code which has an alphabet of approximately 45 characters. Not being able to locate any copies of the JAP broadcasts of that time, it is not quite definite what was used. The best reference we can have is the station report from Cheltenham, which said they monitored all these schedules and found they were all in English and Kana, which means Japanese Morse code. So there is a very strong presumption that it was in the Japanese Morse code and not in the International Morse code. But in either event, it was not in voice. It was not the spoken word.

SENATOR LUCAS. I still don't quite understand when you say it was "probably" in Japanese Morse code. Are there two Morse codes?

CAPTAIN SAFFORD. Yes, sir; the Japanese Morse code of approximately 45 characters, and the English Morse code of 26 characters.

SENATOR LUCAS. Were you intercepting both codes?

CAPTAIN SAFFORD. We were intercepting both codes from time to time. At that time we had approximately 110 radio operators in the United States Navy who were proficient on the Japanese Morse code.

SENATOR LUCAS. One of these codes is easier to intercept, is that it?

CAPTAIN SAFFORD. Any trained operator can intercept the Inter- [3844] national Morse code. The Japanese Morse code requires special training.

SENATOR LUCAS. In other words, any station in the country could intercept the International Morse code?

CAPTAIN SAFFORD. Yes, sir.

SENATOR LUCAS. While it would take a trained operator to intercept the Japanese Morse code?

CAPTAIN SAFFORD. Yes, sir.

SENATOR LUCAS. And you are not positive; you say there is a slight possibility that it would have been in the International Morse code?

CAPTAIN SAFFORD. Yes, sir; because we can't produce any message sent around that time sent from Station JAP. I have requested them, and none can be furnished. [...]

[3848] SENATOR LUCAS. I see. [...] May I have Circulars 2353 and 2354? I now direct your attention, Captain, just for a moment or two, to Circulars 2353 and 2354, with which you are familiar, of course. [...] Now, you state:

> The warning was not sent in the manner prescribed by #72 or #73, but was a mixture.

Will you explain that to the committee, please?

CAPTAIN SAFFORD. Yes, sir. We expected at the time, both Army and Navy, that the reason for possibly having these two different set-ups was that instructions on the warning which was contained in Circular 2353 would be used on the voice broadcast from Tokyo and that the words appearing in 2354 would be used on the Morse code broadcast from Tokyo.

Therefore, I was quite astonished when I found words which I expected would come by voice only, appearing in the Morse code broadcast.

SENATOR LUCAS. Can you explain that?

CAPTAIN SAFFORD. It was our failure, the Army and Navy, to understand exactly what distinction the Japanese themselves did make between the two forms which they had provided in these two messages. If I may —

SENATOR LUCAS. Pardon me, sir.

CAPTAIN SAFFORD. If I may continue, please.

SENATOR LUCAS. Yes, sir.

CAPTAIN SAFFORD. 2353 simply said, "Daily Japanese language short wave news broadcast," and that in the broad sense and maybe the proper sense could apply to any form of Japanese, whether written [3849] or spoken. We possibly jumped at conclusions. I know that the FCC were given those words and they were told it would come by voice; the Army did that.

SENATOR LUCAS. Now, in this same statement you follow up by saying:

> The warning was not sent in the manner prescribed by #72 or #73, but was a mixture. The GY watch officer was not sure of it so he called you and you came in early and verified it.

Now you are talking to Kramer. In other words, when this mixture message came in there wasn't anybody that was certain as to whether or not this was it or not; that is correct, isn't it?

CAPTAIN SAFFORD. That is what appeared at the time, though—

SENATOR LUCAS. Well, now, I am just talking about that time.

CAPTAIN SAFFORD. That was my belief at the time.

SENATOR LUCAS. Yes, sir; that was your belief at the time and you so stated to Kramer 2 years afterward or more, that when this message came in, it was a mixture between these two circulars that had been sent out by Japan, and there wasn't anybody at that time that thoroughly understood what this message was; that is correct, isn't it?

CAPTAIN SAFFORD. Because it was—

SENATOR LUCAS. Now, just wait a minute. Not "because." Is that true or not? I am just taking your own words here to Kramer and you can qualify it later on, but I am just asking a simple question as to whether or not when this message came in, that you men there who saw it first and before Kramer got them did not believe that it was a mixture between the two messages and you did not know what it meant.

CAPTAIN SAFFORD. The watch officer that received it was not certain if it was what we were looking for or not.

SENATOR LUCAS. That is right. Well, counsel calls my attention and Senator Ferguson from Michigan, and they are correct; you were not there when it came in at all?

CAPTAIN SAFFORD. I was not there when it came in myself personally. I did not see it until Kramer took it in and showed it to me. [...]

[3850] SENATOR LUCAS. Now, when you came in that morning, where did you find Kramer?

CAPTAIN SAFFORD. When I think about that afterward I cannot remember anything about that particular day prior to seeing Kramer and holding up a sheet of paper and saying, "Here it is" or "This is it." It was a very simple statement which contained the word "it," "it" referring to the winds message.

SENATOR LUCAS. Well, now, that is practically all you remember with respect to this message known as the winds execute message? You talked to Kramer about it and he held it up and you saw these three words written on it, and he said, "This is it," and that is the last time you ever saw the message?

CAPTAIN SAFFORD. I read it over. He explained it was the genuine execute of the winds code. I saw the writing, and it was sent up to Admiral Noyes immediately and never sent back to my section.

SENATOR LUCAS. Now how do you account for the Japanese not going through, word by word, with their circulars, either 2353 or 2354, on an important message of this kind? If you fellows had it mixed up, would not the Japs have it mixed up also?

CAPTAIN SAFFORD. The Japanese had both forms, and so did we, so whatever we received we could understand.

SENATOR LUCAS. Well, you did not understand it, the watch officer did not understand it when it came in, and you were, 2 years later, asking Kramer for information about this very thing.

[3851] CAPTAIN SAFFORD. The watch officer had been informed that if it came by voice, it would be in the form given in circular 2353, and if it came in the Morse code, it would be in the form given in Circular 2354. The watch officer was not a Japanese translator and therefore he was confused, because he recognized the words, but he was still uncertain because it did not come in in the form he expected it.

I think it was sent out the way the Japanese intended to send it, but it did not come in in the form in which we expected to receive it.

SENATOR LUCAS. Captain, Circular 2353 is clear and free from ambiguity, is it not?

CAPTAIN SAFFORD. Yes, sir.

SENATOR LUCAS. And so is Circular 2354?

CAPTAIN SAFFORD. That is correct.

SENATOR LUCAS. The winds execute message following this circular was probably the most important message that Japan sent, unless it was the 14 parts message?

CAPTAIN SAFFORD. Yes, sir.

SENATOR LUCAS. All right. Now, isn't it a fair assumption to believe that, in view of the fact that Japan was sending this implementing message, they would either send it as set forth in Circular 2353 or as set forth in Circular 2354, so that the Japanese nationals throughout the world would not be confused about it?

CAPTAIN SAFFORD. That is correct.

SENATOR LUCAS. Well, they did not do that, did they, according to what you saw on this sheet?

CAPTAIN SAFFORD. Yes, sir; they did, according to what I saw on the sheet. [...]

[3852] SENATOR LUCAS. Your memory up to this point, Captain, has been consistent on one thing, and that is that you saw these three words, or these three phrases, in the middle of the message. That is correct, isn't it?

CAPTAIN SAFFORD. And immediately adjacent to each other.

SENATOR LUCAS. Yes. But you have never testified that you saw these three phrases at the end of the message, on this teletype message?

CAPTAIN SAFFORD. That is correct.

SENATOR LUCAS. And you never testified at any time that when Kramer talked with you about it and you read this message over, as you just told me you did, and understood it, you never testified that each sentence was repeated twice on this teletype message?

CAPTAIN SAFFORD. I have never testified that.

SENATOR LUCAS. Yes. And the reason that you have not, is because you only saw, as I understand it, these three phrases in the middle of the message?

CAPTAIN SAFFORD. The reason I did not is because it did not stick out in my memory or did not strike me as particularly important, so it would be something that would stay in my memory.

SENATOR LUCAS. Captain you could not say that this would not be important, could you? Here you are looking now for the implementing message, and you know exactly what this circular says that the Jap Government has to do in order to make this a really genuine implementing message.

In other words, they use these phrases in the middle, they use them at the end, and they repeat the sentence twice. Here is a serious situation. Here is Japan getting ready to go to war with the United States upon this kind of an implementing message, and certainly it must have been important to you or you would not be before this hearing now.

CAPTAIN SAFFORD. The significant part of the winds message; that is, the code words compromising the winds message, in this broadcast were underscored and Kramer and I at that time were both thoroughly sure that this was the genuine execute of the winds message.

SENATOR LUCAS. Well, Captain, how could you be? How could you and Kramer be certain of that, if you believed that the Japanese were going to follow out what they said in Circular 2353?

CAPTAIN SAFFORD. Because I, at least, considered that the repetition at the end, either in the case of this message or the other message, was just as a safe precaution to insure that the highly important words were received in case there was difficulty in receiving at the time.

SENATOR LUCAS. When did you think about that?

[3853] CAPTAIN SAFFORD. At the time.

SENATOR LUCAS. I see. In other words, you did not think that it was important to have these three phrases at the end, or that they be repeated twice. You thought any place that you saw them, either in the center of the message or at the end of the message was sufficient to tell you that there was war with the United States?

CAPTAIN SAFFORD. It was where the words appeared together in a contradictory sense and making no possible weather forecast, but in the middle of the Japanese language short wave news broadcast as set out herein. That was the all-important thing.

Senator Lucas. You can reach that conclusion, Captain, but as one member of the committee, where a nation is sending out an implementing message of this kind which means war, it seems to me, in order that they might notify their nationals, without any question they would follow that message to the letter. They had some reason to send this type of a message in the beginning. It was either the making or breaking of Japan, that is how important it was. And you, 2 years later, Captain, were still thinking about the mixed message that came in at that time when you wrote to Kramer.

Captain Safford. What I meant by "mixture" was what we considered the voice form being sent in Morse code. That was the only mixture I had reference to.

Senator Lucas. "The warning was not sent in the manner prescribed by 72 or 73." That is what we are talking about right here, 72 and 73, these two circulars, and you did state, "It was not sent in the manner prescribed by 72 or 73 but was a mixture." That is what you are talking about.

Captain Safford. That was a very vague statement given to Kramer.

Was Kramer Pressured to Alter His Testimony That the Winds Message Was Received?

ALWIN D. KRAMER, TRANSLATION SECTION,
COMMUNICATIONS DIVISION, NAVY DEPARTMENT

Joint Congressional Investigation

[3964] MR. MURPHY. Now, did you have any information as to his—he said that for a long time he had a certain attitude toward what happened at Pearl Harbor and then he made a change. Did he ever tell you why he made the change?

CAPTAIN KRAMER. The first indication I had of what I might term bitterness on the part of Captain Safford toward any other officers in the Navy Department was Captain Safford's second letter to me.

MR. MURPHY. That was the one I read in detail on the record?

CAPTAIN KRAMER. Dated, I believe, January 22, 1944.

MR. MURPHY. Right. Now, then, you went to the hospital at Bethesda on the 28th of September, 1945, did you not?

CAPTAIN KRAMER. Yes, sir.

MR. MURPHY. And you had a visit from Captain Safford on October the 3rd, that is right, isn't it?

CAPTAIN KRAMER. Approximately that date, yes, sir.

MR. MURPHY. What was the purpose of that visit?

CAPTAIN KRAMER. Quite frankly, Mr. Murphy, I was somewhat surprised at that visit. My relations with Captain Safford have been, I believe, cordial; I believe they still are. They have never been intimate to the extent of myself or my wife making social calls on Captain Safford and his wife. It was purely office and official contacts. That is part of the reason at my surprise at his visit to me at the hospital. It was not too surprising, however, inasmuch as he was a long-time acquaintance of mine.

We discussed a few things, not bearing on Pearl Harbor. We played a game of chess that evening. He brought me a box of chocolates, for which I thanked him, naturally.

Source: Pearl Harbor Attack, *volume 9.*

He called again about 3 or 4 days later and picked up a book which he had left with me, a book of cartoons, on his first visit. Our conversations then were of the same character. We may have played a game of chess then, too. He was one of probably six or eight visitors I had during that first few weeks there.

MR. MURPHY. Well, at any rate did you ever discuss Pearl Harbor with him while you were at the hospital?

CAPTAIN KRAMER. No, sir; we did not because all our contact was in the company of other patients in the hospital.

MR. MURPHY. Now, I notice here a headline in a New York paper, "Key Pearl Harbor Witness Vanishes."

CAPTAIN KRAMER. I was made aware of that headline, yes, sir.

[3965] MR. MURPHY. Now, can you tell us where you were on that particular day? This is a headline of the New York Journal-American of Friday, November the 9th, 1945. Where were you that day? Or at least it had reference to your vanishing. Did you leave the hospital?

CAPTAIN KRAMER. The day before, Mr. Murphy, my wife arrived in Washington from Florida. After one or two discussions with my doctors, and I believe on my request, I was permitted to what is termed "subsist" out of the hospital.

My wife contacted that afternoon the Red Cross in the hospital about locating a room near the hospital. We got such a room and stayed there that night. The following day, since it was several days before I had any appointment for further treatments, my wife and I went to Washington shopping. I got permission from the doctor before I left the hospital.

I learned on returning to the hospital the following morning from the nurse that on the previous afternoon there had been another visitor trying to see me. The visitor was described to me as a woman. From the description I could not determine who it might have been. It was that morning about 9:15 in the company of my wife at the hospital that I was preparing to leave the hospital again, having gotten the doctor's permission to do so, to go into town, when the medical officer in charge, Dr. Duncan, informed me that he had a phone call just then from the Navy Department to the effect that a Mr. Gearhart and Mr. Keefe were on their way out there to interview me. It was not until Mr. Keefe, I believe, explained to me that it was his secretary or someone from his office that had come out the day before that I first had any clue as to who my previous day's visitor was.

MR. MURPHY. Now, there have been statements in the press — and I am reading now from the New York Times of November the 12th, the byline of C. P. Trussel, a very able and distinguished writer for that great paper — there is a statement there that —

> Navy Captain issues a denial that he had been beset and beleaguered; asserted that he was feeling very well and would appear before the committee prepared to state fully "anything I know that they may want to know."

Now, were you ever beset or beleaguered by anybody in regard to this case? And, if so, I think the committee are entitled to every detail.

CAPTAIN KRAMER. At no time have I been what is termed beset and beleaguered, sir.

MR. MURPHY. There is a statement further in this article that—

> Captain Kramer had been badgered and beset by an effort to breakdown his testimony.

Now, do you know of anybody and if you do I think we ought to have the details.

CAPTAIN KRAMER. That statement, sir, is false.

SENATOR LUCAS. Did Trussel make those statements?

MR. MURPHY. No; Mr. Trussel is not making them himself but quoting a very distinguished gentleman, not the writer.

MR. GEARHART. Name him. Don't hold it back.

MR. MURPHY. Now, then, I come to the Washington Times-Herald, the United Press.

SENATOR LUCAS. What is the date of that?

MR. MURPHY. I don't know the date of this but it is current or about the same as the New York Times. This is the Washington Times- [3966] Herald and the only reason I think is pertinent to go into these maters is that the composite mind of America is influenced by everything they hear on this case and I think we ought to go into the whole story. I see here a statement:

> I stand exactly on my statement that Kramer is being badgered and beset. Here is the most important witness in the investigation. He entered the Naval Hospital under orders. They took away his uniform, gave him pajamas, bathrobe and slippers. His meals were served in a ward from September 28 to the morning of November 7. I know that Kramer is chafing under this restraint.

Were you chafing under any restraint at the hospital?

CAPTAIN KRAMER. I was getting restless in the hospital because that was the longest hospitalization I had ever had. My previous hospitalizations in the Navy had never been of more than a few days duration.

In that respect I might refer back to about 15 years ago when I was operated on for tonsilectomy in the Navy Hospital in Boston. The normal period in such operations, I was informed, was to keep the patient in the hospital not less than a week. After 3 days following my operation I walked out of the hospital and returned to my ship. I again was "chafing," if you want to use that term, sir.

MR. MURPHY. Well, I am just quoting from the paper, sir.

CAPTAIN KRAMER. Yes, sir.

MR. MURPHY. I now quote from the Washington Post, something by the Associated Press, that you were being—quoted a distinguished gentleman—that you were being badgered to—

change his original testimony, meaning he was being badgered to change his original testimony.

Had anybody asked you to change your original testimony?

CAPTAIN KRAMER. At no time during my hospitalization at Bethesda Naval Hospital has anything in connection with decryption or testimony been brought up in any conversation in which I engaged.

MR. MURPHY. There is also a statement in this same piece from the Washington Post by the Associated Press, not that of the Associated Press writer, but that of a distinguished gentleman, that the Navy was holding you incommunicado.

CAPTAIN KRAMER. That statement is incorrect, sir.

I have previously indicated that I had a number of visitors, and I made some phone calls as well.

MR. MURPHY. I am referring now to another story from another issue of the Washington Times Herald, an article by an able writer, Ted Lewis, in which he quotes another distinguished gentleman, other than the one who had made the previous statement, to the effect that there was a missing winds message of December 6, 1941, which purportedly showed that the Japs were committed to immediate attack.

You do not know anything about any message of December 6, do you?

CAPTAIN KRAMER. I do not, sir.

MR. MURPHY. I now quote from the Scranton Times of Scranton, Pa., United Press dispatch of November 7:

> The Navy today denied Republican charges that a potential witness in the Pearl Harbor inquiry had been "broken in mind and body" and was being held incommunicado in a hospital psychopathic ward.

[3967] Were you broken in mind or body?

CAPTAIN KRAMER. I do not believe so, sir.

MR. MURPHY. You were in this room for several days were you not?

CAPTAIN KRAMER. Yes, sir.

MR. MURPHY. And under questioning by members of this committee yesterday morning and yesterday afternoon, this morning and this afternoon?

CAPTAIN KRAMER. Yes, sir.

MR. MURPHY. Now, when you were at the hospital, you were interviewed, were you?

CAPTAIN KRAMER. By Mr. Keefe and Mr. Gearhart, yes, sir.

MR. MURPHY. Did you tell them what you know about this inquiry, and what facts you knew?

CAPTAIN KRAMER. Our discussions lasted approximately 4½ hours, interrupted in the early part of those discussions by some members of the press. I believe we covered most of my story that I had given in previous hearings and have given in this hearing in those conversations.

MR. MURPHY. Do you feel you told them the truth at that time?
CAPTAIN KRAMER. I did, sir.
MR. MURPHY. Is what you are telling today and told yesterday under oath different in any respect from what you told them at that time?
CAPTAIN KRAMER. In no respect whatsoever, sir.
MR. MURPHY. My reason for going into this is, if there is one single individual who has approached you in any way, low or high, no matter who he is, in any way to attempt to influence your testimony, I think in fairness to yourself, and the members of this committee, we ought to know about it.

Was there ever any such person?
CAPTAIN KRAMER. There was never any such person, sir.
[4074] MR. KEEFE. Captain Kramer, what is your age?
CAPTAIN KRAMER. About forty-two and a half, sir.
MR. KEEFE. You graduated from the Naval Academy when?
CAPTAIN KRAMER. 1925, sir.
MR. KEEFE. You and Captain Safford have always been, at least up until now, good friends, have you not?
CAPTAIN KRAMER. Unless testimony I have given before this hearing has altered his views I do not think our relations have changed in any respect, sir.
MR. KEEFE. That is not an answer to my question. You have been good friends, have you not?
CAPTAIN KRAMER. Yes, sir; office friends, not social friends.
MR. KEEFE. I was a little disturbed by some testimony that you gave yesteryear with respect to a visit by Captain Safford to you in the hospital.
CAPTAIN KRAMER. Yes, sir.
MR. KEEFE. Am I to assume that you intended to convey the impression that that was a gratuitous visit on the part of Captain Safford which your relations with him did not justify?
CAPTAIN KRAMER. That is not quite the impression I intended to convey; no, sir. I was somewhat surprised at that visit but not at all too surprised, I believe I expressed myself.
MR. KEEFE. Well, you stated that he had brought you a box of candy.
CAPTAIN KRAMER. That is correct, sir.
MR. KEEFE. As though that were wholly unexpected and perhaps had some sinister purpose behind it. Did you mean anything like that?
CAPTAIN KRAMER. None whatsoever, sir. I believe it is customary in making visits to patients in a hospital to bring things of that nature.
MR. KEEFE. Why, of course, and you did not intend by that statement that you made yesterday to imply that Captain Safford had any sinister purpose in visiting you at the hospital, did you?
CAPTAIN KRAMER. None whatsoever, sir.
MR. KEEFE. No. Or that he came out there for the purpose of trying to enlist your aid in connection with testimony to be given before this committee?
CAPTAIN KRAMER. None whatsoever, sir.

MR. KEEFE. He did not even discuss Pearl Harbor with you at the time he visited you at the hospital, did he?

CAPTAIN KRAMER. That is correct, sir.

MR. KEEFE. You played a game of chess?

CAPTAIN KRAMER. Yes, sir.

MR. KEEFE. Did he visit you more than once?

[4075] CAPTAIN KRAMER. On two occasions, sir.

MR. KEEFE. Now, you stated yesterday that you had about eight visitors, you think, while you were at the hospital.

CAPTAIN KRAMER. Yes, sir.

MR. KEEFE. Will you tell us who those visitors were bsides Captain Safford?

CAPTAIN KRAMER. I did not expect to be questioned on that point, Mr. Keefe.

MR. KEEFE. If there is anything—

CAPTAIN KRAMER. I believe I could refresh my memory in detail on that. Offhand I can recall the name of one of them, Mister—rather, retired Maj. A. B. C. Graves, who is a member of the Washington Chess Divan, of which I have been a member.

MR. KEEFE. Did any person other than Mr. Gearhart and myself talk to you about Pearl Harbor at any time that you were at the hospital?

CAPTAIN KRAMER. That is precisely accurate, sir, except one patient in the hospital, namely, a former classmate of mine, a Commander Powell, who was in a room near mine in the hospital. In the course of our general conversations I mentioned the fact that I was engaged at the time of Pearl Harbor in handling cryptographic material and I undoubtedly mentioned the fact and the thought I might be a witness before the contemplated hearing, this hearing.

MR. KEEFE. Commander Powell was a classmate of yours?

CAPTAIN KRAMER. Yes, sir.

MR. KEEFE. He had been retired from the Navy for some years and had come back into the Navy?

CAPTAIN KRAMER. Yes, sir; during the war.

MR. KEEFE. Mrs. Powell and Mrs. Kramer were friends, too, were they not?

CAPTAIN KRAMER. Mrs. Kramer has never met Mrs. Powell until recently, last fall.

MR. KEEFE. I see, but she met Mrs. Powell then?

CAPTAIN KRAMER. Yes, sir.

MR. KEEFE. Are those all the people that you can recall? Commander Powell was a patient suffering from arthritis, was he not?

CAPTAIN KRAMER. I am not sure what the diagnosis in his case was, Mr. Keefe.

MR. KEEFE. Well, in any event he was taking treatment out there?

CAPTAIN KRAMER. Yes, sir.

MR. KEEFE. Now, then, you have told us of some General or some man that was in some chess divan. You talked about chess?

CAPTAIN KRAMER. There was one other individual from the chess divan. Just which one I do not recall at the moment.

MR. KEEFE. Of course, the reason that I ask these questions is because the hospital record which I have examined only shows the visit of Captain Safford. You are sure that there were others?

CAPTAIN KRAMER. I am positive of that, sir. In connection with the hospital record I would like to point out that it was not until last month that I was aware of a hospital rule to the effect that patients leaving the hospital during the day should sign out in a book. That, incidentally, Mr. Keefe, is the reason I believe why you were not able to be informed on the occasion of the day before our [4076] interview last fall of where I was. I had apparently violated a hospital regulation in that respect.

MR. KEEFE. Well, Mr. Gearhart and I did speak to you at the hospital?

CAPTAIN KRAMER. Yes, sir.

MR. KEEFE. And we had about a 4½-hour conversation with you?

CAPTAIN KRAMER. Which I would characterize as very pleasant in nature.

MR. KEEFE. A very pleasant conversation. There was no attempt to bulldoze you or change your opinion or anything of that kind, was there?

CAPTAIN KRAMER. None whatsoever, sir.

MR. KEEFE. And Mrs. Kramer was present during the entire course of that conversation?

CAPTAIN KRAMER. Yes, sir.

MR. KEEFE. And Captain Duncan was kind enough to serve us a luncheon while we were sitting in the room?

CAPTAIN KRAMER. A brief lunch, yes, sir.

MR. KEEFE. You recall that very well?

CAPTAIN KRAMER. Yes, sir.

MR. KEEFE. Now, you had been chafing some because of the fact that you were required to stay out there in the hospital, weren't you, Captain?

CAPTAIN KRAMER. Yes, sir.

MR. KEEFE. And you had expressed that to your Commander friend and others that came to see you, hadn't you?

CAPTAIN KRAMER. I believe I expressed it only to Commander Powell, who was the only patient I had previously known.

MR. KEEFE. Yes, and you gave expression to the fact that you felt if you could get word to Ross McIntire you might be permitted to leave the hospital, didn't you?

CAPTAIN KRAMER. I don't recall that statement.

MR. KEEFE. You don't recall that?

CAPTAIN KRAMER. No, sir.

MR. KEEFE. You were clothed in pajamas and bathrobe, were you not?

CAPTAIN KRAMER. That was customary for all patients.

MR. KEEFE. Why, exactly. There was nothing unusual about it.

CAPTAIN KRAMER. None at all, sir.

Was Kramer Pressured? 193

MR. KEEFE. You were not permitted to eat at the officers' mess out there, were you?

CAPTAIN KRAMER. No, sir. The meals were served to all patients in that particular part of the hospital on trays.

MR. KEEFE. Exactly. Now, the day before Mr. Gearhart and I came out your uniform was restored so that you could go with Mrs. Kramer on a shopping tour?

CAPTAIN KRAMER. That is correct, sir. She had arrived just a few days before.

MR. KEEFE. Yes. And there had been some publicity in the newspapers about the speech that had been made on the floor of Congress the day before, hadn't there?

CAPTAIN KRAMER. I became aware of that, yes, sir.

[4077] MR. KEEFE. Yes. And the next day was the day that your uniform was restored to you and you were permitted temporary leave from the hospital, isn't that true?

CAPTAIN KRAMER. I am not sure which event preceeded or followed which, Mr. Keefe. I undoubtedly could refresh my memory on that by going over it in more detail. I know, however, that the proximate and prime cause of the uniform being restored was so that I could leave the hospital with my wife who had just arrived there.

MR. KEEFE. Yes.

CAPTAIN KRAMER. Before that there was no reason for my subsisting out.

MR. KEEFE. Yes. Now, you first went to the hospital in August, did you not?

CAPTAIN KRAMER. Yes, sir.

MR. KEEFE. About the 28th of August?

CAPTAIN KRAMER. That may be correct, sir. I believe it is.

MR. KEEFE. Yes, I checked it.

CAPTAIN KRAMER. Yes, sir.

MR. KEEFE. And then you went back to the hospital the 23d of September.

CAPTAIN KRAMER. About that date I believe, sir.

MR. KEEFE. And in the meantime had you been down to Miami with your family?

CAPTAIN KRAMER. On sick leave, yes, sir.

MR. KEEFE. Now, you, Captain Kramer—and I want this to be said in the record—had, prior to that time, rendered a most distinguished service to your country, there is no question about that fact. That should appear clearly. Now, you would say also that Captain Safford had rendered a most distinguished service to his country, would you not?

CAPTAIN KRAMER. Mr. Keefe, I have always had a very high regard for Captain Safford's professional abilities.

MR. KEEFE. Well, have you had a regard for him in any other respect?

CAPTAIN KRAMER. As a personal friend I had a regard for him which warranted the continuance of that friendship, yes, sir.

MR. KEEFE. Yes. And you feel that way today, do you not?

CAPTAIN KRAMER. I do, yes, sir.

Mr. Keefe. Now, did you express any concern to any of your friends over the fact that you viewed with some apprehension the necessity for your appearing before this Congressional investigating committee?

Captain Kramer. At no time do I recall making expressions of that nature, sir. I have never been in a state of apprehension that I am aware of in any hearing I appeared before.

Mr. Keefe. After you left the hospital did you visit the Public Relations Department of the Navy Department?

Captain Kramer. I did not, sir.

Mr. Keefe. Did anybody visit you from that Department?

Captain Kramer. No, sir.

Mr. Keefe. Were you given any instructions as to statements to be issued or not to be issued?

[4078] Captain Kramer. None whatsoever, sir. If you will recall, during the course of our conversation at the Naval Hospital, Captain Duncan broke into our discussions with words to the effect that the press was outside and champing at the bits to get an interview from me. I expressed myself in answer to Captain Duncan along the lines that it appeared as though I could not avoid such an interview and that it might just as well take place now.

With that expression of my opinion I ask Mrs. Kramer to leave the room; certain members of the press came in and I extemporaneously dictated a statement. On the completion of that statement I asked the correspondent who took it down what service he represented, turned to Captain Duncan, the medical officer in charge of the hospital, and requested him to obtain a copy of that statement and furnish it to the Navy Department Public Relations Officer because any further statement I might have occasion to make to the press would be of identical tenor.

Mr. Keefe. I see. Do you recall at that time that when Captain Duncan came in he stated that he had communicated with the Public Relations Department of the Navy and that it was all right for them to take pictures or for you to make a statement? Do you recall him making this statement?

Captain Kramer. I believe that at one time, either just before or just after that interview with the press, he indicated that the Public Relations Office desired to arrange an interview in the Navy Department that afternoon.

Mr. Keefe. No; I am asking you that specific question.

Isn't it a fact before any newspaper reporters or photographers were in that there was some objection expressed by me to the fact of their taking pictures or having newspaper reporters there and did not Dr. Duncan say that he had taken the matter up with the Public Relations Department of the Navy and that it was all right to take the pictures and make a statement at that time?

Captain Kramer. You are very likely precisely accurate in that respect, sir.

Mr. Keefe. All right. I don't like this "very likely" and "very probably." Isn't that it exactly.

CAPTAIN KRAMER. I used that "very likely," Mr. Keefe, because I do not recall precisely. If I attempted to refresh my memory I probably could.

MR. KEEFE. Isn't that precisely correct, Captain Kramer?

CAPTAIN KRAMER. I think it is, sir.

MR. KEEFE. Yes, you think it is, of course.

Well, now, Pearl Harbor happened, and the Secretary of the Navy flew out to Pearl Harbor to see what had happened, and while he was gone the first person that talked to you about the situation, as I understand your testimony, was the Under Secretary of the Navy, Mr. Forrestal, then acting as Secretary of the Navy.

He requested you, during the absence of Secretary Knox, to prepare a file showing the intercepts, is that correct?

CAPTAIN KRAMER. Mr. Forrestal did not request me. I was directed, as I recall, by Captain McCollum to prepare a folder, which I was given to understand Mr. Forrestal desired to see.

[4079] MR. KEEFE. Well, all right, we will go through the chain of command, then. It went from Forrestal to your superior, McCollum, and from McCollum to you; is that right?

CAPTAIN KRAMER. That is undoubtedly correct, yes, sir.

MR. KEEFE. By virtue of that order, or command, you then assembled the file and went to Mr. Forrestal?

CAPTAIN KRAMER. Accompanied by Captain McCollum, yes, sir.

MR. KEEFE. So you and Captain McCollum discussed the intercepts for the first time during the absence of Secretary Knox with Under Secretary, and Acting Secretary, Forrestal?

CAPTAIN KRAMER. Yes, sir.

MR. KEEFE. Now, following that, who was the next person that you talked with, that you can now recall, with respect to Pearl Harbor, and the incidents prior thereto, during the month of December, or at any other time, in relation to Pearl Harbor?

CAPTAIN KRAMER. Other than the usual conversations I might have had with normal recipients of this traffic, the identical type of conversations that I would have had through 1941. The only time I discussed in detail any events connected with Pearl Harbor was when I testified before the court of Admiral Murfin with one exception; that was Admiral Halsey.

MR. KEEFE. All right.

Now, you did talk with Admiral Halsey. When was that, and where?

CAPTAIN KRAMER. About May 1944, at the headquarters building of Admiral Halsey in Noumea, New Caledonia.

MR. KEEFE. Was that after you had received the letter from Captain Safford which has been introduced in evidence?

CAPTAIN KRAMER. Some months after, yes, sir.

MR. KEEFE. And what was the occasion of your talk with Admiral Halsey?

CAPTAIN KRAMER. A letter from Admiral Kimmell to Admiral Halsey. It was a personal letter.

Four. American Penetration of Codes

MR. KEEFE. Did you see the letter?
CAPTAIN KRAMER. I did, sir.
MR. KEEFE. All right.
Is that letter in existence?
CAPTAIN KRAMER. I do not know whether the original is or not, sir. I have a copy of it.
MR. KEEFE. Well, where is the copy?
CAPTAIN KRAMER. Here [handing document to Mr. Keefe].
MR. KEEFE. Now, as I understand it, Admiral Halsey called you to his command post, or office, and told you that he had received a letter from Admiral Kimmel?
CAPTAIN KRAMER. Yes, sir.
MR. KEEFE. How did you get the copy of that letter?
CAPTAIN KRAMER. The letter requests that I prepare answers in the form of a deposition to certain questions propounded in that letter.
MR. KEEFE. Did you prepare such answers?
CAPTAIN KRAMER. I prepared no deposition as such. I did prepare, however, an answer to Captain Safford's second letter, which I felt [4080] was in the nature of a deposition, in case I wanted to comply with Admiral Kimmel's request.
MR. KEEFE. Well, did you comply with Admiral Kimmel's request?
CAPTAIN KRAMER. I did not, sir, other than what I have outlined.
MR. KEEFE. Well, did you give to Admiral Halsey the answers to the questions that Admiral Kimmel had asked?
CAPTAIN KRAMER. Well, when I went to Admiral Halsey's office, at his request, he showed me the letter, which I read. He indicated that he would leave it entirely to me as to whether or not I should comply with that request.

After reading the letter, I felt that hte questions covered in that letter were of such limited character as regarding the events preceding Pearl Harbor, that a broader picture of events should be given Admiral Halsey.

In fact, my idea was to give a pretty thorough picture of the events as I knew them to Admiral Halsey, and request his advice on what I should do.

I did not, during the course of that first interview.

What I did request, however, was that I be given that letter, and I had in mind preparing a full reply to Captain Safford's second letter, which I felt would pretty thoroughly cover those events, that I would like a few days to prepare that reply and would then have something to show him, and would give him a fairly comprehensive picture of it. [. . .]

[4184] SENATOR FERGUSON. Well, are there any other officers that you have discussed it with not as to detail?
CAPTAIN KRAMER. Yes, sir; there are.
SENATOR FERGUSON. And will you name them?
CAPTAIN KRAMER. Colonel Laswell, Commander Rennick, Commander Benedict, Commander Hudson. In any case officers attached to the fleet radio

unit at Pearl Harbor who were long-standing friends of mine and working in this kind of work.

SENATOR FERGUSON. Did you ever discuss it with Bratton?

CAPTAIN KRAMER. Not that I have any recollection of, sir.

SENATOR FERGUSON. You have had no conversations whatever with Bratton about the testimony or about the Pearl Harbor matter?

CAPTAIN KRAMER. No, sir.

SENATOR FERGUSON. Since the Navy board?

CAPTAIN KRAMER. Either before or after the Navy board, sir.

SENATOR FERGUSON. Did you discuss it with Baecher?

CAPTAIN KRAMER. There was some discussion concerning the availability of records to which I for the first time had access in December last year and chiefly my discussion with Baecher was concerning appointments with counsel for this committee and Mr. Baecher. Details concerning the content of my prior testimony or of testimony I would give I did not discuss with Mr. Baecher.

SENATOR FERGUSON. And he asked you nothing about any of the points that you have covered?

CAPTAIN KRAMER. No, sir.

SENATOR FERGUSON. Can you tell me just what the occasion was that you took these letters to him and the Halsey memorandum? Had he asked you or did you just volunteer that?

CAPTAIN KRAMER. I volunteered that, sir.

SENATOR FERGUSON. There wasn't any request?

CAPTAIN KRAMER. No, sir; it was not.

SENATOR FERGUSON. Well, you were greatly worried, were you not, sometime in September and October, you were worried?

CAPTAIN KRAMER. Of what year, sir?

SENATOR FERGUSON. This last year, 1945.

CAPTAIN KRAMER. About what, sir?

SENATOR FERGUSON. Well, I am just asking you whether you were worried?

CAPTAIN KRAMER. Not that I have any recollection of, no, sir.

SENATOR LUCAS. Unless it is about Pearl Harbor I think it is an improper question to ask him.

SENATOR FERGUSON. This is in relation to Pearl Harbor or I would not have asked him.

SENATOR LUCAS. You said "about anything."

CAPTAIN KRAMER. I had some concern about my health. I don't think I recall any worry, sir.

SENATOR FERGUSON. There was nothing worrying you at that time that you went to the hospital?

[4185] CAPTAIN KRAMER. No, sir; there was not.

SENATOR FERGUSON. Did you know that a letter had been written to your wife requesting her to come up on account of you worrying about something?

CAPTAIN KRAMER. With respect to my health, yes, sir.

SENATOR FERGUSON. Well, no, worrying about Pearl Harbor—or not Pearl Harbor but having something on your mind that you were greatly concerned with?

SENATOR LUCAS. Mr. Chairman, I think this is a highly improper question to ask this witness.

SENATOR FERGUSON. It only relates to Pearl Harbor.

CAPTAIN KRAMER. I am willing to answer that question.

SENATOR LUCAS. Well, I know, but there is a limit to everything. The Senator from Michigan now is asking this question about whether the witness was worrying about anything.

SENATOR FERGUSON. No, about Pearl Harbor.

SENATOR LUCAS. But you don't go back to Pearl Harbor. If you confine it to Pearl Harbor, all right.

CAPTAIN KRAMER. I would like, Senator Lucas, to answer that question.

THE CHAIRMAN. The Chair thinks the witness is willing to answer that question and probably can do so satisfactorily.

CAPTAIN KRAMER. At no time while I was in the Naval Hospital at Bethesda, either for the check-up during August or for my subsequent stay in the hospital in September or October, did I have any worries or concern about what I knew about Pearl Harbor, or any discussions with anyone about either my prior testimony, or what I knew about Pearl Harbor.

I did have a brief discussion, which I have previously indicated in my testimony, with a classmate of mine, namely, Commander Powell, to the effect—and this bears particularly on your question, sir—that I might be called as a witness before the contemplated congressional hearing.

SENATOR FERGUSON. That is what I am talking about, Pearl Harbor.

CAPTAIN KRAMER. Yes, sir.

SENATOR FERGUSON. I am not talking about anything else.

CAPTAIN KRAMER. Yes, sir.

SENATOR FERGUSON. All right.

Now you had some concern as to whether or not you would be called as a witness?

CAPTAIN KRAMER. No concern whatsoever sir. It was simply a conversation in which Halsey mentioned, I believe, as I now recollect it, something to the effect that I was working on things connected with Pearl Harbor in Washington at that time.

SENATOR FERGUSON. Did you appreciate at that time that your testimony, that is, your so-called affidavit which you say now you did not swear to, but you considered it as such, that if you died, it was to be taken as your evidence in any case in which it might arise, and what you said at the Pearl Harbor board, that there may be a conflict in those two statements?

CAPTAIN KRAMER. I was unaware of any such conflict, sir.

[4186] SENATOR FERGUSON. And therefore, there was no concern over the fact that you had a memorandum, and you had also testified in relation to the matter before the Pearl Harbor board?

CAPTAIN KRAMER. That is precisely correct, sir.

SENATOR FERGUSON. You had also testified before the Hewitt committee. Now, was there any concern over the fact that there may be a conflict between your testimony, that is, your memorandum and your testimony before the Pearl Harbor board, and your testimony before the Hewitt committee?

CAPTAIN KRAMER. None whatsoever, sir. I at no time had concern about the few facts with which I was familiar concerning Pearl Harbor.

SENATOR FERGUSON. And, as I understand it, as far as you were concerned, there were no conflicts between those three?

CAPTAIN KRAMER. That is correct, sir.

SENATOR FERGUSON. Were you concerned over your testimony before this board, that it might conflict with one or more of the testimonies that you had given?

CAPTAIN KRAMER. None whatsoever, sir. In fact, it was not until I began studying these documents in December last, that I was aware of such conflicts.

SENATOR FERGUSON. When did you discover that there were some conflicts?

CAPTAIN KRAMER. I learned of certain minor discrepancies, such as the fact that I had previously testified that Commander Wellborn was in Admiral Stark's office on Sunday morning, but it appeared to be not true, inasmuch as Commander Wellborn was not in the Navy Department on Sunday, or at least Sunday morning at all, during the luncheon engagement which I previously testified to at Admiral Stark's home in talking with Captain McCollum.

SENATOR FERGUSON. I do not want any more detail on that, because you have already covered that; isn't that true?

CAPTAIN KRAMER. Yes, sir.

[3967] MR. MURPHY. Now, sir; I would like to review with you your testimony before the Hewitt inquiry. You stated at page 128:

> The evaluation was normally done by Commander McCollum, the head of the Far Eastern Section, or Admiral Wilkinson, but I gave them the benefit of my opinion about it too.

Is that so?

CAPTAIN KRAMER. That is correct, sir.

MR. MURPHY. You stated on page 129, that you had seen those two dispatches set forth on pages 154 and 155 of Exhibit 1. That would be Circular 2353 and Circular 2354, would it not?

CAPTAIN KRAMER. Yes, sir.

MR. MURPHY. Then you were asked if you had seen the dispatch marked "exhibit No. 3" from Alusna, Batavia, and you said:

> I do not recall having seen that.

Which one was that? Would that be the one sent to the Pacific, or would that be the so-called Foote dispatch?

CAPTAIN KRAMER. No, sir; it would be the dispatch from the United States Naval Liaison Officer stationed in Batavia.

MR. MURPHY. And distinct from either 2353, 2354, and the so-called dispatch that we received by way of Admiral Hart?

CAPTAIN KRAMER. That is right, sir.

[3968] MR. MURPHY. At page 130, you stated:

> We were very interested in seeing any of this traffic after the thing was set up, which was about the end of November, but traffic did not appear in this system until the 7th of December and the latter part of December, 1941.

I take it at that time you were talking about the hidden word dispatches.

CAPTAIN KRAMER. Mr. Murphy, until I was shown a photostat of the hidden word message during Admiral Hewitt's hearing, I was still under the impression that the dispatch received Sunday morning was a winds message.

MR. MURPHY. Is is not a fact that from December 7, 1941, down to the time you testified before Admiral Hewitt, you thought the December 7 dispatch was an execute of the winds code?

CAPTAIN KRAMER. Yes, sir; that is correct.

MR. MURPHY. Now, I take you to the bottom of page 130:

> CAPTAIN KRAMER. That is correct. That refreshes my memory now. I remember now that you remind me of it, that these reams of plain language traffic that we were getting in, several weeks before Pearl Harbor, were searched for that indicator. That, however, I didn't recall specifically, because I didn't do the searching. It was done by the GY watch officers.
>
> ADMIRAL HEWITT. I believe that about the middle of the first week of December, there was a teletype message which, to the best of your recollection, one of the watch officers had in his possession and which was subsequently delivered to Admiral Noyes. Will you tell me about that to the best of your recollection?
>
> CAPTAIN KRAMER. I previously testified on that matter at Pearl Harbor, Admiral. I would like to go over that previous testimony again in the light of thinking it over since that time.
>
> I had no recollction of that message at the time it was first mentioned to me in the spring of 1944. However, after being given some of the details of the circumstances surrounding it, I did recall a message some days before 7 December 1941, I believe about the middle of the week 1–7 December, and I do recall definitely being shown such a message by the GY watch officer and walking down with him to Captain Safford's office, and being present while the GY watch officer turned it over to him.
>
> A brief conversation ensued, and Captain Safford then took it, I assumed, to Admiral Noyes, since that message we had all been on the qui vive about for a week or ten days.
>
> That is the last I saw of such a message.
>
> ADMIRAL HEWITT. Can you recall what the general subject of the message was?

Was Kramer Pressured?

Now this is important. You speak up above about the one on December 7 and here, as I understand it, you are describing the one you saw with Safford.

> ADMIRAL HEWITT. Can you recall what the general subject of the message was?
>
> CAPTAIN KRAMER. It was, as I recall it, a "winds" code message. The wording of it I do not recall. It may have been, "Higashi no kaze ame," specifically referring to the United States, as I have previously testified at Pearl Harbor, but I am less positive of that now than I believe I was at that time. The reason for revision in my view on that is the fact that in thinking it over, I have a rather sharp recollection in the latter part of that week of feeling there was still no overt mention or specific mention of the United States in any of this traffic, which I was seeing all of and which also was the only source in general of my information since I did not see, as a rule, the dispatches from the Fleet Commanders or going outto them from Operations.

Is your memory more clear now than it was then on that subject, or do you still feel the same way?

CAPTAIN KRAMER. I still feel the same way regarding the precise wording of that piece of teletype. I, however, am thoroughly convinced from my study of the papers in the last few days, in the last few weeks, that the United States did not appear on that thing. That is my current conviction.

[3969] At the time I was testifying in previous hearings I had not thought particularly about this. In fact, the first time that there was occasion to think about it at all was in preparing my reply to Captain Safford's first letter, in which there is no mention or reference to what country was involved.

MR. MURPHY. Well, Admiral Hewitt then said to you:

> Then it is still your belief, the best you can recall in view of that, there was no indication—
>
> CAPTAIN KRAMER. I would like to continue that statement, Admiral, by saying: For that reason I am now at least under the impression that the message referred to England and possibly the Dutch rather than the United States, although it may have referred to the United States, too.

CAPTAIN KRAMER. That is simply because I was unpositive, and still am unpositive, of the precise wording.

MR. MURPHY. Then Admiral Hewitt says:

> Or possibly it may have referred to Russia?
> CAPTAIN KRAMER. I just don't recall.

Now Admiral Hewitt said:

> Reference to one or more of the messages supplied by the FCC is in Exhibit 65. Can you recall whether any of those may have been seen by you?

Is it your recollection that you did or did not see any of those?
CAPTAIN KRAMER. I believe I saw some of those; yes, sir.
MR. MURPHY. You said then:

> CAPTAIN KRAMER. This document 1 is not a message and document 4 is the one of the 8th of December about midnight GMT. I may have seen these specific messages. I cannot be certain, however, because we saw a great many messages of this kind in looking for this particular type of "winds" code message. When we started monitoring all Japanese plain language some weeks before Pearl Harbor, the volume of material coming in was simply tremendous, swamping. We had only three linguists at the time for translation purposes, with a pretty heavy volume of coded traffic concerning the negotiations. Consequently, we felt the extra burden of having to scan all this Japanese plain language stuff and there were many instances of weather occurring in that, but because of the fact that the particular code thing we were looking for, we felt it was incumbent on us to examine it all. The reason I cannot state specifically that these particular ones were ones I had seen, but they were of the same nature as many I did see.

Then at the bottom of the page Admiral Hewitt said:

> My understanding is that when that was first decoded, the word "minami," which related to the United States, was overlooked, so that the translation merely referred to England. Is that your recollection?
> CAPTAIN KRAMER. Last summer when that question of the late morning of 7 December had come up at Pearl Harbor, my recollection had been that it was a "winds" message. It wasn't until I saw these exhibits yesterday afternoon—

and that would be sometime between May and July of 1945, would it not?
CAPTAIN KRAMER. That is correct, sir.
MR. MURPHY. Your testimony was on Tuesday, May 22, 1945, so I take it that you saw the message on May 21, the day before.
CAPTAIN KRAMER. I believe that is correct, sir. [...]
[4054] SENATOR FERGUSON. Now, Captain, do you reconcile your testimony before the Pearl Harbor Navy Board, the Hewitt committee, and this committee, as far as the winds message is concerned? You know what I speak of when I say wind message. This is the one implementing the wind messages.
CAPTAIN KRAMER. Yes, sir.
SENATOR FERGUSON. Now, do you claim that they are consistent?
CAPTAIN KRAMER. I would state in that respect that they are not consistent, that until a few days ago I was testifying purely from memory after several years, that only in the last few days has my memory been refreshed from an examination of these documents in that respect, sir.
SENATOR FERGUSON. In other words, you don't claim now, and I am going to ask you later exactly what documents you had to refresh your memory, but you don't claim now that your testimony in relation to the winds message is consistent?

CAPTAIN KRAMER. It is not inconsistent in any respect except as to the date involved.

SENATOR FERGUSON. Now, you say that your testimony is the same except as to date?

CAPTAIN KRAMER. I believe that is the case, sir.

SENATOR FERGUSON. Now, I just want to take a short time, if I may, on this testimony. This I am taking from the Pearl Harbor Court of Inquiry of 1944.

MR. MURPHY. Page?

SENATOR FERGUSON. On the bottom of page 956:

> Because of that special arrangement for this particular plain language message, when such a message came through, I believe either the third or the fourth of December—

You were not certain. You are not really contradicting the date there.

CAPTAIN KRAMER. No, sir.

SENATOR FERGUSON (reading):

> —I was shown such a message by the GY watch officer, recognizing it as being of this nature, walked with him to Captain Safford's office, and from that point Captain Safford took the ball. I believe Captain Safford went directly to Admiral Noyes' office at that time. Again, because of the fact that this was a plain language message, and because of the fact that special arrangements had been made to handle this Japanese plain language message which had special meaning, I did not handle the distribution of this particular message, the one of the 3rd or 4th.

Now, that is perfectly consistent with your present testimony, is it not?

CAPTAIN KRAMER. I believe it is, yes, sir.

SENATOR FERGUSON. Because you used the two dates.

CAPTAIN KRAMER. What was that last remark, Senator?

[4055] SENATOR FERGUSON. You used the two dates there, the 3d or 4th.

CAPTAIN KRAMER. Yes, sir. My impression was a few days before Pearl Harbor, probably about the middle of the week.

SENATOR FERGUSON (reading):

> Q. You say it is your recollection that you received some Japanese plain language words which corresponded with the language set out in Document 15; is that correct?
> A. My statement was, not that I received it, but I was shown it.
> Q. Can you recall from looking at Document 15, which Japanese language words you received?

That is question 34.

> A. Higashi no kazeame, I am quite certain. The literal meaning of higashi no kazeame is east wind rain. That is plain Japanese language. The sense of

that, however, meant strained relations or a break in relations, possibly even implying war with a nation to the eastward, the United States.

Now, it was not suggested in the question any Japanese words. Nothing was suggested in the question. It says:

> Can you recall from looking at Document 15 which Japanese language words you received.

And you answered in that language.

Now, is that consistent with your present testimony?

CAPTAIN KRAMER. I believe it is, sir, in the light of what I stated yesterday afternoon in that regard, that until I testified before that hearing I had had no occasion whatsoever to recall or refresh my memory. I do not believe it was ever discussed as to what country was involved in that wind message which I saw. My reaction at the time when that question was first propounded was that in view of the fact we were in the midst of a serious war with Japan, it of course must have been the United States.

I had well in mind the Japanese expressions referring to the United States.

SENATOR FERGUSON. But wouldn't it stand to reason that a spontaneous answer made by you at that time, and after you had received Captain Safford's memorandum and had answered him on the 28th or sometime about that time, the 22d of December 1943, your answer that you had been thinking about this, wouldn't a spontaneous answer be correct? Do you now dispute that answer?

CAPTAIN KRAMER. I was faulty in my recollection at that time, yes, sir.

SENATOR FERGUSON. And you want to now dispute that answer?

CAPTAIN KRAMER. Yes, sir. I think I have clearly indicated that fact already in this hearing.

SENATOR FERGUSON. Well, you told me you thought your testimony was correct, that you didn't want to change it except as to date?

CAPTAIN KRAMER. On that point, Senator, I pointed out yesterday, I think, that later on in that hearing I testified to the effect that in all this traffic, which was my primary source of information at the time of Pearl Harbor, there was still nothing to indicate Japanese overt intentions toward the United States, except the message from Tokyo to Berlin at about the end of November.

SENATOR FERGUSON. Well, that was an overt act, was it not; that was a proposition that they were going to war?

CAPTAIN KRAMER. Yes, sir.

[4056] SENATOR FERGUSON. Now, do you swear, as you did swear, as you did swear before the Pearl Harbor Board, before three of your own admirals, that that statement is false, that I read to you?

CAPTAIN KRAMER. That is my present belief; yes, sir.

SENATOR FERGUSON. Is it any more than your belief? Are you certain about it?

CAPTAIN KRAMER. It is conviction, too, sir.

SENATOR FERGUSON. So, then, you contradict your testimony in its entirety as far as that answer is concerned?

CAPTAIN KRAMER. So far as that point is concerned; yes, sir.

SENATOR FERGUSON (reading):

> Q. Do you remember in what form this communication was that you saw which contained the words about which you have testified, higashi no kazeame?
> A. I am almost certain it was typewritten. I believe it was on teletype paper.

Is that true or false?

CAPTAIN KRAMER. That is still my recollection on that, sir.

SENATOR FERGUSON. Is that correct?

CAPTAIN KRAMER. I believe it is; yes, sir.

SENATOR FERGUSON. Then you saw those words on the typewritten paper?

CAPTAIN KRAMER. I saw certain words on this typewritten paper which I have repeatedly emphasized I do not precisely recall. It was, and this is the only thing on which I am certain of in that respect, of the winds code characters.

SENATOR FERGUSON. I read you another question, question number 143:

> Q. Were you the officer who went to the Communications Officer and said, "Here it is"?
> A. I believe I used that expression when I accompanied the watch officer to Commander Safford's office.

Now, is that a true or false answer?

CAPTAIN KRAMER. That could very well be true; yes, sir.

MR. MURPHY. For the record, that is on page 980 of the Naval Court of Inquiry.

SENATOR FERGUSON. Now, you appeared before the Hewitt committee, did you not?

CAPTAIN KRAMER. I did, sir.

SENATOR FERGUSON. Had you talked to anyone before you appeared at the Hewitt Committee?

CAPTAIN KRAMER. Yes, sir; I did.

SENATOR FERGUSON. With whom did you talk?

CAPTAIN KRAMER. To an assistant of Admiral Hewitt's, a Lieutenant or Lieutenant Commander Sonnett.

SENATOR FERGUSON. Will you tell me your conversation with him?

CAPTAIN KRAMER. I saw him perhaps three or four times. The total time of those several talks I do not believe amounted to more than three-quarters of an hour. The nature of those conversations were of precisely the same kind that I had engaged in on occasions in the past when I was involved in legal duties in the Navy, namely—

SENATOR FERGUSON. Are you a lawyer?

CAPTAIN KRAMER. No, sir. Every line officer, however, is required to take examinations on Navy law for each promotion in normal times.

[4057] SENATOR FERGUSON. All right. Did he make any suggestions to you, did he show you any papers?

CAPTAIN KRAMER. I recollect being shown no papers, sir, although he may have. I believe some dispatches were shown me. I recollect being shown no copies of the transcript of previous hearings I testified before, Admiral Murfin's. It was chiefly conversation with regard to discrepancies between my testimony and other witnesses before previous hearings.

SENATOR FERGUSON. And what he did was to discuss with you the discrepancy between your testimony and other witnesses who testified before the Navy Board?

CAPTAIN KRAMER. That is in effect correct.

SENATOR FERGUSON. And therefore I assume that he pointed out what the other witnesses had testified to and what you had testified to?

CAPTAIN KRAMER. The chief subject of conversation was concerning this winds thing in which it appeared my discrepancies chiefly rested.

SENATOR FERGUSON. Now, he stated to you then that your testimony was not in accordance with other witnesses' testimony [...] in relation to the winds message, wasn't it then by necessity necessary for him to tell you what these other witnesses had testified to?

CAPTAIN KRAMER. Just what his source of information was in making statements to me I do not know, sir.

SENATOR FERGUSON. What did he say to you about the other testimony?

CAPTAIN KRAMER. That my testimony differed from other witnesses.

[4058] SENATOR FERGUSON. How did it differ?

CAPTAIN KRAMER. In respect primarily to the existence of any wind-system message.

SENATOR FERGUSON. I take it then that he stated to you that other people had testified that it didn't exist?

CAPTAIN KRAMER. Yes, sir.

SENATOR FERGUSON. And you had testified that it did exist?

CAPTAIN KRAMER. Yes, sir.

SENATOR FERGUSON. That is correct?

CAPTAIN KRAMER. That is correct, sir.

SENATOR FERGUSON. And what did he say about that, what was wrong about that?

CAPTAIN KRAMER. Whatever he said about that I do not precisely recall, Senator, but I insisted on the accuracy to my best recollection of what I had previously testified to.

SENATOR FERGUSON. And did you so testify before him?

CAPTAIN KRAMER. I did not testify before him, but before Admiral Hewitt, I believe in his presence.

SENATOR FERGUSON. In other words, you kept to that first testimony before Admiral Hewitt; you didn't change?

CAPTAIN KRAMER. To my first testimony before Admiral Murfin and his court.

SENATOR FERGUSON. In other words, what Sonnett told you didn't cause you to change your testimony and you kept to the same testimony before Admiral Hewitt?

CAPTAIN KRAMER. In most respects no change whatsoever, sir.

SENATOR FERGUSON. Was there any relation to the winds message?

CAPTAIN KRAMER. The only respect in which it differed — and, incidentally, I might state I never read to date the transcript of either the Court of Inquiry or the Board of Investigation, except certain parts of my testimony in the Court of Inquiry, not all of it, and such parts as appear in the Naval Narrative — I stated that in the light of thinking about that thing since my previous testimony, in which I believe he pointed out to me what you have just pointed out to me, that I testified it referred to the United States, that I believed that recollection was false at the time of these conversations. At the time of these conversations I was still unaware of what my subsequent testimony before Admiral Murfin's Board was, which I have referred to.

SENATOR FERGUSON. But didn't he tell you what your testimony was before the Murfin Board?

CAPTAIN KRAMER. No, sir; except in general terms.

SENATOR FERGUSON. Well, now, did he tell you they were only taking testimony of those witnesses that had seen the winds code?

CAPTAIN KRAMER. That was not the impression I gathered whatsoever, sir. I gained the distinct impression that the chief purpose of Admiral Hewitt's inquiry or investigation was to fill in the gaps in previous hearings, specifically this I had first-hand knowledge of from being in the South Pacific, to get the testimony of Captain McCollum and Admiral Wilkinson who had not previously testified before a naval inquiry, also to reconcile discrepancies before this previous hearing.

[4059] SENATOR FERGUSON. And he stated that the discrepancies were so that you would have an opportunity to change your testimony if you wanted to?

CAPTAIN KRAMER. If I wanted to; yes, sir.

SENATOR FERGUSON. Now, I want to read from the Hewitt investigation. Your testimony was taken on the 7th and 8th days.

MR. MURPHY. What page?

SENATOR FERGUSON. 151. I am going to read the record of the 8th day before Admiral Hewitt. It is the 23d day of May 1945. Your previous testimony had been on the 22d day of May 1945. [Reading]:

> Pursuant to notice, the investigation met at the offices of the General Board, Navy Department, at 2 p.m., Wednesday, 23 May 1945.

> Present: Admiral H. Kent Hewitt, U.S.N.; Mr. John S. Sonnett; Lt. Comdr. Benjamin H. Griswold, U.S.N.R.; and Ship's Clerk Ben Harold, U.S.N.R.
> ADMIRAL HEWITT. Careful consideration has been given to the evidence concerning the so-called "winds" message with a view to determining whether or not Read Admiral Leigh Noyes, U.S.N. formerly Director of Naval Communications, should be called as a witness. It appears from the testimony of Captain Safford that he thought that a "winds" message relating to the United States was received about 4 December 1941 and was shown to him by Captain Kramer and a watch officer and then delivered to Admiral Noyes. It appears from the testimony of Captain Kramer that he believes that there was some such message at about that time, but that he cannot recall whether or not it referred to the United States, and he is under the impression that it referred to England and possibly to the Dutch rather than to the United States although it *may*—

and "may" is underscored,

> —have referred to the United States also. Captain Kramer believed that the message in question was delivered to Admiral Noyes. There is yet no other evidence to the effect that a "winds" code message relating to the United States was received.
> Upon review of the sworn testimony of Admiral Noyes, given before the Naval Court of Inquiry, it appears that he recalled no such message and that he did not believe that any such message relating to the United States had ever been received by the Navy, although he had some recollection of a "false alarm." Accordingly, I find that no useful purpose would be served by calling Admiral Noyes as a witness in this investigation, and direct that the portions of his previous testimony relating to this subject be incorporated in this record. This decision will be reconsidered should further evidence be developed indicating that a useful purpose would be served by reexamining Admiral Noyes.
> (The extracts of testimony of Rear Admiral Leigh Noyes, U.S.N., before the Naval Court of Inquiry, follow.)

And then they put in certain questions and certain answers.
Now, is his description of your testimony a fair analysis of your testimony?
CAPTAIN KRAMER. I believe it is, sir.
MR. MURPHY. Will the Senator yield?
SENATOR FERGUSON. Yes.
MR. MURPHY. At page 7969 of the Naval Court of Inquiry, question 96:

> Q. Do I understand you to mean that your Section could not have stated categorically that the message meant war or merely a break in diplomatic relations but that all three of those possibilities were available to anyone interpreting that message?
> A. That is precisely correct. I can definitely state that I would not interpret that message as meaning definitely war.

[4060] That is also in the Naval Court of Inquiry.
CAPTAIN KRAMER. Yes, sir.

SENATOR FERGUSON. Are you through, Mr. Murphy?

MR. MURPHY. Yes, sir.

SENATOR FERGUSON. Coming back to your testimony, Captain Kramer, testifying before Admiral Hewitt, after your memory had been refreshed as to whether or not it conflicted with other witnesses, you said this:

> I would like to continue the statement, Admiral, by saying for that reason I am now at least under the impression that the message referred to England and possibly the Dutch rather than the United States, although it may have referred to the United States, too.
>
> Or possibly it may have referred to Russia? —

Hewitt said. Said Captain Kramer:

> I just don't recall.

CAPTAIN KRAMER. In that connection, Senator, I would like to point out that my only intention in stating that I did not recall was that I did not and still do not recall precisely the wording of that piece of teletype paper.

SENATOR FERGUSON. All right.

Now, I want to read some answers that are in Admiral Noyes' testimony and ask you if you can enlighten me on those answers. Did you ever talk to Admiral Noyes on this question?

CAPTAIN KRAMER. I have never seen Admiral Noyes since a few days, possibly as late as a month, after Pearl Harbor.

SENATOR FERGUSON. Did you talk to him about Pearl Harbor?

CAPTAIN KRAMER. I recollect no conversations although there may have been.

SENATOR FERGUSON. Just recently did you meet with any admirals or any Navy men to discuss your testimony or discuss Pearl Harbor?

CAPTAIN KRAMER. Yes, sir.

SENATOR FERGUSON. Who were they?

CAPTAIN KRAMER. Admiral Stark, Admiral Schuirmann and Captain McCollum.

SENATOR FERGUSON. And where did you meet and when?

CAPTAIN KRAMER. At Admiral Stark's home last fall.

SENATOR FERGUSON. About when?

CAPTAIN KRAMER. It was, I believe, the middle or latter part of September.

SENATOR FERGUSON. That was after this inquiry was started?

CAPTAIN KRAMER. I do not believe the inquiry had started then but was directed to be started.

MR. KEEFE. Will the Senator, as we are going along, to save time later, will you ascertain whether or not this meeting wasn't just before Captain Kramer went to the hospital?

SENATOR FERGUSON. Was it, Captain, just before you went to the hospital?

Captain Kramer. It was a few days before I went to the hospital for the second time. The first time I had gone there for a routine check-up and remained there for about a week, following which I was given sick leave and went to Miami.

Senator Ferguson. But this second time was before you went back to the hospital the second time?

[4061]   Captain Kramer. That is correct, sir.

Senator Ferguson. All right. Now, how long were you, Admiral Stark, Admiral Schirmann, and Captain McCollum together?

Captain Kramer. For a period of about 1 hour, perhaps one hour and a half, most of which time we were at lunch.

Senator Ferguson. Well, did you discuss Pearl Harbor?

Captain Kramer. We discussed some aspects of it; yes, sir.

Senator Ferguson. What were the aspects?

Captain Kramer. The principal one that stands out in my mind now, and I have referred to being refreshed on this point before this hearing by Captain McCollum, is with respect to the presence or absence of Admiral Stark's flag secretary, Commander Wellborn, or of Captain McCollum in Admiral Stark's office that Sunday morning.

Senator Ferguson. How did you get to Admiral Stark's home? I mean were you invited, called up, or by letter or what?

Captain Kramer. Yes, sir; I had a short note from him inviting me to a luncheon.

Senator Ferguson. At a specific time?

Captain Kramer. At a specific date and time; yes, sir.

Senator Ferguson. Did he tell you who would be there?

Captain Kramer. No, sir. I did not know until I arrived there.

Senator Ferguson. Well, now, going back to this question, one of the questions brought up was as to what time Admiral Stark got down and whether there was a conference in his office at a certain time Sunday morning?

Captain Kramer. That was the chief point that now stands out in my memory that we specifically discussed. The other things that we discussed were of a very general nature. It was largely and primarily a social affair and we discussed old times at that luncheon.

Senator Ferguson. Well, at that time Pearl Harbor was rather old.

Captain Kramer. Of course it was, sir.

Senator Ferguson. Yes. And do you now tell us that that is all of the conversation that you had at this meeting with Admiral Stark as it related to Pearl Harbor?

Captain Kramer. Senator, at no time during that luncheon do I recall that any details such as this winds message were discussed. It was very general in nature.

Senator Ferguson. Did you find out or ask Admiral Stark where he was Saturday night that you could not reach him on the telephone?

CAPTAIN KRAMER. That point came up, too; yes, sir.

SENATOR FERGUSON. And what did he say as to where he had been?

CAPTAIN KRAMER. My recollection now is that he does not or did not remember to this date where he was that particular night.

SENATOR FERGUSON. Did you mention that you had tried to reach him?

CAPTAIN KRAMER. I did, sir.

FDR on the Final Pre-War Diplomatic Intercept: "This Means War"

LESTER ROBERT SCHULZ, PRESENT WHEN THE
COMMUNICATION WAS READ BY THE PRESIDENT

Joint Congressional Investigation

[4659]   MR. RICHARDSON. Will you state your full name, please?
COMMANDER SCHULZ. Lester Robert Schulz.
MR. RICHARDSON. How long have you been in the Navy, Commander?
[4660]   COMMANDER SCHULZ. Since June 1930, beginning as a midshipman.
MR. RICHARDSON. Were you in Washington during November and December 1941?
COMMANDER SCHULZ. Yes, sir: I was.
MR. RICHARDSON. What was your assignment for duty in Washington during the first week of December?
COMMANDER SCHULZ. I was under instruction in the Office of Naval Communications for communication intelligence. That was my permanent assignment. However, I was on temporary duty under verbal orders at the White House as a communications assistant to the Naval Aide, then Captain Beardall. Also, I had gone to Warm Springs in the same capacity the previous week end. Thus, my return to Washington, I believe, was Tuesday of that week.
MR. RICHARDSON. You were under Admiral Beardall?
COMMANDER SCHULZ. Yes, sir; that is correct.
MR. RICHARDSON. Who others of the Navy were occupying the same duty, a similar duty there under Beardall?
COMMANDER SCHULZ. On the 6th of December, I believe the morning of the 6th there was an Ensign Carson who was sent up to assist me. Actually he performed no duties that day and was simply being instructed and informed as to what his duties would be.
MR. RICHARDSON. What is your present assignment now?
COMMANDER SCHULZ. I am under orders at present to be executive officer of the *Indiana*, a battleship.

Source: Pearl Harbor Attack, *volume 10*.

MR. RICHARDSON. Were you on duty at the White House in Admiral Beardall's office there on the night of December 6, 1941?

COMMANDER SCHULZ. I was on duty in the White House. Admiral Beardall had no fixed office in the White House at that time. He conducted his business for the most part in the Navy Department in the Navy Building and I was given a small office in a corner of the mail room, a closed office, but it was not a place used by Admiral Beardall.

MR. RICHARDSON. That was at the White House?

COMMANDER SCHULZ. Yes, sir; it was.

MR. RICHARDSON. Do you recall Captain Kramer coming to the White House on the evening of December 6 to deliver any papers?

COMMANDER SCHULZ. Yes, sir; I do.

MR. RICHARDSON. About what time did he come?

COMMANDER SCHULZ. Between 9 and 10; I should say about 9:30.

MR. RICHARDSON. In the evening?

COMMANDER SCHULZ. In the evening; yes, sir.

MR. RICHARDSON. Who was there besides you?

COMMANDER SCHULZ. No one else of the Navy.

MR. RICHARDSON. To whom, if anyone, did Captain Kramer hand his papers?

COMMANDER SCHULZ. He handed them to me. They were in a locked pouch.

MR. RICHARDSON. Was that the customary way in which dispatches that were being delivered there were delivered?

COMMANDER SCHULZ. Material of that category was so delivered.

MR. RICHARDSON. What did you do with the locked pouch when it was handed to you?

[4661] COMMANDER SCHULZ. I took it from the mail room, which is in the office building, over to the White House proper and obtained permission to go up on the second floor and took it to the President's study.

MR. RICHARDSON. Did you go alone?

COMMANDER SCHULZ. I was accompanied by someone from the usher's office and announced to the President. However, then I was alone.

MR. RICHARDSON. But Captain Kramer did not go with you?

COMMANDER SCHULZ. That is correct, sir.

MR. RICHARDSON. How long from the time the papers were placed in your hands by Captain Kramer was it before you went to the President's study?

COMMANDER SCHULZ. About 5 minutes, I would say.

MR. RICHARDSON. Whom did you find in the study when you arrived there?

COMMANDER SCHULZ. The President was there seated at his desk, and Mr. Hopkins was there.

MR. RICHARDSON. That is Mr. Harry Hopkins?

COMMANDER SCHULZ. Yes, sir; that is correct.

MR. RICHARDSON. You knew him?

COMMANDER SCHULZ. Yes, sir. I had met him the previous day.

MR. RICHARDSON. And you knew the President?

COMMANDER SCHULZ. Yes, sir.

MR. RICHARDSON. Was the pouch still locked?

COMMANDER SCHULZ. I had a key to the pouch. I do not recall just when I unlocked it. In all likelihood it was after I was in the study, however.

MR. RICHARDSON. What did you do after you entered the study?

COMMANDER SCHULZ. I was announced and I informed the President that I had the material which Captain Kramer had brought and I took it out of the pouch.

MR. RICHARDSON. Did you make any further statement at the time with reference to the material, as to your having been told that it was important or not?

COMMANDER SCHULZ. That I do not recall, sir, but I believe that the President was expecting it. As I recall, he was.

MR. RICHARDSON. Why? What makes you believe that? Was there anything said, I mean, that would indicate that?

COMMANDER SCHULZ. When Admiral Beardall instructed me to stay and meet Captain Kramer and receive the material, he told me oif its important nature.

MR. RICHARDSON. Now, wait just a moment there.

COMMANDER SCHULZ. And my recollection was also that it was of such importance that the President expected to receive it.

MR. RICHARDSON. Before Captain Kramer came did you have a talk with Admiral Beardall with reference to the possibility of papers being delivered in the immediate future?

COMMANDER SCHULZ. Yes, sir; I did. That is why I stayed.

MR. RICHARDSON. What did Admiral Beardall say to you?

COMMANDER SCHULZ. He told me that during the evening Captain Kramer would bring up some magic material and that I was to take it and give it immediately to the President and he gave me the key to the pouch so that I could take it out and deliver it.

[4662] MR. RICHARDSON. That is the substance of your conversation with Admiral Beardall?

COMMANDER SCHULZ. Yes, sir; that is right.

MR. RICHARDSON. Well, now, when you presented the material to the President, was it in the pouch?

COMMANDER SCHULZ. To the best of my recollection I took it out of the pouch and handed it to him. The papers were clipped together. There were perhaps 15 typewritten pages and they were fastened together in a sheaf and I took them out of the pouch and handed them to the President personally.

MR. RICHARDSON. You know now what we mean when we talk about the first 13 parts of the 14-part message; you know what I am talking about?

COMMANDER SCHULZ. Yes, sir.

MR. RICHARDSON. Are you able to state now whether among the papers which were delivered to the President there were this 13 parts of what was eventually the 14-part message?

COMMANDER SCHULZ. No, sir; I cannot. I did not read the message. I have only learned of its substance through information that has been divulged during this inquiry, from newspapers and so on.

MR. RICHARDSON. All right. Now, what happened when you delivered these papers to the President? You remained there?

COMMANDER SCHULZ. Yes, sir; I remained in the room.

MR. RICHARDSON. What happened?

COMMANDER SCHULZ. The President read the papers, which took perhaps 10 minutes. Then he handed them to Mr. Hopkins.

MR. RICHARDSON. How far away from the President was Mr. Hopkins sitting?

COMMANDER SCHULZ. He was standing up, pacing back and forth slowly, not more than 10 feet away.

MR. RICHARDSON. Did the President read out loud when he was reading the papers?

COMMANDER SCHULZ. I do not recall that he did.

MR. RICHARDSON. All right. Now go ahead and give us in detail just what occurred there, if you please, Commander.

COMMANDER SCHULZ. Mr. Hopkins then read the papers and handed them back to the President. The President then turned toward Mr. Hopkins and said in substance—I am not sure of the exact words, but in substance—"This means war." Mr. Hopkins agreed, and they discussed then, for perhaps 5 minutes, the situation of the Japanese forces, that is, their deployment and—

MR. RICHARDSON. Can you recall what either of them said?

COMMANDER SCHULZ. In substance I can. There are only a few words that I can definitely say I am sure of, but the substance of it was that—I believe Mr. Hopkins mentioned it first—that since war was imminent, that the Japanese intended to strike when they were ready, at a moment when all was most opportune for them—

THE CHAIRMAN. When all was what?

COMMANDER SCHULZ. When all was most opportune for them. That is, when their forces were most properly deployed for their advantage. Indochina in particular was mentioned, because the Japanese forces [4663] had already landed there and there were implications of where they should move next.

The President mentioned a message that he had sent to the Japanese Emperor concerning the presence of Japanese troops in Indochina, in effect requesting their withdrawal.

Mr. Hopkins then expressed a view that since war was undoubtedly going to come at the convenience of the Japanese, it was too bad that we could not strike the first blow and prevent any sort of surprise. The President nodded and then said, in effect, "No, we can't do that. We are a democracy and a peaceful people." Then he raised his voice, and this much I remember definitely. He said, "But we have a good record."

The impression that I got was that we would have to stand on that record, we could not make the first overt move. We would have to wait until it came.

During this discussion there was no mention of Pearl Harbor. The only geographic name I recall was Indochina. The time at which war might begin was not discussed, but from the manner of the discussion there was no indication that tomorrow was necessarily the day. I carried that impression away because it contributed to my personal surprise when the news did come.

MR. RICHARDSON. Was there anything said, Commander, with reference to the subject of notice or notification as a result of the papers that were being read?

COMMANDER SCHULZ. There was no mention made of sending any further warning or alert. However, having concluded this discussion about the war going to begin at the Japanese convenience, then the President said that he believed he would talk to Admiral Stark. He started to get Admiral Stark on the telephone. It was then determined—I do not recall exactly, but I believe the White House operator told the President that Admiral Stark could be reached at the National Theater.

MR. RICHARDSON. Now, was it from what was said there that you draw the conclusion that that was what the Whte House operator reported?

COMMANDER SCHULZ. Yes, sir. I did not hear what the operator said, but the National Theater was mentioned in my presence, and the President went on to state, in substance, that he would reach the admiral later, that he did not want to cause public alarm by having the admiral paged or otherwise when in the theater, where, I believe, the fact that he had a box reserved was mentioned and that if he had left suddenly he would surely have been seen because of the position which he held and undue alarm might be caused, and the President did not wish that to happen because he could get him within perhaps another half an hour in any case.

MR. RICHARDSON. Was there anything said about telephoning anybody else except Stark?

COMMANDER SCHULZ. No, sir; there was not.

MR. RICHARDSON. How did he refer to Admiral Stark?

COMMANDER SCHULZ. When he first mentioned calling him, he referred to him as "Betty."

MR. RICHARDSON. Was there any further discussion there before you left?

[4664] COMMANDER SCHULZ. No, sir. To the best of my knowledge that is all that was discussed. The President returned the papers to me, and I left the study.

MR. RICHARDSON. That is all you know about it?

COMMANDER SCHULZ. Yes, sir; that is all.

MR. RICHARDSON. I have no further questions.

THE CHAIRMAN. What time would you say you went to the President's study that night?

COMMANDER SCHULZ. It was approximately 9:30.
THE CHAIRMAN. How long were you there altogether?
COMMANDER SCHULZ. I would say about one-half hour, sir.
THE CHAIRMAN. One-half hour?
COMMANDER SCHULZ. Yes, sir.
THE CHAIRMAN. So you left there about ten?
COMMANDER SCHULZ. Yes, sir.
THE CHAIRMAN. Then where did you go?
COMMANDER SCHULZ. Then I went back to the office which I mentioned before.
THE CHAIRMAN. Back to what you call the situation room?
COMMANDER SCHULZ. No, sir. The situation room was a later development, after the war began.
THE CHAIRMAN. Oh, I see. You went back to the place from which you departed to deliver the message?
COMMANDER SCHULZ. Yes, sir; that is correct. [...]
[4665] SENATOR FERGUSON. I just want to take the situation after you left the President's study. You then returned, as I understand it, to the mail room?
COMMANDER SCHULZ. Yes, sir; that is correct.
SENATOR FERGUSON. And the mail room had these long tables in it?
COMMANDER SCHULZ. Yes, sir; that is right.
SENATOR FERGUSON. Now, was Captain Kramer sitting at those tables when you went back, at one of the tables?
COMMANDER SCHULZ. It is my collection that he was.
SENATOR FERGUSON. And then did you return to Captain Kramer this pouch? Is that your recollection.
COMMANDER SCHULZ. That is my recollection. The happenings during that particular period are somewhat hazy but I know that I did not have the papers the next day. Further, I hadn't too suitable a place to put them during the night because of their high secrecy classification.
SENATOR FERGUSON. You had worked in the Naval ONI so that you knew how secret these papers were and how valuable they were?
COMMANDER SCHULZ. I was in the Communications Division rather than ONI.
SENATOR FERGUSON. All right, Communications.
COMMANDER SCHULZ. However, I knew of their nature and their general source because of their importance.
SENATOR FERGUSON. And, therefore, you wouldn't have cared to keep them at home or where you stayed, and you did not leave them anywhere in the White House?
COMMANDER SCHULZ. I would not have kept them under any circumstances, no, sir. [...]
[4670] MR. KEEFE. All right. Now, when the President got through

reading it, as I understood your testimony, he showed it to Hopkins and said, "This means war," and Hopkins concurred.

COMMANDER SCHULZ. Yes, sir. The words may not be exact but that is the substance.

MR. KEEFE. Then the discussion went on between Mr. Hopkins and the President as to possibly where the Japs might strike and you remember discussions of Indochina?

COMMANDER SCHULZ. That is correct, sir.

MR. KEEFE. But there was no mention of Pearl Harbor or Hawaii?

COMMANDER SCHULZ. That is cocrect, sir.

MR. KEEFE. Or any other places that you recall?

COMMANDER SCHULZ. No other places that I recall; none that I recall.

MR. KEEFE. Do you recall with any degree of certainty, Commander, just what the conversation was with respect to the transmission of this message direct to the Emperor of Japan and how that came into the conversation?

COMMANDER SCHULZ. It came into the conversation when the disposition of forces in Indochina was mentioned, and the way it came [4671] in was that in this message to the Emperor it is my understanding that the presence of Japanese forces in Indochina was mentioned and that the — I have never read the message, if I may say, Congressman, I would like to have you understand that — but, however, I recall mention being made, the President quoting from this message that he drafted to the effect that he had told Hirohito that he could not see how it could be held that there was any danger to peace in the Far East as far as the United States was concerned if there were no Japanese forces in Indochina.

In other words, we were not going to attack Indochina, nor was anyone else. Therefore, the presence of Japanese forces in Indochina was for an aggressive purpose or for ulterior purposes on the part of the Japanese. We ourselves held no threat for Indochina.

That also is in substance, but I do remember that point being brought out.

MR. KEEFE. Did you get the impression from that conversation that the message to the Emperor had been sent, or was going to be sent?

COMMANDER SCHULZ. I cannot recall that definitely, sir.

MR. KEEFE. Now when the President said he wanted to get in touch with "Betty," did he seem to know where "Betty" Stark was that night?

COMMANDER SCHULZ. No, sir; not initially, at least, because I recall that he started to place a telephone call for Admiral Stark.

MR. KEEFE. Then did word come back that Admiral Stark was at the National Theater? Is that what I understood you to say?

COMMANDER SCHULZ. Word came back that that was where he might be reached. Personally, I have no knowledge that he was there, but the President was informed that that was where the admiral had either left word or else someone who could get in touch with him expected to find him there.

MR. KEEFE. And then the President indicated that he would not bother calling him to the phone, that he would get him later after the theater was over?

COMMANDER SCHULZ. Yes, sir; that is correct.

MR. KEEFE. That is the impression you got?

COMMANDER SCHULZ. Yes, sir.

MR. KEEFE. That is because he felt Admiral Stark's leaving his box in the theater might cause some speculation and arouse some public discussion, or alarm.

COMMANDER SCHULZ. Yes, sir; that was my impression.

MR. KEEFE. Now when you got to the President's study the only people who were there were the President and Harry Hopkins?

COMMANDER SCHULZ. Yes, sir; that is correct.

MR. KEEFE. That is all.

Did the Japanese Suspect Their Codes Were Broken?

THEODORE S. WILKINSON, DIRECTOR OF NAVAL INTELLIGENCE

Joint Congressional Investigation

[1815] SENATOR BREWSTER. Did you have any reason to suspect, during the period between October and December 7, 1941, when you were functioning as Director of Naval Intelligence, that the Japs suspected that we were breaking any of their codes?

ADMIRAL WILKINSON. Yes. I do not know specifically in that period but there had been a message which I recall somewhere around October, I think, that the Germans had informed the Japs that there were indications that we were breaking some of their codes. Several messages that were sent from Japan indicated that they wished their agents to be particularly careful in their reports to protect their codes.

SENATOR BREWSTER. Have you located the messages which contained those references to the German warning?

ADMIRAL WILKINSON. I think I can find one, sir.

SENATOR BREWSTER. I would like to ask counsel whether they have located those.

MR. GESELL. No; we have not, the ones I believe the Senator refers to.

SENATOR BREWSTER. What steps have you taken?

SENATOR FERGUSON. Mr. Chairman, may I refresh Mr. Gesell's memory? I had a request in for such information and I am sure that my letter states definitely that there were no such codes—I mean no such messages. Do you recall that, Mr. Gesell?

MR. GESELL. No; I do not.

MR. MITCHELL. I think there were one or two messages such as the Admiral speaks of in Exhibit 1.

MR. MURPHY. And there is also a reference in Matsuoka's message to Hitler that might lead to such an inference.

MR. GESELL. I thought the Senator was referring to ones other than in the exhibit.

Source: Pearl Harbor Attack, *volume 4.*

Senator Ferguson. I am. The letter maybe might refresh you.

Senator Brewster. Well, I have a letter from Mr. Mitchell saying that there was no evidence that the Japanese had any knowledge that we were breaking their codes or suspected it, and that the evidence was all to the contrary. Do you recall that letter, Mr. Mitchell?

Mr. Mitchell. Yes. That is based on a report from the department of whom we made inquiry.

Senator Brewster. Yes.

Mr. Mitchell. I did not know it, personally. I forwarded to you their report.

Senator Brewster. Yes.

Mr. Mitchell. But I think there are one or two messages in exhibit 1 that makes the same report, that the Japs were at one time fearful of certain ones of their codes being broken.

Senator Brewster. Well, I have one here, and it is dated the 23d day of June 1941, from Tokyo to Mexico. It appears on page 122 of the intercepts, concerning military installations, ship movements, and so forth and it says:

> Furthermore, since the Panama Legation, in their #62* from Panama to me, mentioned the question of a trip, get in touch with them regarding date and time of arrival. (American surveillance will unquestionably be vigilant. There are also some suspicions that they read some of our codes. Therefore, we wish to exercise the utmost caution in accomplishing this mission. Also, any telegrams exchanged between you and Panama should be very simple.)

[1816] Now, that, of course, is squarely in conflict with the report which apparently the Navy Department gave you, is it not, indicating that at least the Japanese suspected that we were breaking their code.

Mr. Mitchell. I assume the Navy kept right on cracking them, so we can assume the Japs did not know that. I suppose that is why they made that statement. Obviously that one message contains a suspicion that we might be.

Senator Brewster. Yes.

Mr. Mitchell. But we kept right on breaking them, and I assume that, if the Japs had known we had broken them they would have fixed them up.

Senator Brewster. I am asking for information.

Mr. Mitchell. Well, you asked me if they were not in conflict?

Senator Brewster. Yes, and you agreed that it is. Now, the intercepts run from July 1 to December 7 and I asked some time ago for the earlier intercepts, after I was refused permission to examine the files, as I was reliably informed that there were five cablegrams which made very specific reference to this matter of which the admiral now speaks, that the Germans had apparently discovered something of this kind and communicated it to the Japanese in this interchange of messages between Berlin and Tokyo regarding this and in this matter—I am simply citing reports which the admiral confirms now, or at least intimates in his reference to the Germans, I say I am at least surprised that the Navy would give you the information that there was nothing to indicate this, if there are four or five messages of this character in their files.

MR. MITCHELL. To be specific, do I understand you would like to have any intercepts back to January 1, 1941, of this type that indicate the suspicion, is that what you are interested in?

SENATOR BREWSTER. Well, I certainly am, but I also call attention to my letter of November 15, in which I acknowledge the receipt of these intercepts from July 1, to December 8, and added I would greatly appreciate if you would send me another copy of this material, as well as a copy of all such intercepted messages between January 1 and July 1, 1941.

To that, I, as far as I know, have received no reply. That was a month ago.

I think you will remember, Mr. Mitchell, 10 days ago, in executive session, I spoke of this matter as a matter that I thought was of considerable interest, in view of the very great emphasis which had been placed on the complete ignorance of the Japanese of the fact that we were breaking their code.

MR. MITCHELL. I understand what you are especially interested in is the messages that have to do with the question of whether the Japs suspected our cracking the code. It is so much easier to get results if we know what we are after. I am just asking you the question, to get an indication as to what you are really interested in. ... [1817] I have been sitting here wondering just what the special significance and the importance in this inquiry is the question [1818] of whether prior to June 1941, or at any time, the Japs suspected that we were cracking their code. I confess it would help me a bit to work this thing out, if I knew just what bearing it has on the case.

I am probably dumb about it, but I do not quite grasp it. I have an idea that maybe that attitude may have had something to do with the fact that maybe I did not follow up your request as diligently as I otherwise would.

SENATOR BREWSTER. I should be very happy to give you what is in my apparently simple mentality. The first thing which has interested me a great deal on this particular episode, Mr. Mitchell, is if what Admiral Wilkinson now says is correct, then the Navy has not been giving you complete or accurate information when they tell you there was nothing to indicate that the Japs knew or suspected that we were breaking their codes. ... The second point, I had thought that one of the very outstanding matters that had been emphasized here, and in fact you yourself examined General Marshall at great length regarding this very matter in connection with the Dewey episode, that a great state secret existing here was magic, and that the Japs had no knowledge or suspicion that we were breaking their codes, and apparently very great importance has been attached to that throughout this hearing.

If there is anything to indicate that is not so, we must all, to some extent, revise our estimate of the situation in the light of that possibility or probability. At least that is my observation in all this evidence. I cannot otherwise reconcile the whole Dewey episode.

Now, if, back in May or June 1941, there were messages indicating that the

Japs suspected that this was happening, if it was of great importance, I cannot understand why this has not been developed. I cannot understand why the Navy will tell you there was nothing to indicate it. If it is not of any importance, why do not they just simply give us the facts and the messages, and if it is of importance, and there is any suggestion of concealment, that is something we must take into account. ...

[1819] THE VICE CHAIRMAN. ... I have heard every witness who has testified, and my clear impression is that the remark just made by Admiral Wilkinson is the first intimation that has come out in the course of this hearing that the Japanese had ever suspected that their code might have been broken. I know other witnesses have been asked the question whether there was anything to indicate that Japan had ever suspected that the code had been broken, and their testimony was that there was nothing to indicate it, until just at this moment when Admiral Wilkinson had made the remark in response to the question, and I think that is the first intimation that has come to the committee that anybody thought Japan might have had any knowledg that the code had been broken.

SENATOR BREWSTER. Mr. Chairman, I thank you very much for that observation, and I hope you agree with me that this does have a distinct relevance in establishing it.

THE VICE CHAIRMAN. Of course, if the Senator wants information, I am sure counsel will cooperate in every possible way to secure it, and to give it to the Senator when it is secured. ...

[1821] SENATOR BREWSTER. May I just ask that Admiral Wilkinson will check on those cablegrams, the intercepts during the noon hour so we can get this thing clarified?

ADMIRAL WILKINSON. My only recollection was a dispatch from Berlin, I think to Tokyo, indicating that the Germans thought we might be reading the Japanese codes and warning them about it.

SENATOR BREWSTER. I understood there were five messages on this subject between Tokyo and Washington. I would like to have a complete file.

THE VICE CHAIRMAN. Admiral, you understand the Senator's request?
ADMIRAL WILKINSON. Yes.
THE VICE CHAIRMAN. You will make every effort to comply with it?
ADMIRAL WILKINSON. Yes, sir.

MR. MURPHY. Mr. Chairman, I would like to have the record note that not one question was asked the witness in the last half hour.

THE VICE CHAIRMAN. The committee will stand in recess until 2 o'clock. ...

THE VICE CHAIRMAN. The committee will be in order. Senator Brewster will resume his inquiry.

SENATOR BREWSTER. Admiral, were you able to secure those wires during the recess? I think they were radiograms.

[1822] ADMIRAL WILKINSON. I have not been able to locate it to date. The liaison officer for the Navy Department has made the specific inquiry for that dispatch. I have talked to my predecessor, Admiral Kirk, who says he recalls it as a message from the Japanese Ambassador in Berlin to the home office in Tokyo, that the German Foreign Minister Von Ribbentrop had advised him that there were indications that the Americans were breaking Japanese codes.

I may state, of course, that there were a number of codes, some of which are relatively simple and can be readily broken, others are more complex, and the very reading of one code would not be any assurance that others or the entire bulk of them were being broken. The only indication would be with respect to such a message that we were at least attacking their codes.

I do not know that in the late fall, in the early fall and the late fall, we had some worries about the Japanese finding that out and the Japanese suspicions, although we did not believe from the tenor of their dispatches that they were convinced at all that we were breaking them, and those worries occasioned our tightening up of security concerning intercepts and occasioned our being particularly careful about broadening in any degree the text or even knowledge obtained from the text of such messages.

SENATOR BREWSTER. When you say there are different codes, how frequently are they changed ordinarily?

ADMIRAL WILKINSON. Again it is a matter for a communicator to give expert knowledge, but there is in general, I understand, two types of concealed message. One is a code and the other is a cipher applicable to that code. The code is contained in a book and to change it you have to issue another book. The cipher may be changed from day to day and often is.

You must first break the cipher on any message before you can tell what the concealed message is and then you must have the code to know what the words which have now been derived, or the groups which have now been derived, mean under that code.

Answering your question directly then, the ciphers were very frequently changed, sometimes from day to day, and the codes would not be changed so often, perhaps once a month or even a year or more.

SENATOR BREWSTER. How many are they likely to have in use at any one time? How many would they be likely to have in use at any one time, of codes as distinct from the ciphers?

ADMIRAL WILKINSON. Oh, perhaps 10 or 12: A diplomatic code, a naval attaché's code, a military, a consular, some very secret codes for each of those and some day to day codes.

SENATOR BREWSTER. And the interpretation of any one was dependent either upon breaking it as you did or upon having the code book to enable you to easily translate it?

ADMIRAL WILKINSON. Yes. And the knowledge that we were attacking a code would not be particularly significant as it is more or less of an international practice. The knowledge that we had succeeded in breaking some of the simpler codes would not be particularly significant. If they knew definitely we had broken their most secret codes it would be a matter of great concern.

Did the Japanese Suspect?   225

SENATOR BREWSTER. It is not considered that there is anything particularly reprehensible in this practice, is it? Isn't it a rather well- [1823] recognized practice in the international code of morality that that is done by all governments in the interest of their national security?

ADMIRAL WILKINSON. I think so. I do not think that governments are particularly desirous to admit it, but I think it has been done in the past, sir.

SENATOR BREWSTER. Yes.

ADMIRAL WILKINSON. Whether it is being continued today in all countries I do not know.

SENATOR BREWSTER. Wasn't there a rather conspicuous case in our own history during and after the last war about certain translations that were made in time of peace?

ADMIRAL WILKINSON. My recollection is not authentic at all but I know that in the last war we did have a so-called Black Chamber.

SENATOR BREWSTER. Yes.

ADMIRAL WILKINSON. And that sometime after the last war I believe the then Secretary of State decided that he would abolish it completely and all such activities on our part were then discontinued for a time.

THE VICE CHAIRMAN. If you will permit me, Senator, you and the Senator were both referring to the last war. You are talking about World War I?

ADMIRAL WILKINSON. Yes, World War I. This one is too recent to be known as the last war.

THE VICE CHAIRMAN. Well, both of them are last wars now.

SENATOR BREWSTER. Was that discontinued at that time when Henry L. Stimson was Secretary of State?

ADMIRAL WILKINSON. I do not know.

SENATOR BREWSTER. I think it was.

Now, have counsel been able to secure any further information about these messages? Have they made any inquiries from the Navy Department about it?

MR. MITCHELL. They are hard at work, and so is the Army. ...

[1859] THE VICE CHAIRMAN. The committee will be in order.

Does counsel have anything at this time?

MR. MITCHELL. Yes, Mr. Chairman.

Yesterday we had up an inqury made of counsel by Senator Ferguson, I think, under date of November 16, in which he said, "Please obtain for me all information that any of the services or the Government had that Japan knew we had broken their code."

There was a response from me immediately on the 17th, which said:

> With reference to your letter of November 16 requesting "all information that any of the services or the Government had that Japan knew we had broken their code," there is no indication that Japan ever knew it. All information would indicate the contrary.

Now, yesterday I made the mistake, without checking up on the fact, of saying or thinking that I had submitted that request to the Navy or the Army, and they had reported and it was on the basis of their report that I made that statement, and as the result of that there were some imputations made on the good faith of the Army and Navy in not producing what we asked for.

I want to say that imputation is not justified because I now find I never did ask for that material, and that this answer that I made was made based on my own impression of what they were asking, and what the evidence was at that time. I am quite willing to be open to criticism for not having followed it up, although at that time we were pretty busy just getting started, and possibly I might be forgiven for that.

THE VICE CHAIRMAN. I am sure we all recognize that.

MR. MITCHELL. At any rate, we had the inquiry made. Bear in mind that this inquiry, as I interpret it, I am quite sure referred to what the Japs knew about our breaking the code prior to Pearl Harbor.

[1860] I was not thinking of any information about that in 1944 when Marshall wrote his letter, because we had not asked that they produce any of these intercepts at that day, so I was referring to what the conditions were prior to Pearl Harbor, and I also feel quite sure, although the request is not limited to that—

SENATOR FERGUSON. That is all I was referring to, Mr. Mitchell. There is no misunderstanding about that.

MR. MITCHELL. There is no misunderstanding about that.

I also want to say at that time this was in the singular, and I was thinking of the diplomatic code, the magic or the purple stuff, so I wrote and told him I did not know of any evidence of that kind. I should have asked the Departments for it, but I am glad to make it clear or to get straightened out on it.

SENATOR BREWSTER. I think I had some correspondence also. Did you check that?

MR. MITCHELL. Our file clerk was not able to get in from Virginia this morning. She has been ill for a week. She went away yesterday. We will have to let that go, a little.

THE VICE CHAIRMAN. We will take judicial knowledge of the weather conditions today. All of us had a hard time getting here.

MR. MITCHELL. There is a communication from you, I am quite certain.

SENATOR BREWSTER. Yes, along the same line.

MR. MITCHELL. I have not heard from the Navy this morning on this, but the Army comes in, having worked hard on this subject with a number of intercepts during the months of April and May 1941, intercepts of Jap messages between Berlin and Tokyo, Tokyo and Washington is one of them, two, three, four of them. They all indicate a suspicion on the part of Japan that we were cracking one or more of their codes.

SECTION FIVE

Evaluating the Pearl Harbor Commanders: Negligent, Malinformed by Their Superiors, or Just Plain Unlucky?

The Impressions, Priorities, and Dangers Implied by the Navy Department in Its Communications with Pearl Harbor

ADMIRAL HUSBAND E. KIMMEL,
COMMANDER-IN-CHIEF, U.S. PACIFIC FLEET

Joint Congressional Investigation

PART II—INFORMATION RECEIVED AND ACTION TAKEN

[2511] In this part of my statement, I shall describe the information available to me prior to the attack and the actions which I took upon the basis of that information. I shall deal with the following topics:

First, the information furnished to me by the Navy Department, prior to October 16, 1941;

Second, the dispatches sent to me by the Navy Department from October 16, 1941, to and including November 27, 1941;

Third, the meaning of the so-called war warning dispatch of November 27, and related information;

Fourth, my decisions and actions from November 27 to the time of the attack.

1. *Information and dispatches, January–October 1941.* — In February 1941, when I became commander in chief, I was somewhat familiar with the tense situation in the Pacific. During the year 1941 I received dispatches and letters from the Chief of Naval Operations [2512] which might be broadly described as "war warnings." On January 21, 1941, he sent a dispatch to the commander in chief which stated:

> The international situation continues to deteriorate. It now appears to me that if war eventuates its general character will be according to plan DOG my memorandum to the Secretary. If this estimate proves correct I contemplate ordering mobilization according to plan RAINBOW THREE with following modifications Atlantic Fleet principal concentration New England and Canada execute all tasks except affirm except early reenforcement from Pacific and

Source: Pearl Harbor Attack, *volume 6.*

much stronger British Isles detachment. Pacific Fleet waiting attitude or execute assigned tasks in Area eastward of 160 degrees east depending on action by Japan. Asiatic Fleet cannot expect early reenforcement alert status or carry out tasks according to circumstances.

On February 3, 1941, the Chief of Naval Operations sent me a dispatch from the United States naval attaché in London which stated:

> I have been officially informed that Japanese are apparently planning an offensive on a large scale presumed against Indo-China Malay Peninsula or the Dutch East Indies no doubt to be coordinated with attack on Great Britain approximately February 10. It is definite that the Jap and German relations are becoming more intimate and that the Japs are conducting a hatred campaign against the British even in ordinarily pro-English press also two large Japanese merchant vessels sailings have been cancelled. Reports believed reliable state that all Jap shipping being called home to be taken over by the government. Request your knowledge of this. The Japanese mediating Thai Indo China scene meeting abroad Jap cruiser. Price of umpire's services unreliably reported to be bases on the west coast of Siam that are usable by light craft for cutting Singapore communications via the Malacca Straits.

On July 13, 1941, the Chief of Naval Operations sent me a dispatch which stated:

> The unmistakable deduction from information from numerous sources is that the Japanese Government has determined upon its future policy which is supported by all principal Japanese political and military groups. This policy probably involves war in the near future. An advance against the British and Dutch cannot be entirely ruled out. However, CNO holds the opinion that Jap activity in the south will be for the present confined to seizure and development of Naval, Army and Air bases in Indo-China * * *

The dispatch predicted that Japan's major military effort would be against Russian maritime provinces. It also stated that all Japanese vessels in United States Atlantic ports had been ordered to be west of the Panama Canal by the 1st of August.

On July 3, 1941, the Chief of Naval Operations sent me another dispatch. This reported that the Japanese Government had issued orders that certain Japanese vessels in the North Atlantic and Caribbean areas pass through the Panama Canal to the Pacific. Under these orders all Nipponese merchant vessels would be clear of the Caribbean and North Atlantic areas by July 22. It related information from unusually reliable Chinese sources that within two weeks Japan would abrogate the neutrality treaty with Russia and attack. The dispatch concluded as follows:

> That present strength and deployment of Nip Army in Manchuria is defensive and the present distribution of the Japanese Fleet appears normal, and *that*

is capable of movement either north or south. That a definite move by the Japanese may be expected during the period July 20–August 1 is indicated by the foregoing. [Italics supplied.]

[2513] On July 25, the Chief of Naval Operations sent me a dispatch in which the Chief of Staff joined. This advised that on July 25 the United States would employ economic sanctions against Japan. It stated in part:

> * * * The Chief of Naval Operations and the Chief of Staff do not anticipate hostile reaction by Japan through the use of military means but you are furnished this information in order that you may take appropriate precautionary measures against possible eventualities. Action being initiated by the United States Army to call the Philippine Army into active service at an early date. This dispatch is to be kept secret except from immediate Army and Navy subordinates.

In addition to these dispatches the Chief of Naval Operations' letters to me show recurrent tension in the international situation during 1941. His letters use such expressions as:

> What will happen in the Pacific is anyone's guess. (Memorandum of May 14, 1941.)

An open rupture was described as a possibility on July 24, 1941, "Obviously, the situation in the Far East continues to deteriorate; this is one thing that is factual." (July 31, 1941.)

> * * * Also the seriousness of the Pacific situation which continues to deteriorate. (August 21, 1941.)
> I have not given up hope of continuing peace in the Pacific, but I could wish the thread by which it continues to hang were not so slender. (August 28, 1941.)
> P. S. I have held this letter up pending a talk with Mr. Hull who has asked me to hold it very secret. I may sum it up by saying *that conversations with the Japs have practically reached an impasse.* (September 23, 1941.)

None of these letters or dispatches warned of an attack in the Hawaiian area, or indicated that an attack there was imminent or probable. None of these letters or dispatches directed an alert in the Hawaiian area against an overseas attack.

On the contrary, on February 1, 1941, the Chief of Naval Operations wrote me on the subject of "Rumored Japanese attack on Pearl Harbor."

He stated that Mr. Grew had telegraphed the State Department on January 27, 1941:

> The Peruvian minister has informed a member of my staff that he has heard from many sources, including a Japanese source that in the event of trouble breaking out between the United States and Japan, the Japanese intend to make a surprise attack against Pearl Harbor with all of their strength and

employing all of their equipment. The Peruvian minister considered the rumors fantastic. Nevertheless, he considered them of sufficient importance to convey this information to a member of my staff.

The letter from the Chief of Naval Operations added:

> The Division of Naval Intelligence places no credence in these rumors. Furthermore, based on known data regarding the present disposition and employment of Japanese naval and army forces, *no move against Pearl Harbor appears imminent or planned for in the foreseeable future.* [Italic supplied.]

This estimate as to the improbability of a move against Pearl Harbor was never withdrawn.

Consider my situation as Commander in Chief of the Pacific Fleet at the time I received, by letter and dispatch, these ominous predictions of Japanese aggression in the Far East.

[2514] I was carrying out an intensive training program to prepare the fleet for war. I was under specific injunction to continue that program. In an official letter to me on April 31, 1941 (Serial 038612), the Chief of Naval Operations wrote:

> In the meantime I advise that you devote as much time as may be available to training your forces in the particular duties which the various units may be called upon to perform under your operating plans. The time has arrived, I believe, to perfect the technique and the methods that will be required by the special operations which you envisage immediately after the entry of the United States into war.

On November 24, 1941, the Chief of Naval Operations sent me a dispatch stating that the chances of a favorable outcome of negotiations with Japan were very doubtful and that, in his opinion, an aggressive movement in any direction, including an attack on the Philippines or Guam was a possibility. Admiral Stark testified before the Naval Court of Inquiry that he did not intend that the Pacific Fleet should discontinue its training program upon receipt of this dispatch, 2 weeks before the attack.

I was not expected to discontinue training for all-out security measures, concentrated on the defense of the Hawaiian Islands, every time an alarming dispatch was received from Washington predicting Japanese aggression in the Far East. Indeed, had I done so, the training program would have been curtailed so drastically that the fleet could not have been prepared for war.

During the time these dispatches were sent, the Navy Department knew just what my program in Hawaii was. My fleet-operating schedules were filed with the Navy Department, where the location and movement of substantially every ship in the fleet was known at all times. No dispatch or letter contained any order or suggestion for departure from my operating schedules. On May 24, 1941, the Navy Department sent me the following dispatch.

> The Department in the interest of morale will consider visits of small detachments or individual ships to the Pacific Coast. *It is not desired that detachments of such size make these visits as to indicate the breaking up or reducing the Hawaiian concentration.* Your recommendations are requested. [Italics supplied.]

When the War and Navy Departments wishes to put the forces in Hawaii on alert against attack, they could and did use appropriate language to that end. The dispatch of June 17, 1940, from the War Department to the Hawaiian garrison demonstrated this. That dispatch stated:

> Immediately alert complete defensive organization to deal with possible trans-Pacific raid, to greatest extent possible without creating public hysteria or provoking undue curiosity of newspapers or alien agents. Suggest maneuver basis Maintain alert until further orders. Instructions for secret communication direct with Chief of Staff be furnished you shortly. Acknowledge.

In reply to Admiral Richardson's dispatch reporting the actions taken by the fleet forces to cooperate with the Army in maintaining the "alert," the Navy Department directed him to continue such cooperation.

[2515] It is one thing to warn commanders at a particular base of the probable outbreak of war in theaters thousands of miles away, knowing and expecting that they will continue their assigned tasks and missions.

It is quite another thing to warn commanders at a particular base of an attack to be expected in their own locality.

In 1941, we of the Pacific Fleet had a plethora of premonitions, of generalized warnings and forebodings that Japan might embark on aggressive action in the Far East at any one of the variously predicted dates. After receipt of such warnings, we were expected to continue with renewed intensity and zeal our own training program and preparations for war rather than to go on an all-out local alert against attack.

In the year 1941, the international situation was grave and, at times, tense. However, preparing the fleet for war through an intensive training program had to go on. There was a vital element of timing involved in determining when the fleet should curtail training for all-out war measures. Maximum security measures, consistent with the maintenance of the training program, were already in effect in the fleet. When would Japanese-American relations reach the point that all training should cease and all-out war dispositions should be made? This was what we needed to know in the Pacific in the year 1941.

Throughout 1941, the Navy Department had several courses open. It could furnish me directly with the best evidence of Japanese intentions and plan—the intercepted Japanese military and diplomatic messages. This would have given me an opportunity to judge for myself the gravity and intensity of the crisis as December 7, 1941, approached, and the probability of a Japanese attack on Hawaii. The Navy Department failed to do this. The Navy Department did not permit me to evaluate for myself the intercepted Japanese military and diplomatic messages.

Another course of action then remained. That was to issue an order which would have directed dispositions of the fleet to guard against an attack in Hawaii. The message of June 17, 1940, "be on the alert against hostile overseas raid," was such an order. It would have had the same effect in December of 1941 as it had in June of 1940. Such an order was not given.

Further, the War and Navy Departments could have ordered the local commanders of the Hawaiian Coastal Frontier, Admiral Bloch and General Short, to execute the Joint Coastal Frontier Defense Plan. This was not done.

The Navy Department could have given the order to mobilize under the War Plan. This order would have had a definite meaning. It would have placed the fleet on an all-out war basis. The order to mobilize did not authorize acts of war. The dispatch of January 21, 1941, indicated that mobilization would be ordered when war was imminent. The order to mobilize was not given.

[2516] In the dispatches I received on and after October 16, 1941, I was not given available information as to the actual status of Japanese-American negotiations and as to Japanese military plans; nor was I given orders for alert against an attack on Hawaii. These dispatches had the same tenor as the warnings which had previously been sent in February, June, and July 1941 predicting probable Japanese action thousands of miles from the Hawaiian area.

2. *Dispatches from October 16, 1941, to and including November 27, 1941* — On October 16, 1941, the Chief of Naval Operations sent the commanders in chief, Atlantic, Asiatic, and Pacific Fleets, the following dispatch:

> The resignation of the Japanese Cabinet has created a grave situation. If a new cabinet is formed it will probably be strongly nationalistic and anti-American. If the Konoye Cabinet remains the effect will be that it will operate under a new mandate which will not include reapprochement with the U.S.
> In either case hostilities between Japan and Russia are a strong possibility. Since the U.S. and Britain are held responsible by Japan for her present desperate situation there is also a possibility that Japan may attack these two powers. In view of these possibilities you will take due precautions including such preparatory deployments as will not disclose strategic intention nor constitute provocative actions against Japan.

The term "preparatory deployments" used in this dispatch is nontechnical. It has no especial significance other than its natural meaning. After receiving this dispatch, I made certain preparatory deployments. I ordered submarines to assume a war patrol off both Wake and Midway. I reinforced Johnston and Wake, with additional marines, ammunition, and stores and also sent additional marines to Palmyra Island. I ordered the commandant of the Fourteenth

Naval District to direct an alert status in the outlying islands. He did so and reported his action to me.

I placed on 12 hours' notice certain vessels of the fleet which were in west coast ports, held six submarines in readiness to depart for Japan, delayed the sailing of one battleship which was scheduled to visit a west coast navy yard. I dispatched 12 patrol planes to Midway with orders to carry out daily patrols within 100 miles of the island, and placed in effect additional security measures in the fleet operating areas.

On October 22, I reported by letter all these dispositions to the Chief of Naval Operations.

I might say I summarized all these movements in a letter and the reports had previously been made in movement reports.

By letter dated November 7, 1941, the Chief of Naval Operations specifically approved these dispositions. He wrote:

> OK on the dispositions which you made in connection with the recent change in the Japanese Cabinet.

The naval court of inquiry found:

> He (Admiral Kimmel) did not interpret the dispatch of 16 October as directing or warranting that he abandon his preparations for war. He held daily conferences with his subordinate commanders and the members of his Staff, all experienced officers of long service and sought by every means to ascertain wherein his interpretation might be incorrect. The consensus throughout was that no further steps were warranted by the information at hand.

[2517] In the dispatch of October 16, 1941, I was advised that there was a possibility Japan would attack the United States and Great Britain. But this advice was given a definite meaning by the Chief of Naval Operations in a letter to me on October 17, in which he said:

> Personally I do not believe the Japanese are going to sail into us and the message I sent you *merely stated the "possibility"*; in fact I tempered the message handed to me considerably. (Italic supplied.)

This letter made it clear to me that when Admiral Stark stated certain Japanese action to be "possible," he meant that it was not probable.

In his letter of October 17, 1941, the Chief of Naval Operations enclosed a "Memorandum for the CNO" from Captain R. E. Schuirmann, who was in charge of the Navy's liaison with the State Department. Admiral Stark stated in his letter that this memorandum by Captain Schuirmann "sums up my thoughts better than I have been able to set them down."

The dispatch of October 16 and the Schuirmann memorandum were not consistent. The dispatch of October 16 began: "The resignation of the Japanese

Cabinet has created a grave crisis." The memorandum began: "I believe we are inclined to overestimate the importance of changes in the Japanese Cabinet as indicative of great changes in Japanese policy of thought or action."

The memorandum stated:

> Present reports are that the new Cabinet to be formed will be no better and no worse than the one which has just fallen.

The memorandum was to the effect that the Japanese military would determine Japan's policy regardless of the Cabinet in power.

On November 24, I received a dispatch from the Chief of Naval Operations which was addressed to me, the Commander in Chief of the Asiatic Fleet, and the commandants of the Eleventh, Twelfth, Thirteenth, and Fifteenth Naval Districts. This dispatch read as follows:

> Chances of favorable outcome of negotiations with Japan very doubtful. This situation coupled with statements of Japanese Government and movements their Naval and Military forces indicate in our opinion that a surprise aggressive movement in any direction including attack on Philippines or Guam is a possibility. Chief of Staff has seen this dispatch concurs and requests action addressees to inform Senior Army Officers their areas. Utmost secrecy necessary in order not to complicate an already tense situation or precipitate Japanese action. Guam will be informed separately.

Under date of November 25, the Chief of Naval Operations wrote me a letter which reached me on December 3. This letter contained a postscript added after a "meeting with the President and Mr. Hull today." The dates of the conference and the postscript are not known to me. In the postscript he wrote:

> * * * *From many angles an attack on the Philippines would be the most embarrassing thing that could happen to us. There are some here who think it likely to occur. I do not give it the weight others do, but I included it because of the strong feeling among some people. You know I have generally held that it was not time for the Japanese to proceed against Russia. I still do. Also I still rather look for an advance into Thailand, Indochina, Burma Road area as the most likely.*
> [2518] I won't go into the pros or cons of what the United States may do. I will be damned if I know. I wish I did. The only thing I do know is that we may do most anything and that's the only thing I know to be prepared for; or we may do nothing—I think it more likely to be "anything." (Italic supplied.)

On November 27, the Chief of Naval Operations sent to me and to the Commander in Chief of the Asiatic Fleet, the following dispatch:

> This dispatch is to be considered a war warning. Negotiations with Japan looking toward stabilization of conditions in the Pacific have ceased and an aggressive move by Japan is expected within the next few days. The number and

equipment of Japanese troops and the organization of naval task forces indicates an amphibious expedition against either the Philippines Thai or Kra Peninsula or possibly Borneo. Execute an appropriate defensive deployment preparatory to carrying out the tasks assigned in WPL 46. Inform District and Army authorities. A similar warning is being sent by War Department. SPENAVO inform British. Continental Districts Guam Samoa directed take appropriate measures against sabotage.

On the same day I received two other dispatches from the Chief of Naval Operations, which affected my current estimate of the situation, as well as my subsequent dispositions.

The first of these dispatches was as follows:

Army has offered to make available some units of infantry for reenforcing defense battalions now on station if you consider this desirable. Army also proposes to prepare in Hawaii garrison troops for advance bases which you may occupy but is unable at this time to provide any antiaircraft units. Take this into consideration in your plans and advise when practicable number of troops desired and recommended armament.

The second of these dispatches was as follows:

In order to keep the planes of the 2nd marine aircraft wing available for expeditionary use OpNav has requested and Army has agreed to station 25 Army pursuit planes at Midway and a similar number at Wake provide you consider this feasible and desirable. It will be necessary for you to transport these planes and ground crews from Oahu to these stations on an aircraft carrier. Planes will be flown off at destination and ground personnel landed in boats essential spare parts tools and ammunition will be taken in the carrier or on later trips of regular Navy supply vessels. Army understands these forces must be quartered in tents. Navy must be responsible for supplying water and subsistence and transporting other Army supplies. Stationing these planes must not be allowed to interfere with planned movements of Army bombers to Philippines. Aditional parking areas should be laid promptly if necessary. Can Navy bombs now at outlying positions be carried by Army bombers which may fly to those positions for supporting Navy operations. Confer with Commanding General and advise as soon as practicable. (Italics supplied.)

3. *Analysis of the so-called "war warning" dispatch of November 27, 1941, and related information.* — The so-called "war warning" dispatch of November 27 did not warn the Pacific Fleet of an attack in the Hawaiian area. It did not state expressly or by implication that an attack in the Hawaiian area was imminent or probable. It did not repeal or modify the advice previously given me by the Navy Department that no move against Pearl Harbor was imminent or planned by Japan. The phrase "war warning" cannot be made a catch-all for all the contingencies hindsight may suggest. It is a characterization of the specific information which the dispatch contained.

[2519] The dispatch warned of war—where?

In the Far East. The dispatch stated:

> The number and equipment of Japanese troops and the organization of Naval task forces indicates an amphibious expedition against either the Philippines, Thai, or Kra Peninsula or possibly Borneo.

Thus the Philippines, Thai, and the Kra Peninsula were stated to be expected objectives of Japan. When it came to "possible" objectives, Borneo was the only one specified. Hawaii was not mentioned. As the Naval Court of Inquiry points out, "No reference was made to the possibility of an aggressive movement in any direction as had been done in the dispatch of 24 November." This indicated to us in the fleet that since the earlier dispatch, the Navy Department had obtained later information, on the basis of which it could specify both probable and possible Japanese objectives.

Moreover, the two other dispatches which I received on November 27, in addition to the so-called "war warning" dispatch were affirmative evidence that the War and Navy Departments did not consider hostile action on Pearl Harbor imminent or probable.

One of these dispatches proposed that I send 25 Army pursuit planes by aircraft carrier to each of the islands of Wake and Midway. The other dispatch proposed the reenforcement of Marine defense battalions on Midway and Wake with Army troops.

About the same time General Short received a dispatch from the War Department which stated that the Army proposed to take over the defense of these islands from the marines.

Thus, the dispatches sent from the War and Navy Departments were in disagreement on the very fundamentals of the project.

The proposed exchange of Army troops for marines on the outlying island bases was not feasible. General Short and I had extensive conferences on the subject. I learned that the Army had no guns, either surface or antiaircraft to equip any troops which might relieve or reenforce the marines. Thus, if the marines were withdrawn, their equipment and arms would have to be left for the Army. I did not have sufficient additional supplies to reequip and rearm the marines removed. The marines stationed on the island were trained, acclimated and efficient beyond standards which could be immediately obtained by Army troops relieving them. The Army had nothing in its organization comparable to a Marine defense battalion, so that the Army garrison would have required a new table of organization. The proposed relief of the marine garrisons by Army troops would necessarily disrupt the defense of the islands during the period that one garrison was preparing to depart and the other was being installed.

Furthermore, at Wake, the more westerly of the two islands, there were no harbor facilities or anchorage. Material and personnel had to be landed from ships under way in an open seaway. Ships had been delayed in unloading at Wake for as long as 28 days due to bad weather. It was not unusual for a ship to take as much as 7 or 8 days. Extensive unloading of men and material from ships at Wake, in the face of any enemy operation, would be impossible.

[2520] I believe that responsible authorities in Washington would not plan or propose a project for shifting garrisons under such circumstances, if they considered that enemy action against these outlying bases was imminent.

I promptly recommended to the Chief of Naval Operations that the marines should not be withdrawn from the outlying islands until the Army had received arms and equipment for its defense battalions and had adequately trained them.

The replacement of Marine planes on the islands of Wake and Midway with Army pursuit planes, as proposed by Washington, was also impracticable. At conferences with the Army on this matter, the Commanding General of the Hawaiian Air Detachment stated that the Army pursuit planes could not operate more than fifteen miles from land, nor could they land on a carrier. Consequently, once they were landed on one of the outlying islands they would be frozen there. Their fifteen-mile limit of operation radically restricted their usefulness in the island's defense. I so advised the Chief of Naval Operations by dispatch and letter.

The Army pursuit planes which it was proposed to send to outlying islands from Oahu on November 27 constituted approximately 50 percent of the Army's pursuit strength on Oahu. The very fact that the War and Navy Departments proposed their transfer from Hawaii indicated to me that responsible authorities in Washington did not consider an air raid on Pearl Harbor either imminent or probable.

In brief, on November 27, the Navy Department suggested that I send from the immediate vicinity of Pearl Harbor the carriers of the fleet which constituted the fleet's main striking defense against an air attack.

On November 27, the War and Navy Departments suggested that we send from the island of Oahu, 50 percent of the Army's resources in pursuit planes.

These proposals came to us on the very same day of the so-called "war warning."

In these circumstances no reasonable man in my position would consider that the "war warning" was intended to suggest the likelihood of an attack in the Hawaiian area.

From November 27 to the time of the attack, all the information which I had from the Navy Department or from any other source, confirmed, and was consistent, with the Japanese movement in southeast Asia described in the dispatch of November 27.

On November 30, the Navy Department sent me for information a dispatch addressed to the Commander in Chief of the Asiatic Fleet. [2521] This stated there were indications that Japan was about to attack points on the Kra Isthmus by overseas expedition. The Commander in Chief of the Asiatic Fleet was directed to scout for information of Japanese movements in the China Sea.

On December 1, the Navy Department sent me for information another dispatch which it addressed to the Commander in Chief of the Asiatic Fleet, describing a Japanese intrigue in Malaya. Japan planned a landing at Khota Baru in Malaya in order to entice the British to cross the frontier from Malay into Thailand. Thailand would then call Britain an aggressor, and call upon Japan for aid. This would facilitate the Japanese entry into Thailand as a full-fledged ally, and give Japan air bases in the Kra Peninsula, and a position to carry out any further operations along Malaya.

From the commander in chief of the Asiatic Fleet, from the China coast, and other sources, we had reports of the development of a Japanese amphibious expedition headed south. Movements of troops, tanks, amphibian boats, landing craft, transports, and naval vessels had been sighted moving to the Kra Peninsula.

On December 6, 1941, the commander in chief of the Asiatic Fleet reported various large Japanese forces apparently making for Kohtron. These consisted of one 25-ship convoy with an escort of 6 cruisers and 10 destroyers, and another 10-ship convoy with 2 cruisers and 10 destroyers. The scouting force of the Asiatic Fleet had sighted 30 ships and one large cruiser anchored in Camranh Bay in Indochina. Incidentally, Kohtron is in Indochina.

In short, all indications of the movements of Japanese military and naval forces which came to my attention confirmed the information in the dispatch of 27 November—that the Japanese were on the move against Thailand or the Kra Peninsula in southeast Asia.

The fortnightly "Summary of Current National Situations" issued by the Office of the Chief of Naval Operations under date of December 1, 1941, stated on page 1 "Strong indications point to any early Japanese advance against Thailand."

The same publication, on page 9, under the heading "The Japanese Naval Situation," stated definitely "Major capital ship strength remains in home waters as well as the greatest portion of the carriers."

On December 3, 1941, I received intelligence that Japanese consular and diplomatic posts at Hong Kong, Singapore, Batavia, Manila, Washington, and London had been ordered to destroy most of their codes. This dispatch stated "most of their codes and ciphers"—not all—a point which was noted by me and my staff at the time. This information appeared to fit in with the information we had received about a Japanese movement in southeast Asia. Japan would naturally take precautions to prevent the compromise of her communication system in the event that her action in southeast Asia caused Britain and the United States to declare war, and take over her diplomatic residences.

[2522] In addition to actual observation, there was another way of obtaining some indications of Japanese Fleet movements. This was the system of so-called traffic analysis. It rested on an attempted identification of call signs of various enemy ships and of subdivision commanders in the enemy fleet. The call sign is a group of letters and numbers used by a ship to identify itself much as a radio station announces itself as "Station WABC." The location of the ships from whence the call signs emanate is made by direction finders. In 1941 we had direction finders at Manila, Guam, and Pearl Harbor. We made a daily traffic analysis. I went over the material with care. [...]

[2523] As to the Japanese carriers, during the 6 months preceding Pearl Harbor, there existed a total of 134 days—in 12 separate periods—each ranging from 9 to 22 days, when the location of the Japanese carriers from radio traffic analysis was uncertain.

In brief, in the week immediately prior to Pearl Harbor, I had no evidence that the Japanese carriers were en route to Oahu. Radio traffic analysis did not locate their positions. But this was not a new or unusual condition. It was inherent in the changes of call signs. It had existed on 12 other occasions over a 6-months' period.

The dispatch of November 27 stated that Japanese-American negotiations looking toward stabilization of conditions in the Pacific had ceased. The Navy Department did not let this statement stand without modification. On November 29, 2 days later, the Navy De- [2524] partment sent me a dispatch, which quoted the War Department's message to General Short of November 27. It stated:

> Negotiations with Japan *appear* to be terminated with only the barest possibility of resumption. [Italic supplied.]

This dispatch came to me near the end of "the next few days" set forth in the dispatch of November 27 as the period within which the Japanese action would come. Further, there was a public resumption of Japanese-American negotiations after November 27. The public press and radio news broadcasts contained accounts that negotiations were continuing after November 27 and after November 29. In the absence of more authoritative information, I took account of this public information as to diplomatic developments. This suggested a lessening of the emergency which prompted the so-called "war warning" dispatch.

The Navy Department did not inform me of the contents of the American note to Japan on November 26, or that the prevalent opinion in the Navy Department was that the proposals contained in that note were so drastic as to make Japanese acceptance of them impossible. In a letter of November 14, the Chief of Naval Operations sent me a copy of a memorandum for the President signed by himself and General Marshall. This memorandum advised against direct United States intervention in China and recommended specifically that "no ultimatum be delivered to Japan."

I was not informed that the Japanese were continuing the negotiations after November 26 only as a device to cover up their plans. The Navy Department knew this to be the fact. I was not informed that, upon receipt of the American note of November 26th, the Japanese considered that negotiations had not merely ceased but that relations with this country were ruptured. The Navy Department knew this to be the fact.

Five. Evaluating the Commanders

The statement in the Navy Department's dispatch to me to the effect that negotiations had ceased on November 27 was a pale reflection of actual events; so partial a statement as to be misleading. The parties had not merely stopped talking. They were at swords' points. So far as Japan was concerned, the talking which went on after November 26 was play-acting. It was a Japanese strategem to conceal a blow which Japan was preparing to deliver. That strategem did not fool the Navy Department. The Navy Department knew the scheme. The Pacific Fleet was exposed to this Japanese stratagem because the Navy Department did not pass on its knowledge of the Japanese trick.

In the November 29 dispatch after quoting the Army message, the Chief of Naval Operations added the following direction:

> WPL-52 is not applicable to Pacific Area and will not be placed in effect in that area except as now in force in South East Pacific Sub Area and Panama Naval Coastal Frontier. Undertake no offensive action until Japan has committed an overt act. Be prepared to carry out tasks assigned in WPL-46 so far as they apply to Japan in case hostilities occur.

WPL-52 was the Navy Western Hemisphere Defense Plan No. 5. Under this plan the Atlantic Fleet had shooting orders. It was [2525] charged with the task of destroying German and Italian naval, land, and air forces encountered in the area of the western Atlantic. The southeast Pacific sub area covered the area from the coast of South America to a distance of 700 miles westward. Here the southeast Pacific naval force had similar shooting orders and a similar task. In the dispatch of November 29, the Chief of Naval Operations informed me that WPL-52 was not applicable to the Pacific. This was to impress upon me the fact that I did not have shooting orders and that I was not to shoot until Japan had committed an overt act. Although this dispatch was sent me for information I was as much bound by these orders as though I had been an action addressee.

Incidentally, when I received that dispatch, I considered that a modification of the orders I have received in the war-warning dispatch, and that I was to be governed by the provisions of this dispatch. I can see no other interpretation, and I thought that the Navy Department had been brought into accord with the orders that had been issued by the War Department, and I thought that was what they were doing when they sent that dispatch.

This same note of caution is in the dispatch of October 16, 1941:

> You will take due precautions including such preparatory deployments as will not disclose strategic intention nor constitute provocative action against Japan.

Again in the War Department dispatch, quoted to me by the Chief of Naval Operations in his message of November 29:

> The United States desires that Japan commit the first overt act. * * * Measures should be carried out so as not repeat not alarm civil population or disclose intent.

The Pacific Fleet was based in an area containing over 130,000 Japanese, any one of whom could watch its movements. You can appreciate the psychological handicaps orders of this kind placed upon us. In effect, I was told:

> Do take precautions.
> Do not alarm civilians.
> Do take a preparatory deployment.
> Do not disclose intent.
> Do take a defensive deployment.
> Do not commit the first overt act.

One last feature of the so-called "war-warning" dispatch remains to be noted. This is the directive with which it closed:

> Execute an appropriate defensive deployment preparatory to carry out the tasks assigned in WPL-46.

Under WPL-46 the first task of the Pacific Fleet was to support the forces of the Associated Powers (Britain, the Netherlands, and the United States) in the Far East by diverting enemy strength away from the Malay barrier.

The Navy Department emphasized this instruction by repeating it on November 29. The dispatch of that date directed:

> Be prepared to carry out the tasks assigned in WPL-46 so far as they apply to Japan in case hostilities occur.

Thus in two separate dispatches I was ordered by the Navy Department to have the Pacific Fleet ready to move against the Marshalls upon the expected outbreak of war in the Far East.

[2526] This was a determinative factor in the most difficult and vital decisions I had to make thereafter. There was not a hint in these two dispatches of any danger in the Hawaiian area. [. . .]

[2529] 4. *Action taken and decisions made after November 27, 1941.* — The War Plan of the Pacific Fleet (W. P. Pac-46) prescribed a definite plan of operations to enable the fleet to carry out its basic task of diverting Japanese strength away from the Malay barrier, through the denial and capture of positions in the Marshalls.

THE CHAIRMAN. "The Marshalls" refers to the islands and not to the general?

ADMIRAL KIMMEL. How is that?

THE CHAIRMAN. The word "Marshall" there refers to the islands and not to the general?

ADMIRAL KIMMEL. This refers to the Marshall Islands to the east of the Carolina Islands in the Pacific.

THE CHAIRMAN. Go ahead.

ADMIRAL KIMMEL. This plan was called the Marshall reconnaissance and raiding plan. Under the plan, Task Force 2, under the command of Admiral Halsey, was to depart from Pearl Harbor one one J-day; i.e., one day after hostilities with Japan began. This task force, consisting of the carrier *Enterprise* with battleships and destroyers, was to proceed toward Taongi Atoll in the northern Marshalls. Task Force 1 under the command of Admiral W. S. Pye, was to depart Pearl Harbor above five J-day, so as to rendezvous with Admiral Halsey's task force at a designated point on eleven J-day. From six J-day to nine J-day, Admiral Halsey's task force was to reconnoiter by air the atolls of the Marshall Islands for the purpose of determining the best objectives for a raid. About 10 J-day, Task Force 3, under the command of Admiral Wilson Brown, was to join Task Force 2 under Admiral Halsey, and thereafter operate as a part of that force. After the rendezvous of the task force on 11 J-day, the commander in chief of the fleet would direct Admiral Halsey to commence the attacks on the selected islands of the Marshalls group. Admiral Halsey's battleships would then be transferred to Task Force 1, which would operate as a covering force for Halsey's raiding force. On about 13 J-day, Task Force 2 would attack the selected objectives with air and surface forces.

Thus our plans called for a strike at the Marshalls very shortly after J-day — when hostilities commenced. We were conscious of the great value of speed in setting this expedition in motion. Its prime purpose was to divert Japanese strength from the Malay Barrier. If it were delayed, its entire purpose and value would be frustrated.

Under this plan of operations, the patrol planes of the Pacific Fleet had an essential role. The plan provides:

> (d) *Task Force Nine* (Patrol Plane Force) coordinate operations of patrol planes with those of other forces as follows:
>
> (1) Prior to Five J-Day advance maximum practicable patrol plane strength to WAKE, MIDWAY, and JOHNSTON, leaving not less than two operating squadrons at OAHU.
>
> (2) JOHNSTON-based planes, during passage of units of other forces to the westward, search along the route of advance from the vicinity of JOHNSTON to longitude one hundred seventy-eight degrees west.
>
> [2530] (3) MIDWAY-based planes search sectors to the southwestward of MIDWAY to prevent surprise attack across that sector on units operating toward the MARSHALLS.
>
> (4) WAKE-based planes make preliminary air reconnaissance of TAONGI and BIKAR on Five J-Day, or as soon thereafter as practicable, and acquaint *Commander Task Force Two* with the results. Thereafter, conduct search, to the extent that available planes and supplies will permit, to prevent surprise attack from the westward by enemy surface forces on own units operating toward the MARSHALLS.
>
> (5) On completion of the raiding operations of *Task Force Two* resume normal operations as required by paragraph 3242 b. of the Fleet Operating Plan.

The mere recitation of these tasks demonstrates the vital air reconnaissance required of the patrol plane force. Without it, the task forces might be exposed to surprise attack if they entered the dangerous Marshall area. It was an indispensable feature of the entire operation.

Beginning November 30, 1941, I made a daily memorandum entitled "Steps to be taken in case of American-Japanese war within the next 24 hours." The last form of this memorandum I reviewed and approved on the morning of December 6, 1941. In it I attempted to keep the basic plan of the raid on the Marshall Islands up to date and in conformity with the existing dispositions of fleet units. The last issue of this memorandum, dated December 6, 1941, is as follows:

>1. Send dispatch to Pacific Fleet that hostilities have commenced.
>2. Send dispatch to task force commanders:
>(a) WPL 46 effective (Executive O-1A R5 except as indicated in (b) and (c) below). (The submarine and patrol plane plans will become effective without special reference to them.)
>(b) Commence sweeping plan, including cruiser operations west of Napo Shoto, cancelled.
>(c) Raiding and reconnaissance plan effective, modified as follows: Delay reconnaissance until Task Forces Two and Three are joined; Batdiv One join Task Force One; Commander Base Force send two tankers with utmost dispatch to rendezvous with Task Force Three to eastward of Wake at rendezvous to be designated.
>(d) Comairbatfor and units in company with him (Taskfor 8) return to Pearl at high speed, fuel and depart with remainder of Taskfor Two, less BBs, to join Task Force Three.
>(e) Lexington land Marine aircraft at Midway as planned (p. m. 7 Dec) and proceed with ships now in Company (Taskfor 12) to vicinity of Wake.
>(f) Comtaskfor Three proceed to join Lexington group. Return DMS to Pearl.
>3. (a) Do not modify the movements of Regulus at Midway (departing 9th), nor ships bound to Christmas and Canton.
>(b) Direct that William Ward Burrows continue to Wake but delay arrival until 10th. Direct that *Lexington* group send two destroyers to join Burrows prior to her arrival at Wake.
>(c) Do not withdraw any civilian workmen from outlying islands.
>(d) Provide two destroyers to escort *Saratoga* from longitude 150° west to Pearl Harbor.
>(e) Do not change passage of shipping to and from Manila, nor send any added escorts, nor dispose any cruisers toward California or Samoa until further developments occur.

The provisions of the memorandum were coordinated with the basic plan for the Marshall raid. The "VP plans" which were to "become effective without special reference" were the plans for the operation of the patrol-plane force. Paragraphs 2 (c), (d), and (e) had reference to the existing disposition of fleet units on December 5 and 6. Admiral Halsey at that time was returning from an expedition to Wake Island with a task force specially constituted for that purpose [2531] and called Task Force 8. I planned to have him return to Pearl Harbor to refuel before joining Task Force 3 on the expedition to the Marshalls. The carrier *Lexington* on December 6 was en route to Midway. She was in a task force specially constituted for that purpose and called Task Force 12. In the event of hostilities I planned to have the *Lexington* carry out the Midway expedition and proceed to Wake, there to be joined by the commander of Task Force 3 of which the *Lexington* was a regular component. Admiral Wilson Brown, the commander of Task Force 3, on December 5 was engaged in operations in the vicinity of Johnston Island. I planned to have him leave that area and join the *Lexington* group, thereby bringing together all elements of Task Force 3. Task Force 3 would then be joined by Admiral Halsey's Task Force 2. When these task forces joined, they would proceed with the reconnaissance features of the raiding plan as a preliminary to the actual raids on the Marshall Islands.

This initial expedition was to continue operating as long as we could supply it with fuel. We estimated that it would require continuous operation of maximum patrol plane strength from 4 to 6 weeks. Additional expeditions were to be undertaken as rapidly as events and forces permitted.

I shall now describe the nature and extent of distant reconnaissance from the Hawaiian area on and after November 27, 1941.

By dispatch on November 27, the Navy Department had urged me to send Army pursuit planes to Midway and Wake by aircraft carrier. I replied by dispatch that on November 28 I was sending a carrier to Wake with Marine fighter planes, and that I expected thereafter to send other Marine planes to Midway.

I considered the Navy Department's suggestion that planes be sent to Wake and Midway to be sound. It was desirable that the defenses of these outlying islands should be as strong as possible. The planes which went to Wake were, of course, not enough to save that island. Together with its other defenses, they could make the capture of that island sufficiently costly to justify sending them there. The actual results in the defense of Wake after December 7 demonstrated that fact.

The sending of the carrier task forces to Wake and Midway did more than reinforce the air defenses of the islands. It permitted a broad area to be scouted for signs of enemy movement along the path of the advance of these task forces to the islands and their return to Oahu. In addition, they were in an excellent position to intercept any enemy force which might be on the move.

On November 28, Admiral Halsey left Pearl Harbor en route to Wake in command of Task Force 8, consisting of the carrier *Enterprise*, 3 heavy cruisers and 9 destroyers. He carried out morning and afternoon searches to 300 miles with his planes for any sign of hostile shipping.

On December 5, 1941, Admiral Newton left Pearl Harbor en route to Midway in command of Task Force 12, consisting of the carrier *Lexington*, three heavy cruisers, and five destroyers. Newton, like Halsey, conducted scouting flights with his planes to cover his advance.

[2532] On December 5, Admiral Wilson Brown left Pearl Harbor en route to Johnston Island with Task Force 3 to conduct landing exercises.

Thus by December 5 there were at sea three task forces of the fleet, each deployed in a different area. The *Lexington* and the *Enterprise* were each conducting air searches. It was a more intensive search in the areas covered than could have been made by patrol planes based on Oahu. Further, as they approached the outlying islands, these searches were conducted at a much greater distance from Oahu than any patrol plane based on Oahu could travel.

In addition to the operations of these task forces, other distant reconnaissance was conducted by the fleet after November 27.

Upon receipt of the so-called war warning dispatch of November 27, I ordered a squadron of patrol planes to proceed from Midway to Wake and search the ocean areas en route. While at Wake on December 2 and 3, they searched to a distance of 525 miles. These orders were executed.

I also ordered another squadron of patrol planes from Pearl Harbor to replace the squadron which went from Midway to Wake. This squadron of patrol planes left Pearl Harbor on November 30. It proceeded to Johnston Island. On the way to Johnston, it searched the ocean areas. It then proceeded from Johnston to Midway, making another reconnaissance sweep on the way. Upon reaching Midway, this squadron of patrol planes conducted distant searches of not less than 500 miles of varying sectors from that island on December 3, 4, 5, and 6. On December 7, five of these Midway-based patrol planes were searching the sector 120° to 170° from Midway, to a distance of 450 miles. An additional two patrol planes of the Midway squadron left at the same time to rendezvous with the *Lexington* at a point 400 miles from Midway. Four of the remaining patrol planes at Midway, each loaded with bombs, were on 10-minute notice as a ready striking force.

When the *Enterprise* completed its delivery of planes to Wake, I withdrew a squadron of patrol planes from Wake. This squadron then proceeded to Midway, searching the ocean areas en route. It then moved from Midway to Pearl Harbor, conducting a reconnaissance sweep en route.

In the week before December 7, these reconnaissance sweeps of the patrol plane squadrons moving from Midway to Wake; from Pearl Harbor to Johnston and from Johnston to Midway; from Wake to Midway and Midway to Pearl Harbor, covered a total distance of nearly 5,000 miles. As they proceeded, each squadron would cover a 400-mile strand of ocean along its path. They brought under the coverage of air search about 2,000,000 square miles of ocean area.

In addition to these reconnaissance sweeps, submarines of the fleet on and after November 27 were on war patrols from Midway and Wake Islands continuously.

At Oahu before the attack, there were 49 patrol planes which were in flying condition. Eight other planes were out of commission and undergoing repair. In addition, on December 5, a squadron of patrol [2533] planes returned to Pearl Harbor after an arduous tour of duty at Midway and Wake. This squadron consisted of obsolete PBY-3 planes, approaching 18 months' service and overdue for overhaul. It was not available for distant searches.

The 49 flyable patrol planes on Oahu were part of the planes which had arrived during the preceding 4 weeks—18 on October 28, 24 on November 23, and 12 on November 28. These planes were of the PBY-5 type. They were experiencing the shake-down difficulties of new planes. There was considerable difficulty due to the cracking of new engine sections, which required replacement. A program for the installation of leakproof tanks and armor on these planes was underway. The leakproof tanks and armor were necessary to make these planes ready for war. That work had to be carried out in Hawaii. Under war plans the planes were to operate from advance bases, Midway, Wake, Johnston, Palmyra Islands. There, they would operate from aircraft tenders. There were no facilities at those advanced bases to complete important material installations. The planes had to be in the highest condition of fighting efficiency before they left Oahu.

There was a total absence of spare parts for these planes.

There were no spare crews.

To insure an island base against a surprise attack from fast carrier-based planes, it is necessary to patrol the evening before to a distance of 800 miles on a 360° arc. This requires 84 planes on one flight of 16 hours. Of course, the same planes and the same crews cannot make that 16-hour flight every day. For searches of this character over a protracted period, a pool of 250 planes would be required. These are fundamental principles. You will find them in the testimony of expert aviation officers before the naval court; and in the very comprehensive letter Fleet Admiral Nimitz wrote to the commander in chief, United States Fleet, on January 7, 1942, on the subject Airplane Situation in Hawaiian Area.

It is clear that I did not have a sufficient number of planes to conduct each day a 360° distant search from the island of Oahu. That fact is beyond controversy.

A search of all sectors of approach to an island base is the only type of search that deserves the name. The selection of one sector around an island for concentration of distant search affords no real protection. After a while it may furnish some insurance that the enemy, having knowledge of the search plan, will choose some other sector within which to make his approach. The search concentrated on the so-called "dangerous sector" then ceases to offer much prospect of detecting the enemy. Admiral Nimitz put the matter clearly in his official letter on the subject. He said:

> It cannot be assumed that any direction of approach may safely be left unguarded. The fuel problem is no deterrent, for the approach was made from the north on 7 December. Increase in difficulty of the logistic problem would not be proportionately great if even an approach from the east were attempted. At the same time, as discussed above, neglect of any sector is apt soon to be known.

Tactical discussions now of what was the most dangerous sector around Oahu before December 7 do not reach the heart of the problem which I faced.

[2534] The Secretary of the Navy in his endorsement to the record of the Naval Court of Inquiry has stated:

> There were sufficient fleet patrol planes and crews, in fact, available in Oahu during the week preceding the attack to have flown, for at least several weeks, a daily reconnaissance covering 128° to a distance of about 700 miles.

This statement assumes a 25-mile visibility for each patrol plane engaged in the search. It further assumes that I could have used all the patrol plane force for this type of search alone without keeping any planes in reserve for emergency searches or to cover movements of ships in and out of the harbor and in the operating area.

If I instituted a distant search of any 128° sector around Oahu on and after November 27, within the foreseeable future, I would have deprived the Pacific Fleet of any efficient patrol plane force for its prescribed war missions.

In the secret investigation before Admiral Hewitt, from which I was excluded, Vice Admiral Bellinger, who commanded my patrol plane force, testified:

> Q. Assuming that on December 1, 1941, you had received a directive from Admiral Kimmel to conduct the fullest possible partial reconnaissance over an indefinite period of time, could you have covered 128 degrees approximately on a daily basis and for how long?
> A. It could have been done until the failure of planes and lack of spare parts reduced the planes to an extent that it would have made it impossible. *Perhaps it could have been carried on for two weeks,* perhaps, but this estimate is, of course, very vague and it is all based on maintaining planes in readiness for flight. (Italic supplied.)

This testimony reflected the conditions in the patrol plane squadrons as I knew them on November 27 and thereafter.

Captain Ramsey, the executive officer of the patrol wing, testified before the Naval Court of Inquiry as follows:

> * * * As nearly as I could estimate the situation and in view of our almost total lack of spare parts for the PBY-5 planes, I believe that three weeks of intensive daily searches would have been approximately a 75 percent reduction in material readiness of the entire outfit and we would have been placing planes out of commission and robbing them for spare parts to keep other planes going. The pilots, I believe, could have kept going approximately a six-weeks period, but at the end of that time they would have all required a protracted rest period.

The patrol planes in Oahu were not uselessly employed prior to the attack. They were not standing idle. There was a definite program for their operation which was consistent with creating and preserving their material readiness for war. In the week preceding the attack, there was a daily scout by patrol planes on Monday, Tuesday, Wednesday, and Thursday, of a sector to the north and northwest of Oahu to a distance of 400 miles, after which the planes required maintenance and upkeep. This was not distant reconnaissance, as such, although the distance covered was greater than that searched at the time of the 1940 alert. In addition, there was the daily dawn patrol out 300 miles to cover the areas where the fleet operated.

I had been ordered, not once but twice, to be prepared to carry out the raids on the Marshalls under WPL-46, which meant the extended use of the fleet patrol planes from advanced bases in war operations.

[2535] I had to decide what was the best use of the patrol planes as a matter of policy for the foreseeable future, and with their war task in front of me.

Had I directed their use for intensive distance searches from Oahu, I faced the peril of having these planes grounded when the fleet needed them and when the war plan was executed.

I had no way of knowing that the war was to start on the 7th of December. I could not decide the matter on the basis of 5 days or 10 days of distant searches.

I did not have the intercepted Japanese dispatches pointing to Pearl Harbor as a probable point of attack.

I knew that any search I could make, straining the planes to the breaking point, was in its nature partial and ineffective.

I took account of my resources. They were slender.

I took account of my probable future needs and of my orders from the Navy Department.

I decided that I could not risk having no patrol plane force worthy of the name for the fleet's expected movement into the Marshalls.

I considered the nature and extent of the distant reconnaissance I was effectuating with my task forces at sea and the patrol plane sweeps to and from the outlying islands.

I considered the necessity of permitting the essential replacement and material upkeep program for the new patrol planes in Oahu to be continued to get them into war condition.

I considered the need for patrols of the fleet operating areas against the submarine menace and these I carried out.

I considered the need for some reserve of patrol planes for emergency distant searches.

I considered the need for patrol planes in covering fleet movements in and out of the harbor—which might have to be quickly and unexpectedly executed.

I considered the endurance of my patrol-plane manpower—and the absence of any spare crews.

I decided that I could not fritter away my patrol-plane resources by pushing them to the limit in daily distant searches of one sector around Oahu—which within the predictable future would have to be discontinued when the patrol planes and crews gave out.

The three admirals who composed the Naval Court of Inquiry scrutinized my decision after extensive testimony. Each of the admirals could view the matter from the point of view of the commander in the field. They summarized the problem:

> The task assigned the Commander in Chief, Pacific Fleet, was to prepare his Fleet for war. War was known to be imminent—how imminent he did not know. The Fleet planes were being constantly employed in patrolling the operating areas in which the Fleet's preparations for war were being carried on. Diversion of these planes for reconnaissance or other purposes was not justified under existing circumstances and in the light of available information.
>
> If so diverted, the state of readiness of the Fleet for war would be reduced because of the enforced suspension of Fleet operations.
>
> The value of the Fleet patrol planes to the Fleet would be reduced seriously after a few days because of the inability of planes and crews to stand up under the demands of daily long-range reconnaissance.

The court concluded (finding XIII):

> The omission of this reconnaissance was not due to oversight or neglect. It was the result of a military decision, reached after much deliberation and con- [2536] sultation with experienced officers and after weighing the information at hand and all the factors involved.

I shall now discuss the dispositions of the capital ships of the Pacific Fleet on and after November 27. On November 28 Admiral Halsey left for Wake with a carrier task force and on December 5 Admiral Newton left for Midway with another carrier task force. These missions were in pursuance of an explicit suggestion from the Navy Department. When Admiral Halsey left for Wake on November 28 the three battleships of his task force accompanied him out of Pearl Harbor so as to avoid creating the impression that there was anything unusual about the movement of his task force. However, immediately on clearing the channel Admiral Halsey diverted his battleships and instructed them to carry out exercises in the Hawaiian area. He then headed west with the remainder of his task force.

It would have been unwise for Admiral Halsey to have taken along the battleships. The maximum speed of the battleships was 17 knots. The fleet units which he took to Wake could make 30 knots. To take his battleships with him would have meant the loss of 13 knots of potential speed. He was bound for dangerous waters where curtailed speed might spell disaster. He needed all the mobility his force could attain. Three battleships did not furnish sufficient supporting strength to warrant the risks of reduction in speed and mobility which their presence in the expedition to Wake would entail. Moreover, it was necessary to complete the Wake operation as quickly as possible so that the ships engaged might be ready for further eventualities.

Almost evern disposition which I made in the Pacific with the forces available tome had its cost. In sending the two carriers to Wake and Midway, I took from the immediate vicinity of Pearl Harbor, for the time being, the fleet's air strength. We had no carrier left in the Hawaiian area. The *Saratoga*, the third carrier of the Pacific Fleet, had been undergoing repair and overhaul on the west coast. The advisability of using her to transfer a squadron of Marine fighter planes from San Diego to Hawaii was suggested by the Chief of Naval Operations on November 28.

The absence of the carriers from the Hawaiian area temporarily limited the mobility of the battleships which were left behind.

While the carriers were absent on the assigned missions to Midway and Wake, the battleships force was kept in Pearl Harbor. To send them to sea without air cover for any prolonged period would have been a dangerous course. The only effective defense at sea from air attack, whether it be a bombing attack or a torpedo-plane attack, is an effective air cover. Surface ships, such as destroyers and cruisers, are much less effective against an air attack. That is so today. It was the more so prior to 7 December because of the existing inadequacies of antiaircraft guns.

The carriers furnished air coverage for the battleships at sea. The few planes that battleships and cruisers carry for use by catapult are not fighters. Their function is only scouting and reconnaissance. They are ineffective as a defense against enemy air attack. The battleships at sea without carriers had no protection from air bombing attack. In Pearl Harbor they had the protection of such antiaircraft [2537] defenses as the Army had. At sea, in deep waters, there were no physical barriers to the effectiveness of torpedo-plane attack. In Pearl Harbor, where the depth of water was less than 40 feet, a torpedo-plane attack was considered a negligible danger. The battleships of the fleet at sea, without carriers, sighted by a force of such character as to have a chance of a successful air attack on the Hawaiian Islands appeared to be more subject to damage than in port.

Vice Admiral Pye, commander of the Battle Force, and I discussed these considerations in a conference after the receipt of the so-called war-warning dispatch.

At the time of our discussion—at that time and later—we did not have before us the intercepted Japanese messages indicating that the ships in port in Pearl Harbor were marked for attack. We had no information that an air attack upon Pearl Harbor was imminent or probable. The fact that the Navy Department proposed at this time that our carriers be sent to the outlying islands indicated to us that the Navy Department felt that no attack on Pearl Harbor could be expected in the immediate future.

All the dispositions of my task forces at sea, as well as the presence of the battleships in port, were known to the Navy Department. Admiral Stark, the Chief of Naval Operations, testified before the Roberts Commission as follows:

> What we expected him (Admiral Kimmel) to do was to get more planes and personnel, and so on, out to Wake and Midway, if possible, and to send his task forces—some task forces to sea in readiness to catch any raiders, which he

did. He did that. *We knew it. We knew these task forces were at sea. He informed us that one was returning from having put the people ashore at Wake, that certain planes had been sent to Midway, and were expected to go on the fifth or sixth day down to Wake, and we knew the schedule of the ships that were in port, and at that particular time out of the three task forces, there were two scheduled to be in port. Actually there was less than one and a half in port. He kept the others at sea. He had taken those measures which looked absolutely sound. It was a safe assumption that other measues had been taken of a similar nature.* (Italics supplied.)

Upon receipt of the so-called war warning dispatch of November 27, 1941, I issued orders to the fleet to exercise extreme vigilance against submarines in operating areas and to depth bomb all contacts expected to be hostile in the fleet operating areas. My dispatch of November 28 to the fleet containing this order was forwarded to the Navy Department on that day. On December 2, I wrote to the Chief of Naval Operations directing his personal attention to this order. The Navy Department, in the 10 days prior to the attack, did not approve or disapprove my action.

For some time there had been reports of submarines in the operating areas around Hawaii. During the first week of February 1941, a submerged submarine contact was reported about 8 miles from the Pearl Harbor entrance buoys. A division of destroyers trailed this contact for approximately 48 hours, after which the contact was lost. The destroyers were confident it was a Japanese submarine. I was not fully convinced, but made a complete report to Naval Operations, stating the action taken and adding that I would be delighted to bomb every suspected submarine contact [2538] in the operating area around Hawaii. I was directed by dispatch not to depth bomb submarine contacts except within the 3-mile limit.

A similar contact at approximately the same position was made about the middle of March. Again the destroyers were confident that they had trailed a Japanese submarine. Again the evidence was not conclusive because the submarine had not actually been sighted.

On September 12, 1941, I wrote to the Chief of Naval Operations and asked him "What to do about the submarine contacts off Pearl Harbor and the vicinity." I stated, "As you know, our present orders are to trail all contacts but not to bomb unless they are in the defensive areas. Should we now bomb contacts without waiting to be attacked?"

On September 23 the Chief of Naval Operations replied to my question in a personal letter. He stated:

> The existing orders, that is not to bomb suspected submarines except in the defensive sea areas, are appropriate. If conclusive, and I repeat conclusive, evidence is obtained that Japanese submarines are actually in or near United States territory, then a strong warning and threat of hostile action against such submarines would appear to be our next step.

Five. Evaluating the Commanders

No conclusive evidence was obtained until December 7, 1941.

The files of the Commander in Chief, Pacific Fleet, contain records of at least three suspicious contacts during the 5 weeks preceding Pearl Harbor.

On November 3, 1941, a patrol plane observed an oil slick area in latitude 20–10, longitude 157–41. The patrol plane searched a 15-mile area. A sound search was made by the U.S.S. *Borden,* and an investigation was made by the U.S.S. *Dale,* all of them producing negative results. On November 28, 1941, the U.S.S. *Helena* reported that a radar operator without knowledge of my orders directing an alert against submarines was positive that a submarine was in a restricted area. A search by a task group with three destroyers of the suspected area produced no contacts. During the night of December 2, 1941, the U.S.S. *Gamble* reported a clear metallic echo in latitude 20–30, longitude 158–23. An investigation directed by Destroyer Division Four produced no conclusive evidence of the presence of a submarine. On the morning of the attack, the U.S.S. *Ward* reported to the Commandant of the Fourteenth Naval District that it had been attacked, fired upon and dropped depth charges upon a submarine operating in the defensive sea area. The Commandant of the Fourteenth Naval District directed a verification of this report with a view to determining whether the contact with the submarine was a sound contact or whether the submarine had actually been seen by the *Ward*. He also directed that the ready-duty destroyer assist the *Ward* in the defensive sea area. Apparently, some short time after reporting the submarine contact, the *Ward* also reported that it had intercepted a sampan which it was escorting into Honolulu. This message appeared to increase the necessity for a verification of the earlier report of the submarine contact.

Between 7:30 and 7:40 I received information from the Staff Duty Officer of the *Ward*'s report, the dispatch of the ready-duty [2539] destroyer to assist the *Ward*, and the efforts then under way to obtain a verification of the *Ward*'s report. I was awaiting such verification at the time of the attack. In my judgment, the effort to obtain confirmation of the reported submarine attack off Pearl Harbor was a proper preliminary to more drastic action in view of the number of such contacts which had not been verified in the past.

Did War Department Communications with the Army Commander in Hawaii Imply an Imminent Danger?

LIEUTENANT GENERAL WALTER C. SHORT,
COMMANDING GENERAL, HAWAIIAN DEPARTMENT

Joint Congressional Investigation

[2975] MR. KAUFMAN. Now, coming down to the summer of 1941, you read in the paper, of course, about the deterioration of relations as between the Japanese and the United States?

GENERAL SHORT. I did.

MR. KAUFMAN. And you knew of the freezing of Japanese funds in the United States?

GENERAL SHORT. Yes, sir.

MR. KAUFMAN. And you knew of the oil embargo against Japan?

GENERAL SHORT. Yes, sir.

MR. KAUFMAN. And the embargo against scrap and ammunition?

GENERAL SHORT. Yes, sir.

MR. KAUFMAN. Did that create in you a consciousness that trouble might come with Japan?

GENERAL SHORT. Yes, sir; but I was also told by the War Department that they did not expect a reaction causing the use of military forces on account of these acts. In their message of July 25, they stated definitely they did not expect a military reaction.

MR. KAUFMAN. They said that in July 1941?

GENERAL SHORT. Yes, sir; on July 25.

MR. KAUFMAN. And did you get any further advice from Washington that they did not expect military action?

GENERAL SHORT. No, sir. The only further advice that might be construed to that effect was on the 20th of October after the joint message had been sent on the 16th predicting certain attacks by the Japanese.

The War Department sent me a message on the 20th stating, while the

Source: Pearl Harbor Attack, *volume* 7.

situation continued to be tense, that they did not expect any abrupt change in the relations between the United States and Japan.

MR. KAUFMAN. Now, after this message from the War Department on the 26th of July—is that correct?

GENERAL SHORT. The 25th.

MR. KAUFMAN. The 25th of July 1941, there was nevertheless, great concern about the air defenses at Hawaii?

GENERAL SHORT. Yes, sir.

[2976] MR. KAUFMAN. As a result of which, General Martin made a report in August of 1941, which is Exhibit 13 in this proceeding. Are you familiar with that report?

GENERAL SHORT. I am very familiar with it.

MR. KAUFMAN. And in that report he made many suggestions for the improvement of the air defenses in Hawaii?

GENERAL SHORT. That is correct.

MR. KAUFMAN. And you approved that report, did you not?

GENERAL SHORT. I went over that report very carefully, and personally added the 36 torpedo bombers to what we required.

After talking it over with General Martin, he agreed with my suggestion. I reviewed that report very carefully before it went to Washington.

MR. KAUFMAN. You approved that report, and this is a photostatic copy of your approval of that report [handing document to General Short]?

GENERAL SHORT. That is correct.

MR. KAUFMAN. I will ask that that be marked as an exhibit. A copy of it has been handed to the members of the committee.

THE VICE CHAIRMAN. It will be so received. What exhibit number will that be?

MR. KAUFMAN. Exhibit 138.

(The document referred to was marked "Exhibit No. 138.")

MR. KAUFMAN. General, on the basis of the report of General Martin, another agreement was made between the Army and Navy with respect to the use of planes for reconnaissance and other things, and that is known as the Martin-Bellinger agreement, is it not?

GENERAL SHORT. I do not think that was made as the result of the study. That was just a natural follow-up on the agreement that Admiral Bloch and I had made.

MR. KAUFMAN. That is correct.

So that we have it, General, in connection with your appointment, you recognized the importance of the Hawaiian Department; you recognized the deterioration of relations between Japan and the United States throughout the summer of 1941, you had in mind the letter from the War Department of July 25, that they did not anticipate any action by Japan, and we come now to the telegram that you received from the War Department, the one of November 27. Have you got it before you?

General Short. Yes, sir.

Mr. Kaufman. Before you received this telegram, did you see a telegram sent to the Navy Department dated November 24?

General Short. Yes, sir. I was a little uncertain whether I had actually received it, or just had it read to me, but a naval officer before the Roberts board stated that he definitely gave me a copy, which he undoubtedly did.

Mr. Kaufman. In the hearings before the Roberts Commission your recollection was that you had not seen the telegram of November 24?

General Short. I believe I stated that I remembered seeing it, but I had been unable to find it in my headquarters, and I thought perhaps I had not actually received it.

But in view of what the naval officer stated, I am sure I must have actually received it.

[2977] Mr. Kaufman. Captain Layton testified that he had actually given it to you.

General Short. Actually delivered it to me, and talked to me about it.

Mr. Kaufman. You saw it and you did receive it, according to the testimony of Captain Layton, prior to the receipt of the telegram of November 27?

General Short. That is correct.

Mr. Kaufman. From the War Department?

General Short. That is correct.

Mr. Kaufman. So that on the 24th you received information from the commander in chief of the Pacific Fleet, as follows:

> Chances of favorable outcome of negotiations with Japan very doubtful.

That was a definite statement, was it not?

General Short. Yes, sir.

Mr. Kaufman. It goes on to say:

> This situation, coupled with statements of Japanese Government, and movement their naval and military forces indicate in our opinion that a surprise aggressive move in any direction including attack on the Philippines or Guam, is a possibility.

Now, I take it from your statement, General, that you said that language excluded Hawaii, because of the mention of the Philippines or Guam.

General Short. What I intended to say was that I felt certain that if the Navy Department believed an attack on Hawaii was probable, they would have mentioned it, the same as they did the Philippines. "In any direction—"

Mr. Kaufman. Well, they said—

Senator Brewster. Let him finish.

Mr. Kaufman. I am sorry.

General Short. "In any direction" might mean anywhere in the world, but they specifically stated that they did expect an attack toward the Philippines or Guam. I believe if they had been convinced of the same thing in Hawaii, they would very definitely have included Hawaii specifically, and not leave it to be included in the "in any direction."

MR. KAUFMAN. Well, do you mean to say, General, that with information of that kind, you were justified in not going on an all-out alert?

GENERAL SHORT. I think very definitely that I was. The fact that the War Department did not even inquire or give me any direct information to justify it.

MR. KAUFMAN. This was directed to be sent to you for your information?

GENERAL SHORT. That is correct.

MR. KAUFMAN. A specific direction to you?

GENERAL SHORT. Yes, sir.

MR. KAUFMAN. So that when the Navy Department said "aggressive movement in any direction," did it not mean in the direction in which they directed this message to go for information?

GENERAL SHORT. I would not say so. If you take it literally, I feel absolutely confident, if they had any idea that Hawaii was to be directly included, if there was a direct probability that they would have said so. There would be no purpose in leaving me to guess.

[2978] MR. KAUFMAN. Did you expect the War Department to be able to tell you the exact place of an attack?

GENERAL SHORT. I believe the War Department actually had the information 4 hours before the attack, so they could have told me the exact place.

MR. KAUFMAN. Now, we are 2½ weeks before the 4 hours of the attack. We are on the 24th of November, General.

GENERAL SHORT. The War Department could at least give me their best estimate, and I would like, when you get to November 29, to read to you what the man who wrote the estimate had to say about it.

MR. KAUFMAN. Coming back again, General, to the 24th, you said that the failure in this dispatch to name Hawaii as the place of possible attack, the same as the Philippines or Guam excluded from your consideration Hawaii as a probable point of attack.

GENERAL SHORT. It indicated to me that they did not feel that Hawaii was definitely a point of probable attack. It was a possible place of attack, of course, but I am 100 percent confident, if they had believed it was a probable place of attack, they would have so stated it.

MR. KAUFMAN. Did it prompt you to ask for any instructions from the War Department?

GENERAL SHORT. It did not.

MR. KAUFMAN. We go now to the telegram of November 27. That was a direct telegram to you?

GENERAL SHORT. Yes, sir.

MR. KAUFMAN. It states.

> Negotiations with Japan appear to be terminated to all practical purposes, with only the barest possibility that the Japanese Government might come back and offer to continue.

that is a very definite statement, is it not?

GENERAL SHORT. It is a very indefinite statement. It says that they are to all practical purposes, but there is a possibility that they may come back. And they did come back. I knew it only from the papers. I knew that the negotiations were continuing.

The War Department knew definitely there was a de facto rupture, and the Japanese were just stalling. They intercepted a message that told them that very positively.

MR. KAUFMAN. You regard that as an indefinite statement?

GENERAL SHORT. A very indefinite statement.

MR. KAUFMAN. Then it follows, with the statement: "Action unpredictable."

It says:

> Japanese future action unpredictable, but hostile action possible at any moment.

Was that an indefinite or definite statement?

GENERAL SHORT. Certainly, when you say a thing is unpredictable, it is not a definite statement. You say that something is possible, and they did not indicate the type of hostile action, they just said "hostile action," and I would say again that is a very indefinite statement.

MR. KAUFMAN. You did not believe that that was sufficient to put you on notice to go on an all-out alert?

[2979] GENERAL SHORT. I did not. I thought the War Department was perfectly capable of writing a positive and definite instruction if they wanted to give one.

MR. KAUFMAN. You did not make any inquiry from the War Department?

GENERAL SHORT. I did not.

MR. KAUFMAN. Well, you did get a definite instruction in this dispatch, did you not?

GENERAL SHORT. I got certain missions assigned, as will appear later in the message.

MR. KAUFMAN. It says:

> If hostilities cannot comma repeat cannot comma be avoided the United States desires that Japan commit the first overt act.

GENERAL SHORT. Yes, sir.

MR. KAUFMAN. That is a definite statement?

GENERAL SHORT. That is a definite statement if they didn't go ahead and modify it by the next sentence. Then you change it into an indefinite statement.

MR. KAUFMAN. But that statement, you agree, is definite?

GENERAL SHORT. If you stop there I agree that is definite.

MR. KAUFMAN. Then it says:

> This policy should not comma repeat not comma be construed as restricting you to a course of action that might jeopardize your defense.

GENERAL SHORT. You immediately have qualified it and it is no longer a definite statement. It is an indefinite statement.

MR. KAUFMAN. You have one definite statement and one indefinite statement?

GENERAL SHORT. They are joined together.

MR. KAUFMAN. Did what you claim to be inconsistencies in that statement prompt you to make any inquiry from Washington?

GENERAL SHORT. It did not.

MR. KAUFMAN. And you didn't do so?

GENERAL SHORT. No, sir. I was satisfied of one thing, that their prime desire was to avoid war, and to not let any international incident happen in Hawaii that might bring on war.

MR. KAUFMAN. It says:

> You are directed to take such reconnaissance and other measures as you deem necessary.

GENERAL SHORT. Yes, sir.

MR. KAUFMAN. But these measures should be carried out so as not to alarm the civil population.

So that you did have a broad directive?

GENERAL SHORT. Always qualified. [...]

[2982] MR. KAUFMAN. The telegram of November 27 says:

> You are directed to take such reconnaissance and other measures as you deem necessary.

GENERAL SHORT. That is correct.

MR. KAUFMAN. Let us go to the first directive. You are directed to undertake such reconnaissance —

GENERAL SHORT. As I deem necessary.

MR. KAUFMAN. As you deem necessary.

Did you take any reconnaissance at that time?

GENERAL SHORT. I did not deem any was necessary because it was the Navy's function, definitely agreed upon in the plan, to conduct the long-distance reconnaissance.

Mr. KAUFMAN. Did you make inquiry from the Navy as to whether they were at that time making reconnaissance?

GENERAL SHORT. I knew they were sending out three task forces. I discussed it fully with them that morning. They were sending a task force to Wake to send out additional Marine planes. They were sending out to Midway to send out additional Marine planes. They were going to send one to Johnston Island. And I actually got permission to send a staff officer along because they were going to conduct a landing exercise which I wished my G-2 section to understand. I knew they were making perimeter reconnaissance from Johnston and Wake to Midway. I did not know the details of that reconnaissance but I knew it would take place.

Mr. KAUFMAN. You knew that the task force to Johnston Island did not leave until December 5?

GENERAL SHORT. It was later, but the other two were leaving early.

Mr. KAUFMAN. Admiral Halsey left on the 29th?

GENERAL SHORT. The 28th or 29th.

Mr. KAUFMAN. 28th or 29th.

GENERAL SHORT. Yes, sir.

Mr. KAUFMAN. Those were the only two task forces that were out?

GENERAL SHORT. The only two task forces going out right at that time.

Mr. KAUFMAN. Now, the joint agreement between yourself and Admiral Bloch contemplated long-range reconnaissnce from the islands, did it not?

GENERAL SHORT. It contemplated it not just from the island. Whatever long-range reconnaissance was necessary. And, as I understand Admiral Kimmel's attitude, it was that with the perimeter reconnaissance from Johnston, Wake, and Midway, there was a very great saving in planes, that he could accomplish more than he could with the same number of planes from Oahu. And it was a logical thing to do, not to send them all out from Oahu.

Mr. KAUFMAN. General, let us come back to the 27th of November. You were directed to take reconnaissance?

GENERAL SHORT. As I deemed necessary?

GENERAL SHORT. As you deemed necessary?

GENERAL SHORT. Yes, sir.

Mr. KAUFMAN. In other words, in order to have reconnaissance, effective reconnaissance, radar stations have to be in operation, do they not?

[2983] GENERAL SHORT. The radar did not make distant reconnaissance. We thought at that time it was limited to 75 or a hundred miles. We discovered that under very exceptional circumstances we actually got 132 miles. It was not an instrument for distant reconnaissance.

Mr. KAUFMAN. That was not put into alert, was it?

GENERAL SHORT. That was put into alert during what I considered the most dangerous hours of the day for an air attack, from 4 o'clock to 7 o'clock a. m. daily.

Mr. KAUFMAN. And did you report that to the—

GENERAL SHORT. I did not.

MR. KAUFMAN. Just putting the radar station into operation is not effective unless there is the information center that works with it?

GENERAL SHORT. The information center was working with it.

MR. KAUFMAN. Was working with it?

GENERAL SHORT. Was working with it; yes, sir.

MR. KAUFMAN. Now, General, did you later on that day see the dispatch that Admiral Kimmel received from the Navy Department?

GENERAL SHORT. Yes, sir. I think Lieutenant Burr testified that he actually brought it to me personally.

MR. KAUFMAN. That was after you had replied to the War Department?

GENERAL SHORT. Probably sometime in the next hour or two.

MR. KAUFMAN. And when you saw the words "war warning" did that create any impression on your mind?

GENERAL SHORT. No more so than the fact that they had said before that the Japs would probably attack.

MR. KAUFMAN. Had you ever in your experience seen a message to a field commander using the words "This is a war warning"?

GENERAL SHORT. No, sir; but I knew that the Navy messages were habitually rather more aggressive than the Army. On October 16 we had a message in which they said Japan would attack. On October 20 I had one from the War Department saying they didn't expect any. My message said nothing about a war warning and his did. I think the Navy messages were inclined to be more positive, possibly you might say more alarming, in the context.

MR. KAUFMAN. So that the war warning, you just regarded it as aggressiveness of the Navy, and paid no particular attention to it?

GENERAL SHORT. No particular attention to those words.

MR. KAUFMAN. I direct your attention to the telegram to the commander in chief of the Pacific Fleet which says:

> The number and equipment of Japanese troops and the organization of naval task forces indicates an amphibious expedition against either the Philippines, Thai, or Kra Peninsula or possibly Borneo.

That is for information, is it not?

GENERAL SHORT. Yes, sir; and indicated definitely to me they were attacking toward the Western Pacific.

MR. KAUFMAN. Then it goes on with a directive to the commander in chief of the Pacific Fleet.

GENERAL SHORT. Yes, sir.

MR. KAUFMAN. To —

> Execute an appropriate defensive deployment preparatory to carrying out the tasks assigned in WPL-46.

[2984] GENERAL SHORT. Yes, sir. I thought sure that that included distant reconnaissance and as I remember Admiral Kimmel told me that he had tightened up all along the line, as I think he expressed it.

MR. KAUFMAN. Now, you had occasion to see Admiral Kimmel within a few days after the receipt of the dispatches of November 27?

GENERAL SHORT. I had a conference with Admiral Kimmel on December 1. I had another conference with Admiral Kimmel on December 2. I had another conference with him on December 3.

MR. KAUFMAN. Did you—

SENATOR BREWSTER. Let him finish.

MR. KAUFMAN. Yes.

GENERAL SHORT. I was going to say, one of my staff officers, my staff officer used for liaison with the Navy, had a conference with his gunnery officer on the 4th. I think that was the last conference we had before the attack.

MR. KAUFMAN. General, did you at any time tell Admiral Kimmel that you had alerted only against sabotage?

GENERAL SHORT. I don't know that I said that specifically. However, there was never any doubt in my mind that he knew exactly the status. Lieutenant Burr was detailed as a liaison from the Navy to the G-3 section. He sat in with our G-3 section, which was our operations section, which controlled all the alerts, all the war plans, everything of that kind. He knew everything that my staff knew. He had just one duty and that was to keep his headquarters informed of exactly what we were doing.

MR. KAUFMAN. Now, can you account, General, for the testimony given by Admiral Kimmel before this committee to the effect that he did not know that you had alerted only against sabotage? He testified further that he thought you had gone on an all-out alert and that he didn't know that you had anything else but an all-out alert.

GENERAL SHORT. The only way I can account for that would be poor staff work on the part of the staff of the Fourteenth Naval District. As I say, their liaison officer must have known exactly. We had furnished them with 10 copies of our staff operating procedure, which somebody in that naval staff certainly must have dug into and known what it meant. Why it did not get to Admiral Kimmel I do not know.

SENATOR LUCAS. General Short, will you give the committee the name of that liaison officer?

GENERAL SHORT. Lieutenant Burr. I don't know his initials. B-u-r-r.

SENATOR LUCAS. Thank you.

MR. KAUFMAN. Now, General—

MR. KEEFE. Mr. Chairman, may I suggest, in the interest of saving time, that counsel ask General Short at this time what an all-out alert would mean to an observer who knew nothing about it. What would they have to do so that someone in Hawaii would know that they were on an all-out alert if one was ordered and they went on such an alert.

Mr. Kaufman. What would be an all-out alert, General?

General Short. An all-out alert would cause every officer and every enlisted man in every organization to move to battle positions. Men would be moving all over the islands, in helmets, full [2985] field equipment, by motor, and otherwise. There would be men on every road.

Mr. Kaufman. And do you feel that was contrary to the instructions of the War Department not to alarm the civilian population?

General Short. I would say that it would mean to the civilian population and any Japanese agents that we were taking up our definite battle positions. There couldn't be any mistake about it.

Mr. Kaufman. Even though it was done under the name of war games, or whatever you wanted to call it?

General Short. If we had had time to make a previous announcement, which we usually did if we were going into maneuvers, and a little build-up, we probably could have deceived the average citizen. We probably could not have deceived a Japanese agent who had the message.

Mr. Kaufman. So you want the committee to understand that you had that problem in mind, so as not to circumvent or go contrary to the decision of the War Department?

General Short. I did.

Mr. Murphy. Counsel, as long as you are going into that, I suggest that we might complete the picture and ask the witness why he didn't go into alert No. 2, which provided protection against a submarine and an air attack. Alert No. 2.

Mr. Kaufman. General, will you first describe what alert No. 2 was. We have No. 1, against sabotage, and No. 3, an all-out alert. What was alert No. 2?

General Short. Alert No. 2 was a defense against sabotage and uprisings and, in addition, a defense against an air attack or against an attack by surface and subsurface vessels.

Mr. Kaufman. Will you tell us why you didn't put that into effect?

General Short. All of the coast artillery, all of the antiaircraft artillery, and all of the air would have immediately taken up their duties as described in that alert. Part of the coast artillery was right in the middle of the town. Fort de Russy was within two or three blocks of the Royal Hawaiian Hotel. The public couldn't help seeing that they were manning their seacoast guns. Placing live ammunition. Some of the guns were practically in the middle of the park. The bombers would have all gone to outlying islands, except the B-17's which could not, because the landing gear was not along. So there would have been a considerable amount of activity. Again perhaps the average citizens wouldn't have understood fully but if there was a Japanese agent, who knew what he was looking for, he would have known perfectly. [. . .]

[3026] The Vice Chairman. All right. Now, then, the Navy message of November 27, the so-called war warning message, you are thoroughly familiar with that?

General Short. Yes, sir.

THE VICE CHAIRMAN. And you saw it at the time Admiral Kimmel received it?

GENERAL SHORT. Yes, sir.

THE VICE CHAIRMAN. And you conferred with him about it?

GENERAL SHORT. I am sure that I talked pretty thoroughly about that on the 1st and the 3d—well, the 1st, 2d, and 3d of December.

THE VICE CHAIRMAN. Well, that was received—

GENERAL SHORT. Oh, no. On the 24th you are talking about?

THE VICE CHAIRMAN. No.

GENERAL SHORT. The one on November 27?

THE VICE CHAIRMAN. I am talking about the one on November 27.

GENERAL SHORT. I talked pretty thoroughly with him about that. We had talked immediately previously on that morning about the situation and the message of the 24th and there was really no additional information of an enemy in the message on the 27th that was not in the 24th.

THE VICE CHAIRMAN. Well, it was received in Hawaii on the 27th, the day it was sent?

GENERAL SHORT. That is correct, the afternoon of the 27th.

THE VICE CHAIRMAN. And you were familiar with it on that day?

GENERAL SHORT. Yes, sir.

THE VICE CHAIRMAN. And the opening words there:

> Consider this dispatch a war warning—

you say it did not mean anything special to you?

GENERAL SHORT. It meant no more than saying that Japan was going to attack some place. It is the same thing.

THE VICE CHAIRMAN. I see. And I believe you stated yesterday that you never had seen those words used in any dispatch before?

GENERAL SHORT. I did not remember that I had; no, sir.

THE VICE CHAIRMAN. I recall that Admiral Kimmel stated that he had never seen those words used before.

GENERAL SHORT. Yes, sir.

THE VICE CHAIRMAN. And I was just wondering why it was that those words that you had never seen in a dispatch before did not mean something more to you than you here indicate?

[3027] GENERAL SHORT. Well, if you analyze them they really are not nearly as definite, they mean not nearly as much as to say that Japan is going to attack the Philippines or Borneo because you are saying there that war is imminent and you are saying where it is imminent.

THE VICE CHAIRMAN. Well, this says:

> Consider this dispatch a war warning.

General Short. Yes, sir.

The Vice Chairman. That is a pretty definite statement, General.

General Short. Well, I think if they tell you that the Philippines are going to be attacked that is equivalent to a war warning.

The Vice Chairman. Well, that would be definite, too.

General Short. I think probably that was the reason that it did not have any particular effect on me, because the one on the 24th had stated that they expected Japanese action in any direction, including the Philippines and Guam.

The Vice Chairman. Well, you had the impression in your mind at the time from the information contained in the Navy message of November 24th that hostilities were indicated?

General Short. That the Navy definitely believed they were indicated.

The Vice Chairman. All right. Then 3 days later on the 27th, you saw this message, "Consider this dispatch a war warning."

General Short. Yes, sir.

The Vice Chairman. With the knowledge in your mind that you had already been notified that hostilities were imminent?

General Short. Yes, sir.

The Vice Chairman. And then here comes a message:

> Consider this dispatch a war warning.

You did not give any special meaning to that?

General Short. I thought it was just a reiteration of what had been said. [. . .]

[3040] The Vice Chairman. Did you and Admiral Kimmel keep each other thoroughly informed as to all information you received?

General Short. I will tell you what the practice was.

Whenever he received a message that directed the message be transmitted to me or that the Chief of Staff concurred in this message he furnished me with a copy. He did not furnish me with copies of other messages. He frequently, when we were together, told me of some other information but the only thing that I got from the Navy were the messages that he was told to deliver to me.

The Vice Chairman. All you got from Admiral Kimmel were the messages that he was told to deliver to you?

General Short. As far as messages were concerned. As I say, there were times when he picked up items of interest that he told me of.

The Vice Chairman. That was more or less accidental?

General Short. Yes, sir.

The Vice Chairman. How about the messages received by you, did you promptly inform Admiral Kimmel of what they contained?

General Short. I don't think I received any message that I didn't send to him, because I didn't have more than a half-dozen. I think every message that I got either showed that it was going to him or I sent him a copy.

The Vice Chairman. You feel sure then that you kept him fully informed as to all information received by you through messages but he did not do the same thing to you?

[3041] General Short. Well, I would say there was this difference. I got such a limited number of messages and only the very important messages. I got a message on July 8, on July 25, and on October 20, and November 27, and then one on the 7th, that came after the attack. I think those five were the only messages from July on that I received pertaining to the situation, the international situation, and I am quite sure that they were all furnished to him, to the Navy. They, on the other hand got, I think, much more information and lots of it, apparently, that they didn't feel I had any interest in or that they assumed I had received.

The Vice Chairman. How about these code messages, about burning the codes, was that conveyed to you?

General Short. That was not.

The Vice Chairman. It was not conveyed to you?

General Short. Not conveyed to me.

The Vice Chairman. The Navy had it?

General Short. Yes, sir.

The Vice Chairman. And did not tell you anything about it?

General Short. No, sir; and there was no direction in those messages that they should.

The Vice Chairman. So unless there was a definite direction in the Navy message to tell you about it, why, you were not told?

General Short. I think that is absolutely correct.

The Vice Chairman. All right.

Now, General, I would just like to ask you this question, with all deference and proper respect but if the messages sent, that is, if the messages not sent to you from Washington which you think should have been sent had made no more impression than the messages that were sent to you from Washington, what difference do you think it would have made?

General Short. I don't think that is a correct statement at all. There was never a message received by me that didn't make an impression. It may not have made the impression on me that you get from it or you think it should have made, but I never received a message from Washington that I didn't analyze carefully and make up my mind what the message meant.

The Vice Chairman. And you think these messages that were not sent to you from Washington would have been more important to you than those that were sent?

General Short. There were two that could hardly fail. The intercept which was the bombing plan of Pearl Harbor and the message stating that the ultimatum would be delivered at 1 p. m., which could have been sent to me 4 hours before the attack, and reached me 7 hours after the attack. Those two messages would definitely have meant something to me.

The Rejected Proposal for an Additional Warning to Kimmel

ARTHUR H. McCOLLUM, CHIEF, FAR EASTERN SECTION,
OFFICE OF NAVAL INTELLIGENCE

Joint Congressional Investigation

[3381] MR. KAUFMAN. Captain, where were you born?
CAPTAIN MCCOLLUM. I was born in Nagasaki, Japan.
MR. KAUFMAN. And how long have you been in the Navy?
[3382] CAPTAIN MCCOLLUM. I have been in the Navy for 28 years continuously.
MR. KAUFMAN. Will you tell us briefly your experience in the Navy?
CAPTAIN MCCOLLUM. I was appointed of the Naval Academy in 1917 by the late Senator Bankhead, of Alabama. I was graduated in 1921, in June.

I served for 6 months on the battleship *Arkansas* and for 2 months on the destroyer *Argonne* en route to the Orient. I arrived in Japan, in Tokyo, in March of 1922 for the purpose of studying the Japanese language. I remained, I think it was, until 1925.

During that period, for 4 months I served with the destroyers of the Asiatic Fleet who were at that time serving in conjunction with Japanese destroyers assisting the Army planes flying around the world in 1924. Most of that service was in the Kurile Islands, where I spent nearly 6 weeks at that time.

I returned to the United States in June of 1925, went to submarine school, finished there and in June 1926 I was assigned to duty on board the U.S.S. *O-7*, a submarine operating out of the Canal Zone. I served in that submarine for 2½ years, the last of which I was in command of it. I shifted from the U.S.S. *O-7* to executive officer of a larger submarine, the *S-11*, returned to the United States in that ship in June of 1928 and was ordered to duty as assistant naval attaché at the American Embassy in Tokyo. I arrived in Tokyo in about October of 1928 and served on that up until June of 1930.

I returned then to the United States and served for 3 years on the battleship *West Virginia*. In 1933, I returned to the Navy Department as head of the Far Eastern Division of the Office of Naval Intelligence. In February of 1935 I was

Source: Pearl Harbor Attack, *volume 8.*

detached from that duty and ordered to San Pedro, Calif., to set up a special Intelligence Office to work in conjunction with the staff of the commander in chief of the fleet, at that time, Admiral Reeves, to make an effort to stop the Japanese espionage attack on the vessels of our fleet.

I completed that duty in 1936 and was assigned as assistant operations officer and fleet intelligence officer on the staff of the commander in chief of the United States Fleet, Admiral A. J. Hepburn. I continued in that duty until about February 1, 1938. The last 7 months of that duty I was acting operations officer of the fleet, having no senior in that billing.

I spent then 2 months on temporary duty here in the Navy Department in connection with the installing of a new system for keeping check of the movements of vessels of the fleet; was assigned to the command of the destroyer *Jacob Jones*. In the course of that cruise I was detached from the command of the *Jacob Jones* in the latter part of September of 1939, returned to the United States, and was assigned to duty in the Division of Naval Intelligence, where I was detailed as officer in charge of the far eastern section.

I was relieved from that duty in October of 1942, was ordered as operations officer on the staff of the commander of the Southwest Pacific force, which was later called the Seventh Fleet, which was that part of the Navy serving under General MacArthur's orders, his over-all command. Upon arrival I was directed by the admiral to assume duty as intelligence officer of that fleet and served and developed an intelligence organization for him.

[3383] I served as inteligence officer of that fleet until about May 1 of 1945, when I returned to this country. I am now assigned as commanding officer of the heavy cruiser *Helena*.

MR. KAUFMAN. During the months of October and November 1941 what was your assignment?

CAPTAIN MCCOLLUM. I was head of the far eastern section of the Division of Naval Intelligence. I might add that from the 25th of August until about the 14th of October I was absent from the United States.

MR. KAUFMAN. You returned here around the 14th of October 1941?

CAPTAIN MCCOLLUM. That is correct, sir.

MR. KAUFMAN. And you continued as chief of the far eastern section until October of 1942?

CAPTAIN MCCOLLUM. That is correct, sir.

MR. KAUFMAN. And who was the counterpart of your particular position in the Army?

CAPTAIN MCCOLLUM. Colonel Bratton.

MR. KAUFMAN. Now, as part of your duties as chief of the far eastern section was it part of your duties to keep track of the fleet movements, of the Japanese fleet movements, and will you explain to the committee the manner in which that was done?

CAPTAIN MCCOLLUM. It was. I had a special section in my office who were charged with that particular duty. We had a large chart spread on the wall with

270   Five. Evaluating the Commanders

the ocean divided up into certain zones to which we had given names. All sorts of information concerning the movements of any Japanese man-of-war were entered on a card and that card index was kept together and daily or more often as necessary pins representing the various ships of the fleet were moved around on this chart, and for my own purposes there was a sheet summarizing the situation.

MR. KAUFMAN. Did the time come in November 1941 when you determined that the Intelligence Office in Washington had lost track of part of the Japanese fleet?

CAPTAIN MCCOLLUM. By the time you speak of, we were almost wholly dependent on one form of radio intelligence for information concerning the Japanese fleet which was not on the China coast. That form is known as traffic analysis, whereby inferences are drawn from such things as the volume of radio traffic and call signs and so on.

Those inferences were drawn and were made based largely on radio intelligence by that particular section of the Communications Intelligence organization. Their conclusions were then submitted to my office.

Radio intelligence, of course, has very definite limitations. If the man you are trying to find out about does not use the radio, radio falls down. After a fleet has been in port a certain length of time, in the absence of other information, that is, information other than radio intelligence, such as sight contact or some other report from an observer, unless the call signs of those ships are heard very definitely and plotted in by compass a doubt arises as to whether those ships are where radio intelligence thinks that they are. That situation existed, to my mind, from about the middle of November on.

MR. KAUFMAN. And as a result of that doubt did you dispatch to the commander of the Asiatic Fleet a dispatch which is dated No- [3384] vember 24, 1941, part of exhibit 37 [handing document to witness]?

CAPTAIN MCCOLLUM. Yes, sir, I drafted that dispatch and it was released by my chief, Admiral Wilkinson.

MR. KAUFMAN. And in reply to that dispatch did you get communications from the commander in chief of the Asiatic Fleet and the commander in chief of the Pacific Fleet which are referred to on page 7610 of the record before this committee, pages 7610 and 7611 [handing transcript to witness]?

CAPTAIN MCCOLLUM. Yes, sir.

MR. KAUFMAN. On or about December 1, 1941, did you cause to be prepared a memorandum showing the disposition or location of the Japanese fleet?

CAPTAIN MCCOLLUM. May I just see it, sir? I think I know what you mean, Mr. Counsel, but I would just like to refresh my mind, sir.

(The document referred to was handed to the witness.)

CAPTAIN MCCOLLUM. Yes, sir; this is a routine report on this particular subject and under the office orders that existed at the time, while that is dated December 1, the information and the time, the dead line for preparing this report was about 2 days before that, sir.

MR. KAUFMAN. And in that memorandum that you prepared you indicated that part of the Japanese fleet was in Japanese home waters?

CAPTAIN MCCOLLUM. That is correct, sir.

MR. KAUFMAN. That is in Exhibit 85 before this committee.

On or about December 6 did you prepare another memorandum as to the disposition of the Japanese fleet [handing document to witness]?

CAPTAIN MCCOLLUM. December 6?

MR. KAUFMAN. December 1.

CAPTAIN MCCOLLUM. No, sir. This memorandum that you have shown me here on December 1 is a memorandum which I personally prepared covering the development of the entire situation, the general location on the idea of the Japanese fleet and it is only one part of it. This summarizes the situation and is an attempt to show what to my mind was the very critical situation that had been brought about step by step.

MR. KAUFMAN. And was that communicated to the commander in chief of the Pacific Fleet?

CAPTAIN MCCOLLUM. So far as I know it was not, sir. This thing was actually drafted by me on the Friday and Saturday preceding.

If I remember correctly, December 1 was Monday. I polished it up in some aspects and took it to my chief, Admiral Wilkinson, early Monday morning in finished form. He read this document over, directed me to wait in his office and disappeared. He came back in about 10 minutes and said:

> You be ready to go to the office of Admiral Stark with me between 11 and 11:30 this morning, and make a number of copies of this thing that you have given me.

I did that and at the time stated I appeared in Admiral Stark's office. Present in that office at the time were Admiral Stark, Chief of Naval Operations, Admiral Ingersoll, the Assistant Chief of Naval Operations, Admiral Turner, the Director of War Plans, of course my chief, Admiral Wilkinson, and one or two other flag officers—I believe Admirals Brainard and Noyes.

[3385] At the direction of Admiral Wilkinson copies of this memorandum were passed to each of the flat officer present. I then read the memorandum personally and engaged a discussion at that time and pointed out that in my opinion war or rupture of diplomatic relations was imminent, and I requested information as to whether or not the fleets in the Pacific had been adequately alerted.

I was given a categorical assurance by both Admiral Stark and Admiral Turner that dispatches fully alerting the fleets and placing them on a war basis had been sent. I had seen no such dispatches at that time.

MR. KAUFMAN. Were you informed at that time of the war message sent by Admiral Stark to the commander in chief of the Pacific Fleet under date of November 27?

CAPTAIN MCCOLLUM. Not except in the form of the assurance that adequate information in alerting the fleet had been sent.

Five. Evaluating the Commanders

MR. KAUFMAN. In connection with the preparation of the memorandum to which you have just referred did you rely to any extent on the traffic analysis reports received by you from Admiral Kimmel?

CAPTAIN MCCOLLUM. Oh, yes. I might point out that the best stations for traffic analysis were at Corregidor, the radio intelligence center there, and at Hawaii on Oahu. We were dependent on those places for our information here.

. . .

[3388] CAPTAIN MCCOLLUM. After submitting my memorandum to Admiral Wilkinson and through him to the Chief of Naval Operations—

MR. KAUFMAN. You are referring now to exhibit what? Exhibit 81?

CAPTAIN MCCOLLUM. The December 1, 1941. [Continuing:] I was put in the rather difficult position of not personally knowing what had been sent out to the fleet. Possibly it was none of my business. As I pointed out to you, the basis of this memorandum—the information it was based on—was actually as of about the 28th of November. As time went on we had sent out dispatches to our naval attachés in Tokyo, Pieping, Bangkok, and Shanghai to destroy all of their codes, and to report by the use of a code word, and those codes were destroyed.

We were getting reports from our observers of the Japanese task force which was moving down the Kra Peninsula. Our planes were sighting forces moving; our submarines were trailing them. We had some little information in addition. I still did not know what had been sent to the fleet.

I drafted a rather brief dispatch, outlining the information pretty much as is in this memorandum, but greatly condensed. I went further and stated that we felt everything pointed to an imminent outbreak of hostilities between Japan and the United States. That dispatch was taken by me to my Chief, Captain Hurd, and together we went in to see Admiral Wilkinson. We did it in view of the fact that the function of evaluation of Intelligence, that is, the drawing of inferences therefrom, had been transferred over to be a function of the War Plans Division.

I was directed to take that dispatch and present it for the consideration of Admiral Turner, the Director of the War Plans Division, which I did.

Admiral Turner read the dispatch over. He then made a number of corrections in it, striking out all except the information parts of it, more or less, and then showed me for the first time the dispatch which he had sent on the 27th, which I believe is referred to as the "war warning" dispatch, and the one which was sent, I believe, on the 24th—wasn't it?

MR. KAUFMAN. That is right.

CAPTAIN MCCOLLUM (continuing). Which preceded that dispatch, and said did not I think that was enough. I said, "Well, good gosh, you put in the words 'war warning.' I do not know what could be plainer than that, but, nevertheless, I would like to see mine go too."

He said, "Well, if you want to send it, you either send it the way I corrected it, or take it back to Wilkinson and we will argue about it"—or words to that effect.

I cannot presume to remember precisely.

I took it back to Admiral Wilkinson and discussed it with him, and he said, "Leave it here with me for a while," and that is all.

Now, I would like it understood that merely because this was prepared on a dispatch blank in no sense means it was an official dispatch. [3389] It was merely my recommendation to my seniors which they were privileged to throw in the wastebasket, I imagine. It was in no sense a part of the official file. It is nothing other than a recommendation for the dispatch officer. I have written dozens of dispatches for the admiral, and he could either throw them away, or use them. There was no record kept of that sort of thing.

MR. KAUFMAN. That dispatch, or that memorandum that you prepared had no relation or no reference at all, to the winds execute message?

CAPTAIN MCCOLLUM. No, sir.

MR. KAUFMAN. And if Captain Safford says that the dispatch or memorandum that you prepared had relation to the winds execute message, what is your version of it?

CAPTAIN MCCOLLUM. I think Safford would be misinformed in that. He has judged my intentions in what motivated me, sir, and I believe I am a better judge of that than he is, although I do not impugn his motives whatsoever. He may sincerely believe that to be true, sir.

MR. KAUFMAN. Captain Safford testified at one place that the last paragraph of your memorandum or dispatch had particular reference to the winds execute message, and a suggestion by you that you wanted to avoid another Port Arthur.

CAPTAIN MCCOLLUM. No, sir; I could not have done anything like that, Mr. Counsellor, when I did not have the winds execute message.

MR. KEEFE. May I inquire, Mr. Chairman? Am I correct in the understanding that this purported message drawn by Captain McCollum is not in evidence, and is not in existence?

CAPTAIN MCCOLLUM. As I explained, sir, this sort of thing was merely my recommendation on a dispatch blank, drafted in dispatch form.

MR. KEEFE. But it is not in existence?

CAPTAIN MCCOLLUM. No, sir, it is not in existence, sir.

MR. KEEFE. You are testifying from recollection?

CAPTAIN MCCOLLUM. That is correct, sir.

MR. KEEFE. As to what was written in it?

CAPTAIN MCCOLLUM. That is correct, sir. . . .

SENATOR LUCAS. May I make an inquiry at this point?

As I understand you, sir, Admiral Wilkinson did not act on your recommendation.

CAPTAIN MCCOLLUM. That, Senator, I do not know, sir. I do not know what further Admiral Wilkinson did with it. He may have gone up with it to higher authority, and it was turned down, or he may have decided not to go further with it, sir.

Senator Lucas. As far as the evidence is concerned, there is no evidence in the record that any dispatch of this character was ever sent?

Captain McCollum. There is no evidence that any dispatch of this character was ever sent.

Senator Lucas. By the Chief of Naval Operations?

[3390]   Captain McCollum. That is correct, sir; no dispatch was ever sent.

Mr. Keefe. Does the evidence disclose the date of this alleged conversation, or the writing of this dispatch?

Captain McCollum. These things are entirely memory on my part, sir. There is no record of this thing at all. As I explained to you, this was drawn up and written on the dispatch form. When the dispatch does not go, you wind it up, and throw it in the waste basket. That is what happened probably in this case.

Mr. Keefe. Do you recall the date that this took place?

Captain McCollum. It was either the 4th or 5th, sir.

Mr. Keefe. Of December?

Captain McCollum. Yes, sir.

Senator Ferguson. That would be on a Saturday or a Friday?

Captain McCollum. Yes, sir. It was about that time.

The Scrambler Phone Controversy

LIEUTENANT GENERAL WALTER C. SHORT,
COMMANDING GENERAL, HAWAIIAN DEPARTMENT

WALTER C. PHILLIPS, CHIEF OF STAFF
UNDER GENERAL SHORT, HAWAIIAN DEPARTMENT

CARROLL A. POWELL, SIGNAL CORPS,
U.S. ARMY, WASHINGTON, D.C.

Roberts Commission

GENERAL GEORGE C. MARSHALL, CHIEF OF STAFF, U.S. ARMY

Joint Congressional Investigation

LIEUTENANT GENERAL WALTER C. SHORT,
Commanding General, Hawaiian Department

[46] Apparently later that morning the War Department got some alarming information. I have no way of knowing how they got the information. However, they filed at 12:18, Eastern Standard Time, December 7, which is 6:45 our time here, Honolulu — they filed a message with the R. C. A. to ask me and General Martin — that message had to be encoded before it was filed. I think the estimate of an hour would be an extremely short time for the encoding of the message and filing it with R. C. A. Our experience would indicate a great deal more time for that. We cut that down as a minimum.

Here is what the message said, and this to my mind is the most important thing I received from the War Department:

> 529 7th Japanese are presenting at 1 p. m. Eastern Standard Time today what amounts to an ultimatum also they are under orders to destroy their code machine immediately stop. Just what significance the hour set may have we do not know but be on alert accordingly stop. Inform naval authorities of this communication.

Sources: Pearl Harbor Attack, *volume 22;* Pearl Harbor Attack, *volume 3* (General Marshall only).

In view of what happened it is perfectly apparent that they destroyed their code machines in order to put into use a new code that they knew nobody had broken or could get their information.

That message, as I say, was filed at 6:48 in Washington. It was received here by the R. C. A. at 7:33. I do not know what caused the R. C. A. to delay delivering the message immediately because it would have to be delivered by a messenger, but I suspect that at the time the messenger was getting under way, the attack, which was at 7:55, had started, and the messenger did not care to be roaming around during an attack, and it was brought to the Signal Office at 11:45. It was decoded and delivered to the Adjutant General of the Department at 2:58 in the afternoon. You can see the time it took to decode it, so I do not think I am very much wrong when I say that it must have taken at least one hour to decode it; so that if we assume that they started to encode it that they had the information as early as 5:45 Honolulu Time. If they had telephoned me urgent, telephoned the corps in the clear, I could have had the information at 6 o'clock in the morning without any question at all because we talk repeatedly and when we get the call through I receive these things in around 15 minutes.

On that point also we have one of these *speech scramblers,* and there is one in the office of the Chief of Staff. While they are not considered as safe as code, they are reasonably safe.

If they had felt this was a probability of an attack on Honolulu, they could have put the call through, and if they felt there was a [47] possibility of an attack certainly then they had *every great duty* to get that information to me as rapidly as possible, and if that call was put through to me and got to me as early as 2 o'clock, or I should say 6 o'clock, which was two hours in which to arrange everything and make absolutely ready for a Japanese attack.

As I say, that reached me seven hours after the attack. During the attack that morning I had gone to our defense command post and told Colonel Phillips to call the Chief of Staff and get the information as soon as it was decoded. He asked if we had received a message, but we had not received it even then.

THE CHAIRMAN. Can you tell me at what hour Phillips telephoned?

GENERAL SHORT. I left this office sometime around 8:35 or 8:40 and Colonel Phillips put in the call and I went to the command post. I don't know how long it took to get the call through but my feeling is sometime around, it must have been around 9 o'clock. Anyway it was before 2:58 in the afternoon. That was all that was said at that time. Apparently the War Department became aware a little later of the significance of the message and of our not getting it until seven hours after the attack.

WALTER C. PHILLIPS,
Chief of Staff under General Short, Hawaiian Department

[147] GENERAL MCCOY. I understand that he established immediately what you call your advanced—

COLONEL PHILLIPS. Command post.

GENERAL MCCOY. Command post, in the crater?

COLONEL PHILLIPS. Yes, sir.

GENERAL MCCOY. Do you remember about what time that was established?

COLONEL PHILLIPS. Very shortly; I should say around 9, perhaps 9 o'clock, 9:30, it was being opened.

GENERAL MCCOY. It was functioning, then, during most of the succeeding raids?

COLONEL PHILLIPS. Yes, sir.

GENERAL MCCOY. That is, I take it there were three raids, were there?

COLONEL PHILLIPS. There were three to my knowledge. I remained here, sir.

GENERAL MCCOY. That is, you remained in this building?

COLONEL PHILLIPS. I remained in this building, my office just in there (indicating). We had our scrambled phone to Washington in this little booth right here, and I was directed to remain here and did not go to the forward command post until Tuesday following the attack.

GENERAL MCCOY. Who was in charge of it during the Sunday morning after it was established?

[148] COLONEL PHILLIPS. General Short was there himself, G-3 was there, and the bulk of G-2; the headquarters commandant, Major Henderson, was there establishing the post, and he of course is—

GENERAL MCCOY. That was the normal arrangement for it?

COLONEL PHILLIPS. That was the normal arrangement, yes, sir. Normally the Chief of Staff, of course, would have been there; but due to our telephone arrangement with Washington and the necessity that the Department Commander felt for getting information to Washington and from Washington I remained near this phone and did all the talking with the War Department.

GENERAL MCCOY. How many times did you talk with them that day? Do you remember?

COLONEL PHILLIPS. Two or three, sir.

GENERAL MCCOY. Did you take a transcript of your conversation?

COLONEL PHILLIPS. I did not, sir. Most of them were in the—first call I put in at the direction of the Department Commander, General Marshall.

GENERAL MCCOY. The Chief of Staff, you mean?

COLONEL PHILLIPS. To the Chief of Staff, yes, sir.

GENERAL MCCOY. You talked to him personally?

COLONEL PHILLIPS. Yes, sir.

GENERAL MCCOY. How many times that morning?

COLONEL PHILLIPS. We only called once, as I recall.

GENERAL MCCOY. Did he call you back at any time that day?

COLONEL PHILLIPS. I believe he did, sir. There is a record of that. There is a record of the number of calls.

GENERAL MCCOY. Yes. Could you sit down and think it over and dictate the nature of your conversation to General Marshall?

COLONEL PHILLIPS. Yes, sir.

GENERAL MCCOY. I think it would be well.

THE CHAIRMAN. Will you make a memorandum to do it and come back later when we have got through these other matters?

COLONEL PHILLIPS. Yes, sir.

GENERAL MCCOY. Was there any other time between November 27 and December 7 that the Department Commander or you talked with the Chief of Staff or anybody else in the War Department about the measures taken for security here?

COLONEL PHILLIPS. I did not, sir, and I do not believe that the Department Commander did.

GENERAL MCCOY. Was it customary in time of crisis to use the telephone with the office of the Chief of Staff in Washington?

COLONEL PHILLIPS. It was used very very seldom, sir.

GENERAL MCCOY. Why was that the case? That is, I mean it is the quickest means of communication.

COLONEL PHILLIPS. Yes, sir.

GENERAL MCCOY. Now, why was it not used in time of emergency more frequently, say?

COLONEL PHILLIPS. I could not say as to that, sir.

GENERAL MCCOY. Did you possibly feel that it was not as safe as a code message by radio?

COLONEL PHILLIPS. No, sir. With this phone it's a highly secret arrangement. It's a scrambled phone, and we feel its use is ex- [149] tremely — that is limited; we shouldn't use it but on a highly important — or for highly important calls. That is the impression that the Department Commander gave me. It is the most secret, we think. I don't know.

GENERAL MCCOY. And it is certainly the quickest?

COLONEL PHILLIPS. No question about that, sir.

GENERAL MCCOY. You talk in the open, and it scrambles itself?

COLONEL PHILLIPS. That's right. You raise a little plug on the phone itself. There are definite instructions as to how to place the call. The operator says, "Go ahead," and you pull out this little plug, and that scrambles your conversation.

GENERAL MCCOY. Both ways?

COLONEL PHILLIPS. Both ways. He pulls out the plug on his phone.

ADMIRAL STANDLEY. That is understood beforehand?

COLONEL PHILLIPS. Oh, yes, yes, sir.

GENERAL MCCOY. Have you any such arrangement with the Navy here on the Island?

COLONEL PHILLIPS. No, sir.

GENERAL MCCOY. Do you have a direct line between commanders-in-chief and the commander here?

COLONEL PHILLIPS. We have in the forward C. P.

GENERAL MCCOY. But not here?

COLONEL PHILLIPS. Not here, no, sir?

GENERAL MCCOY. It would go here through the city central, would it?

COLONEL PHILLIPS. Yes, sir. Well, no. We have cables here direct to Pearl Harbor but no direct connection. The forward C. P., we have a phone directly—onto the Department Commander's desk directly from the Commander in Chief of the Pacific Fleet.

GENERAL MCCOY. How would you get the Commander in Chief normally here at headquarters?

COLONEL PHILLIPS. Call Pearl Harbor, sir.

GENERAL MCCOY. That would go into a military central, would it?

COLONEL PHILLIPS. Yes, sir, right here, sir.

GENERAL MCCOY. It would not go downtown to the civilian central?

COLONEL PHILLIPS. No, sir, I do not believe so. I believe that is correct, sir.

GENERAL MCCOY. In other words, there is a military central here and a naval central down at the—

COLONEL PHILLIPS. A naval central down there.

GENERAL MCCOY. At Pearl Harbor?

COLONEL PHILLIPS. Yes, sir.

CARROLL A. POWELL,
Signal Corps, U.S. Army, Washington, D.C.

[237] THE CHAIRMAN. Now, since you have been here before, Colonel, have you investigated the atmospheric and radio conditions on the Island of Oahu on the morning of December 7?

COLONEL POWELL. I did not investigate the atmospheric conditions but just took our log that we worked with from Washington and the trouble we had that morning.

At 1:40 a. m. we were contacted with Washington. Our frequently here was 8160. Washington's was 8860. We had been contacting them previously and we were clearing corrections. We had been clearing corrections, errors, and we had a readability of four, which is very poor.

At 2:40 a. m. we were still clearing our corrections of the previous errors and had a readability of four. The frequency was the same.

At 3:40 a. m. we were still clearing our corrections. The readability was the same. It was very difficult to get anything through that morning. . . .

[243] GENERAL MCCOY. In other words, you would assume that had the attack not occurred that normally that interference would be atmospheric?

COLONEL POWELL. Yes, that is what I thought about it, because we have been having that same experience right along. This is a bad time of the year to transmit with our transmitter to Washington. We might be a complete day without communication to Washington due to atmospheric conditions, the time of the moon and so on, that sometimes no one was able to transmit to Washington.

THE CHAIRMAN. The same thing does not necessarily apply to their ability to transmit to you because their station is more powerful?

COLONEL POWELL. Yes.

THE CHAIRMAN. But as it was, your reception was very bad that morning?

COLONEL POWELL. Yes.

THE CHAIRMAN. Any other questions?

GENERAL MCCOY. Didn't you have some questions you wanted to ask concerning this scrambled telephone?

THE CHAIRMAN. When was your scrambled telephone instrument installed here?

COLONEL POWELL. It was about a year ago. It is a very secret thing. Very few people know about it.

THE CHAIRMAN. We are keeping everything secret, but we have got to know the facts.

COLONEL POWELL. Yes.

THE CHAIRMAN. Because it was so very secret, was there any understanding here that it should be used only in emergency cases, or was it generally used?

COLONEL POWELL. It was only for the use of the commanding general and the chief of staff. Nobody else used it or had the key to it except the commanding general and the chief of staff.

THE CHAIRMAN. That would indicate that it was an emergency service?

COLONEL POWELL. Yes, a confidential service.

THE CHAIRMAN. A confidential service.

COLONEL POWELL. Yes. It is fairly confidential, but it is not secret by any means.

THE CHAIRMAN. Why not?

COLONEL POWELL. Just because of the mechanics of the thing. Our transmission to San Francisco is all scrambled by the Mutual Telephone Company.

THE CHAIRMAN. That is the Mutual Telephone Company here?

COLONEL POWELL. Yes, and the R. C. A. at San Francisco. For scrambling done here, a radio or an ordinary receiver could not pick up that message.

[244] THE CHAIRMAN. If I had an ordinary receiver I would hear a series of queer words which did not mean anything?

COLONEL POWELL. That is correct.

THE CHAIRMAN. And the Mutual office here has to advise San Francisco which dial they are using in order to unscramble it?

COLONEL POWELL. Yes.

THE CHAIRMAN. Then San Francisco has got to set its dial at a certain point?

COLONEL POWELL. Yes.

THE CHAIRMAN. So that San Francisco will hear it clearly?

COLONEL POWELL. Yes.

THE CHAIRMAN. They have the same system from San Francisco into Washington?

COLONEL POWELL. Yes.

THE CHAIRMAN. So that if anybody was going to listen in on another set, he would have to know which dial they are going to use to get it?

COLONEL POWELL. He would not know the type of instrument?

THE CHAIRMAN. The type of instrument?

COLONEL POWELL. Yes.

This scrambler here has an addition to the scrambler, put in by the Mutual Telephone Company so that the message is double scrambled. A very interesting thing happened. We installed the outfit about a year ago, and the telephone circuit from Tokyo uses the same scrambler as this Mutual does from here to San Francisco.

So when we put this on the circuit, Tokyo called up right quick and wanted to know what we had done to the circuit between Honolulu and San Francisco because they said they could not understand it and wanted to know what was being done to it; so we have been watching that telephone circuit and reading it all the time—everything that goes on.

THE CHAIRMAN. Is that telephone circuit a radio circuit?

COLONEL POWELL. Yes.

THE CHAIRMAN. It is not run on a cable?

COLONEL POWELL. No, sir. The only cable is the cable company.

THE CHAIRMAN. I thought this was a wire?

COLONEL POWELL. It is simply a radio.

GENERAL MCCOY. So they could listen in?

COLONEL POWELL. Yes.

GENERAL MCCOY. And you put in a second scrambler to cover that?

COLONEL POWELL. Yes. That is what they called up for and wanted to know what we had done to the circuit.

THE CHAIRMAN. You do not know if they ever found out or not?

COLONEL POWELL. No, sir. We just told them something had happened, or Mutual told them something had happened to the circuit, and that is all.

I have been assured by the board in Washington that, so far as this particular circuit ever getting out of the United States, that does not mean it makes it private because they can undoubtedly find out that, I suppose, or shift it or make it themselves; so it is not a secret means of transmission. It is what you might call a private means of communication.

[245] THE CHAIRMAN. But rather dangerous to use?

COLONEL POWELL. Yes.

GENERAL MCCOY. What caused it to be put in? Was it put in on your recommendation?

COLONEL POWELL. No, sir; it was a system put in under orders of the Secretary of War, I understand, in that he wanted to talk to all commanding generals in the area in the United States, and then he had one put in over here in Puerto Rico—no, in Panama, so he could have a private means of communication so everybody would not be able to listen in on his conversation.

282   Five. Evaluating the Commanders

GENERAL MCCOY. Do you know whether there are any Japanese in the telephone central office here?

COLONEL POWELL. There are no alien Japanese in the telephone central, and the Department Commander has placed me in kind of charge of the telephone company, and they have cooperated very well and have removed all aliens from the telephone circuits going to the mainland, and have eliminated them from all very important key jobs. They had no aliens, but only people of Japanese ancestry, which they have taken out.

GENERAL GEORGE C. MARSHALL,
Chief of Staff, U.S. Army

[1212] SENATOR FERGUSON. Did you ever notify General Short that you found it impossible or that you were not furnishing him all available G-2 data for reasons of security?

GENERAL MARSHALL. No, sir; I have no recollection of that.

SENATOR FERGUSON. So then he could not have any knowledge as to whether or not he was getting all that G-2 had or had not?

GENERAL MARSHALL. Presumably so. Here is the message I was referring to.

SENATOR FERGUSON. Will you read it?

GENERAL MARSHALL. It is dated Washington, D.C., July 8, 1941. It is only the later portion I refer to, but I will read it all (reading from Exhibit No. 32):

> Hawaiian Department, Fort Shafter, T. H.
> Nine two four seven AGMC for your information deduction from information from numerous sources if that Japanese Government has determined upon its future policy which is supported by all principal Japanese political and military groups Period This policy is at present one of watchful waiting involving probable aggressive action against maritime provinces of Russia if and when Siberian garrison has been materially reduced in strength and it becomes evident that Germany will win a decisive victory in European Russia Period Opinion is that Jap activity in the south will be for the present confined to seizure and development of naval army and air bases in Indochina although an advance against the British and Dutch cannot be entirely ruled out Period Neutrality pact with Russia may be abrogated Period They have ordered all Jap vessels in US Atlantic ports to be west of Panama Canal by first August Period Movement of Jap shipping from Japan has been suspended and additional merchant vessels are being requisitioned.

Signed "Adams," who was the Adjutant General.

I was referring specifically to the last sentence which is taken almost entirely from magic, other portions were in magic, but—that came to us in various ways—but the last sentence was from magic direct.

SENATOR FERGUSON. When you sent the message on the 7th, General, that is, the noon on the 7th, did you consider the question of security?

GENERAL MARSHALL. Do you mean, Senator, in relation to the form of the message?

SENATOR FERGUSON. Yes; both the form and the means of sending it.

GENERAL MARSHALL. I only knew that it would be encoded, which is done very rapidly on a type machine and automatically. My only recollection regarding the security aspect — and it is difficult for me to state this with any assurance that I am being accurate because I am confused in back sights — was we must be sufficiently secure to prevent some claim of overt act on our part and, therefore, the telephone was ruled out.

Now, I am not at all certain that that did rule out the telephone. That might have been an afterthought after the event; I do not know.

SENATOR FERGUSON. I want to talk to you about that for a moment.

GENERAL MARSHALL. But I assume that this message — in fact, I had [1213] seen that this message to which you just referred was going to be enciphered in secure code and decoded in that manner.

SENATOR FERGUSON. Well, you felt rather sure at that particular moment that you were sending this message that something would happen somewhere at 1 o'clock, or prior to 1 o'clock?

GENERAL MARSHALL. Something of some serious nature was going to be synchronized with that 1 o'clock.

SENATOR FERGUSON. Yes. Well, then, you were thinking about the question of security and as to whether or not you would use the telephone. Now, how could the use of that telephone to Hawaii have been an overt act of war by America against Japan in alerting Hawaii?

GENERAL MARSHALL. I think, Senator, that the Japanese would have grasped at most any straw to bring to such portions of our public that doubted our integrity of action that we were committing an act that forced action on their part.

I say again I am not at all clear as to what my reasons were regarding the telephone because 4 years later it is very difficult for me to tell what went on in my mind at the time. I will say this, though: It was in my mind regarding the use of transocean telephone.

Mr. Roosevelt, the President, had been in the frequent habit of talking to the Prime Minister by telephone. He also used to talk to Mr. Bullitt when he was Ambassador in Paris and my recollection is that that was intercepted by the Germans.

I had a test made of induction from telephone conversations on the Atlantic cable from Gardner's Island. I found that that could be picked up by induction. I talked to the President not once but several times. I also later, after we were in the war, talked with the Prime Minister in an endeavor to have them be more careful in the use of the scrambler. I believe it is understood what that is.

SENATOR FERGUSON. Yes.

GENERAL MARSHALL. Because in our terminology that is private and not secret. A casual person listening in would not know what we were talking about. The person intent and with the facilities for breaking through in your communications can do it. It was long after we were in the war before we were able to install a scrambler system, which is now in vogue and which is quite elaborate, that was felt to be secret. Therefore, whether or not our overseas communication, overseas telephone communication, was secure or not was a question. I might go—

SENATOR FERGUSON. Will you explain for our benefit now what a scrambler is?

GENERAL MARSHALL. A scrambler is a machine which takes your conversation and mixes it up into something that sounds like Chinese; that is the nearest I can give you.

SENATOR FERGUSON. Almost like static, isn't it?

GENERAL MARSHALL. Well, no; it is not a roar so much as it is just a hash of sounds and if you press a certain button it comes to you in understandable English. Now, a person—

SENATOR FERGUSON. In other words, you unscramble it.

GENERAL MARSHALL. Yes, sir; you unscramble it, anyone at the other end if he has the machine and presses the button.

SENATOR FERGUSON. All along the line it is scrambled and in that machine it is unscrambled?

[1214] GENERAL MARSHALL. Until it gets to the other end of the line.

Now, I might illustrate a little further our telephone reactions because I undertook to try one officer for the use of the telephone from Panama, which we found all taken down here and that was furnished to me in writing by a naval intercept, where they were checking on the time and indiscretions of that nature.

I called this commander to get him up here, the officer going to Panama and the commander going the other way and then I found myself in the same difficulty with the commander in his conversation from Hawaii and then we hung up on him.

I had several conversations with the western defense commander and I hung up the phone because of the indiscretions in the excitement and argument that were being made over the phone. We were always in danger of that and we were quite aware of it, because the telephone is a very easy instrument to tap and the radio telephone, I believe, is even easier, but I want to repeat again that I have no clear recollection whatsoever as to my own reactions as to why I did not attempt to telephone at this time, but I have one conclusion that I think is quite accurate, that I certainly would have called up General MacArthur first.

SENATOR FERGUSON. You had a scramble telephone to Hawaii and the Philippines at that time?

GENERAL MARSHALL. I don't know about the Philippines but I know we had it in to Hawaii.

SENATOR FERGUSON. Had you ever talked to General Short on the scramble telephone?

GENERAL MARSHALL. I do not recall, sir.

SENATOR FERGUSON. Did you have a line to General MacArthur?

GENERAL MARSHALL. We had a means of telephone communication but I do not recall whether or not we had a scrambler.

SENATOR FERGUSON. Did you talk to General MacArthur the first 7 days of December 1941?

GENERAL MARSHALL. No, sir; and I do not recall I ever did talk to him on the telephone.

SENATOR FERGUSON. You do not recall that you ever talked to him?

GENERAL MARSHALL. Then or since.

SENATOR FERGUSON. On the telephone?

GENERAL MARSHALL. On the telephone. . . .

[1288] SENATOR FERGUSON. All right. Now I want to ask you in relation to the use of the telephone as an overt act to Hawaii, compared to this action, [sending a telegram] as to how you would compare it.

GENERAL MARSHALL. I would say the use of a telephone depended on what was being said on the telephone.

SENATOR FERGUSON. Well, to alert the Hawaiians.

[1289] GENERAL MARSHALL. That is a matter of judgment, Senator.

SENATOR FERGUSON. I just want your explanation of it.

GENERAL MARSHALL. I will go into this first, the question of the air flight. General Arnold discussed that with the Secretary of War, because we regarded it as a very delicate proposition. We could not figure any other way how to obtain this information. We thought it was very important that we should know. We thought it possible that by flying at a high altitude we might get by with the thing without more than a Japanese objection to our coming into their mandated area. However, we had to accept the possibility that they would seize upon this as an overt act.

As to the telephone message, I feel if they knew exactly what we were doing, which they would have ascertained from the telephone message, that there were two factors involved: One was the explanation of why we took that action, which was the receipt of a magic message, the only way we could obtain that, and the other was the fact we were alerting the garrisons which they could construe as a hostile act.

Now there was brought to my attention in that connection an item of my testimony on page 3109, lines 8 and 9—no, I am wrong. I will strike that all out. It does not apply to this.

That is the best answer I can give you, Senator. I will say this, though, in conclusion, that my comments about the telephone, where I explained my own state of mind in general regarding the serious aspect of the telephone, should not be read in the light of assuming that that was definitely why I did not telephone, because just exactly why I did not telephone I do not undertake to explain right now, because I am too involved in back sights to try to determine definitely what was going on in my head at that particular moment.

There was the question of time involved. The only thing I can say, I am quite certain I am right, is had I telephoned I would have telephoned to the Philippines first.

SENATOR FERGUSON. Now, would alerting our own Army on the Philippines, from a military standpoint, be an overt act against any country?

GENERAL MARSHALL. I would not consider it as such. . . .

[1431] MR. KEEFE. Well, when you were before the Army Board, General Marshall, there were some questions asked you at that time as to why you did not use the telephone, and you gave quite a long answer, if you recall, and in your answer you referred to the fact that, oh, it [1432] would have required getting those fellows out of bed out there in Hawaii at that hour. Do you remember that?

GENERAL MARSHALL. Well, I was talking about the time involved, and I was multiplying it by the number of places involved.

MR. KEEFE. And was that one of the reasons why you decided not to use the telephone, that perhaps it would take time getting the fellows out of bed in Hawaii?

GENERAL MARSHALL. I think you are giving a considerable emphasis to the "bed." I was talking about the time required to get the people on the phone and giving them the communication at the hour that the message would come in.

Shortages of Military Equipment

LIEUTENANT GENERAL WALTER C. SHORT, COMMANDING GENERAL, HAWAIIAN DEPARTMENT

Navy Court of Inquiry

[169] 1. Q. Will you please state your name, rank, and present status, General Short?

A. Major General Walter C. Short, U.S. Army (Ret).

2. Q. What was your station and duty on 7 December 1941?

A. I was commanding the Hawaiian Department. I was stationed at Fort Shafter, Territory of Hawaii.

3. Q. When did you assume that duty?

A. February 7, or it might be carried on the War Department's records as the 8th. The War Department records will show February 7 or 8, 1941.

[170] 4. Q. When were you relieved of this duty?

A. December 16, 1941.

5. Q. I show you a document which is marked Exhibit 6 before this court for identification, and it is entitled Joint Army and Navy Action 1935. Generally, speaking, are you familiar with the provisions of this document?

A. I am generally familiar with it.

6. Q. I show you page five of this document, under paragraph nine, the general subject matter of determination of methods of coordination, and ask you, had unity of command been placed in effect in the Hawaiian area prior to 7 December 1941?

A. It had not.

7. Q. So far as you were concerned, had any consideration been given to placing unity of command in effect under the provision that it might be done by the commanders of local forces?

A. As long as I had communication with the War Department, I would have not considered it without consulting them.

8. Q. Under Chapter Two, Article 9, subsection b. (3), what officer did you deal with as Commander of Naval Forces in the Hawaiian area?

A. I dealt with two officers; primarily, on routine matters, with Admiral

Source: Pearl Harbor Attack, *volume 32*.

Bloch, the Commandant of the 14th Naval District, and on matters of immediate importance with Admiral Kimmel, with Admiral Bloch usually present—the three of us in the discussion.

9. Q. In matters affecting the defenses of Pearl Harbor, what officer in the Navy, in the Hawaiian area, did you usually have dealings with?

A. The same reply pertains. When it was routine I dealt with Admiral Bloch. When it got beyond routine I usually dealt with both Admiral Bloch and Admiral Kimmel together.

10. Q. Was it the practice in the Hawaiian area to hold conferences on military matters affecting the defenses of Pearl Harbor?

A. We had no stated time set for holding conferences, but whenever Admiral Kimmel or I either got anything of prime importance from the Navy or War Department, we practically always had a personal conference.

11. Q. How would you describe the relations between yourself and the Commander-in-Chief Pacific Fleet—as cordial, strained, cooperative, or what language would you use?

A. I would say that they were extremely friendly, cordial, and cooperative. We were on a very friendly basis personally, as well as officially. We played golf together about every other Sunday, and the Sundays we didn't play golf, very frequently Admiral Kimmel dropped in to see me in the morning; because his family was away he came to my quarters more than I went to his.

12. Q. I show you a document marked Exhibit 7 before this court of inquiry, which purports to be JCD-42. If you recognize this document, will you state what it is?

A. The full name of the document is "Joint Coastal Frontier Defense Plan, Hawaiian Coastal Frontier," and that is the way we usually designated it, rather than leaving out the word "frontier." [...]

[171] 19. Q. Now was the whole Exhibit, this JCD-42, in effect on 7 December 1941?

A. Yes, sir, before that date it had been amended, so that the amendment would be included in it.

20. Q. Adverting to this same Exhibit, would you please read Article 14?

A. Reading:

> TASKS. a. JOINT TASK To hold OAHU as a main outlying naval base, and to control and protect shipping in the Coastal Zone.
>
> b. ARMY TASK. To hold OAHU against attacks by sea, land, and air forces, and against hostile sympathizers; to support the naval forces.
>
> c. NAVY TASK. To patrol the Coastal Zone and to control and protect shipping therein; to support the Army forces.

21. Q. Adverting to Article 17 of JCD-42, which states that the Commanding General of the Hawaiian Department shall provide for the beach and land, seacoast and anti-aircraft defenses of OAHU, with particular attention to the Pearl Harbor Naval Base, will you please state in general terms what provisions

Military Equipment 289

had been made to carry out the Army's undertaking in this respect prior to 7 December 1941?

A. The Army had provided proper defenses—harbor defenses, anti-aircraft defense, aircraft defenses, communications, and aircraft warning service. I say in general terms that would be the answer.

22. Q. On 7 December 1941, would you state what your opinion was as to whether the dispositions that had been made were adequate to meet the Army's undertaking under this section.

A. I am not sure that I know just what you mean by that—whether the dispositions would be provided for in our plans or whether the dispositions we were actually occupying at the minute.

23. Q. I shall rephrase my question. Will you state what your opinion was on about 7 December 1941 as to whether the Army had adequately provided the materiel and [172] the personnel to carry out the requirements of Article 17, section a., that I read you in my question a moment ago?

A. The materiel of the harbor defense, on the average, yes, as pertaining to the harbor defenses proper. As pertaining to the anti-aircraft, there was a shortage of allotted guns, I think of twelve 3-inch anti-aircraft guns. There was a shortage of the 37-millimenter; we had 20 out of 140. In the 50-calibre guns, we had 180 out of, I think, 345, so there was a shortage of equipment that had been allocated that we were trying to get; and when it came to the personnel, there was a decided shortage of personnel in the Coast Artillery, which resulted in practically all our organizations having two assignments. They had to man harbor defense guns and anti-aircraft, and if you had gotten both kinds of attack at the same time, it would have been impossible to man all the equipment. If you got one attack at a time, there was sufficient personnel to man the equipment. That covers, I think, the harbor defenses. On the question of the air force, we had nothing like enough to carry out our mission properly. We had made a study, had it written; we felt we should have 180 B-17s for long-distance reconnaissance and for bombers. We actually had 12, and only 6 of them in commission. We required approximately 200 pursuit planes. We had, I think, something like 105 P-40s, and 80 of them were in commission, but the others could have been put in commission fairly soon. On the anti-aircraft warning service, we had a program approved and funds allocated for the construction of six fixed stations and six mobile stations. Originally, the program had called for only three fixed stations and had been increased some time along in perhaps September or October, I don't remember the date, from three to six. None of the fixed stations and had been increased some time along in perhaps September or October, I don't remember the date, from three to six. None of the fixed stations on Oahu were to be placed at as great an altitude as 10,000 feet, and on the other islands at the highest suitable point we could get, which we hoped would give us 200 miles effective radius. None of those were in action. The parts had not all been received; certain articles, cable and material of that kind, were essential before we could construct the station, and it had not been received, so no fixed stations were operating. The six mobile stations were in condition to operate and were all stationed on the Island of Oahu. I believe that about covers the points. [...]

24. Q. Adverting to your answer with reference to anti-aircraft guns in the Pearl Harbor area. Had you made any estimate of the number of anti-aircraft guns, together with their calibre, which you considered adequate for the defense of this base against an aircraft attack?

A. In addition to what had been allocated there, we were supposed to have twenty-four, 90-millimeter guns, fixed at the time the allocation was made, and we had felt that with the exception of Kaneohe Bay — the Army had not assumed the responsibility for the defense of Kaneohe Bay then — that the equipment, if we got it all, would be fairly satisfactory. Shortly after I got there, I strongly recommended to the War Department that the Hawaiian Department assume the responsibility for the defense of Kaneohe Bay because it was like shutting your front door and leaving your back door open if you [173] didn't. We asked for a garrison for Kaneohe Bay which had never been approved up to that time because they said no approval would be given until after the limit of the strength of the Hawaiian garrison was lifted, which was placed then at 59,000, and we had asked them to raise it to 71,500 so that we could provide some additional personnel for Coast Artillery, Engineers, Air Corps, and a garrison for Kaneohe Bay.

25. Q. Do you consider, General, that if you had gotten all the 90-millimeter guns that were allocated to you, that you would or would not have still been short of anti-aircraft fire to defend Oahu?

A. We could have done pretty well, diregarding Kanoehe Bay, and the allocation, when it was made, did not include Kaneohe Bay.

26. Q. Do you consider that 90-millimeter guns are effective against high-altitude bombers?

A. Probably not as effective as your 5-inch, but they were the most effective thing the Army had.

27. Q. Now, adverting to your aircraft warning service. You have told us what some of the technical equipment was that you had. What was the status of training of personnel in your aircraft warning service?

A. They were not expert by any means. We started our training, I think, about the last of October or the first of November, when we really got enough of our equipment to begin training our men. As the first step in our training, we had earlier sent 15 men to sea with the Navy to learn something of the operation of the naval radar before we got any of our equipment. Our operators had gotten to the point where they were fairly satisfactory. As I say, the whole thing was new. The Army had just recently gone into it and they were by no means expert but had been working hard at it for at least a month, a little more than a month, and could be counted on to do fairly satisfactory work.

28. Q. What communication facilities did you have between this aircraft warning service and the Commandant, 14th Naval District?

A. We had several types of communication with the Commandant of the 14th Naval District. We had commercial telephones and we had a very fine cable system, Army cable system, that looped the island and went into, I think, your switchboard of the 14th Naval District. I don't think it went to a direct line to the Commandant. We also had messenger service by plane from the headquarters of the Department, these small messenger planes to Hickam Field, which was right alongside of Pearl Harbor, that we could use in case other signals went out. We had in operation, in addition to radar, about a hundred lookout stations throughout the island, and the Navy had some signal stations that they based on the island at various places and quartered with the Army troops, and they had communications with their own naval crew.

29. Q. You have mentioned something to the effect that there were about 100 lookouts. What were those lookouts?

A. Those were regular Coast Artillery stations with communications and everything of that kind. They served as a combination for spotting ships, or they would have spotted planes if they were visible.

30. Q. As a general statement, where were these lookouts stationed?

[174] A. They were pretty much on the high ground around the whole island.

31. Q. Of Oahu?

A. Of Oahu.

32. Q. What sort of communication did they have?

A. They were tied in with the cable that circled the island so they had instant communication, practically.

33. Q. Were these lookouts continuously on watch day and night?

A. They were not. They would have been if we had considered the situation such as to go on that type of alert.

34. Q. The point I would like to have you answer is whether these lookouts were or were not stationed on the morning of 7 December 1941?

A. They were not because they were not alerted for aircraft attack or for attack by a landing force, or an all-out attack.

35. Q. But you did have provision for that in your plans?

A. Our plans were very complete for that and we had lots of training in it, and if we had been on Alert No. 2 instead of Alert No. 1—

36. Q. Do you consider that your personnel were adequately trained to fulfill those duties?

A. They were.

37. Q. Was your aircraft warning service in direct communication with the Commander-in-Chief of the Pacific Fleet? You have said that it was in communication with the Commandant of the 14th Naval District.

A. I think we were connected with the switchboard at Pearl Harbor, and it would be the naval communication through the switchboard to the Commander of the Fleet.

38. Q. Did the Navy have a liaison officer, or any other personnel, assigned to the aircraft warning service?

A. I will have to answer that a little fully. On August 5, 1941, I wrote a letter to Admiral Kimmel pointing out the desirability of a naval liaison officer, and I think it was the 24th day of November that Lieutenant Burr—who was the naval liaison officer in G-3—was requested to set up liaison offices with the Navy because we were then working enough of these services that it was desirable to have it. I don't know whether they had actually reported on December 7th, or not. I thought they had. I thought they were actually working daily from November 24th to December 7th. I don't believe that I personally visited the anti-aircraft warning information room between the hours of 4:00 and 7:00. I visited it two or three times during that period but not between the prescribed hours and I can't say whether there was a naval officer there on duty, or not, when I visited it, or whether there was a naval officer on duty daily between November 24th and December 7th.

39. Q. In your testimony as regards the aircraft warning service, I don't recall that you mentioned anything concerning sound detectors. Did you have any such materiel?

A. We had sound detectors. We felt that as soon as our radar was operating 100 per cent that the sound detectors would have little value and I don't think we were manning them when we look at the shortage of the personnel because they were so much less valuable than the radar, as long as the radar was working.

[175] 40. Q. Then am I to understand that your position is this: That you had some sound detectors—

A. We had some sound detectors and we were using some of them because we didn't have the radars where we were sure of them at that time. We didn't have our fixed stations on December 7th. For that reason, the sound detectors were still valuable on account of the height of the mountains. We might have gotten them when they were close to the mountains, where we wouldn't have gotten them with the mobile stations.

41. Q. Do I understand you to say that these sound detectors were not in use on the morning of 7 December 1941?

A. They definitely were not because the command was not alerted that way.

42. Q. Was there any organization in the Island of Oahu for civilian aircraft squadrons or lookouts?

A. There was not. May I add there, that the limited terrain of the island was such that plotting by an individual was of very little value because the distance was so short, before the report could be made the aircraft would be upon us and considering that, we had not organized civilian lookouts.

43. Q. Had you ever considered the practicability or the desirability of having an aircraft patrol organized?

A. I didn't think that the aircraft patrol would be of any value for anything but submarines, considering the distance that we were supposed to go out. As far as air went, it would have been of no value.

44. Q. Would you give the court an opinion of the efficacy of the aircraft warning service as you had it set up; not as it was operated but as it was set up on the morning of 7 December 1941, to perform the functions for which an aircraft warning service would be provided?

A. Those mobile sets were supposed to be effective about 75 to 100 miles. Actually, under favorable conditions one morning, one set picked up enemy planes at 132 miles. There was one great handicap: They were not at sufficient height when the enemy planes came in and apparently turned to the east of the Koolau mountain range, and they lost them because of the intervening body of mountains. Now with the higher one, if we had had the one fixed station on Kaala in operation it might not have lost them.

45. Q. As I understand it, the Commanding General of the Hawaiian Department was responsible for the defense of Pearl Harbor? Is that correct?

A. Supported by the naval forces.

Army-Navy Cooperation at Pearl Harbor—and Its (Severe) Limits

ADMIRAL HUSBAND E. KIMMEL,
COMMANDER-IN-CHIEF, U.S. PACIFIC FLEET

Joint Congressional Investigation

[2572] MR. RICHARDSON. Now, the fact is, Admiral, is it not, that as a matter of naval policy you were directed to carry on and maintain a defensive position in the Pacific?

ADMIRAL KIMMEL. Yes.

MR. RICHARDSON. And the only departure that was contemplated in WPL-46 was a raiding move toward the mandated islands?

ADMIRAL KIMMEL. The most important part of any defensive attitude is the offensive action you take to carry it out. We speak of defensive in the sense of strategic defensive, not a tactical defensive.

MR. RICHARDSON. Well, with the size of fleet that you had in Hawaii during the summer of 1941 you were not in a position to inaugurate a grand offensive?

ADMIRAL KIMMEL. No, no.

MR. RICHARDSON. Against the Japanese Fleet?

ADMIRAL KIMMEL. A main offensive involved going into the Japanese waters. What we had there would permit us to make raids on the Marshalls. This was a Navy Department plan, and I was carrying out the plan. We hoped to divert the strength of the Japanese away from the Malay Barrier, to ease the pressure on the British and Dutch, and to do as much damage as we could to the enemy.

Incidentally, we had Wake Island and we planned, in the days before Pearl Harbor, that we could use Wake Island as more or less of a bait to catch detachments of the Japanese Fleet down there.

MR. RICHARDSON. Now, Admiral, if you had any naval disaster in the Hawaiian area, was there any place you could look for immediate aid?

ADMIRAL KIMMEL. Well, we could look for immediate aid by planes from the coast, that they would send out.

Incidentally, I have been informed, although not in detail, that in the days

Source: Pearl Harbor Attack, *volume 6.*

immediately after the attack on Pearl Harbor a great many planes of good type did appear there.

MR. RICHARDSON. Then the only relief they could give to you would come from the mainland?

ADMIRAL KIMMEL. Oh, yes.

MR. RICHARDSON. And from the mainland bases?

ADMIRAL KIMMEL. That is right.

MR. RICHARDSON. So that, as a matter of fact, Admiral, it can be fairly stated, can it not, that your main defense for yourself in the Pacific lay in your own hands and that of the Army at Hawaii?

ADMIRAL KIMMEL. Oh, yes; we were out there.

MR. RICHARDSON. Now you not only found when you went there, Admiral, a shortage of planes which could make recon- [2573] naissance and planes which could attack upon a reconnaissance, but you also found the base deficient in antiaircraft defenses, did you not?

ADMIRAL KIMMEL. And in fighter planes.

MR. RICHARDSON. Leaving the fighter planes, there was also a shortage of antiaircraft guns, was there not?

ADMIRAL KIMMEL. Yes.

MR. RICHARDSON. And part of your requests to Washington asked for an assignment of more of those guns?

ADMIRAL KIMMEL. That is right.

MR. RICHARDSON. Were they an essential part of the defense of the base?

ADMIRAL KIMMEL. Yes; I think so.

MR. RICHARDSON. Those guns would be ordinarily under the control of the Army, would they not?

ADMIRAL KIMMEL. Yes, but we wanted additional antiaircraft guns for our outlying island bases. We requested that on many occaions. . . .

MR. RICHARDSON. Yes. Admiral, I plead guilty to the fact of not being able all the while to separate in my mind the Army and the Navy in Hawaii, but that is due to the fact, and I am going to ask you, whether you didn't enter into a cooperative defense arrangement in late 1941 in which you were both for one and one for both?

ADMIRAL KIMMEL. I entered into that early in February of 1941. I issued a letter which is entitled "2 CL-41." The date of the first letter was early in February, and about 2 or 3 weeks later we replied to that. I wanted to get something out right away and that is the reason we hurried with the first one.

[2574] Two or three weeks later we revised it, and issued another one in the latter part of February, and by that time we felt that we had covered the point with the equipment and the forces we had in pretty good shape.

That letter stood until the 14th of October of 1941, when we issued another letter.

Incidentally, I might tell you a little bit about my activities in regard to getting an agreement betwixt the air forces out there. Immediately I got this responsibility, or knew I was going to have it, I started to work on the Army, and when General Short arrived I went out to call on General Short before he had taken over his command. I went out in civilian clothes. I realized the importance of cooperation betwixt the services.

I found General Short a very likable gentleman, and subsequently a very able Army officer. I broached the subject of some kind of an agreement whereby the efforts of the Army air and the Navy air could be coordinated on the island of Oahu and in the Hawaiian area.

I found General Short very much of the same mind, and we set in motion the studies which eventually resulted in the agreement to use what we had jointly.

That agreement was sent on to Washington. Eventually, we got out the estimate of the situation, which Admiral Bellinger and General Martin had a great deal to do with drawing up, and the coordination betwixt the two services was of a higher degree there than any other area that I had ever known prior to that time.

I issued an order that every Navy squadron of planes on wheels was to land on each of the Army fields, and to be serviced there and to get ammunition and bombs so they would know how to do it, and General Short did the same thing for the Army.

Now, those were the steps that we took in trying to utilize to the best advantage the facilities and the forces that we had.

MR. RICHARDSON. Those steps were made necessary, Admiral, by your shortage in equipment?

ADMIRAL KIMMEL. No, in any event it would have been very desirable, especially as regard air. I am talking now of the air of the Army and the air of the Navy, which was temporarily based on shore at any one time.

MR. RICHARDSON. Then, as a matter of fact, Admiral, for the Navy you did assume a protection to the base which, under better conditions you wouldn't have had to assume?

ADMIRAL KIMMEL. I tried to insure that we would have all of our forces actively take part in the defense of the Islands. . . .

[2581] MR. RICHARDSON. Did you have any knowledge, or did you direct any member of your staff to get specific knowledge as to the status of readiness of the Army's antiaircraft batteries immediately prior to the attack on December 7th?

ADMIRAL KIMMEL. That was a matter which was covered in my fleet security order, and all of that work was delegated to the commandant of the Fourteenth Naval District, who was the naval base defense officer; he was also the commander of the Hawaiian coastal frontier, and, as I indicated yesterday, with General Short was charged with the defense of the Hawaiian coastal frontier by the Navy Department and as a naval base defense officer to coordinate whatever fleet effort could be available with that of the Army, and I read from specification "G" of 2 CL-41, dated October the 14th, 1941:

(6) The Commandant Fourteenth Naval District is the Naval Base Defense Officer. As such he shall:

(a) Exercise with the Army joint supervisory control over the defense against air attack.

(b) Arrange with the Army to have their anti-aircraft guns emplaced.

(c) Exercise supervisory control over naval shore-based aircraft, arranging through Commander Patrol Wing TWO for coordination of the joint air effort between the Army and Navy.

(d) Coordinate Fleet anti-aircraft fire with the base defense by:

(1) Advising the Senior Officer Embarked in Pearl Harbor (exclusive of the Commander-in-chief, U.S. Pacific Fleet) what condition of readiness to maintain.

(2) Holding necessary drills.

(3) Giving alarms for: attack, blackout signal, all clear signal.

(4) Informing the Task Force Commander at sea of the attack and the type of attacking aircraft.

(5) Arranging communication plan.

(6) Notifying all naval agencies of the air alarm signal prescribed.

Admiral Bloch, I might say, was the commander in chief of the United States Fleet just prior to Admiral Richardson. Admiral Richardson relieved him as commander in chief of the United States Fleet. I relieved Richardson, as you recall.

Admiral Bloch was an accomplished officer, an officer in whom I had the highest confidence and still have and I had turned over this matter to him, not to a member of my immediate staff, and he did, I believe, a great many things. You will get him here, you will have him testify.

MR. RICHARDSON. Well, did you understand, Admiral, that it was Bloch's duty under your direction to see to it that the Army anti-aircraft batteries were in a state of readiness to defend that base?

ADMIRAL KIMMEL. Well, insofar as the Navy had any responsibility for it, yes, but now I think maybe it would be well for me to go into that a little bit in regard to General Short's alert.

In the late afternoon of November 27, 1941, Captain Earle, Admiral Bloch's Chief of Staff, brought to me a copy of the message which General Marshall had sent to General Short. General Short had sent a copy to the Naval Base Defense Officer, Admiral [2582] Bloch. I read General Marshall's message. I noted the language that Short's measures were not to alarm the civilian population or disclose intent. I also noted the order directing General Short to report the measures taken by him to General Marshall. The officer who brought me the message informed me, "The Army has gone on an alert." The next morning my Chief of Staff confirmed this report with information about Army troop movements.

I conferred with General Short on November 28 about the messages each of us had received on the 27th. We discussed these dispatches in all aspects. We considered, as we did frequently before and did later, the probabilities and possibilities of an air attack on Pearl Harbor. In this connection there was discussion of the effect of the suggestion from Washington that 50 Army pursuit planes be sent by aircraft carriers to Wake and Midway. I understood the Army was on an alert and that the alert was against sabotage among other things, although I do not now recall General Short specifically mentioning the details of his alert.

During 1941 I went to sea with the fleet on maneuvers whenever that was possible. I also expected that if war came and the fleet left Pearl Harbor on an operation, I would be far from Pearl Harbor. Consequently, I knew there was need to have a naval officer permanently based in Pearl Harbor to coordinate the use of the naval units which might be in Pearl Harbor at that time in the base defense. [. . .]

Admiral Bloch, the commandant of the Fourteenth Naval District, was the naval base defense officer. He was invariably in attendance at my conferences with General Short. He has testified at some length before the Naval Court as to his activities prior to the attack in carrying out the duties assigned to him under the provisions of my orders which I have just read. He will be a witness here. I do not wish to anticipate his testimony. However, I will give you certain highlights of his activities, as testified to before the Naval Court of Inquiry, because I was generally familiar with them prior to the attack.

In February 1941 he had urged upon General Short the necessity of emplacing his mobile antiaircraft guns in the field. He personally examined the plans for location of all Army antiaircraft weapons that were to be emplaced. His subordinates were in constant touch with Army representatives.

[2583] In October or November 1941 General Short had explained to him the difficulties General Short had emplacing certain of the Army's mobile antiaircraft guns. Sites were not on Government land. Fire-control communications were out in weather and subject to deterioration. It was difficult for personnel comprising the gun crews to be quartered and subsisted.

To help obviate this last problem for the Army, the Navy was actually making arrangements on December 7 to mess and quarter Army gun crews on Navy reservations.

I considered I had done everything I could prior to the attack to strengthen the Army antiaircraft defense of Pearl Harbor. As late as December 2, in an official letter to the Chief of Naval Operations, I pointed out that "the Army is not only lacking antiaircraft guns for outlying bases, but has a serious shortage on Oahu." I had appointed a responsible naval officer to exercise with the Army joint supervisory control over the defense against air attack and to arrange with the Army to have their antiaircraft guns emplaced. From everything I knew, he had been active and diligent in following the matter up. Of course, the Army had its difficulties some of which I have mentioned. Neither I nor Admiral Bloch could solve them. Moreover, if I had constantly intruded into the day-to-day coordination of Admiral Bloch and General Short on this matter I might very well have undone all my security order, 2 CL-41, was designed to accomplish, the working out of a permanent Army-Navy local defense coordination which would have to continue in my absence and that of the fleet.

I knew that General Short had been ordered to report the measures he took in response to his message of November 27 from General Marshall. This meant the joint participation of General Marshall and General Short in the character of the alert assumed in Hawaii. I thought that General Marshall and General Short knew better than I what specific Army measures should be adopted to perform adequately the Army mission of defending the naval base at Pearl Harbor and at the same time of complying with the restrictions involved of not alarming the civilian population nor disclosing intent.

MR. MURPHY. Mr. Chairman, could I inquire from what the witness is reading? Is it from a previous record or what?

THE VICE CHAIRMAN. Mr. Murphy has inquired, Admiral, as to what it is you have been reading from?

ADMIRAL KIMMEL. A memorandum which I prepared.

MR. MURPHY. Your own memorandum?

ADMIRAL KIMMEL. Yes.

MR. MURPHY. All right.

MR. RICHARDSON. Did you know, Admiral, what General Short's first alert was?

ADMIRAL KIMMEL. You mean No. 1 alert, as you call it?

MR. RICHARDSON. That is it.

ADMIRAL KIMMEL. I did not know he had but one kind of an alert.

MR. RICHARDSON. What kind of alert did you think he had?

ADMIRAL KIMMEL. I thought he had an alert where he put his people on the alert.

MR. RICHARDSON. Did you know at the time you talked with General Short that his No. 1 alert was simply against sabotage?

ADMIRAL KIMMEL. I did not know he had a No. 1 alert. I think I have found out since, however, that this No. 1, 2, and 3 alert business was put into effect on the 5th of November of 1941. Prior to that they had an alert and a nonalert status.

MR. RICHARDSON. Did you know from any conversation you had with General Short or any reported to you by your staff that Short had responded to the dispatch from Marshall with a notice on his part to Marshall that he had put in this first alert against sabotage?

ADMIRAL KIMMEL. I never saw Short's reply and was never informed of it.

MR. RICHARDSON. You never knew anything about it?

ADMIRAL KIMMEL. That is right.

MR. RICHARDSON. In your opinion, under the circumstances that there faced you would an alert against sabotage have been in accordance with what you were contemplating under the order that you have just referred to concerning a defense of Pearl Harbor?

ADMIRAL KIMMEL. I had taken the steps to put the ships of the fleet on an alert some time before—I mean to put them in shape where they could go on an alert very quickly a long time before. I had provided—I mean I had made sure that the ammunition for the guns was available, that the crews were on board and that a certain proportion of them would be manning the guns. At sea we had full security measures in effect and in port we had the security measures in effect which we felt that the situation demanded at the time and there was very little more that we could have done in port than what we did. [...]

[2596] ADMIRAL KIMMEL. You have said I feared an air attack. I felt always that an air attack was a possibility. I felt that I would have been remiss if I had not called the attention of the Navy Department and the War Department, with all of the force at my command, to the necessity of providing against every contingency in Hawaii.

At no time did I consider that an air attack was any more than a possibility under the conditions that we had out there. What the events of a war might bring forth was quite a different thing.

MR. RICHARDSON. We might just as well explain it now. Why do you suggest that you did not think an air attack was more than a possibility? What were the reasons why it not only could not have been limited to a possibility, but that it was not a probability?

ADMIRAL KIMMEL. Well, I knew the difficulties of an overseas expedition such as that. I knew the short range, the steaming range of the Japanese aircraft carriers. I very much doubted their ability to plan and execute an attack such as they made. We had had various reports on the Japanese Air Force, and I think not only I, but all the Navy Department were very much surprised at the efficiency of their air force and the manner in which they conducted that attack.

Now, the hazard that they undertook when they came there was something that I thought they would never take a chance on.

MR. RICHARDSON. You also knew by December 7—

ADMIRAL KIMMEL. And I might add that I gathered this opinion after a great deal of thought and a great deal of consultation with the best naval minds we had, and I think those naval minds were right in Hawaii at the time I was there.

MR. RICHARDSON. You knew, Admiral, of the burning of the Japanese codes by December 7, did you not?

ADMIRAL KIMMEL. You mean the message of December 3?

MR. RICHARDSON. That is one of them. There was more than one with reference to the burning of codes, was there not?

ADMIRAL KIMMEL. There was only one that I recall at the moment. There was a message of December 3 which said the Japs were burning most of their codes and ciphers in London, Hongkong, Batavia, Washington, and so forth.

MR. RICHARDSON. What would that indicate to you?

ADMIRAL KIMMEL. At that time it indicated to me, in conjunction with the other messages I had that Japan was taking precautionary measures preparatory to going into Thai, and because they thought that the British or the Americans, or both of them, might jump on them and seize their codes and ciphers after they went into Thailand.

Now, that was the interpretation we gave on it at that time.

Now incidentally, I would like to add another thing to that. That message came to me. It had nothing in it directing me to pass this on to General Short. That was a procedure that the Navy Department always used when they had an important message that they wanted me to give to General Short. I tried to give everything that I thought would be of interest to General Short to him anyhow.

But when the Navy Department sent me an important message which they thought should be conveyed to General Short they put that [2597] in the message. They did not put it in this message, and that in itself lent some weight to my construction of it.

MR. RICHARDSON. Did you advise General Short about it?

ADMIRAL KIMMEL. I did not personally, no, but you will hear from him about whether he heard about it or not.

MR. RICHARDSON. Did you instruct any of your staff to advise General Short?

ADMIRAL KIMMEL. I did not. I did not advise my staff to instruct General Short to do a great many things, but they did.

MR. RICHARDSON. They did what?

ADMIRAL KIMMEL. I say I did not instruct my staff to instruct General Short to do a great many things that they did automatically. Most of his information he got from the commandant of the district.

As I have tried to tell you, this liaison with the district on matters of that kind was more direct that it was with my fleet staff.

Now the district got everything that I did.

MR. RICHARDSON. I was just going to ask you, do you know that Admiral Bloch got this information with reference to the burning of codes?

ADMIRAL KIMMEL. Oh, yes.

MR. RICHARDSON. Then from your plan of operation that you had there you would expect that information to go from Bloch to Short or his staff?

ADMIRAL KIMMEL. To exchange the information, yes.

MR. RICHARDSON. Now you knew also on December 6 about the status which we spoke about this morning of the Jap espionage in Hawaii. You had all the knowledge you ever had up to December 7 about the presence in Hawaii of a flock of Japanese spies that were transmitting information into Tokyo as to the situation in Hawaii?

ADMIRAL KIMMEL. We knew about that, yes.

MR. RICHARDSON. You knew also on December 6 about these reports which had frequently come to you of military movement by Japan on the Asiatic Coast?

ADMIRAL KIMMEL. Oh yes, yes. That was following the pattern that was laid down in the messages of the 24th and 27th.

MR. RICHARDSON. Now, Admiral, it is also a fact, isn't it, that on December 6 it was reported to you by one of your staff, under circumstances showing his nervous interest in the fact, that for 6 days the Japanese carriers had been lost?

ADMIRAL KIMMEL. I thought I covered that pretty completely.

MR. RICHARDSON. You did. Let me finish.

And in response to his anxiety about it you made the remark, "Do you expect me to believe that the carriers are coming around Diamond Head?"

Now do you recall the incident and will you give us your version of it?

ADMIRAL KIMMEL. You are talking about the twinkle in my eye, I suppose.

MR. RICHARDSON. Well, that is part of it.

ADMIRAL KIMMEL. I do not recall the exact words that I used to Captain Layton, but I was very much interested in the location of all Japanese ships, not only the carriers but the other types. I felt if I could locate the carriers I would be able to determine pretty closely [2598] where the main Japanese effort was going to be. [...]

[2740] SENATOR LUCAS. And you conveyed the crystallization of those ideas on [potential dangers to Hawaii] to General Short, I take it.

ADMIRAL KIMMEL. I should say so, the things that he was interested in.

SENATOR LUCAS. Did you see General Short every day and discuss with him the military and naval situation around the island of Oahu from the time you received the war-warning message up to the attack?

ADMIRAL KIMMEL. No, sir; I did not see him every day, but to the best of my recollection betwixt November 27 and December 7 I had conferences with him on four or five different occasions.

SENATOR LUCAS (reading): [...]

> ADMIRAL KIMMEL. We had several conferences.
>
> GENERAL MCCOY. My remembrance is that he spoke of a prior conference with you.
>
> ADMIRAL KIMMEL. That is correct, sir. [...]
>
> GENERAL MCCOY. Immediately prior to the attack.
>
> ADMIRAL KIMMEL. Yes, sir, that is correct.
>
> GENERAL MCCOY. And we asked him to give us some idea of what you talked about,—
>
> ADMIRAL KIMMEL. Yes, sir.
>
> GENERAL MCCOY. —to see what effect these dispatches [from Washington] had on the two of you.
>
> ADMIRAL KIMMEL. Yes, sir.
>
> GENERAL MCCOY. Talking it over together.
>
> ADMIRAL KIMMEL. Yes, sir.
>
> GENERAL MCCOY. And the dispatch that we had particularly in mind, I think, at the time, was this one that was the war warning on the 27th.
>
> ADMIRAL KIMMEL. Yes, sir.
>
> GENERAL MCCOY. Apparently General Short didn't remember that at all. He had received no copy of it. That is, he had the record looked up. He didn't remember it at all, but he said he felt that you must have mentioned it to him, although he couldn't remember it, and his records and his file over there do not show that it was ever furnished him.

ADMIRAL KIMMEL. Well, General, I not only sent that war warning to General Short, to the best of my knowledge and belief, but—
GENERAL McCOY. I understand from your records that you had sent him a paraphrase.
ADMIRAL KIMMEL. Yes, sir.
GENERAL McCOY. Would that paraphrase use the term "war warning," do you think?
ADMIRAL KIMMEL. Oh, yes.
ADMIRAL REEVES. Yes, sir; we had a paraphrase, or he read it, because they were not the same in literal wording, but "war warning" was in both dispatches, the paraphrase and the original.
[2741] GENERAL McCOY. It made no impression, as I remember, on General Short, however.
ADMIRAL KIMMEL. No, I don't think it did.
GENERAL McCOY. He said, however, that he felt you had shown everything you had received.
ADMIRAL KIMMEL. I was going to add, General, that I believe that in my own office I showed him these dispatches and discussed them with him.

Is that still your best memory on that question, Admiral?
ADMIRAL KIMMEL. I think you can search your record a little further—
SENATOR LUCAS. I am going to.
ADMIRAL KIMMEL (continuing). And find that I subsequently testified that on the afternoon of November 27, when I received this war warning, I immediately sent for—well, my Intelligence officer brought it in. I told him to prepare a paraphrase of it and give it to General Short. That he did and the message was delivered to General Short's headquarters, there is no question about that, on this afternoon or evening of November 27.
MR. MURPHY. Will the gentleman yield?
ADMIRAL KIMMEL. And General Short subsequently, I think, arrived at the same conclusion.
MR. MURPHY. Will the gentleman yield?
SENATOR LUCAS. He may have arrived at the same conclusion thereafter but at this particular time he apparently was not certain as to whether or not the message was ever delivered and you were.
ADMIRAL KIMMEL. Yes; I was certain. I was certain then and the only trouble was that at that particular instant I wanted it checked to make sure that my subordinate had carried out the orders I gave him. I subsequently found out he had.
MR. MURPHY. I believe the record will show that the gentleman, the admiral, referred to Layton as being an idiot because he did not carry out the order which he was given, I believe. He was given it and told to deliver it personally but did not deliver it personally. He gave it to a subordinate and the subordinate did not deliver it personally. He gave it to some other subordinate of the Army, according to the testimony.
ADMIRAL KIMMEL. That is correct.
MR. MURPHY. And the record will show the admiral calling Layton an idiot before the Board because he did not do what he was told.

SENATOR LUCAS. Well, is there any question about whether or not Short did finally get the message?

ADMIRAL KIMMEL. I think there is no question but what he received it.

SENATOR LUCAS. I now turn briefly to the radar question which has been discussed quite a little.

ADMIRAL KIMMEL. What is that, sir?

SENATOR LUCAS. I am going to talk to you now about radar for just a few moments. After November the 27th, Admiral, when you went on a 24-hour alert, I call it that, maybe that is not quite correct, did you have any conversation with General Short about the condition of the Army warning service at that time?

ADMIRAL KIMMEL. My best recollection is that I was informed by General Short at about this time that he could give us a coverage of 150 to 200 miles. Subsequently General Short corrected [2742] me to say that he had told me a hundred miles. At any rate, I was informed that the Army radar was manned and that, as far as I was concerned, suited me.

Subsequently I found that the Army radar had been manned daily from 4 o'clock in the morning until 6 p.m. and eventually changed to 4 in the morning until 4 p. m. This is all second-hand. I did not go to the place to see it. That eventually, the day before the attack, one of General Short's subordinates told them they need not man it after 7 o'clock and up to the including Saturday preceding the attack they had been manning it from 4 o'clock in the morning until 4 in the afternoon.

I did not inquire of General Short the hours that he was keeping in manning his radar, nor did I inquire of him the status of his information center. That was an Army responsibility. I had been informed that the radar was in operation and I presumed that General Short—and I always thought he was perfectly competent to set the hours for manning his radar.

SENATOR LUCAS. Admiral, in view of the deficiencies and the inadequacies and the vulnerability of the fleet that we have testified to here and all agreed on wasn't it almost your duty to find out definitely whether or not the radar was working in line with the warning that was given in that war message?

ADMIRAL KIMMEL. I thought I knew. You must trust somebody. I couldn't do everything.

SENATOR LUCAS. I appreciate that you must trust someone, but under the orders that you were operating on at that time and the agreement that you entered into for the coastal defense of the island it was the duty, as I understand it—if I am wrong you will correct me—for the Navy to have a liaison man between the Army and the Navy so that they could properly obtain just what those who were experimenting or operating radar were doing. Am I correct about that?

ADMIRAL KIMMEL. The responsibility for the information center and the Army radar was entirely an Army function. I received a letter from General Short, as I testified to already before this committee, on August 5 requesting that I detail a liaison officer to work with his forces in the development of radar. I did so detail an officer, Commander Curts, who was my fleet communication officer at that time, and this liaison officer, my understanding of it at the time, which was never changed, was that he was to furnish them with technical advice and information. He was in nowise to be a watch stander in the information center.

SENATOR LUCAS. Who was to be a watch stander?

ADMIRAL KIMMEL. That was a function of the Army; and the Army commander, if he wanted a naval officer in there, he could have requested a naval officer, and one naval officer would not have been sufficient. He would have required several.

And, furthermore, had he requested these several watch standers to stand watch in the information center he would undoubtedly have submitted that request to Admiral Bloch, who was the commandant of the district and the man who was working with him in connection with all those affairs.

I believe that Admiral Bloch has stated he never received a request.

[2743] Now, I would like to make clear that the man sitting in the operations center and the people to whom the Army refers as liaison officers were in effect officers detailed to stand watch in the information center. An Army officer who had the information in regard to the Navy planes could have done that job, in my opinion, quite as well as a naval officer could have done it and, likewise, an Army officer detailed — I mean a naval officer detailed to follow Army planes. The only advantage in having a naval officer to look out for naval planes or an Army officer to look out for Army planes was that they probably knew the means of getting information. They could not sit in the information center and tell which planes were operating. They had to get that information from the people who were ordering the operations and directing the operations.

Now again I would like to add there was one other thing that I did. A few weeks, I forget the exact date, before the attack a member of my staff came to me and said the Army had requested the services of Lieutenant Taylor. Lieutenant Taylor was a young naval officer who had been operating with the British and who had some knowledge of the operation of an information center, and I sent Lieutenant Taylor to report to the Army and they had complete control over his movements from that time until December 7 and how much longer I have forgotten. At any rate, Lieutenant Taylor did everything that he could to assist the Army in getting organized and improve their center. I felt that having done those things I had done all that I could to assist the Army in getting their radar business in operation.

SENATOR LUCAS. My inquiries have been directed to radar primarily for this reason: Everyone knew about the vulnerability of the fleet out there.

ADMIRAL KIMMEL. That is right.

SENATOR LUCAS. Everybody knew that there was no long-range reconnaissance going on.

ADMIRAL KIMMEL. That is right.

Senator Lucas. Everybody knew that there were no surface ships that were patrolling wide areas because it was not feasible to do that.

Admiral Kimmel. That is right.

Senator Lucas. There were no submarines at that particular time.

Admiral Kimmel. Because we did not have any.

Senator Lucas. You did not have any.

Admiral Kimmel. No.

War Drills Preparing for Conflict

MAJOR GENERAL HENRY T. BURGIN, IN CHARGE
OF ARMY ANTI-AIRCRAFT FORCES, HAWAII

Army Pearl Harbor Board

[1355] 1. COLONEL WEST. General, will you please state to the Board your name, rank, organization, and station.

GENERAL BURGIN. Henry T. Burgin; Major General, Army of the United States. My station is Fort Shafter, T. H., I presume.

2. GENERAL GRUNERT. General Burgin, the Board is after facts as to what happened prior to and during the attack on December 7. Because of your assigned duties at that time, we hope we can get some facts from you, and also probably get leads to others who have such facts. [...] Now, according to the Roberts Commission testimony, you evidently believed that Short counted on the Navy for warning of a sea approach, through the sources of Navy scouting, and you stated that Short expressed himself forcibly that no enemy ships could get close enough to land a plane. Why this belief, do you know?

GENERAL BURGIN. It should be "launch a plane." I did not say "land a plane."

3. GENERAL GRUNERT. To "launch a plane"?

[1356] GENERAL BURGIN. Launch a plane from a carrier.

4. GENERAL GRUNERT. Did you concur with Short in that belief, or had you given the matter thought?

GENERAL BURGIN. I concurred in General Short's belief, and I got it from conversations with General Short and others. We had no means whatsoever, so far as the Army was concerned, of getting information. We had no surface ships. We did have some planes. It was my understanding that those planes of the Army operated under the Navy so far as scouting purposes went, patrol purposes. Those patrols were seen to go out every morning, come back late afternoon. I was never shown or didn't attempt to see what routes they took, where they went, or what sectors they covered, but in my mind, and I am sure, in that of General Short's, was the idea that the Navy was doing the scouting, and that from the Navy we would get our information, should the enemy approach.

Source: *Pearl Harbor Attack*, volume 28.

5. GENERAL GRUNERT. But you never knew just what scouting the Navy was doing, if any?

GENERAL BURGIN. I never knew positively, no, only I saw these scouting planes go out and come back. It was not my business and I didn't bother to look into it.

6. GENERAL GRUNERT. What were they — the Navy PBYs?

GENERAL BURGIN. A great many were Navy PBYs, some of them were Army bombers.

7. GENERAL GRUNERT. Tell me, first, just what did you command at that time?

GENERAL BURGIN. I commanded what was known at that time as the Coast Artillery Command, consisting of a seacoast artillery plus all the antiaircraft artillery in the Hawaiian Department.

8. GENERAL GRUNERT. What was the Fifty-Third Coast Artillery Brigade? What was that?

GENERAL BURGIN. That was antiaircraft artillery, composed of the Sixty-Fourth Regiment, the Two Hundred Fifty-First Regiment, and the Ninety-Eighth, which came in just before the attack, two or three months before.

9. GENERAL FRANK. A National Guard regiment?

GENERAL BURGIN. The Two Hundred Fifty-First was the only National Guard regiment.

10. GENERAL GRUNERT. Now, it appears that you had in that brigade a brigade SOP of November 26, 1941, which charged each unit with responsibility for its own security against air and ground forces, and with the maintenance of air guards and dispersion of personnel and matériel, and which provided for alarms for air attack. Now, was this in conformity with the Department SOP of November 5, or was that your own idea, or what?

GENERAL BURGIN. At this time, I don't recollect whether it exactly conformed to the Department SOP. I believe it did. In addition to that, the idea behind that particular paragraph is the same old idea that you have with an infantry company marching along the highways. They were cautioned to be ready to shoot, to disperse, and every man shoot at the plane, should they be attacked. The same idea was behind this — each individual unit to look after itself, in so far as strafing planes were concerned, and keep dispersed.

11. GENERAL GRUNERT. Was this both in post and while out?

[1359] GENERAL BURGIN. Everywhere, the idea behind it. That is followed even today in all these units. They are scattered as much as you can, dug into the ground, hidden.

12. GENERAL GRUNERT. How did that work out during the attack?

GENERAL BURGIN. I did not have a chance to check it, because we were not particularly attacked. They had one target to go after, which was Pearl Harbor, and they went after it. They did it, and did the strafing of airfields, serious strafing, but so far as my AA units, they were not attacked seriously. There were probably half a dozen men injured from attack during the whole day.

13. GENERAL GRUNERT. Under that SOP, which required each unit to take care of itself, did that include preparing the necessary air-raid shelters and the preparation of slit trenches, and all other requirements to ward off an air attack?

GENERAL BURGIN. I do not think that would be in that particular paragraph, but that is SOP to do that when you go out into a field position for battle, and the men actually did it without having to be told, when they went out.

14. GENERAL GRUNERT. In the various garrisons in which your troops were stationed, were such precautionary measures taken prior to December 7?

GENERAL BURGIN. You mean, were slit trenches made, and so forth? No, they were not.

15. GENERAL GRUNERT. Was that done, shortly after December 7?

GENERAL BURGIN. Immediately after, and during.

16. GENERAL GRUNERT. Now, there is a statement in your testimony, I believe, to the effect that you turned your anti-aircraft over to the Interceptor Command for drills, prior to December 7, and on that date, for action. Was the Interceptor Command then in being?

GENERAL BURGIN. The Interceptor Command was being organized. It was never in being and functioning, as it should have been. It was only a temporary measure; but that particular feature of Interceptor Command controlling AA fire was jealously guarded by the air people, and we had constant training and maneuvers, practice, where that particular thing was stressed, and the anti-aircraft was turned over the interceptor command.

17. GENERAL FRANK. On what date?

GENERAL BURGIN. A peculiar thing attaches to that. For at least six weeks or two months prior to December 7, we had, every Sunday morning, one of these exercises with the Navy. Our AA would go out in the field and take their field positions. They would know that the Navy was coming in, with carrier-based planes, and they would simulate an attack on the island, and we put our guns out mainly along the roadways, sometimes in position, and practiced simulating fire against this simulated attack made by the Navy. And we were out just one week prior to December 7.

18. GENERAL FRANK. On Sunday?

GENERAL BURGIN. On Sunday; but, by some stroke, we did not go out on December 7. The fleet was in the harbor.

The interceptor command never got into being actually as a bona fide interceptor command, for weeks after December 7; but we were practicing as an interceptor command, through General Davidson, all the time.

[1358]   19. GENERAL GRUNERT. During these practices and exercises, did the thing work?

GENERAL BURGIN. It worked, yes, because we would get the information of the planes coming in, and immediately the interceptor command would take over. All that is, so far as turning it over the interceptor command, is that the interceptor command tells you when to hold fire and when to resume fire. If he doesn't want you firing, he tells antiaircraft to hold fire, and under the orders we have to hold fire.

20. GENERAL GRUNERT. Now, suppose that the interceptor command as had been working during these drills and exercises, was in being on December 7, and had been working as it had been working during the drills and exercises: what difference would it have made in warding off the attack or in minimizing the effect of the attack, in your opinion?

GENERAL BURGIN. In my opinion, none.

21. GENERAL GRUNERT. Why not?

GENERAL BURGIN. Because we didn't have ammunition with our mobile antiaircraft. If they had been out in the field without any ammunition, they would have been worse off than they actually were.

22. GENERAL GRUNERT. That brings me to my next line of questioning.

What did you have out with your antiaircraft batteries such as existed on December 7th? Where were they? In what condition were they to go into action?

GENERAL BURGIN. They were all ready to go into action immediately, with the exception that the mobile batteries did not have the ammunition. The fixed batteries along the seacoast, those batteries bolted down to concrete, had the ammunition nearby. I had insisted on that with General Short in person and had gotten his permission to take this antiaircraft ammunition, move it into the seacoast gun battery positions, and have it nearby the antiaircraft guns. It was, however, boxed up in wooden boxes and had to be taken out. The ammunition for the mobile guns and batteries was in Aliamanu Crater, which, you may know or may not, is about a mile from Fort Shafter, up in the old volcano. The mobile batteries had to send there to get ammunition. In addition to that, the mobile batteries had to move out from the various posts to their field positions. They were not in field positions.

23. GENERAL GRUNERT. What proportion of mobile to fixed, approximately? Two or one? Three to one?

GENERAL BURGIN. I can give you that exact figure from some notes here.

24. GENERAL GRUNERT. I can probably refresh your memory by your saying—

GENERAL BURGIN. 26.

25. GENERAL GRUNERT. Location of 60 mobile and 26 fixed antiaircraft guns?

GENERAL BURGIN. Yes, 26 fixed guns and 60 mobile at the time of the attack.

26. GENERAL GRUNERT. And then there were 26 fixed antiaircraft guns which had the ammunition alongside and ready for action?

[1359] 27. GENERAL FRANK. In boxes.

28. GENERAL GRUNERT. Was that ammunition for the fixed guns boxed or uncased?

GENERAL BURGIN. It was boxed.

29. GENERAL GRUNERT. But how long approximately would it take to unbox it and get it into action?

GENERAL BURGIN. It depends on the batteries. Some of them had ammunition immediately available; that could be done in a very few minutes, four or five: they get enough ammunition out to begin firing, and continue to unbox. The batteries at Fort Weaver that is across the other side of Pearl Harbor, a little longer, because this ammunition was at Fort Kamehameha, had to be carried across the channel. But for the other fixed batteries I would say they could have been firing within five minutes, as far as the ammunition was concerned. They did begin firing; they went into action, three of those batteries. Three of those batteries got into action promptly.

30. GENERAL GRUNERT. They didn't get into action for the first wave of the attack, did they?

GENERAL BURGIN. That I don't know. These waves, I have never found anyone yet who could distinguish the difference in waves and how many waves actually came in here, as a matter of fact.

31. GENERAL GRUNERT. Did you have any information that was gotten out to the batteries in time for them to get into action before the attack actually struck?

GENERAL BURGIN. Oh, no; we knew nothing about the attack until the torpedoes dropped.

32. GENERAL GRUNERT. Then, you succeeded, through your own request, in getting boxed ammunition with your fixed antiaircraft batteries, which consisted of approximately 26 guns?

GENERAL BURGIN. Right.

33. GENERAL GRUNERT. But you were not successful or did you attempt to get ammunition to keep with your mobile batteries that could have gone into position with their ammunition without having to wait to draw it?

GENERAL BURGIN. Yes, sir, we did. I would like to answer that a little more elaborately. You may recollect yourself the great difficulty in prying loose ammunition from our storehouses and from the ordnance during peacetime. It was almost a matter of impossibility to get your ammunition out because in the minds of everyone who has preservation of ammunition at heart it goes out, gets damaged, comes back in, and has to be renovated. The same was especially true here. It was extremely difficult to get your ammunition out of the magazines. We tried the ordnance people without results. General Max Murray and myself went personally to General Short. General Murray pled for his ammunition for the field artillery. I asked for ammunition for the antiaircraft. We were put off, the idea behind it being that we would get our ammunition in plenty of time, that we would have warning before any attack ever struck.

34. GENERAL FRANK. Was that putting off made directly by the Commanding General or by a staff department?

GENERAL BURGIN. Both; staff departments first, then the Commanding General in person.

[1360] 35. GENERAL FRANK. Supported them?

GENERAL BURGIN. In his own office, to General Murray and to me.

36. GENERAL FRANK. Well, what were the staff departments who opposed it?

GENERAL BURGIN. The Gs; G-4s, the Ordnance.

37. GENERAL FRANK. And their reasons were?

GENERAL BURGIN. Same old reason, that they didn't want to issue any of the clean ammunition, let it get out and get dirty, have to take it back in later on and renovate it; and, besides, we would get our ammunition in plenty of time should any occasion arise.

38. GENERAL GRUNERT. Then it was just a question of maintenance and preservation. Did the question of possible sabotage come into it; do you know?

GENERAL BURGIN. That is quite true; the sabotage was foremost in everybody's mind. As long as the ammunition could be left locked up in the magazines, it was pretty safely guarded and could not be tampered with to any great extent.

29. GENERAL GRUNERT. Still, you being on an outpost here, with some intimation, at least, of the imminence of an attack, the guns were no good without ammunition?

GENERAL BURGIN. Quite true, sir.

40. GENERAL GRUNERT. And, therefore, what warning in the matter of time did you figure you should have in order to get your guns in position and your ammunition there with the guns to fire? Had that been practiced?

GENERAL BURGIN. We had many, many practices and tested that out, and it varied from the battery's position, where it started to where it wound up, and other things, but six hours was considered to be the maximum.

41. GENERAL GRUNERT. Six hours.

GENERAL BURGIN. Day and night. We went out daytime and we went out nighttime.

42. GENERAL GRUNERT. You actually took the live ammunition out there to practice handling it?

GENERAL BURGIN. No.

43. GENERAL GRUNERT. And to practice taking it out there?

GENERAL BURGIN. No, I never took live ammunition on any practices. That was done once. I can't say this for a fact, though, because I don't know. I was only told it was done before I came here, at one time. The ammunition was taken out. There was a flurry and a scare, and the then there was all hell to pay when the ammunition came back in and had to be cleaned up, put back in the ordnance magazine. That, however, is not my personal knowledge.

44. GENERAL GRUNERT. Was there any question in your mind as to the ammunition not being put out there because it might alarm the public or indicate the intent of what was about to happen?

GENERAL BURGIN. The idea never occurred to me at the time. Looking back at the message General Short had, not to alarm the public, there is a possibility that was in his mind. I couldn't alarm the public in this way: to move one of these batteries out to take the position in a private field was practically impossible prior to December 7th. As soon as you got off the highway, the owner, the manager, the topside man, all ran onto General Short's neck: The Army is trespassing [1361] on their land. Get to hell out of there. You had to do all these maneuvers on Army land or on the highways.

45. GENERAL GRUNERT. All right. Now, how many of the mobile positions for the 60 mobile guns were on such private land that you had to trespass to put them in position? Do you recall that?

GENERAL BURGIN. I can look here and refer to this bulletin.

46. GENERAL GRUNERT. Go ahead.

The actual number doesn't make so much difference. I would like to have an idea of what the percentage is, if possible.

GENERAL BURGIN. About 40 percent were on private land.

47. GENERAL GRUNERT. And the other 60 percent, then, could have been put in position without going on private land?

GENERAL BURGIN. Wait a minute. I have included those fixed batteries. Make that higher. That percentage, at least 50 percent of the mobile batteries were on private land.

48. GENERAL GRUNERT. I believe General Short stated something to the effect that under Alert No. 1 each battery had a skeleton crew with it. Would that refer to the fixed batteries or to the mobile or to both?

GENERAL BURGIN. It referred to both as far as sabotage meant only.

49. GENERAL GRUNERT. But your mobile batteries had to move out from their location to go into a position, and then none of these mobiles went out in their position, and they had skeleton crews?

GENERAL BURGIN. I don't quite understand your question. I am sorry.

50. GENERAL GRUNERT. Here, your fixed batteries are fixed and they undoubtedly had a skeleton crew there to prevent sabotage.

GENERAL BURGIN. Right.

51. GENERAL GRUNERT. In other words, your skeleton crews to prevent sabotage came in, as far as your mobile batteries are concerned, as if they were at the post and had not moved out into position?

GENERAL BURGIN. They were taken more or less as a regiment or a battalion on the post and the sabotage guards did not necessarily go down to the battery itself.

52. GENERAL GRUNERT. There was not, then, much of a sabotage problem as far as guards were concerned, within the post itself?

GENERAL BURGIN. No, sir.

53. GENERAL GRUNERT. You may have answered this, but I will ask it again: What instructions, if any, prevented the antiaircraft command from having ammunition at the guns? Were they any instructions or could you not get the ammunition?

GENERAL BURGIN. There were no instructions forbidding the antiaircraft or any other outfit from having the ammunition, but it was just impossible to pry the ammunition loose from the Ordnance, the G-4's, or from General Short himself. . . .

[1370] 132. GENERAL RUSSELL. As a matter of fact, therefore, the action which would have been required under Alert 3 had never been taken on this island?

GENERAL BURGIN. In so far as the guns going actually in positions, digging their revetments, putting in their bunkers, that had never been done, so far as the mobile, in all their positions; in some, it had.

133. GENERAL RUSSELL. Elsewhere in your testimony you referred to "turning the town up-side-down," or language similar its meaning to that.

GENERAL BURGIN. I see I will have to curb my language.

134. GENERAL RUSSELL. No, we are just attempting to get at the thought behind the language. We are not interested in the language. Do you think that going all-out on Alert No. 3 would have resulted in disturbing the people of the City of Honolulu?

GENERAL BURGIN. I do.

135. GENERAL RUSSELL. Is there in your mind some thought that there would have been developed a considerable opposition among the influential civilian population here on the island toward the results of Alert No. 3?

GENERAL BURGIN. I think there is no doubt about it, in the world.

136. GENERAL RUSSELL. In other words, if General Short had ordered Alert No. 3—and I am asking this question in the interest of clarity—if General Short had ordered Alert No. 3 and thrown all of his people into readiness for immediate combat, including the issuing of ammunition, it might, or, in your opinion, it would have provoked opposition on the part of some of the responsible and influential civilian population here on the island?

GENERAL BURGIN. I feel positive it would.

137. GENERAL GRUNERT. Even though he might have explained that to the influential citizens, there would still have been opposition?

GENERAL BURGIN. I don't believe you could have explained it, at that time. . . .

[1371] 146. GENERAL GRUNERT. These so-called "big, influential people have mostly land and crop interests, have they, where Alert No. 3 might interfere with or disrupt them?

GENERAL BURGIN. That was my idea. That's my idea; yes, sir.

147. GENERAL RUSSELL. I want to ask another question in line with this, General. I have gotten the impression from your testimony that the possibility of this opposition might have had a little bit deeper basis than indicated by your answer to General Grunert's last question, which rather limited this opposition to the land owners because of that we would have opposition to the land owners because of disturbing their profits, and whatnot. I had gotten the impression that we would have opposition from influential people on the island, because they did not want the community upset, and the relation between the races

disturbed and their commercial trends broken into. Was that behind this opposition, too?

GENERAL BURGIN. It might have been; I don't know much about that feature of it. I don't see how it would have any bearing on the races, except perhaps the Japanese, they could see we were doing something, and those who wanted to try to get information back to their own country would have that opportunity. That had nothing to do with it in this case, so far as I can see.

148. GENERAL RUSSELL. Going away from that for the minute, you have given considerable testimony about the weapons available to you as antiaircraft commander. We have had testimony to the effect that, first, the weapons available for the protection of Pearl Harbor, of the smaller caliber, were not numerous enough, and were ineffective. What is your opinion on that?

GENERAL BURGIN. They were certainly not numerous enough. They were, however, about as effective as any weapons we had at that time, except for a few experimental models. For example, we had the 3-inch gun, a pretty good old gun in its day. The 90-mm. had hardly come into play up to that time to any great extent; there were some manufactured, some in use, on the mainland. There had been built 12 experimental model 105-mm. They were all sent to Panama, and were on duty down there. They never panned out well, and were discarded; but so far as our heavy equipment, it was pretty good for its day.

149. GENERAL RUSSELL. Did you observe the firing of the batteries in and near Pearl Harbor against the high-altitude Japanese bombers?

GENERAL BURGIN. Yes.

150. GENERAL RUSSELL. What was your impression of that fire?

GENERAL BURGIN. Those bombers never reached any great altitude. As far as I could tell they were never over 11,000 feet, any of them. Any gun we had would reach that, even the old Navy 5-inch, which isn't a very good gun, either; at the time; very low muzzle velocity, very slow fire; also defective ammunition. That is the Navy 5-inch, their main weapon. [...]

[1372] 153. GENERAL GRUNERT. I would like, before you leave that subject, to ask you about the Navy 5-inch ammunition. You say some of it was defective?

GENERAL BURGIN. A great deal of it was defective, and "duds." Unfortunately, the "duds" detonated on contact with the ground. They were not really "duds," so far as contact with any material object was concerned. However, they did not burst in the air. They burst all over town. They burst all over De Russy, where I was. I saw them burst two of them up in the crater on Diamond Head, knocking out one of my mortars. That 5-inch ammunition was falling all over the island. A great many people thought they were Japanese bombs, but only one bomb hit the town of Honolulu, and I think that was an accident. All the rest of them were Navy 5-inch shells.

154. GENERAL GRUNERT. How do you know that to be a fact?

GENERAL BURGIN. I went out and dug up the fragments and looked at the markings on them. I know they were Navy shells; and so does the Navy.

155. GENERAL GRUNERT. Do you know whether or not the Army was blamed for that damage? Do you know whether or not the Army was accused of having poor ammunition, and that they thought it was the Army ammunition that did that?

GENERAL BURGIN. I never heard of that.

Why Military Aircraft Were Not Dispersed on the Ground

LIEUTENANT GENERAL WALTER C. SHORT,
COMMANDING GENERAL, HAWAIIAN DEPARTMENT

Roberts Commission

THE CHAIRMAN. Yes. Now, when I interrupted, you said you had issued orders to have those stations—

GENERAL SHORT. We issued the order by telephone, and there were three reasons why I decided to issue the order for Alert No. 1 rather than for Alert No. 2 or 3. In the first place, with the population we have here there was a very strong possibility of sabotage. Individual sabotage was the thing that I feared more than anything else. I didn't fear uprisings; I didn't think that they would dare take a chance on that.

In the second place, I had no information to indicate an attack, so it did not appear essential to prepare against a real attack. The sabotage was a direct possibility.

In the third place, if I ordered Alert 2 or 3, I interfered very seriously with the training. No. 2 would have interfered seriously, particularly with the air and anti-aircraft training; 3 would interfere seriously with all training. It was impossible to do any orderly training with them on.

THE CHAIRMAN. Were your troops really in need of training?

GENERAL SHORT. We have thousands of new men. Some of them had not completed the 13 weeks' training when we got them over. We have a complete regiment of anti-aircraft that is all draft. We have a regiment of engineers that is very largely draft. Some of them had six or seven weeks when they came over. And we have men that have come and gone through the reception center, draftees from the Territory that had gone in the two Hawaiian National Guard regiments here. So that there was a decided necessity for real training. I will cover that with regard to the air corps a little more.

Now, in the carrying out of anti-sabotage measures it can be done very much better and with less men if the planes and the command are not dispersed too widely. With the Alert No. 1 where we were carrying it out for sabotage the

Source: Pearl Harbor Attack, *volume 22.*

planes were kept in the vicinity of the landing mat or the apron in groups, so they could be guarded very closely. If we had gone to Alert No. 2, then some bombers would have been sent to outlying islands where our garrisons are extremely small, or put in the air, and you cannot keept them in the air indefinitely. The pursuit planes would have been distributed in their bunker all around the perimeter of Wheeler Field and around the perimeter of Bellows Field, and it would take maybe hundreds of men to protect them reasonably well from sabotage.

Now, this was especially true because we had not constructed manproof fencing with floodlights around these fields. I put in for money on the 15th day of May for putting manproof fences and floodlights around all of the critical installations. That part of the money was [37] approved, some on July 11, and on August 12 we got approval for some more. I had asked for $240,000. We got about $200,000. The orders were placed on the mainland for the material because it simply was not available in Honolulu. The defense work has cleaned out practically all essential material here. Up to the time of the attack a small amount of this wire, not all the parts, had been received by constructing quartermaster for the Chemical Warfare, and some ordnance staples. The District Engineer, who does the work for the airfields, had not received any material for fencing on the airfields.

You understand, this is a question of priority. We were not given the top priority. The Navy in certain construction work had the top priority and could get their things through at once. We had to take our turn to get the material. Then we had to take our turn to get it on the boats, and in spite of repeated following up it had not arrived at that time.

THE CHAIRMAN. Do I understand, then, that Hickam Field was open to the road and the adjoining land?

GENERAL SHORT. The back part of Hickam Field was fenced, but there was no fencing off, which we wanted very much to do, of the hangar line from all of the living part of the field, which made the guarding extremely difficult.

And another thing, at Hickam Field it was impossible to completely disperse the planes there on account of the nature of the soil. That is all filled ground, and with those heavy planes that when they are loaded weigh up to 50,000 pounds you didn't dare get them off there. I had asked in February for money to put in runways and bunkers. It could only be done with heavy material. My engineers with their equipment could not do that. I had asked for money for that, and it had been going back and forth ever since that time. I had gone ahead without any money at Wheeler Field and built the bunkers with my aviation engineering troops. I could not do that on account of the nature of the conditions. You can't dig ground there; you run into water. You have to bring in the earth and build it up. [. . .]

[38] Now, to go into the question of the interference with training if I ordered Alert No. 2 or 3, this was particularly true with reference to the training of the air corps and particularly important. As you know, this B-17, the Flying

Fortress, is a plane that has not been distributed to the Army generally very long. We have had some for a few months, and training a complete combat team for that plane, including bombers, takes a very considerable time. We have been required to send nine out of twenty-one bombers to the Philippines with the trained crews. Then we had been told that we were going to have to carry on a large ferrying operation of planes to the Philippines. We had previous to November 27 sent 18 trained combat teams for these ships to the mainland ferry. We had 17 more ready to send. We had also been told that we would get 12 additional planes to make up very soon, so we were trying to train those.

Now, we have to train those crews only six B-17's. We had twelve here but in order to keep the planes going, that were ready, through to the Philippines, we didn't dare let them go on without part replaced. Well, they kept our minimum of spares down to where we could use only six planes. In other words, to train all these extra crews we had only six planes that we could use. So if we put those six planes in a state of readiness and dispersed them and kept them warmed up most of the day, it completely stopped the training and we definitely would not be able to carry out the ferrying mission that we had been ordered to carry out to the Philippines. We were constantly mindful of the fact that we might have to give up our route bases of Midway and Wake and were working just as rapidly as possible to develop an alternate route down by either Palmyra or Christmas and Canton and Suva and Townsville, Australia. We had all of those fields well under construction and were pushing everything [39] to the limit, and we felt like we had to push the training of our combat teams in exactly the same way. So that had a decided influence on deciding to not order an alert that put the air out where they could not train.

This is the reply that I sent in answer to that radiogram of November 27:

> Re your radiogram number four seven two twenty seventh report Department alerted to prevent sabotage period liaison with Navy.

Now, that should have given the War Department very exact information of just what I was doing, of the nature of the alert. I did not say "Alert No. 1." I didn't want anybody to have to run and look up and find out what it was. I said, "Alert against sabotage."

I got a reply back from the Adjutant General the next day:

> 28th. Critical situation demands that all precautions be taken immediately against subversive activities within field of investigative responsibility of War Department Paren see paragraph 3 Mid SC30-45 end paren stop. Also desired that you initiate forthwith all additional measures necessary to provide for protection of your establishments comma property comma and equipment against sabotage comma protection of your personnel against subversive propaganda and protection of all activities against espionage stop. This does not repeat not mean that any illegal measures are authorized stop. Protective measures should be confined to those essential to security comma avoiding unnecessary publicity

> and alarm stop. To insure speed of transmission identical telegrams are being sent to all air stations but this does not repeat not affect your responsibility under existing instructions.

They thought that the question of sabotage, subversive activities, and espionage were so important when they sent me this that they sent a copy right on to the individual air stations to impress them all the more. You will notice here that there was the question that nothing was said about anything but sabotage, subversive activities, and espionage.

I received three message up to that date, October 16, November 27, and November 28. They emphasized right straight throught that we must not disclose our stand and that we must not alarm the population and that we must take measures to protect against sabotage, against espionage, and against subversive action. Nowhere did they indicate in any way the necessity for protecting against attack. They also did indicate definitely that we must avoid publicity and avoid alarming the public. If I ordered a complete alert against attack, it would have alarmed at least the Japanese population.

You will also notice they made no objection whatever to my wire where I stated I was alerted for sabotage. If they had any idea that that was not a correct order, they had all the opportunity from November 27 to December 7 to come back and say, "We do not consider the action taken by you as sufficient and that you should instead take action to defend yourself against air attack."

In other words, I took it as a tacit agreement with the course I had taken and that there was no objection raised, and I cannot see how I could draw any other conclusion.

Now, to show that I was carrying out exactly their instructions in regard to sabotage, on November 29 I sent another wire. I said:

> Full precautions are being taken against subversive activities within the field of investigative responsibility of War Department. Paragraph 3 Mid SC30-45 —

[40] That applies entirely to the delineation between the actions of the FBI, ONI, and G-2 respectively of the military forces, and of the FBI carrying out the work with respect to the civilian population. The three worked very close together.

(Continuing):

> Military establishments including personnel and equipment stop. As regards protection telephone exchanges and highway bridges comma this headquarters by confidential letter dated June 19 1941 requested the Governor of the Territory to use the broad powers vested in him by Section 67 of the Organic Act which provides comma, in effect comma, that the Governor may call upon the commanders of military and naval forces of the United States in the Territory of Hawaii to prevent or suppress lawless violence, invasion, insurrection et cetera stop. Pursuant to the authority stated the Governor on June 20th confidentially made a formal written demand of this headquarters to furnish and

continue to furnish such adequate protection as may be necessary to prevent sabotage comma and lawless violence in connection therewith comma being committed against vital installations and structures in the Territory stop. Pursuant to the foregoing request appropriate military protection is now afforded vital civilian installations stop. In this connection comma at the instigation of this headquarters the city and county of Honolulu on June 30th 1941 enacted an ordinance which permits the Commanding General Hawaiian Department comma to close comma or restrict the use of and travel upon comma any highway within the city and the city and county of Honolulu on June 30th 1941 enacted an ordinance which county of Honolulu comma whenever the Commanding General deems such action necessary in the interest of national defense stop. The authority thus given has not yet been exercised stop. Relations with FBI and all other federal and territorial officials are and have been cordial and mutual cooperation has been given on all pertinent matters.

I want to explain my reason for some time at least—say the last year and a half or two years when during perhaps tests or certain alarming conditions that they have been placing sentinels over essential utilities without any legal authority. I felt that if these sentinels who are protecting transformer stations or waterworks should fire upon someone that I had no legal protection whatever, and that was my reason for calling upon the Governor to make this request. That placed the military command in a much better situation.

Also I had no authority to close roads, and for that reason I asked the City and County Council to give me that authority and assured them that I would only use that when necessary. So I thought that I was in a much better legal status than they had been theretofore.

I will now take up what happened from November 27 to December 6. Alert No. 1 remained in effect. Troops went on with their routine training. The Aircraft Warning Service worked, as part of the interceptor command, was working every morning until 4 and 7 and was working each station on its own from 7 to 11 and was making necessary reports and so forth from 1 to 4 o'clock in the afternoon.

I might explain what we mean by the interceptor command. We have for the purpose of combat, we place pursuit airplanes, anti-aircraft artillery, Aircraft Warning Service, under the command of what we call the interceptor commander. [...]

[82] ADMIRAL REEVES. [...] Alert No. 1 did not require your planes to be in the air?

GENERAL SHORT. No, sir. Alert No. 1 did not cover preparation against an air attack at all. It's sabotage, uprisings, and subversive measures.

ADMIRAL REEVES. Had our pursuit planes been in the air, ordered there as a security measure during the dawn daylight period, they would have been an added security, would they not?

GENERAL SHORT. They probably would have been back on their fields about seven o'clock. I mean, you can't just keep them in the air constantly. We had decided that some two hours before dawn until one hour after dawn was the dangerous time, and just as we were working our interceptor station the chances are that if we had had a dawn patrol out it would have returned before eight o'clock. There is no question, if we had had pursuit in the air fully armed and expected this attack at eight o'clock, why, we probably would have—we might have been able to stop it to a very considerable extent, at any rate. Some of them would have gotten through. We think they had approximately 160 to 180 planes in the attack.

[83] ADMIRAL REEVES. Of course you would adopt security measures at other times than a time when you were expecting an attack, wouldn't you?

GENERAL SHORT. Oh, if you were at war, yes. If you were at war you would carry—you would carry—

ADMIRAL REEVES. Or in case of possibility of war?

GENERAL SHORT. It is determined absolutely by your estimate. My estimate of the situation here was that the only thing that could seriously be expected was sabotage. I was fully prepared against sabotage, and there has been no sabotage from November 27 to this date. Now, there have been people who have been stationed here in years past who have felt that serious things would happen. We have had complete control of that. That was my estimate. My estimate was that the War Department would let me know of a crisis and that the Navy would let me know of the presence of any carriers in Hawaiian waters, and without that there couldn't be an air attack.

ADMIRAL REEVES. In reference to this distant reconnaissance, a carrier operating at high speed, say 30 knots, might have been several hundred miles, perhaps 500 miles away, the night before?

GENERAL SHORT. Oh, yes. No question about that.

ADMIRAL REEVES. So that distant reconnaissance covering the circumference of a circle 500 miles—

GENERAL SHORT. Wouldn't do any good.

THE CHAIRMAN. If what?

GENERAL SHORT. We had planes.

ADMIRAL REEVES (continuing). —did not guarantee that you would be notified of the approach of that carrier?

GENERAL SHORT. Not if it stopped at 500 miles, no. Our plan and the plans we had sent in to the War Department called for reconnaissance out to a thousand and fifty miles, based on very accurate study as to how close they could come, making the most of the use of darkness, don't you see, to get in, and we figured that the distant reconnaissance should go to a thousand and fifty miles. That was as far as our B-17's could carry it; and that that was the—and there is a very long study in the War Department that we put in on that. But as I understand it the Navy is not limited to reconnaissance for their information of hostile ships, and we had a definite line of Mandate Islands, that that was the closest land base that the Japanese could have, and that was 2,100 miles. [...]

[85] THE CHAIRMAN. [...] After all, I am only a layman, but reading the communications of the War and Navy Departments sent to you from the period

of October 16 to November 27 I should have expected when I looked at them that there was a possibility of imminent danger of hostile attack from Japan, a surprise attack.

Did you get that impression, or was there any discussion between you and your Navy colleagues as to that?

GENERAL SHORT. The most positive expression we got over this period was that by—when Admiral Kimmel asked his War Plans Operations Officer what he considered was the possibility of a surprise attack on Oahu, and he said, "None."

If Admiral Kimmel did not agree with that conclusion he made no expression of it to the contrary.

THE CHAIRMAN. If I get the right impression from your testimony, it is this: that while the force knew that Oahu was subject to a surprise attack, none of you envisaged it within a period of days or weeks; is that right?

GENERAL SHORT. I had the feeling, and I know it was on my part and Admiral Kimmel's that as long as he had as much of his exercises of the fleet here in Hawaiian waters, that they would not try to take a chance with a carrier attack. If the fleet had been ordered away from the Hawaiian waters I would have been extremely apprehensive.

I knew that they had a force out constantly, carriers with perhaps 90 planes, scouring the seas, but I did not believe it was possible for them to actually carry through an attack without the Navy getting something and becoming suspicious.

THE CHAIRMAN. Unless I am misinformed, the general understanding in both the Army and Navy has been for many years that a surprise airplane attack might be the method of Japanese attack on Oahu?

GENERAL SHORT. I definitely would have expected it if the fleet had not been here.

THE CHAIRMAN. Well, wouldn't the fleet in Pearl Harbor be a very fine target for such an attack?

GENERAL SHORT. That is true. There were two task forces out at that time with airplane carriers. I believe that is the first time since I came here in February when all the ships have been in the harbor. I did not know until the next day that they were in. They come in and they go out constantly on exercises. I cannot say this is correct, but I think they probably had more battleships here then than at any time since I have been here.

THE CHAIRMAN. You say in your report to the War Department that because of the seriousness of the situation depicted in the Chief of Staff's telegram of November 27 that you ordered Alert No. 1?

GENERAL SHORT. Yes.

THE CHAIRMAN. What did you mean in your statement about "the seriousness of the situation"?

GENERAL SHORT. I figured that we were always in very great danger here from sabotage. Take for instance when they closed down the banks. I thought then that there was a very great possibility that there may be something of that kind, and I put an Alert No. 1 in. I felt that any change in the situation for the worse at all might cause [86] the Japanese agents—as there were some here—to attempt to carry out sabotage operations that would hurt us.

THE CHAIRMAN. From the time you came into the command of this Department, sir, did you have any information of subversive activities of any kind on this island, furnished through your own intelligence, the Naval Intelligence, of the FBI?

GENERAL SHORT. We knew, and we had a list of probably something over 500 people. We had something over 300 we knew and also the consular agents.

I do not believe since I came here that there has been any act of sabotage of any importance at all, but the FBI and my intelligence outfit knew of a lot of these people and knew they probably would watch the opportunity to carry out something.

THE CHAIRMAN. What is the military opinion as to the most dangerous time for an airplane raid on Oahu?

GENERAL SHORT. About dawn or maybe two hours before dawn, because we figure that they will do more damage if they can hit in the dark or just at dawn and get back to their ships. If they attacked entirely at night they might get back to their ships and not be able to land on them. Then they could not land without turning on their lights. I do not think any of them like to land on the ships at night, and we figured they would never attack so early that they would get back to their ships when it would not be daylight, but that they would always attack about dawn.

THE CHAIRMAN. Under the conditions prevailing since you came here, which dawn was the most dangerous dawn from the point of view of attack? Which day of the week?

GENERAL SHORT. Definitely figuring the day of the week, you would probably say they would figure Sunday would be the day that there would be more people off and that the command would be less on Sunday than any other time.

THE CHAIRMAN. What was the condition with respect to leaves over that week-end?

GENERAL SHORT. No different from the other.

THE CHAIRMAN. No different from any other week-end?

GENERAL SHORT. No, sir.

THE CHAIRMAN. But different than week-days, though?

GENERAL SHORT. Our distance is so short that any man can get back to his post in ah hour and can get back to their posts from town within 30 minutes. So with respect to the amount of time involved, the only reason is that Saturday night was the only night they could stay out, because on week-days we worked them hard. They would not have any way of going out because that was the difference between Sunday morning and other mornings.

THE CHAIRMAN. What was the percentage of effectives on station on that Sunday morning?

GENERAL SHORT. I imagine that would run about—
THE CHAIRMAN. Eighty percent?
GENERAL SHORT. Eighty percent or maybe more, because I would say probably 90% of them—they will not get home until 2 or 3 o'clock in the morning, so they are very much discouraged from staying in town.
THE CHAIRMAN. What was the condition of the anti-aircraft crews on that Sunday morning? Were they skeleton crews?
[87] GENERAL SHORT. Yes, skeleton crews at every gun.
GENERAL MCCOY. You mean available for manning?
GENERAL SHORT. No, on account of sabotage we had covered every gun, covered every installation with the men right at the weapon, because we were taking no chance of sabotage.

The Lack of Sabotage at Pearl Harbor

I. H. MAYFIELD, FOURTEENTH NAVAL
DISTRICT INTELLIGENCE OFFICER, HAWAII

Clausen Investigation

FEBRUARY 9, 1942.

Confidential

From: The District Intelligence Officer
 Fourteenth Naval District
To: The District Intelligence Officer
 Third Naval District
Subject: Pearl Harbor, Hawaii, Fifth Column Activities at
Reference: (a) Letter dated 3 January, 1942 from Commandant 3ND to Chief
 of Naval Operations, above Subject.

1. Reference (a) suggests that "there be conveyed to all District Intelligence Offices, such information of Fifth Column activities at Pearl Harbor, as may be useful in connection with the operations of all District Intelligence Office activities."

2. For the purpose of this letter, methods of fifth column activities will be considered to consist of the following:

(a) To conduct accurate espionage work and transmit the results to the enemy.

(b) To demoralize public opinion; to cause panic or confusion; to promote discord and dissatisfaction.

(c) To carry on actual physical sabotage.

(d) To render assistance to invading forces.

3. Referring to Paragraph 2 (a) above, there is no question but that the espionage work of our enemies was carried out in an extremely efficient, thorough and accurate manner. There is also no doubt but that this information was very successfully conveyed to our enemies. The collection of the information was very simple. The geography and topography of the area around Pearl Harbor are such that any one with good eyes (perhaps aided with a pair of field glasses) can observe accurately movements in and out of Pearl Harbor from several highways and roads near Pearl Harbor and also from a great many houses on the heights   [338]   back of Pearl Harbor and Honolulu. There is no question but that the enemy did this in a very thorough and efficient manner. It is also true that they were able to transmit this information very effectively and quickly

Source: Pearl Harbor Attack, *volume 35.*

to their forces at sea. This again is easily explained by the fact that there was no censorship of mail, cables or radio; sampans were operating regularly off shore; there may have been (and probable was) communication by private radio; and there may have been other signalling. Unfortunately, under a democratic form of government, it does not seem possible to take necessary action ahead of time to prevent this sort of thing.

4. Referring to Paragraph 2 (b) above, there were numerous rumors of cars zigzagging along highways to slow up traffic, of cars being parked across roads to tie up or block traffic, of shots being fired from ambush or from automobiles, etc., etc., etc. None of these reports were substantiated.

5. Referring to Paragraph 2 (c) above, there were no real cases of actual physical sabotage. This is somewhat hard to understand as the utilities such as the Hawaiian Electric Company, the Honolulu Gas Company, the Honolulu Rapid Transit Company, the plants and storage tanks of the privately owned oil companies all of which are concentrated in a limited area, the City and Navy yard water supply systems, etc., etc., were not adequately protected. As a matter of fact, a comparatively small group of well trained saboteurs could easily have put them all out of operation in a very short time. This leads to the query as to whether there were no well organized plans to wreck these utilities and services, or whether such plans were and are so well organized that one might assume that instructions had been passed that no action was to be taken at the time as there were no plans to follow up the attack of December 7 with attempts to land and invade the island. This latter assumption may seem to be far fetched, but is being carefully considered and studied. The only real basis for considering it seriously is that there was not a single attempt made to sabotage any of these essential utilities on the morning of December 7.

6. Referring to Paragraph 2 (d) above, there were many reports such as the one about swaths being cut in cane and pineapple fields pointing to important objectives; people signalling enemy planes; etc., etc. All such rumors and reports were checked as expeditiously as possible. None of the cases investigated proved to be authentic.

7. This Subject has been checked thoroughly with the local office of the Federal Bureau of Investigation and with Military Intelligence Division, Hawaiian Department, whose findings coincide with the above.

I. H. MAYFIELD,
A. J. LOWREY,
A. J. LOWREY,
By direction.

The Claim of Alcoholic Impairment of U.S. Service Personnel

MELVIN L. CRAIG, PROVOST MARSHALL,
HAWAIIAN DEPARTMENT

Roberts Commission

THE CHAIRMAN. Your full name?
COLONEL CRAIG. Melvin L. Craig.
THE CHAIRMAN. And your rank?
[183]   COLONEL CRAIG. Lieutenant Colonel.
THE CHAIRMAN. And your commission here in this Department, or your office, the office you hold?
GENERAL MCCOY. Assignment.
COLONEL CRAIG. Provost Marshal.
THE CHAIRMAN. Assignment?
COLONEL CRAIG. Department Provost Marshal.
THE CHAIRMAN. Since when?
COLONEL CRAIG. Since July—it was a year last July, almost two years now.
THE CHAIRMAN. In your official capacity you are supposed to know the conditions within this District with respect to law and order by troops and officers?
COLONEL CRAIG. Yes, sir.
THE CHAIRMAN. What have you to say as to the condition on the night of December 6, 1941?
COLONEL CRAIG. The condition as to law and order on the island of December 6, 1941, was very good.
THE CHAIRMAN. Any reports of misconduct or drunkenness by enlisted personnel?
COLONEL CRAIG. Nothing unusual.
THE CHAIRMAN. What is unusual?
COLONEL CRAIG. Well,—
THE CHAIRMAN. Or, rather, what is usual on a Saturday night?
COLONEL CRAIG. Saturday night we usually have 70, 80 arrests, drunkenness.
THE CHAIRMAN. For drunkenness?

Source: Pearl Harbor Attack, *volume 22.*

COLONEL CRAIG. Yes, sir.

THE CHAIRMAN. And you perhaps had 70 or 80 that night?

COLONEL CRAIG. Yes, sir.

THE CHAIRMAN. That is of enlisted personnel?

COLONEL CRAIG. Yes, sir.

GENERAL MCCOY. What was done with those 70 or 80 on Saturday night?

COLONEL CRAIG. The most of them were returned to their stations. That is, those from Schofield were returned to Schofield; those from Fort Kamehameha were returned to Kam. The other ones were detained, those that were beyond — seemed what we might call passed out — detain those at Fort Shafter guardhouse overnight.

GENERAL MCCOY. How many of those? Do you remember?

COLONEL CRAIG. Well, I should say offhand approximately 25, roughly.

GENERAL MCNARNEY. I think we might have the exact figure.

THE CHAIRMAN. I would like to have the exact figures.

COLONEL CRAIG. I can get the exact figures for you.

THE CHAIRMAN. I would like you to furnish them to us.

COLONEL CRAIG. Yes, sir. [...]

[184] THE CHAIRMAN. That would not a difficult thing to get?

COLONEL CRAIG. No, sir. They have that information right available.

GENERAL MCCOY. I think we might state to the Provost Marshal the reason we are asking these questions.

THE CHAIRMAN. Certainly.

GENERAL MCCOY. So that he could possibly even give us a better picture than what we asked for. For instance, there have been telegrams received by all the members of this Commission, before it left the United States, from certain organizations asking us to investigate what they stated were reports of great revelry and drunkenness on the night of December 6 amongst the officers and soldiers of this command.

COLONEL CRAIG. Yes, sir. Well, I can get that record in figures for you.

[185] GENERAL MCCOY. So that we would like to get a sort of picture, comparative picture, —

COLONEL CRAIG. I see.

GENERAL MCCOY. — that would show just what did occur on that night.

COLONEL CRAIG. Yes, sir. Very well, sir.

GENERAL MCCOY. And comparable notes over a period of, say, some month or two.

COLONEL CRAIG. Yes, sir.

GENERAL MCCOY. Does that cover it from your point of view, Mr. Justice?

THE CHAIRMAN. Yes.

Colonel, where were you on the night of December 6?

COLONEL CRAIG. I think I was home, from my recollection; I just hadn't thought about it, but I think that I was home that night. I don't think I went out anyplace.

ADMIRAL STANDLEY. Where is it?
COLONEL CRAIG. Sir?
ADMIRAL STANDLEY. Where is your home?
COLONEL CRAIG. Right here on Fort Shafter.
GENERAL MCCOY. In other words, you weren't called out during the night?
COLONEL CRAIG. No, sir.
GENERAL MCCOY. Due to any unusual happenings?
COLONEL CRAIG. No, sir.
GENERAL MCCOY. Mobs or brawls or anything like that?
COLONEL CRAIG. No, sir, nothing unusual. [. . .]
[186] ADMIRAL STANDLEY. Yes, I would like to ask: In the number of arrests during the day here or the evening are some of them sent back to barracks?
COLONEL CRAIG. Yes.
ADMIRAL STANDLEY. Without any record?
COLONEL CRAIG. No, sir. We keep a record of them, yes.
ADMIRAL STANDLEY. If you pick them up, take charge of them, there is always a record?
COLONEL CRAIG. That's right, yes, sir.
ADMIRAL STANDLEY. There is a naval patrol—
COLONEL CRAIG. Yes, sir, shore patrol.
ADMIRAL STANDLEY. —in connection with it?
COLONEL CRAIG. They were right next door to my office downtown.
ADMIRAL STANDLEY. And any records they have would be the same as you have? If you pick up a sailor man and turn him over to the patrol you would make a record of it?
COLONEL CRAIG. No, sir, we don't pick up the sailor men. That is done by the shore patrol.
ADMIRAL STANDLEY. Done by the patrol?
COLONEL CRAIG. Yes, sir. They handle all theirs, yes, sir.
THE CHAIRMAN. So they will have in all probability a similar record as to their forces—
[187] COLONEL CRAIG. That's right.
THE CHAIRMAN. That you have with respect to your forces?
COLONEL CRAIG. Yes, sir. [. . .]
GENERAL MCCOY. Were you conscious on Saturday night of any unusually large number of sailors being in town?
COLONEL CRAIG. Yes, sir, I did; I noticed that there were quite a few sailors in town.
GENERAL MCCOY. In other words, you knew the fleet was in the harbor, did you?
COLONEL CRAIG. Well, I noticed that there were an awful lot of sailors in the streets. I didn't know, of course—that's all that I observed. I didn't know that the fleet was in, but it seemed to me there were a lot of sailors in town on

the evening of the 6th. I was down there about 6, between 6 and 7 o'clock, I think it was, and I remember seeing a lot of sailors in the street.

GENERAL MCCOY. But even so, there was nothing that caused you to stay downtown that night due to anything unusual?

COLONEL CRAIG. No, sir, not to the best of my recollection. I think that I was at home that evening; I could check it up with my wife.

GENERAL MCCOY. In other words, it wasn't so outstanding that you remembered anything about it particularly?

COLONEL CRAIG. No, sir.

GENERAL MCCOY. Have you heard any comment in town here among civilians, any charges that the Army or the Navy ran riot that night, a lot of them.

COLONEL CRAIG. No, sir. This is the first I have heard of it. I haven't heard anything like that. [. . .]

FURTHER TESTIMONY

[286] THE CHAIRMAN. Have you the information we requested?

COLONEL CRAIG. Yes, sir, I believe that I have.

On the night of December 6, between 6 p. m. and 6 a. m. the total number of soldiers arrested was 43, and 38 of these men were arrested for being drunk and 4 for being A. W. O. L. Out of these 43, 42 were returned to their organizations and one man was confined.

The civil police record for that night: they had a total of 90 arrests: drunkenness 39, gambling 39, threatening 2, theft 1, auto theft 1, drunk-driving 1, other misdemeanors 3, assault and battery 3. A total of 90.

Comparing that with previous Saturday nights at payday, the night of July 31 from 6 p. m. to 6 a. m. we had 80 arrests. That is soldiers. Out of these, the number that were returned to their organizations was 48.

On the night of August 30 between 6 p. m. and 6 a. m. we had 87 arrests. That is the military. Number of men returned to their organizations was 30. 28 were turned in for safekeeping that night.

[287] In the night of October 1, total number of arrests was 87. Number of men returned to their organizations was 40, and 47 confined.

On September 2 we had 21 arrests, 20 men confined and 1 returned to his organization.

September 30, 79 arrests, 35 returned to their organizations and 44 confined.

Then in November they started to distribute the paydays, and on November 3 Schofield Barracks was paid. Number of arrests was 67. Number of men returned to their organizations was 49. Number of men confined was 18.

And November 7: number of arrests 70, number of men returned to their organizations 10, number of men confined 60.

Then on December 3 — that was the payday before — the total number of arrests that night was 114. 98 of these men were returned to their organizations;

16 were confined. But as far as the records show there was a relatively small number on the night of the 6th.

The civil police on November 15 arrested 74. That's civilians.

THE CHAIRMAN. Yes.

COLONEL CRAIG. Not soldiers.

THE CHAIRMAN. Yes.

COLONEL CRAIG. November 22, 63; November 29, 68.

GENERAL MCCOY. So in every case there were more civilians arrested than soldiers?

COLONEL CRAIG. Yes, sir, it works out about that way. The population of the City of Honolulu and police district #1—that includes just the City of Honolulu and around this area here—that is, men over 21 years of age—is 61,800.

That is as far as I went back; I thought that that was the information the Commission desired.

THE CHAIRMAN. I think that is exactly what we want, sir.

COLONEL CRAIG. Yes, sir.

THE CHAIRMAN. Now, was there anything else that we asked the colonel to get us? I think not.

MR. HOWE. I have nothing else, no, sir.

COLONEL CRAIG. There were no officers on the night of the 6th.

THE CHAIRMAN. No officers detailed?

COLONEL CRAIG. No officers. And, as I stated before, I checked on my activities that night, and I was home at eight o'clock, and I was home all evening until Sunday morning.

THE CHAIRMAN. Thank you very much, sir.

Submarine Contacts Just Outside Pearl Harbor on December 7th

CAPTAIN WILLIAM W. OUTERBRIDGE,
COMMANDING OFFICER, *Ward*

Hewitt Inquiry

[55] ADMIRAL HEWITT. State your name and rank.

CAPTAIN OUTERBRIDGE. William W. Outerbridge, Captain, U. S. Navy.

ADMIRAL HEWITT. You were the Commanding Officer of the WARD on the morning of 7 December 1941?

CAPTAIN OUTERBRIDGE. Yes, sir.

ADMIRAL HEWITT. And during the early hours of that morning, you had several actual contacts with submarines? Is that so?

CAPTAIN OUTERBRIDGE. Several actual contacts?

ADMIRAL HEWITT. Well, reported contacts.

CAPTAIN OUTERBRIDGE. Yes, sir. We had one alert and one actual contact and then later, after the attack, we had several outside.

ADMIRAL HEWITT. There has been reported and logged the conversation which you had with the CONDOR along about 0520 Honolulu time and later there is in evidence and report of your actual attack on the submarine. Will you give me your story of the events of the morning, beginning with the report from the CONDOR about 0400?

CAPTAIN OUTERBRIDGE. That doesn't appear on this record, but she signalled us by flashing light that she believed she had seen an object that looked like a submarine proceeding to the westward, and I believe she had just come out and was sweeping, magnetic sweep out in the channel, but she said, "The submarine is standing to the westward."

ADMIRAL HEWITT. What was her location?

CAPTAIN OUTERBRIDGE. She was in the channel, sweeping with her magnetic sweeps.

ADMIRAL HEWITT. The approach channel to Pearl Harbor?

CAPTAIN OUTERBRIDGE. Outside of the actual channel, between the reefs, but on the approach channel to Pearl Harbor.

Source: Pearl Harbor Attack, *volume 36.*

ADMIRAL HEWITT. Swept channel?

CAPTAIN OUTERBRIDGE. Swept channel, yes, and we went to General Quarters and proceeded to her position, as close as we could get to her without fouling her sweeping gear, and then we stood to the westward, slowed to ten knots, and searched. It was a sonar search. We couldn't see anything.

ADMIRAL HEWITT. About what time did you get that signal?

[56]   CAPTAIN OUTERBRIDGE. We got that signal about 0358, visual signal about 0358, and we searched for about an hour and didn't find anything; so I got in contact with her again and asked her for a verification. Then she said — this is in the record here. We asked her first, "What was the approximate distance and course of the submarine that you sighted?" and she said, "the course was about what we were steering at the time 020 magnetic and about 1000 yards from the entrance apparently heading for the entrance." Well, I knew then that we had been searching in the wrong direction. We went to westward, and, of course, there was still doubt as to whether she had actually seen a submarine because there hadn't been any other conversation, except by flashing light with us, and I wondered whether they were sure or not; so I did ask them, "Do you have any additional information on the sub?" and they said, "No additional information," and I then asked them, "When was the last time approximately that you saw the submarine?" and they said, "Approximate time 0350 and he was apparently heading for the entrance." Then we thanked them for their information and asked them to notify us if they had any more information and then we just kept on searching in our area, in the restricted area outside of the buoys. That was the end of this incident for the first search.

ADMIRAL HEWITT. You made no report of that to higher authority?

CAPTAIN OUTERBRIDGE. No, sir, I didn't make any report of it.

ADMIRAL HEWITT. What was your evaluation of that?

CAPTAIN OUTERBRIDGE. Well, at the time I thought perhaps it wasn't a submarine, because they didn't report it. This conversation was taken over another circuit entirely. This is not in either his log or mine. They didn't report it and I thought if he didn't report it, he must not think it is a submarine. It was his initial report and I thought it may not be. It may have been anything; it may have been a buoy. Since then, I don't believe it was a buoy. I believe the Commanding Officer of the CONDOR saw a submarine. I don't know where he is. I think he was killed, killed in action. But at that time I didn't know whether or not it was a submarine.

ADMIRAL HEWITT. You say you think the Commanding Officer of the CONDOR was killed?

CAPTAIN OUTERBRIDGE. I believe he was killed.

ADMIRAL HEWITT. Do you remember his name?

CAPTAIN OUTERBRIDGE. No, sir, I don't know, but I met some people who told me about him.

ADMIRAL HEWITT. Well, now about the later contact.

CAPTAIN OUTERBRIDGE. The later contact — I turned in again and was sleeping in the emergency cabin, as usual, and Lieutenant Goepner had the deck. He was a j. g. He called me and said, "Captain, come on the bridge." The helmsman was the first one to sight this object and he saw this thing moving. It looked like a buoy to him, but they watched it and after they had watched it for a while, they decided probably it was a conning tower of a submarine, although we didn't have anything that looked like it in our Navy, and they had never seen anything like it. I came on the bridge as fast as I could and took a look at it. I don't know where it appeared to them at first, but at that time it appeared to me to be following the ANTARES in. The ANTARES had been reported to me and at that time I thought [57] the ANTARES had been heading into the harbor. She also had a tow, towing a lighter, and it appeared to me the submarine was following astern of the tow.

ADMIRAL HEWITT. Astern of the tow?

CAPTAIN OUTERBRIDGE. Yes, sir. It may or may not have been. I think other people can testify it was standing in to Honolulu. To me it appeared to be following the ANTARES in and I thought, "She is going to follow the ANTARES in, whatever it is." It was going fairly fast. I thought she was making about twelve knots. It seemed to be a little fast to me. I was convinced it was a submarine. I was convinced it couldn't be anything else. It must be a submarine and it wasn't anything that we had and we also had a message that any submarine operating in the restricted area—not operating in the submarine areas and not escorted—should be attacked. We had that message; so there was no doubt at all in my mind what to do. So, we went to General Quarters again and attacked. That was 0740–0640.

ADMIRAL HEWITT. And you attacked and you reported, I believe that—

CAPTAIN OUTERBRIDGE. Yes, sir, we reported.

ADMIRAL HEWITT. Will you identify those exchanges of messages? Will you identify the messages on the radio log?

CAPTAIN OUTERBRIDGE. Yes, sir. The Executive Officer was on the bridge at the time. We made the attack and we dropped depth charges in front of the submarine. The first report was, "We have dropped depth charges upon sub operating in defensive sea area." I thought, "Well, now, maybe I had better be more definite," because we did fire and if we said we fired, people would know it was on the surface, because saying it was a sub and dropping depth charges, they may have said it might have been a blackfish or a whale. So I said, "We have attacked fired upon and dropped depth charges upon submarine operating in defensive sea area," so they would feel, well, he shot at something. We sent the message at 0653, the second one.

(The radio log of the Naval Radio Station, Bishop's Point, Oahu, containing the conversation between the WARD and CONDOR and the WARD's report of attack upon a submarine, was received and marked "Exhibit 18.")

ADMIRAL HEWITT. What do you feel was the effect of your attack?

CAPTAIN OUTERBRIDGE. I think we sank the submarine.

ADMIRAL HEWITT. What do you base that on?

CAPTAIN OUTERBRIDGE. On the gun hit, only on the gun hit.
ADMIRAL HEWITT. There was a gun hit on it?
CAPTAIN OUTERBRIDGE. There was a gun hit on it, and I looked these submarines over and there is no hatch between the conning tower and the tube of the submarine, where I believe it was hit, right at the waterline, the base of the conning tower.
ADMIRAL HEWITT. And the submarine disappeared after that?
CAPTAIN OUTERBRIDGE. Yes, sir, it disappeared.
ADMIRAL HEWITT. That was before you made the depth charge attack?
CAPTAIN OUTERBRIDGE. Yes, sir, we fired at the submarine before we made the depth charge attack, and as she was going under the stern, we dropped over the depth charges.
ADMIRAL HEWITT. Your depth charges were close to her?
[58]   CAPTAIN OUTERBRIDGE. Yes, sir.
ADMIRAL HEWITT. Definitely?
CAPTAIN OUTERBRIDGE. Definitely, they were there. I didn't claim a kill—
ADMIRAL HEWITT. Whom were those reports addressed to?
CAPTAIN OUTERBRIDGE. I believe it was Commander Inshore Patrol. We were working for inshore patrol, but the interpretation is here—
ADMIRAL HEWITT. You got the calls?
CAPTAIN OUTERBRIDGE. Yes, sir, we got the calls.
ADMIRAL HEWITT. Do you remember what they mean?
CAPTAIN OUTERBRIDGE. No, sir.
ADMIRAL HEWITT. Those were the only reports of that attack you made?
CAPTAIN OUTERBRIDGE. Yes, sir, two messages on that.
ADMIRAL HEWITT. What was your action after the completion of that attack?
CAPTAIN OUTERBRIDGE. Well, I saw one of these large white sampans lying to out there in the defensive area.
ADMIRAL HEWITT. Was that against regulations?
CAPTAIN OUTERBRIDGE. That was against standing rules. They weren't supposed to be in the defensive area, but he was in there. So, I turned around and went after him and we chased him out towards Barber's Point. He was going pretty fast.
ADMIRAL HEWITT. He tried to get away from you?
CAPTAIN OUTERBRIDGE. It appeared that way to me. He could have stopped much sooner, but he appeared to be going around Barber's Point. When we did catch up to him, he came up waving a white flag. I thought that was funny. I thought, "We will just send for the Coast Guard." That was what we always did when we caught a sampan in the defensive area. We sent for the Coast Guard and they were very prompt. They sent a cutter out to take him in.
ADMIRAL HEWITT. Will you identify for the record those two messages you sent about the sampan, which are on the Bishop's Point record?
CAPTAIN OUTERBRIDGE. "We have intercepted a sampan into Honolulu. Please have Coast Guard send cutter to relieve us of sampan." And, "We have

intercepted sampan and escorting sampan into Honolulu. Please have cutter relieve us of sampan." We sent that. That is a little garbled, but that looks like it.

ADMIRAL HEWITT. What was the time of it?

CAPTAIN OUTERBRIDGE. That was 0833 and 0835.

ADMIRAL HEWITT. Well, then, I understand that several days later you saw a midget submarine which was recovered off Bellow's Field. Is that correct?

CAPTAIN OUTERBRIDGE. Yes, sir, that is correct.

ADMIRAL HEWITT. Was the appearance of the conning tower similar to the one that you saw?

CAPTAIN OUTERBRIDGE. Yes, sir.

ADMIRAL HEWITT. What was the condition of that submarine off Bellow's Field? Did it have its torpedoes?

CAPTAIN OUTERBRIDGE. Yes, sir, it was in good condition and I went inside and there was a torpedoman—I believe he was a chief torpedoman—working on the torpedoes, trying to get them out without exploding them, and I saw the torpedoes inside.

[59] ADMIRAL HEWITT. Well, I think, that is all I had planned to ask you. I am naturally interested in any information you can provide on this Pearl Harbor attack. Is there anything that you might think would be pertinent to this investigation that you can volunteer?

CAPTAIN OUTERBRIDGE. Well, I suppose it would be a matter of opinion, which probably wouldn't do you much good, but I was even a little surprised at the attack which followed. I mean I had no idea that the air attack was going to follow. We brought the sampan in and we got another submarine attack. We dropped four depth charges on another submarine in the area. We got depth charges that morning and at 11 o'clock we ran out. When the attack started, we were still at General Quarters. We hadn't secured from the attack. We were still at General Quarters and we saw the planes coming in, but not until after the bombs began to fall, because the bombs were falling on Pearl Harbor, and the Exec and I were standing on the bridge. Lieutenant Commander Dowdy was the Exec and he said, "They are making a lot of noise over there this morning, Captain." I said, "Yes, I guess they are blasting the new road from Pearl to Honolulu." He said, "Look at those planes. They are coming straight down." I looked at them, and he said, "Gosh, they are having an attack over there." I said, "They certainly area," and that was the time the attack actually began.

ADMIRAL HEWITT. That was about 0750?

CAPTAIN OUTERBRIDGE. 0750, yes, sir.

ADMIRAL HEWITT. That must have been about the time, judging from this report here, that you were engaged in bringing the sampan in.

CAPTAIN OUTERBRIDGE. Yes, sir, we were still standing in with the sampan.

ADMIRAL HEWITT. You mentioned just then several other submarine attacks that you had the same morning.

CAPTAIN OUTERBRIDGE. Yes, sir.

ADMIRAL HEWITT. That was after the ones you have already discussed. What were they?

CAPTAIN OUTERBRIDGE. They were good metallic contacts, although I was a little surprised at them at first, before things began to pop. I didn't think we would get so many, but we did get a lot of them. We got good metallic contacts and the only thing to do was to bomb them. They gave us a good sharp echo. We bombed them until we ran out of depth charges and went in and got some more.

ADMIRAL HEWITT. That was in the same general area?

CAPTAIN OUTERBRIDGE. Right in that defensive area.

ADMIRAL HEWITT. Off the entrance to the swept channel?

CAPTAIN OUTERBRIDGE. Yes, sir. There was another thing we saw. That was a lot of explosions along the reefs. I thought that they were explosions of torpedoes fired into the reefs. I didn't see any other submarines the whole morning. We didn't actually see any, but we did see a lot of explosions that looked like shallow water explosions of torpedoes.

ADMIRAL HEWITT. What would make you think they were torpedoes rather than bombs?

CAPTAIN OUTERBRIDGE. They were right along the coast, along the reef, and I didn't see any planes overhead. They were inside the coast [60] in Pearl Harbor, bombing Pearl Harbor, and I didn't think they would all miss that far. I thought they would do better than that. They did do better than that in general.

ADMIRAL HEWITT. Do you recall approximately how many different contacts you bombed?

CAPTAIN OUTERBRIDGE. I think we had three or four that morning, sir.

ADMIRAL HEWITT. After the one—

CAPTAIN OUTERBRIDGE. In the first ten days we had eighteen contacts, day and night, but we didn't actually see any more submarines. I heard that they were there, but we didn't actually see any more. We don't know what the effect of the attacks were on the submarines. There was one other one, on the 2nd of January. We were with our division, making the attack, and the ship astern of us, after I got in port, told us that she saw a submarine come up under our starboard depth charge. I hadn't, up until then, claimed any hit for it. We had a pretty good contact. It was our turn to make the run. We made the run and kept on going, and that is what the Commanding Officer of the ALLEN said. That was the 2nd of January. But we didn't actually see that from the ship.

Why Were There No Torpedo Nets in Pearl Harbor?

ADMIRAL HAROLD R. STARK, CHIEF OF NAVAL OPERATIONS

Joint Congressional Investigation

[2264] SENATOR LUCAS. Admiral Stark, I want to talk just a moment with you about the anti-torpedo baffles that were discussed between yourself and Admiral Kimmel, as I recall, along in the spring of 1941.

ADMIRAL STARK. Yes, sir.

SENATOR LUCAS. I have before me an exhibit that is not in evidence here, a statement made by Admiral Kimmel, in which he refers to an official letter which you wrote and which is a part of Exhibit 49 in the Naval Court of Inquiry, in which is stated the following:

> Consideration has been given to the installation of A/T baffles within Pearl Harbor for protection against torpedo plane attacks. It is considered that the relatively shallow depth of water limits the need for anti-torpedo nets in Pearl Harbor. In addition, the congestion and the necessity for maneuvering room limit the practicability of the present type of baffles.
>
> [2265] Certain limitations and considerations are advised to be born in mind in planning the installation of anti-torpedo baffles within harbors, among which the following may be considered:
>
> (a) A minimum depth of water of 75 feet may be assumed necessary to successfully drop torpedoes from planes. 150 feet of water is desired. The maximum height planes at present experimentally drop torpedoes is 250 feet. Launching speeds are between 120 and 150 knots. Desirable height of dropping is 60 feet or less. About 200 yards of torpedo run is necessary before the exploding device is armed, but this may be altered.

Now, at one time you considered seriously placing these anti-torpedo nets in Pearl Harbor to protect the battleships?

ADMIRAL STARK. Yes, sir.

SENATOR LUCAS. And you, as I understand it, made an exhaustive search with the British as well as our own naval experts and engineers, scientific men, with respect to what could or could not be done in shallow water?

Source: Pearl Harbor Attack, *volume 5.*

ADMIRAL STARK. That is correct.

SENATOR LUCAS. And this letter that you wrote is the consequence of that, am I right?

ADMIRAL STARK. Yes, sir.

SENATOR LUCAS. Well, the Navy Board of Inquiry called this bomb a secret weapon in the nature of a robot bomb which was unknown to the best professional opinion in America at this time. Do you agree with that statement?

ADMIRAL STARK. A robot bomb?

SENATOR LUCAS. This torpedo bomb was in the nature of a secret weapon, they said, along the lines of a robot bomb, which was unknown to the best professional opinion in America at this time. Do you agree with that statement?

ADMIRAL STARK. A robot bomb?

SENATOR LUCAS. This torpedo bomb was in the nature of a secret weapon, they said, along the lines of a robot bomb, which was unknown to the best professional opinion in America and Britain at that time.

I ask if you agree with that? Do you agree that it was unknown to the best American and British opinion at that time, that a bomb of that kind could not operate in water as shallow as it was in Pearl Harbor?

ADMIRAL STARK. No, I did not agree with that. There is a later letter of ours that states that no capital ship was safe in any water which she could float in, where there was sufficient run for the torpedo to arm itself.

However, the letter was further qualified by stating depths which were desirable. I have got the letter here.

SENATOR LUCAS. I wish you would produce that letter and read it into the record, as I have been under the impression that there was an opinion among British and American experts that you couldn't use a bomb of that kind in that shallow water.

ADMIRAL STARK. That was true at the time it was written. There is a later letter of 13 June from the Chief of Naval Operations.

SENATOR LUCAS. 1941?

ADMIRAL STARK. 1941. To the Commandant, 1st, 3d, 4th, 5th, 6th, 7th, 8th, 10th, 11th, 12th, 13th, 14th, 15th and 16th Naval Districts. The subject is:

> Anti-torpedo baffles for protection against torpedo plane attacks.

Then there is a reference to the letter of 17 February, which I believe may be the one you just mentioned:

> 1. In reference (a) the Commandants were requested to consider the employment of and to make recommendations concerning anti-torpedo baffles especially for the protection of large and valuable units of the Fleet in their respective harbors and especially at the major Fleet bases.

[2266] In paragraph 3 were itemized certain limitations to consider in the use of A/T baffles among which the following was stated:

> A minimum depth of water of 75 feet may be assumed necessary to successfully drop torpedoes from planes. About 200 yards of torpedo run is necessary before the exploding device is armed, but this may be altered.

That was in the letter you just referred to. 2:

> Recent developments have shown that United States and British torpedoes may be dropped from planes at heights of as much as 300 feet, and in some cases make initial dives of considerably less than 75 feet, and make excellent runs. Hence, it may be stated that it cannot be assumed that any capital ship or other valuable vessel is safe when at anchor from this type of attack if surrounded by water at a sufficient distance to permit an attack to be developed and a sufficient run to arm the torpedo.

I would like to read the rest of that. If the letter stopped right there, there wouldn't have been any doubt, but it does show that possibility.
Paragraph 3:

> While no minimum depth of water in which naval vessels may be anchored can arbitrarily be assumed as providing safety from torpedo plane attack, it may be assumed that depths of water will be one of the factors considered by an attacking force, and an attack launched in relatively deep water (10 fathoms or more) is much more likely.
> 4. As a matter of information the torpedoes launched by the British at Taranto were, in general, in 13 to 15 fathoms of water, although several torpedoes may have been launched in 11 or 12 fathoms.

In other words, we pointed out the danger that any ship was subject to if she were afloat, had enough water to float in and enough room to fire the torpedo, if they could get the approach, and enough length of run for arming, and we then go on to say, and I would like to repeat that "it cannot be assumed that any capital ship or other valuable vessel is safe when at anchor from this type of attack if surrounded by water," from this type of attack, and then we go on to say that we feel the attacks are more likely where the depth of water is greater.

SENATOR LUCAS. That letter was written in June, 1941?

ADMIRAL STARK. Yes, sir; and a copy of that letter was sent to the commander in chief, Pacific; commander in chief, Atlantic; commander in chief, Asiatic; and commander in chief of some of the naval net depots, Bureau of Ordnance, and OP-12.

SENATOR LUCAS. In view of that discovery in June of 1941 that these torpedo bombs could operate in shallow water, was there anything done by the Navy Department toward the construction of torpedo nets to go into Pearl Harbor?

ADMIRAL STARK. We had directed the Bureau of Ordnance, I have forgotten the date, but it is here, to go ahead and design and develop antitorpedo nets for harbor work. The letter of February 11, which I would like to read, shows the action we took as far back as that, because of this possible contingency.

Senator Lucas. Is it a long letter?
Admiral Stark. No, sir; one page.
Senator Lucas. All right.
Admiral Stark (reading):

> 1. Reference (a) requested information concerning all promising experimental and development work on nets and booms done by the U. S. Navy since March 1940.
> [2267] 2. As far as this Office is aware, no such work has been done other than the making of minor modifications to the Admiralty designs. It is considered that experimental and development work should be undertaken. If necessary, additional personnel for this purpose should be secured.
> 3. There appears an urgent need for an anti-torpedo net which can be laid and removed in certain harbors in a short time for temporary use, and which will give good if not perfect protection from torpedoes fired from planes. The present Admiralty type net is designed to withstand torpedoes and with cutters, and its appurtenances are very heavy. A lighter net which will stop a torpedo not armed with cutters would furnish some protection, especially against torpedoes which would explode on contact with a metal net.
> 4. Effort should be made to reduce the weights of the present Admiralty nes and booms and their appurtenances without reducing their efficiency in order that they may be more readily handled. As a beginning, it is also suggested that plans be made to test sections of the old A/S net and of the new, as well as indicator nets, by attacking submarines. While such tests may duplicate British experiments, valuable lessons may be learned. It is requested that this office be kept informed of development work and all tests and experiments conducted with nets and booms.

That was our initial letter on directing the Bureau of Ordnance to go ahead with that work.
Senator Lucas. The date is February 1941?
Admiral Stark. February 11, 1941; yes, sir.
Senator Lucas. When did you first get any nets?
Admiral Stark. We didn't get any nets until 1942.
Senator Lucas. Do you know why?
Admiral Stark. I have forgotten the date but we did not have them up to the time of Pearl Harbor.
Senator Lucas. Do you know why the delay?
Admiral Stark. The Bureau of Ordnance just didn't produce on it.
Senator Lucas. Was any follow-up made on that letter of February 11 with respect to the Bureau of Ordnance insisting that the nets be produced?
Admiral Stark. Yes, sir; there were several.
Senator Lucas. A lot of ships could have been saved at Pearl Harbor if the nets had been out; isn't that right?
Admiral Stark. If an effective baffle had been there it undoubtedly would have minimized the effect. Of course, the bombs also did considerable damage.
Senator Lucas. I understand the torpedo planes did the real damage to the battleships, according to previous testimony; more than altitude bombs.

ADMIRAL STARK. I think that is correct.

SENATOR LUCAS. Do you know how long it took us to perfect this type of bomb that we could use in shallow water?

ADMIRAL STARK. No; I do not have that information. The Bureau of Ordnance could furnish it.

SENATOR LUCAS. And you don't have the information as to how long it took the Japanese to perfect that type of bomb?

ADMIRAL STARK. No, sir. I remember the original specification. I was Chief of Bureau of Ordnance. Our first specification was 100 knots and 100 feet. We were continually trying to raise the speed and increase the altitude from which they could be fired.

SENATOR LUCAS. Undoubtedly Japan had Pearl Harbor in mind when she first started experimenting with this type of bomb; do you agree?

[2268] ADMIRAL STARK. Unquestionably she had us in mind, just as we had any possible enemy in mind. We were all after a high-dive and shallow-water run.

SENATOR LUCAS. Very few harbors are as shallow as Pearl Harbor, however?

ADMIRAL STARK. Well, it was a shallow-water harbor. So is Colon. So is Guantanamo. So are many others. Too shallow in many cases for comfort. . . .

[2284] MR. MURPHY. In your judgement who was at fault, if anyone, for the failure to have the torpedo baffles or nets on the ships on December 7, 1941? You have already testified that Ordnance was working on it. There were three or four letters between you and Admiral Kimmel on the subject. Do you know of anyone particularly to blame for not having them on that day?

ADMIRAL STARK. I was asked this morning if I instituted any follow-up of my original request of Bureau of Ordnance to design and build those baffles. I perhaps can best answer the question by reading into the record the follow-ups which we made and if the committee so desires I will read them. They are not very long.

MR. MURPHY. I think it is important enough to do it.

THE CHAIRMAN. Read them into the record.

ADMIRAL STARK. The original letter was in February. On April 9, Chief of Naval Operations wrote this letter to Chief of Bureau of Ordnance, inviting attention to certain references and stating that the:

> * * * the Chief of Naval Operations brought forth the necessity for experimental and development work in connection with nets and booms, and especially the need for a light anti-torpedo net. The attention of the Bureau is directed to reference (b) which gives certain details of an apparently much lighter net now used by the Germans.
> Signed: R. E. Ingersoll, Acting.

[2285] On September 16, the Chief of Naval Operations wrote the Bureau of Ordnance.

Subject: Experimental and Developmental Work on Nets and Booms.

with four references.
The letter reads:

> It is suggested that in order that progress may be made in solving some of the problems which confront us, that a small group of officers, engineers and draftsmen be assigned exclusively to planning improvement in net and boom designs and to development and experimental work. The group, it is suggested, may be aided by using the facilities of the Net Depots at Tiburon and Newport. It is suggested that these two depots appear suitable as centers for experimental and development work.
>
> In references (a) and (b) the Chief of Naval Operations indicated the desirability of undertaking some research and development work. Among other suggestions, the need for a lighter anti-torpedo net was stressed, which can be laid and removed in harbors in a short time for temporary use, and which will give good if not perfect protection from torpedoes fired from planes.
>
> Designs are requested to be prepared giving A/T net protection to one or more large ships moored in harbors against torpedo plane attack in which the A/T net may be placed completely around one or more large ships, similar to placing the ship or ships in a "dry dock" of A/T net. It may be assumed that the currents inside of most harbors are not as great as at the entrances, and the moorings of such nets may be of less weight and less extensive than for the present A/T nets which are designed principally for harbor entrances. As such nets may be desired for advance bases, as little weight and volume of material as possible is desirable. As little space as possible should be taken up by the nets in order not to take up too much anchorage space.
>
> Designs of A-T nets which might be attached to booms on ships or floating off of ships at anchor are requested to be prepared in conjunction with the Bureau of Ships. In a design of this type it may be possible to do away with mooring the nets. A net which deflects rather than stops the torpedo may possibly be designed.
>
> Reference (c) is a preliminary Admiralty report on the development of a torpedo net defense for merchant ships at sea. It is requested that the Bureau of Ordnance in conjunction with the Bureau of Ships undertake a similar development work for the protection of ships under way at sea.
>
> It is possible that in our Navy the assumption that has been reached that anchorages protected by nets are secure. Nets are defensive measures, and, in general, are without destructive means. Patrol vessels are required in conjunction with net defenses, and of the two measures of defense, the vessels, capable of offensive action, are probably the more important. It is believed that the tests with nets conducted by the British should be accepted as conclusive. While one test of torpedo firing against an A/T net has been conducted by the Bureau, the torpedo was not equipped with cutters. No other tests have as yet been held. It may be well to repeat and to extend the British tests. It may be worth while to know the exact damage which will be done to an anti-torpedo net from a torpedo fired in the net.
>
> Until the present in great measure reliance in this mode of defense has been placed on British designs, experiments and tests. It is considered that now we should be in a position to take more progressive action. In this letter it is realized that the requests made are not concrete and definite, but serve only to

indicate several of the problems toward the solution of which action may be directed.

On 3 October 1941 the Chief of Naval Operations wrote again to the Chief of Bureau or Ordnance on the same subject, with references and a copy of reference A, which were proceedings of meeting of local joint planning committee, northern California sector, Pacific coastal frontier, of September 17. The letter reads:

> Enclosure (A) is forwarded for information.
> Attention is invited to paragraph 3 of the enclosure. The Chief of Naval Operations considers it urgent to develop an anti-torpedo net which can be made up, towed to a desired location, and quickly laid. The use of pontoons, as suggested, does not appear to solve this question; a reduction in the number of moorings, at present necessary for the standard net, would seem to be required.

[2286] That is the correspondence up to December 7 that Operations had with the Bureau of Ordnance on that subject of getting nets.

MR. MURPHY. What I was referring to previously was the Hewitt report contained in the appendix to Narrative Statement of Evidence which was given to me. On page 43 there is a reference made to a letter of February 15, 1941, from you to Admiral Kimmel and again to a letter of February 17, 1941, from you to Admiral Kimmel and again to a letter by Admiral Bloch of March 20, 1941, and again a letter of June 1941 from you to Admiral Kimmel, to which you referred this morning.

ADMIRAL STARK. Yes, sir.

MR. MURPHY. Now, in the Hewitt report I find the following:

> Admiral Kimmel testified that on this correspondence he based his opinion that there was no chance of an air torpedo attack on Pearl Harbor—and that even after the June letter, he did not think that torpedoes would run in such shallow water. He pointed out that the Navy made no effort to place such nets in Pearl Harbor. He later stated that he did not think an aerial torpedo attack would be made because he did not think such torpedoes would run in Pearl Harbor and did not give this a great deal of consideration for that reason.

In the light of the fact that Bureau of Ordnance were working on it and none had been furnished to Hawaii was Admiral Kimmel justified in that statement?

ADMIRAL STARK. I think the statement is not justified in view of the letter which I read this morning.

MR. MURPHY. The letter in June 1941?

ADMIRAL STARK. Of June 13 of 1941, in which appears the paragraph in part:

> Hence it may be stated that it cannot be assumed that any capital ship or other valuable vessel is safe when at anchor from this type of attack—that is

torpedo attack—if surrounded by water at a sufficient distance to permit an attack to be developed and a sufficient run to arm the torpedo.

Now, you will recall that I follow that with other paragraphs which while not changing that paragraph may have minimized it to the extent that it would not occur.

MR. MURPHY. Yes. Those letters are all in the record and you read them this morning.

ADMIRAL STARK. Yes, sir.

MR. MURPHY. Did Admiral Kimmel have the facilities at Pearl Harbor for manufacturing or preparing torpedo nets?

ADMIRAL STARK. No, sir.

MR. MURPHY. If he had gotten them wouldn't he have to get them through the CNO or would he go direct to Ordnance?

ADMIRAL STARK. Well, he probably would have written us about them. He could have written the Bureau of Ordnance but I think he would have come to us, undoubtedly, on it.

MR. MURPHY. What is your judgment subsequent to June of 1941? Should he or should he not have initiated a move to get them before December and if he did initiate it, in your judgment would they have been available?

ADMIRAL STARK. Well, we had initiated it and we did not have them, but we were pressing the Bureau of Ordnance. You will note that I also mentioned the Bureau of Ships. I remember personally suggesting to the Bureau of Ships the possibility of developing something like our targets to be placed alongside of ships in Pearl Harbor. Just [2287] what they had arrived at at that time I do not know, but they had not produced. [...]

[2350] SENATOR FERGUSON. Admiral, where did you first get the idea that there was a secret weapon used by the way of torpedoes at Pearl Harbor in the initial attack, when did that first come to your attention?

ADMIRAL STARK. I don't recall any particular secret weapon. There was nothing revolutionary, I believe, in anything they used.

SENATOR FERGUSON. In the discussion here a few days ago, as part of your testimony, when you were talking about these torpedo baffles, and as to whether or not we had already equipment to meet such an attack, the words secret weapon were used. They had a torpedo that we knew nothing about and that they were able to launch in 20 or 30 feet of water instead of, as at Taranto, where they had launched it in 60 to 80 feet.

ADMIRAL STARK. That was covered in the letter where they stated no ship could now be considered safe in any depth, that is, any major caliber depth, where there was sufficient room for the run of the torpedo to arm. It was just a progressive step, which I explained in our own experiments we were continually trying to increase the speed of a plane in dropping a torpedo, and also increasing the altitude from which it should be dropped. And the Japs, as shown, had progressed very far in that. And the letter which you read this morning where they spoke about putting some apparatus on the stern of the torpedo, we had already been experimenting with ours, we referred to it as the tail of the torpedo. But I think there was nothing revolutionary except the development had gone further.

SENATOR FERGUSON. As I understand it, the Navy Department never had any complaint because Admiral Kimmel didn't put in these torpedo nets, because they had neither furnished them to him nor had they furnished the equipment with which he could make them?

ADMIRAL STARK. That is correct. He stated, in the first place, that he thought they were not necessary from the information he had, and which later information showed them desirable, but he had no nets which were easy to handle, or baffles. These we were endeavoring to develop and they had not been developed up to December 7.

SECTION SIX
Other Pertinent Data

How the American Fleet Came to Be Permanently Based in Hawaii

ADMIRAL JAMES O. RICHARDSON,
COMMANDER-IN-CHIEF, U.S. FLEET (1940)

Joint Congressional Investigation

[254] From 1936 to 1937 I commanded the destroyers of the scouting force. From 1937 to 1938 I was the Assistant Chief of Naval Operations, during which period the China incident started and during which period the attack on the *Panay* occurred.

From 1938 to 1939 I was the Chief of what was then called the Bureau of Navigation, now known as the Bureau of Naval Personnel.

From 1939, the summer, until 1940 I was commander of the battle force. From 1940 to 1941 I was commander in chief of the United States Fleet. At that time the United States Fleet comprised all combatant ships in commission that were not assigned to the Asiatic Fleet or not operating directly under the Chief of Naval Operations.

I reported for duty as commander of battle force on June 24, 1939. On January 6, 1940, I relieved Admiral Claude C. Bloch as commander in chief of United States Fleet. On the 5th of January 1941 I received a secret dispatch in a code held only by the Chief of Naval Operations and myself informing me that I would be detached on the 1st of February.

On February 1, 1941, I was relieved by Admiral Husband E. Kimmel. At that time the fleet was reorganized, and Admiral Kimmel became commander in chief of the Pacific Fleet and another officer became commander in chief of the Atlantic Fleet.

I departed from Honolulu on February 14, 1941, and on March 25, 1941, I reported for duty as a member of the General Board.

MR. MITCHELL. At that time when you were commander of the United States Fleet was there a separate command known as the commander of the Pacific Fleet?

ADMIRAL RICHARDSON. There was not.

Source: Pearl Harbor Attack, *volume 1.*

Mr. Mitchell. Who was Chief of Naval Operations while you were chief in command of the United States Fleet?

Admiral Richardson. Admiral Harold R. Stark, who was my immediate superior.

Mr. Mitchell. When you were at that time commander of the United States Fleet at what Pacific city or was it on the Pacific side or the Atlantic side that you went to?

Admiral Richardson. When I assumed command of the United States Fleet there was a portion of the fleet serving in the Atlantic. There was a detachment of the United States Fleet serving in the Hawaiian area, known as the Hawaiian detachment, which was composed of heavy cruisers and destroyers, and, if my memory serves me correctly, one aircraft carrier. The Hawaiian detachment was under the command of Vice Adm. Adolphus Andrews, who was also commander of the scouting force.

Mr. Mitchell. Well, were you located on the Pacific coast?

Admiral Richardson. All the fleet in the Pacific assigned to the United States Fleet, that did not form a part of the Hawaiian detachment, was based at San Diego and San Pedro, Long Beach.

[255] Mr. Mitchell. Well, that is where you made your headquarters then?

Admiral Richardson. I actually assumed command of the fleet in the harbor of San Pedro, Long Beach, and I remained there until approximately the 1st of April, when the fleet departed for their annual fleet exercises.

Mr. Mitchell. What was your flagship at that time?

Admiral Richardson. The U.S.S. *Pennsylvania*.

Mr. Mitchell. You say the Pacific Fleet that you were in command of out there that was not included in these other detachments, that was based on the Pacific coast, was ordered out to maneuvers in the spring of 1940?

Admiral Richardson. It had been the custom for many years to have annual fleet exercises, including fleet problems and other exercises under simulated war conditions, where all available ships and aircraft were employed in training.

Mr. Mitchell. What were the base ports of the Pacific Fleet at that time other than the Hawaiian detachment and the Asiatic vessels you spoke of?

Admiral Richardson. Well, each ship had a home port.

Mr. Mitchell. Generally speaking, I mean what were the principal points?

Admiral Richardson. They were based practically all the time at San Pedro and Long Beach but the ships periodically proceeded to Bremerton and to San Francisco for overhaul, and normal operations in training and gunnery exercises were off the coast of southern California.

Mr. Mitchell. When the fleet vessels under your command made that movement in the spring of 1940, to what area did they proceed?

Admiral Richardson. They proceeded to sea divided into two task forces representing opposing fleets and conducted a war game and various exercises and then united with the Hawaiian detachment and proceeded to the Hawaiian area, arriving there on the—I actually arrived at Lahaina Roads at 1500 on April 10.

MR. MITCHELL. Well, you had been ordered to move out into Hawaiian waters after these exercises, or had you—

ADMIRAL RICHARDSON. Each year the fleet exercises were held in a different part of the world, a different part of the ocean, to familiarize the officers with the weather conditions and the terrain and everything else that it was necessary to know and before I became commander in chief the plans for this exercise had already been drawn up and approved and I carried out exercises which were planned by my predecessor.

When I arrived in Pearl Harbor according to the published plan the fleet, with the exception of the Hawaiian detachment, was to depart from the Hawaiian area on the 9th of May—no, the 9th of April. Wait a minute, let me see. No, the 9th of May.

MR. MITCHELL. This is 1940?

ADMIRAL RICHARDSON. 1940;

ME. GEARHART. What was the date?

ADMIRAL RICHARDSON. The 9th of May 1940.

MR. MITCHELL. And you say, do you—

ADMIRAL RICHARDSON. From the Hawaiian area the return would normally have been to the Pacific coast.

[256] MR. MITCHELL. The point is that when you went to Hawaiian waters at that time you expected that that would be a temporary arrangement and that you would shortly return to the Pacific coast?

ADMIRAL RICHARDSON. That was an arrangement the schedule for which had been prepared and approved and was known to all the officers and men in the fleet.

MR. MITCHELL. Well, you understood it was temporary?

ADMIRAL RICHARDSON. Oh, yes.

MR. MITCHELL. Yes. Now, we have a file of correspondence that includes some letters between you and Admiral Stark, Chief of Naval Operations, running from January 1940 to January 1941. You have examined that file and have a copy of it?

ADMIRAL RICHARDSON. Yes, sir. You have supplied me with a copy of that file. [...]

[258] MR. MITCHELL. Well, now, Admiral, I have here a letter dated March 15, 1940.

ADMIRAL RICHARDSON. March what?

MR. MITCHELL. March 15, 1940, addressed to "Dear J. O." and signed "Betty." Who is "J. O.?"

ADMIRAL RICHARDSON. I am J. O.

MR. MITCHELL. Who is "Betty?"

ADMIRAL RICHARDSON. Admiral H. R. Stark.

MR. MITCHELL. Is that the way you usually addressed each other in this personal correspondence?

ADMIRAL RICHARDSON. It was.

MR. MITCHELL. I notice in the letter of March 15, 1940 on page 2 there is a paragraph that reads as follows:

> I still think that the decision to send the detachment to Hawaii under present world conditions is sound. No one can measure how much effect its presence there may have on the Orange foreign policy.

What did the word "orange" stand for in naval parlance? Was it Japan?

ADMIRAL RICHARDSON. Japan.

MR. MITCHELL (reading):

> The State Department is strong for the present set-up and considers it beneficial; they were in on all discussions, press releases, etc.

That is a letter from Admiral Stark to you?

ADMIRAL RICHARDSON. Yes, and that was in reply to my letter to him asking about why the Hawaiian detachment was there, and I would like to invite your attention to the second paragraph in that letter of March 15, 1940.

MR. MITCHELL. When you went there you expected to come back soon and then you found you were not ordered back; that is right, isn't it?

ADMIRAL RICHARDSON. That is true.

MR. MITCHELL. Then you wanted to know why you were kept out there?

ADMIRAL RICHARDSON. That is true. [...]

[259] MR. MITCHELL. [...] Then we pass on to the letter of May 7, 1940, by Admiral Stark to you, and I find that contains this statement:

> When the fleet returns to the Coast (and I trust the delay will not be over two weeks, but I cannot tell) the President has asked that the fleet schedule be so arranged that on extremely short notice the fleet be able to return concentrated to Hawaiian waters. This will present somewhat of a problem in lugging around more oil with you perhaps than usual and keeping more provisions on board, because if action is wanted it will be wanted quickly. As far as I can see, your proposed schedule meets this requirement, and unless you hear to the contrary, you may assume it is O. K.

That is on May 7, 1940, and up to that time you expected to come back in the course of 2 weeks?

ADMIRAL RICHARDSON. No—oh, yes.

MR. MITCHELL. Yes.

ADMIRAL RICHARDSON. I thought it was possible.

MR. MITCHELL. We have here a letter of May 22 that is written by you to Admiral Stark, May 22, 1940, in which you write him:

As you no doubt well appreciate, I now must plan the Fleet schedule, and employment for the next few months. To do this intelligently, however, it is necessary to know more than I know now about why we are here and how long we will probably stay. I realize that the answer to the second question is largely dependent upon the first, and probably also upon further developments, but nonetheless I should have something to go on.

For instance, carrying out even a curtailed gunnery schedule will require wholesale movements of targets, tugs, utility planes, etc., from the Coast. The following are pertinent questions:

(a) Are we here primarily to influence the actions of other nations by our presence, and if so, what effect would the carrying out of normal training (insofar as we can under the limitations on anchorages, airfields, facilities and services) have on this purpose? The effect of the emergency docking program and the consequent absence of task forces during the training period must also be considered.

(b) Are we here as a stepping-off place for belligerent activity? If so, we should devote all of our time and energies to preparing for war. This could more effectively and expeditiously be accomplished by an immediate return to the West Coast, with "freezing" of personnel, filling up complements, docking, and all the rest of it. We could return here upon completion.

As it is now, to try and do both (a) and (b) from here and at the same time is a diversification of effort and purpose that can only result in the accomplishment of neither.

If we are here to develop this area as a peacetime operating base, consideration should be given to the certain decrese in the efficiency of the Fleet and the lowering of morale that may ensue, due to inadequate anchorages, airfields, facilities, services, recreation conditions, for so large a fleet. If only peacetime training is involved, should the Bureau of Navigation and I not be advised so we may remove restrictions on officer details?

Now, with that statement before you, will you state to the committee just what your situation had been up to that time, and how you happened to write that letter?

ADMIRAL RICHARDSON. Well, a fleet composed of a large number of ships and men and planes must secure careful planning, in order that time not be wasted and that something be accomplished. When the fleet went to the Hawaiian area as a part of the fleet exercises, we had [260] a definite schedule of gunnery exercises, steaming competitions, full power drives, inspections, and everything else that is required to keep a fleet busy, and keep them under training.

When the fleet went to the Hawaiian area we did not take with us tugs, targets, target rafts, target planes, towing planes, repair ships; so that if the fleet was to remain in the Hawaiian area, in order that it could be usefully employed, it was essential that I know that we remain there long enough to bring out all of the gear that was necessary for training the ship, for fear that I would start all this material to Hawaii and then, after it once started and got halfway there I would return, and then have to wait for several weeks for it to get back to the normal bases on the west coast, so I could continue training.

So that, from my point of view, my effectiveness in the fleet and continued training in the fleet demanded an early decision, so that plans could be made.

MR. MITCHELL. When did you first learn, and how, that the decision had been made here in Washington to base your fleet at Pearl Harbor instead of on the Pacific coast?

ADMIRAL RICHARDSON. The first notice that I received was a dispatch from the Chief of Naval Operations to the commander in chief, United States Fleet, May 4, which reads —

MR. MITCHELL. What is the date of it?

ADMIRAL RICHARDSON. May 4.

MR. GEARHART. 1940?

ADMIRAL RICHARDSON. May 4, 1940.

> It looks probable but not final that Fleet will remain Hawaiian waters for short time after May 9. Will expect to apprise you further Monday or Tuesday next.

The 4th of May was Saturday. On the 7th of May I received from the Chief of Naval Operations, addressed to CINCUS — CINCUS was the abbreviation for commander in chief United States Fleet —

> CINCUS make immediate press release instructions as follows:
> "I request permission to remain in Hawaiian waters to accomplish some things I wanted to do while here. The Department has approved this request."
> Delay Fleet departure Hawaiian area is for about two weeks prior to the end of which time you will be further advised regarding future movements. Carry out regular scheduled overhauls of individual units, movements of base force units at your discretion.

MR. MITCHELL. Did you issue the press release?

ADMIRAL RICHARDSON. I did.

MR. MITCHELL. You had not requested or asked to be left out there, had you?

ADMIRAL RICHARDSON. I had not. [. . .]

MR. MITCHELL. I refer now to a letter of May 27, 1940, which was written by Admiral Stark to you in response to the letter of May 22 that I just read from, and in which you wanted to know about what you were supposed to do, and he said, among other things:

> [261] Yours of the 22nd just received. I shall endeavor to answer it paragraph by paragraph.
> First, however, I would like to say that I know exactly what you are up against, and to tell you that here in the Department we are up against the same thing.
> Why are you in the Hawaiian area?
> Answer: You are there because of the deterrent effect which it is thought

your presence may have on the Japs going into the East Indies. In previous letters I have hooked this up with the Italians going into the war. The connection is that with Italy in, it is thought the Japs might feel just that much freer to take independent action.

We believe both the Germans and the Italians have told the Japs that so far as they are concerned, she, Japan has a free hand in the Dutch East Indies.

Then later in the letter:

Along the same line as the first question presented, you would naturally ask—suppose the Japs do go into the East Indies? What are we going to do about it? My answer to that is, I don't know, and I think there is nobody on God's green earth who can tell you. I do know my own arguments with regard to this, both in the White House and in the State Department, are in line with the thought contained in your recent letter.

I would point out one thing, and that is even if the decision here were for the U. S. to take no decisive action if the Japs should decide to go into the Dutch East Indies, we must not breathe it to a soul, as by so doing we would completely nullify the reason for your presence in the Hawaiian area. Just remember that the Japs don't know what we are going to do, and so long as they don't know, they may hesitate or be deterred. These facts I have kept very secret here.

The above, I think will answer the question "why you are there." It does not answer the question as to how long you will probably stay. Rest assured that the minute I get this information I will rush it to you. Nobody can answer it just now. Like you, I have asked the question and also—like you—I have been unable to get the answer.

I realize what you are up against in even a curtailed gunnery schedule. I may say that so far as the Department is concerned, you are at liberty to play with the gunnery schedule in any way you see fit, eliminating some practices for the time being and substituting others which you may consider important, and which you have the means at hand to accomplish. Specifically, if you want to cut short range battle practice and proceed with long range practices, or division practices or experimental or anything else, including anti-air, etc., etc., which you think will be to the advantage of the Fleet in its present uncertain status—go ahead. Just keep us informed.

Later on, he says:

You ask whether you are there as a stepping-off place for belligerent activity? Answer: Obviously it might become so under certain conditions, but a definite answer cannot be given as you have already gathered from the foregoing.

I realize what you say about the advantages of returning to the West Coast for the purpose of preparation at this time is out of the question. If you did return, it might nullify the reasons for your being in Hawaii. This very question has been brought up here. As a compromise, however, you have authority for returning ships to the Coast for docking, taking ammunition, stores, etc., and this should help in any case.

He says later:

> You were not detained in Hawaii to develop the area as a peacetime operating base, but this will naturally flow to a considerable extent from what you are up against.
>
> As to the decrease in the efficiency of the Fleet and the lowering of morale due to inadequate anchorages, airfields, service, recreation conditions, for so large a fleet:
>
> I wish I could help you. I spent some of my first years out of the Naval Academy in the West Indies.

Now, that brings to our minds the question of your attitude about the basing of the fleet, and I call your attention to a letter you wrote to Admiral Stark — before we get to that, I have a letter here of June 22, Stark to Richardson.

> [262] Your trip to Washington was held in abeyance because of uncertainty as to the movement of the Fleet in the immediate future. Tentatively, decision has been made for the Fleet to remain for the present where it is. [. . .]

MR. MITCHELL. Had you received any information more definite than that as to the permanency of your station at Pearl Harbor prior to that letter? It says:

> Tentatively decision has been made for the fleet to remain for the present where it is. This decision may be changed at any time.

ADMIRAL RICHARDSON. No, I had received no prior information.

MR. MITCHELL. Well, you had developed by that time very definite ideas in your own mind in opposition to the advisability of basing the fleet at Pearl Harbor, had you not? Will you please state in your own way just what the situation was and what your objections were grounded upon?

ADMIRAL RICHARDSON. My objections for remaining there were, primarily, that you only had one port, secure port, and very crowded, no recreation facilities for the men, a long distance from Pearl Harbor to the city of Honolulu, inadequate transportation, inadequate airfields.

A carrier cannot conduct all training for her planes from the carrier deck. In order to launch her planes she must be underway at substantial speed, using up large amounts of fuel. So that wherever carriers are training their squadrons there must be flying fields available, so that while the ship herself is undergoing overhaul, or repair, or upkeep, the planes may conduct training, flying from the flying fields.

There were inadequate and restricted areas for anchorages of the fleet; to take them in and out of Pearl Harbor wasted time.

Another reason, which was a substantial one: Americans are perfectly willing to go anywhere, stay anywhere, do anything when [263] there is a job to be done and they can see the reason for their being there, but to keep the fleet, during what the men considered normal peacetimes, away from the coast and away from their families, away from recreation, rendered it difficult to maintain a high state of morale that is essential to successful training.

For those reasons, and because I believe that the fleet could be better prepared for war on a normal basis on the west coast, I wanted to return to the west coast.

MR. MITCHELL. There is also a letter from you—or rather a memorandum from the Secretary, it is called, dated September 12, 1940, Will you please turn to that? [...] At the bottom of page 2, under "4 (A)" is the title "Retention of the Fleet in the Hawaiian Area."

Was that statement intended to sum up your views about the retention of the fleet in the Hawaiian area?

ADMIRAL RICHARDSON. It was.

MR. MITCHELL. Would you mind reading that, Admiral?

ADMIRAL RICHARDSON (reading):

> Retention of the fleet in the Hawaiian Area.
>
> (a) From a purely Naval point of view there are many disadvantages attached to basing the fleet in this area, some of which are:
>
> (1) Difficulty, delay and cost of transporting men, munitions, and supplies.
>
> (2) Inadequacy of Lahaina as operating anchorage due to lack of security.
>
> (3) Inadequacy of Pearl Harbor as operating anchorage due to difficulties of entry, berthing and departure of large ships.
>
> [264] (4) Congested and restricted operating areas, in the air and on the surface.
>
> (5) Inadequate facilities for fleet services, training, recreation and housing.
>
> (6) Prolonged absence from mainland of officers and men in time of peace adversely affects morale.
>
> (7) In case of war, necessary for fleet to return to mobilization ports on West Coast or accept partial and unorganized mobilization measure resulting in confusion and a net loss of time.

Shall I continue?

MR. MITCHELL. Yes, I think those are pertinent.

ADMIRAL RICHARDSON (reading):

> If the disposition of the fleet were determined solely by naval considerations the major portion of the fleet should return to its normal Pacific Coast bases because such basing would facilitate its training and its preparation for war.
>
> If factors other than purely naval ones are to influence the decision as to where the fleet should be based at this time, the naval factors should be fully presented and carefully considered, as well as the probable effect of the decision on the readiness of the fleet. In other words, is it more important to lend strength to diplomatic representations in the Pacific by basing the fleet in the Hawaiian area, than to facilitate its preparation for active service in any area by basing the major part of it on normal Pacific Coast bases?
>
> In case our relations with another Pacific nation deteriorate, what is the State Department's conception of our next move? Does it believe that the fleet is now mobilized and that it could embark on a campaign directly from Hawaii or safely conduct necessary training from the insecure anchorage at Lahaina which is 2,000 miles nearer enemy submarine bases than our normal Pacific Coast bases?

MR. MITCHELL. Shortly after that you made a visit to Washington, did you not, Admiral?

ADMIRAL RICHARDSON. I did.

MR. MITCHELL. Do you remember when you reached here and when you left, approximately? You were here on October 8, were you not?

ADMIRAL RICHARDSON. Yes. At 07:07, on October 7. I talked with Stark, Nimitz, Knox. That was my second visit to Washington. I came at that time because the Secretary said he wanted to talk to me. I arrived. I found that they were considering increasing the strength of the Asiatic Fleet, which was under the command of Admiral Hart. And while here I lunched with the President. Had a long talk with him. I saw Dr. Stanley Hornbeck of the Department of State, who was at that time, if my memory serves me correctly, the advisor of the State Department on far eastern affairs.

MR. MITCHELL. In your interviews with the Secretary of the Navy and Admiral Stark, did you take up this question with them of your objections, the objections that you just stated, as to the basing of the fleet in the Hawaiian area?

ADMIRAL RICHARDSON. I think not, because I had given a memorandum to the Secretary and fully stated my views to him. I had sent a copy of it to Admiral Stark, who was thoroughly familiar with my views. And I had sent a copy of part of it to Dr. Stanley Hornbeck of the State Department who knew what I thought. So, if I remember correctly, I did not talk about that with Admiral Stark. I talked primarily about detaching ships from the main fleet to strengthen the Asiatic Fleet.

And the first day I arrived I was suddenly confronted with the fact that 5,000 sailors had landed on the west coast to be turned over to me and I had to find some means of getting them out to Hawaii. So I had to take a carrier—I think it was the *Saratoga*—and use her to [265] transport the men that I was unable to accommodate in ships that had come to the coast with me.

MR. MITCHELL. Well, the White House records show that on October 8, 1940, you had lunch with the President and with Governor Leahy at 1 p. m. Do you remember that?

ADMIRAL RICHARDSON. That is correct.

MR. MITCHELL. Governor Leahy or Admiral Leahy?

ADMIRAL RICHARDSON. Admiral William E. Leahy.

MR. MITCHELL. He was then Governor of Puerto Rico.

ADMIRAL RICHARDSON. Yes. We did not go to the White House office in company. I was invited by the President through the Chief of Naval Operations to lunch at 1 o'clock. When I arrived there I found Admiral Leahy there.

MR. MITCHELL. Will you state in your own way, Admiral, just what occurred at that meeting and what was said about any of these matters we have been referring to?

ADMIRAL RICHARDSON. The President talked to Admiral Leahy about Puerto Rican affairs, and as I was not interested, I remember little of what was said; but I have a vague recollection that one subject under discussion was the question of housing.

The President asked Admiral Leahy his opinion about strengthening the Asiatic Fleet and my recollection is that Admiral Leahy said that whatever you sent out will be lost, therefore I would send the least valuable combatant ships we have, the 7,500 ton cruisers, but I recommended, I personally recommended that none be sent. A decision to send none was reached.

MR. MITCHELL. Admiral Leahy had been Chief of Naval Operations previously?

ADMIRAL RICHARDSON. He had been Chief of Naval Operations. He was Chief of Naval Operations when I was the assistant.

MR. MITCHELL. Then proceed, Admiral, with your statement of what occurred there.

ADMIRAL RICHARDSON. The following statement, because of its importance, I have written out. I wrote it out several weeks ago when it appeared certain, in my mind, that I would, unfortunately, be called before this committee. And with the permission of the Chairman I would like to read this statement—

THE CHAIRMAN. Yes.

ADMIRAL RICHARDSON. Which I prepared in the quiet of my home, where I could think and refresh my memory to a maximum extent possible.

THE CHAIRMAN. You may proceed, Admiral, to do that.

ADMIRAL RICHARDSON. I took up the question of returning to the Pacific coast all of the fleet except the Hawaiian detachment.

The President stated that the fleet was retained in the Hawaiian area in order to exercise a restraining influence on the actions of Japan.

I stated that in my opinion the presence of the fleet in Hawaii might influence a civilian political government, but that Japan had a military government which knew that the fleet was undermanned, unprepared for war, and had no train of auxiliary ships without which it could not undertake active operations. Therefore, the presence of the fleet in Hawaii could not exercise a restraining influence on Japanese action.

[266] I further stated we were more likely to make the Japanese feel that we meant business if a train were assembled and the fleet returned to the Pacific coast, the complements filled, the ships docked, and fully supplied with ammunition, provisions, stores, and fuel, and then stripped for war operations.

The President said in effect, "Despite what you believe, I know that the presence of the fleet in the Hawaiian area, has had, and is now having, a restraining influence on the actions of Japan."

I said, "Mr. President, I still do not believe it, and I know that our fleet is disadvantageously disposed for preparing for or initiating war operations."

The President then said, "I can be convinced of the desirability of returning the battleships to the west coast if I can be given a good statement which will convince the American people and the Japanese Government that in bringing the battleships to the west coast we are not stepping backward."

This is embarrassing.

Later I asked the President if we were going to enter the war. He replied that if the Japanese attacked Thailand, or the Kra Peninsula, or the Dutch East Indies we would not enter the war, that if they even attacked the Philippines he doubted whether we would enter the war, but that they could not always avoid makign mistakes and that as the war continued and the area of operations expanded sooner or later they would make a mistake and we would enter the war.

MR. MITCHELL. Does that complete your statement of the conversation?

ADMIRAL RICHARDSON. That is about all of it. [...]

[270] MR. MITCHELL. What about the second appointment at 12 noon on July 11 with the President? Do you remember about that and what was said?

ADMIRAL RICHARDSON. I believe that that—well, I know that that meeting lasted only a few minutes and I went by to tell the President good-bye and no subjects of any moment were discussed.

MR. MITCHELL. Did you have any appointment with Mr. Hull or Mr. Welles, or both of them, during July 1940? Their record shows an appointment on July 9.

ADMIRAL RICHARDSON. During that visit I saw Secretary Hull and Under Secretary Welles and talked to both of them at the same time, or, rather, I talked to Secretary Hull in the presence of Under Secretary Welles for an hour or so.

I saw Senator Byrnes on the 10th of July. I had lunch with General Marshall on the 10th of July. I saw Dr. Stanley Hornbeck on the 11th of July and outside of naval personnel I think those were the only officials that I saw. I wanted to see the then Congressman Scrugham, who was chairman of the subcommittee of the Appropriations Committee of the House that handled naval appropriations, but he was not in town.

MR. MITCHELL. Do you remember the subject of your discussion with Mr. Hull on that meeting of the 9th of July, what the general tenor of it was?

ADMIRAL RICHARDSON. I saw Mr. Hull to fully explore and learn all that I could as to why the fleet was retained in Hawaii, how long they would probably stay there and what the future intentions were, because I had been directed to retain the fleet in Hawaii and announced that it was retained there at my request and naturally, since I had made no such request, I wanted to know what was back of the whole thing.

I also felt so strongly the need for men that I wanted to impress on both the Secretary of State and the Under Secretary of State that I felt that they should assist insofar as possibly they could in seeing that the fleet was fully manned. [...]

[281] MR. MITCHELL. Now, going back to your visits with Secretary Hull and Secretary Knox, which was your first trip here in 1940, along in [282] July, you said you went to Mr. Hull and others to find out what the situation was, why you were being kept at Pearl Harbor. I neglected to ask you what Mr. Hull said, if he gave the reason for it.

ADMIRAL RICHARDSON. Mr. Hull in a very complete and comprehensive manner presented to me his views of the relationships, relations between the United States and Japan. He felt that we should take a very strong position with respect to Japan and that the retention of the fleet in Hawaii was a reflection of that strong attitude.

I did not receive this impression from Secretary Hull, and I cannot state with certainty how I received it, but I left here with the distinct impression that there was an opinion in Washington that Japan could be bluffed.

MR. MITCHELL. Well, when you were here during that trip you visited with Admiral Stark, I suppose?

ADMIRAL RICHARDSON. I did. I stayed with Admiral Stark at the Admiral's house.

MR. MITCHELL. In your contact with him did you gather any different impression about his attitude toward basing the fleet at Pearl Harbor instead of on our west coast than he expressed in these letters?

ADMIRAL RICHARDSON. It is my belief that had Admiral Stark been uninfluenced by other considerations he would have wholeheartedly agreed with me.

MR. MITCHELL. Well, just what did he say about it in your meetings with him, if you remember.

ADMIRAL RICHARDSON. Well, his letters, I think, in many places show that he hoped that the fleet would return to the west coast, and after the fleet had been in Hawaii for some time he authorized me to return approximately one-third of the fleet to the coast at a time for recreation and replenishment and the securing of additional men, and when he informed me that I might do that he said that he informed me with great pleasure. And I believe that I came with either the first or the second one of those task forces that visited the coast.

MR. MITCHELL. During 1940, when you were in command of the fleet, did you have fleet war games out in the Hawaiian area?

ADMIRAL RICHARDSON. We had, while I was in command of the fleet, only one big fleet exercise which involved two fleet propers. They took place between the first of April and the 9th of May.

MR. MITCHELL. Did any of those exercises involve a simulated air attack by an enemy carrier force?

ADMIRAL RICHARDSON. Those exercises did not. The exercises were planned by my predecessor. They did not include a carrier attack on Pearl Harbor. And joint exercises with the Army were discussed by Admiral Stark with me in letters, and it was too late to modify the plans, and in those exercises the only exercises in which the Army participated was, I believe, on the 8th or 9th of April. I sent some heavy cruisers in to simulate an attempted raid in order to exercise the forces stationed in Hawaii, the Navy patrol planes, in locating the force and the Army bombers in bombing it, and the submarine stations normally in Pearl Harbor in attacking the force, which was simulating an attack, so that there was not a large scale joint exercise between the Army and the Navy in which a carrier raid on installations in Hawaii occurred, although in previous years, when I was in a [283] position other than commander in chief, I had been present in the fleet when such attacks were made. [...]

[285] SENATOR LUCAS. Mr. Chairman. I should like to ask the admiral two or three questions.

In your memorandum of September 12, 1940, to the Secretary of the Navy you submitted a number of pertinent points to be considered, among which were the operations of the fleet and in that part of the memorandum you discussed the problems involved if the fleet was to be retained in Hawaiian waters.

As I understand it, those points of disadvantage that you stressed in that memorandum were purely problems from a naval standpoint and nothing else?

ADMIRAL RICHARDSON. Oh, absolutely.

SENATOR LUCAS. All right. Now, you set forth seven points, seven disadvantages to basing the fleet in that area. Those points have been gone over by counsel and yourself and I was anxious to determine from you as to whether or not at that time you considered the question of the possibility of a hostile air attack from some aggressor nation, in connection with not basing the fleet in the Hawaiian waters?

ADMIRAL RICHARDSON. I had not considered that it was likely that the fleet would be attacked by a carrier raid and I so stated repeatedly in security orders issued to the fleet. [...]

[286] SENATOR LUCAS. This memorandum was in June 1940, and if I understand you correctly, Admiral, the possibility of a hostile air attack on the fleet was not considered in making up the recommendations which the authorities here in Washington should study?

ADMIRAL RICHARDSON. That is correct.

SENATOR LUCAS. And the question of a submarine attack was not considered either in connection with those plans?

ADMIRAL RICHARDSON. I have difficulty in hearing the Senator.

SENATOR LUCAS. I say the question of a submarine attack by a hostile force was not considered in 1940 either?

ADMIRAL RICHARDSON. No. I think my view is clearly presented in a document before the committee which says:

> The security of the Fleet operating and based in the Hawaiian Area may reasonably be based on two assumptions:
> (A) That no responsible foreign power will provoke war, under present existing conditions, by attack on the Fleet or Base, but that irresponsible and misguided nations of such powers may attempt;
> (1) sabotage from small craft on ships based in Pearl Harbor,
> (2) to block the Entrance Channel to Pearl Harbor by sinking an obstruction in the Channel,
> (3) lay magnetic or other mines in the approaches to Pearl Harbor.

So that, actually, before I left the fleet we were sweeping the channel against magnetic mines.

SENATOR LUCAS. How long was it after you gave your seven points of disadvantage to keeping the fleet in Hawaii that the order of Admiral Andrews was issued to start the patrol which you discussed?

ADMIRAL RICHARDSON. Admiral Andrews' order did not start a patrol.

SENATOR LUCAS. What was that order?

ADMIRAL RICHARDSON. It modified the patrol that I had in existence.

SENATOR LUCAS. I see, all right. And when did that patrol go into existence that you had, Admiral?

ADMIRAL RICHARDSON. It started the day that the fleet arrived in the Hawaiian area on the 10th of April.

SENATOR LUCAS. 1940?

ADMIRAL RICHARDSON. 1940, purely as a part of the fleet exercise for training purposes.

SENATOR LUCAS. For training purposes only?

ADMIRAL RICHARDSON. Yes.

SENATOR LUCAS. And how long did that continue?

ADMIRAL RICHARDSON. It continued until, I think, the 30th of December 1940.

SENATOR LUCAS. Well, how did the admiral's order augment that? I had just forgotten your statement a moment ago.

ADMIRAL RICHARDSON. Initially the long-range patrol, so-called, but it was not a long-range patrol, it was to 180 miles centered on Lahaina between the arc of 220 and 235, a I remember, but I can verify that—220 to 335 to 180 miles.

Now, when the Army received an alert Admiral Andrews shifted the center from Lahaina to Pearl Harbor and increased the distance to 300 miles and changed the arc from 180 through west to north. Later on I modified that patrol.

[287] SENATOR LUCAS. Yes. Now, before you leave the patrol, how long did that continue?

ADMIRAL RICHARDSON. The patrol established by Admiral Andrews?

SENATOR LUCAS. That is right.

ADMIRAL RICHARDSON. I am not certain, but I think it continued as long as the Army maintained their alert which was, as I remember, almost a month. [...]

[292] SENATOR BREWSTER. [...] I think it should be clear what was the representation in your letter to which Admiral Stark expressed his view on. It was, as I understand it, your letter of May 13, in which you used the following language [reading]:

> I feel that any move west means hostilities. I feel that at this time it would be a grave mistake to become involved in the West where our interests, although [293] important, are not vital, and thereby reduce our ability to maintain the security of the Western Hemisphere which is vital.
>
> If the Fleet is to go west it can only start, properly prepared, from the West Coast where it can be docked, manned, stocked and stripped, and a suitable train assembled.

> Rest assured that although I am entirely without information I realize your position, and I want you to know that if the situation becomes such that higher authority decides we should go West, all of us are ready to give all we have.

That is the end of the quotation from your letter, to which I understand Admiral Stark in his letter of May 22 replied. [Reading]:

> I agree with the tenor of your letter and you will be glad to know I had already so expressed myself.

Would that lead you to believe, or would that leave you in any doubt, Admiral Richardson, as to the position of Admiral Stark in this matter?

ADMIRAL RICHARDSON. I was never in any doubt about his position.

SENATOR BREWSTER. And what was the situation, Admiral, of the fleet? With the fleet which you had at Pearl Harbor—was it what would be considered in naval parlance as a fleet?

ADMIRAL RICHARDSON. Well, it was a combatant fleet but it did not have in company with it the auxiliaries that would be essential to active operations.

SENATOR BREWSTER. So that if there were hostilities that should develop, what would have been the mission of the fleet under any plans that were in existence?

ADMIRAL RICHARDSON. Under the existing plans it would have been necessary for the fleet to return to the west coast to mobilize, assemble a train, fill the ships with the regulation number of personnel, provisions, supplies, stores, fuel, strip the ships of needless articles which necessarily appear on a ship during a long period of peace and prepare them for offensive operation. [. . .]

[298] MR. GEARHART. Admiral, pursuing the questions that have been asked just a moment ago by the Senator from Maine, I think you testified that the fleet, as you commanded it in 1940, was undermanned, undertrained, understaffed, under provisioned and underammunitioned.

ADMIRAL RICHARDSON. Well, no American force was ever underprovisioned. We eat better than anybody in the world.

MR. GEARHART. But did you have a sufficient supply of edibles to keep you going for a long time, for instance, through a war engagement, a war responsibility?

ADMIRAL RICHARDSON. Well, normally we carried dry provisions for about 60 days, if I remember correctly. Insofar as I remember, there was no question of provisions. The ships did not carry the full wartime allowance of ammunition because of the needless expenditure of fuel in pushing that much weight through the water. There was a deficiency in certain types of ammunition.

[299] For example, we had little, if any bombardment ammunition which would be necessary in effecting a landing.

As to enough men, never within my knowledge, except in war, has the Navy had on board enough men to fight the ship. We have been lucky if we could secure sufficient appropriations to maintain 85 percent of complement. Men of experience were being removed from the ships in order to train new men.

MR. GEARHART. Now to place it on a percentage basis, what would be the percentage of fighting efficiency of the Navy as you commanded it?

ADMIRAL RICHARDSON. Well, that would be a highly theoretical question. No answer would be of any value.

MR. GEARHART. You consider you were 85 percent manned?

ADMIRAL RICHARDSON. Well, we had 85 percent enough men to man the battery and steam at full power for more than a very short time, and as an instrument of war their value was prospective. They could be fully realized in a short space of time by the addition of men, because men in war learn far more rapidly than they do in time of peace.

MR. GEARHART. Well, then, the Navy under your command was not in a condition of readiness to commence the war with Japan?

ADMIRAL RICHARDSON. Absolutely not.

MR. GEARHART. And if it were the policy of the United States to commence a war with Japan the ships would have to return first to the west coast, spending a week in travel and a week in coming back—and how many weeks being put in shape for striking?

ADMIRAL RICHARDSON. Well, in my letter, one of my letters, I stated that in the event active war operations were undertaken it would either be necessary to return to the coast for mobilization or preparation or accept the handicaps of preparing in Pearl Harbor. I could not hazard a guess as to how soon they would be ready from Pearl Harbor, returning to the coast and being ready to start again, because I do not know how quickly you could have assembled the ships, the tankers, and done the training. Actually it was a year or so, was it not?

MR. GEARHART. You say a year or so?

ADMIRAL RICHARDSON. Well, before we really got going well in this war it was not a matter of weeks.

MR. GEARHART. Then in order to prepare the fleet to strike, say, Japan originally, it would have to travel from Hawaii to the United States, spending a week, then uncertain weeks in the United States being equipped for war, and then travel back a week, and that would mean really by leaving it in Hawaii it was 4,500 miles further away from the enemy than it would be if it had been in the United States?

ADMIRAL RICHARDSON. Yes, but I think when you consider the many, many other things that had to be done before active war operations could be undertaken, the question of whether it was in Hawaii or whether it was on the west coast would have little effect on the over-all time, because you had to assemble, train, you might have to build some, you might have to have drydocks, you might have to have repair facilities, you had to have a terrific amount of stores and all kinds of equipment for building roads and airfields, and everything else, none of which was ready.

[300] MR. GEARHART. Yes.

ADMIRAL RICHARDSON. So that the question of whether it was in Hawaii or whether it was on the west coast, when actual war started it was a matter of no moment, in my opinion, because other things controlled the time of getting ready.

MR. GEARHART. Well, considering the other situation, the one which actually happened, by having our fleet in Hawaiian waters we had our fleet 2,500 miles closer to the enemy for their sneak attack?

ADMIRAL RICHARDSON. Do you want an opinion on that?

MR. GEARHART. Yes, unless it is a question of geography, unless it is a matter of going over water, or something else.

ADMIRAL RICHARDSON. In my opinion, Congressman Gearhart, a Japanese fleet that could cross most of the Pacific ocean and deliver an undiscovered attack on Pearl Harbor would quite likely have been able to deliver the same attack on Puget Sound.

MR. GEARHART. Well, that is amazing.

ADMIRAL RICHARDSON. But the whole question is the amount of oil they have got in the ships.

MR. GEARHART. Now you have outlined the deficiencies in our Navy's strength at that time. Were those deficiencies known to the Japanese? Have you any way of knowing whether they were or not?

ADMIRAL RICHARDSON. Well, I never had any doubt that the Japanese knew everything they wanted to know about our fleet, and the Secretary of the Navy told me himself that they knew more about it than I did.

MR. GEARHART. Well, then in the light of what you have just said, do you think that the President was correct when he said he thought the presence of the Fleet in Hawaiian waters had a restraining effect on the Japanese?

ADMIRAL RICHARDSON. I did not think so when I was talking to him, and I have not changed my mind. [...]

[321] SENATOR FERGUSON. I understand that you stated you left the position as commander in chief of the fleet February 1, 1941.

ADMIRAL RICHARDSON. That is correct.

SENATOR FERGUSON. And you at that time were succeeded by Admiral Kimmel?

ADMIRAL RICHARDSON. That is correct.

SENATOR FERGUSON. And you also stated that he was a commanding officer under you in charge of cruisers?

ADMIRAL RICHARDSON. He was a type commander, not commanding officer, because with us commanding officers command a single ship.

SENATOR FERGUSON. I see. Now, do you know how Admiral Kimmel came to succeed you; have you any information on that you could give the committee?

ADMIRAL RICHARDSON. When I was in Washington in October 1940, in conversation with Admiral Stark and Admiral Nimitz, who was then Chief of the Bureau of Navigation, now Bureau of Naval Personnel, I stated that in my opinion they should have in mind the names of officers whom they would consider favorably as the relief of all of the important officers in the fleet, as any officer of the age of most of the flag officers of senior rank might break down in health or might be detached for other reasons, and that in order that they might not be taken unawares I thought they should have a tentative slate of prospective reliefs, and they agreed with me and asked me to suggest the names of possible reliefs.

SENATOR FERGUSON. Did you make any suggestions?

ADMIRAL RICHARDSON. After some consideration I submitted a list of names and in that list was the name of Rear Admiral Husband E. Kimmel.

SENATOR FERGUSON. Will you tell us who else was in the list?

ADMIRAL RICHARDSON. I do not remember with certainty, and I hoped I would not be required to answer that question, because I have very many friends in the Navy and I would hate for them, any of them, to feel that their name was not on that list.

[322] SENATOR FERGUSON. I have no desire to press for an answer.

About how many were in the list, so that they may feel that they were included?

ADMIRAL RICHARDSON. I think probably five or six. [...] When I left Washington in October, Admiral Stark and Admiral Nimitz informed me that it was their belief that I would remain in command until I completed 2 years' service as commander in chief, and I had no reason for suggesting this excepting that when a man is over 60, in a strenuous job, he might not hold out.

SENATOR FERGUSON. What was the normal tour of duty—is that how you express it in the Navy?

ADMIRAL RICHARDSON. That is how we express it, but there is no such thing, because there have been officers remain Commander in Chief one year; there have been officers remain two years. My predecessor remained, I think, 2 years.

SENATOR FERGUSON. The normal, you would say, then, is 2 years—average?

ADMIRAL RICHARDSON. Well, it was not normal for a number of years, and I believe that a feeling grew up in the Navy that a 1-year tenure of office was too short, and there was a tendency, as exemplified by actual practice, to extend the cruise of a commander in chief to 2 years.

SENATOR FERGUSON. Was 13 months an average tour of duty?

ADMIRAL RICHARDSON. I know of one or two flag officers who were detached as commander in chief after 1 year.

SENATOR FERGUSON. When you say the commander in chief, that would be in the same position as you were?

ADMIRAL RICHARDSON. Same way.

SENATOR FERGUSON. Was seniority recognized in the Navy, for instance as it is recognized in the Senate, that the next in line would take your position?

ADMIRAL RICHARDSON. Seniority is recognized in the Navy in the assignment of officers to duty up to and including that of captain, but in the selection of officers for flag assignments an effort is made to base assignments on an estimate of the officer's ability rather than upon his lineal position on the list.

SENATOR FERGUSON. Now, how long of a notice did you have that you were going to be removed, when you were commander in chief of the fleet?

[323] ADMIRAL RICHARDSON. I received a dispatch on 5 January, about 11:30 in the morning Honolulu time, Sunday.

SENATOR FERGUSON. And from whom did you receive that dispatch?

ADMIRAL RICHARDSON. I am not positive. I think it came from the Chief of the Bureau of Naval Personnel, who was Admiral Nimitz, and was charged with the preparation of all orders, but it came to me in a secret code that was held by no one in the fleet except me, and the reason it was in a secret code was that the same message involved many other changes of flag officers, and I was directed in the message to inform all of the officers concerned but to inform no one else in a public release of the impending changes made.

SENATOR FERGUSON. When was the first public release that you were retired from that position as commander in chief of the Navy?

ADMIRAL RICHARDSON. My recollection is that it was on the 6th of January or possibly the 7th, Tuesday. [...] Well, my orders directed me, my orders detaching me from command of the United States Fleet directed me to report to the Secretary of the Navy for duty. I reported, as nearly as I can remember, on the 24th day of March, 1941. I can verify that date.

SENATOR FERGUSON. Well, it is near enough.

ADMIRAL RICHARDSON. By the Secretary of the Navy I was ordered on 25 March 1941 to report duty with the General Board. When I went in to report to the Secretary of the Navy I said, in effect, in my experience in the Navy I have never known of a flag officer being detached from command of the United States Fleet in the same manner that I was, and I feel that I owe it to myself to inquire why I was detached, and he stated that the President would send for me and talk the matter over with me.

[324] SENATOR FERGUSON. Did the President ever send for you and talk the matter over with you?

ADMIRAL RICHARDSON. He did not.

SENATOR FERGUSON. Did you ever seek to go to the President on the matter after being told that he would send for you?

ADMIRAL RICHARDSON. By no means. [...]

SENATOR FERGUSON. Did you have any conversation with the Secretary of the Navy that would indicate that he knew why you were detached?

ADMIRAL RICHARDSON. He said to me, "The last time you were here you hurt the President's feelings."

SENATOR FERGUSON. Did he say what the occasion was that you had hurt the President's feelings?

ADMIRAL RICHARDSON. He did not say.

SENATOR FERGUSON. Did you ask him.

ADMIRAL RICHARDSON. No, sir.

SENATOR FERGUSON. Do you know on what occasion you could have hurt the President's feelings?

The American Fleet 371

ADMIRAL RICHARDSON. Well, it would hurt my feelings if a senior subordinate under me disagreed with me and I couldn't make him change his mind.

SENATOR FERGUSON. Then you feel that probably the conversation that you had then on the—was it the 8th of October at a luncheon with Admiral Leahy and the President—was the occasion that you may have hurt his feelings?

ADMIRAL RICHARDSON. I think so.

SENATOR FERGUSON. That is the occasion that you told us that you were rather definite in your opinions?

[325] ADMIRAL RICHARDSON. Unfortunately, I am definite in most of my opinions. [...]

[339] SENATOR FERGUSON. Mr. Chairman, I would just like to ask the admiral one concluding question, and that is, if he has anything now that he wants to volunteer to the committee, rather than a direct question, relative to this issue that he believes to be relevant.

THE CHAIRMAN. The Chair was about to ask the admiral about the same thing. If the members of the committee are through with their questions, and I assume that they are, Admiral, if you have any further statement that you wish to make, the committee will be glad to receive it.

ADMIRAL RICHARDSON. Mr. Chairman, I thank you for this opportunity to state that I never bore any resentment toward [340] President Roosevelt because of my detachment from command of the United States Fleet.

He was the constitutional Commander in Chief of the Army and Navy. I was one of his senior subordinates; there was a difference of opinion; each of us frankly expressed his views; neither could induce the other to change his opinion; I was relieved of command of the Fleet. Had I been constitutional Commander in Chief of the Army and Navy, I would have taken the same action.

Because of this conviction, on January 28, 1941, 4 days before I was relieved of command of the Fleet with orders to proceed to Washington for duty, I sent to the Chief of Naval Operations by an officer, the following oral message:

> The day I was made commander in chief I realized then and thereafter that the same power which made me commander in chief could unmake me at any time. When I arrive in Washington I shall keep my lips sealed and my eyes in the boat and put my weight on the oar in any duty assigned.

Living up to this resolution has resulted in the circulation of many rumors which bear little relation to fact.

I hope my testimony given here has clarified the situation to some extent.

Wisdom of the Sea Route Chosen by the Japanese

ADMIRAL RICHARD KELLY TURNER,
CHIEF, WAR PLANS DIVISION, U.S. NAVY

Joint Congressional Investigation

[1942]   MR. MITCHELL. Turning to another subject, did you know of the diversion of merchant shipping from the northern ship lanes to the Central Pacific area which occurred in October 1941 and later?

ADMIRAL TURNER. Yes, sir; that subject had been under discussion for some little time between Admiral Ingersoll, Admiral Brainard, whose business it was, and myself, whose interest was in War Plans, and we were prepared to execute that when conditions became tense and we believed that war was imminent. That was initiated by Admiral Ingersoll, who talked to me about it before it was sent out and I was heartily in favor of it.

MR. MITCHELL. There was a large area up there that even normally had a very slight amount of marine traffic in it, was there not?

ADMIRAL TURNER. There was very little marine traffic north of Hawaii, except such as was going to Vladivostok and there wasn't very much of that. By no means all, but a large proportion of the maritime traffic that was going from the United States or from Panama to the Far East went via Hawaii and thence going to Japan would go north to Midway, and going to China I think also went north of Midway. The other that went to South China and the Dutch East Indies and the Philippines went rather close to Guam. The composite great circle course from Puget Sound or from San Francisco, that goes south of the Aleutians to Japan or to China, runs very close to Japan itself and approximately parallel to the general trend of the land.

MR. MITCHELL. Well, that was the traffic that you diverted, was it?

ADMIRAL TURNER. We diverted that and also the traffic that went via Honolulu. We sent that down via Torres Straits, so that the track that the Japanese task force actually took would cross the composite great circle course close to Japan and they would be clear of any traffic that would be there in a very short time and that traffic that went on that composite course went

Source: Pearl Harbor Attack, *volume 4.*

through the normal operating areas where the Japanese held their maneuvers.

SENATOR BREWSTER. Mr. Counsel, I wonder if we could have one of the maps of the Pacific put up, which would enable us to understand very much better this question of the routes, if that map were put up on one of the standards.

MR. MITCHELL. I will have it set up. It is 12 o'clock now.

THE CHAIRMAN. We have changed our schedule to 12:30.

MR. MITCHELL. Oh, we have?

THE CHAIRMAN. Yes.

ADMIRAL TURNER. Those routes illustrate exactly what I have just said.

MR. MITCHELL. Well, now, on the map that has just been placed on the easel, south of the Aleutians, going from our northern Pacific coast, there are a number of lines drawn from the United States over to the Japanese area. Are those lines representative of the ship lanes, so-called, for that traffic?

ADMIRAL TURNER. Yes, sir. That is what is called the composite great circle course.

MR. MITCHELL. And that is the traffic that by these orders was diverted to a southerly course?

[1943] ADMIRAL TURNER. It was that traffic and also all of the traffic that went westward, that is, all of the merchant traffic that went westward from Hawaii. Now, from Hawaii all traffic except naval traffic was sent down around, too, in that direction; some of it had to go via Suva and the Fiji to get water—no, it didn't go that far south. It went through the Solomons. Possibly I had better trace it. [...] All of this traffic, this traffic—

SENATOR BREWSTER. You will have to identify it a little more because in the record that won't be clear.

ADMIRAL TURNER. I beg your pardon. All of the composite great circle routes from San Francisco and from Puget Sound which went to the Asiatic points, either to Japan or to China or even around to the Philippines and Malasia, plus all the traffic that went from Hawaii to Japan, to China direct, to the Philippines, was diverted south roundabout to go first east—the Puget Sound and San Francisco ships were sent first to Hawaii and then all ships from Hawaii, merchant ships, went approximately west of Howell and Baker Islands, through the Solomons, then west of the Santa Cruz Islands, thence south of New Guinea and through Torres Strait, which is between Australia and New Guinea. We had Australian pilots to take them through there.

We for a time sent some of the naval traffic which had freight for Guam and the Philippines, direct from Honolulu to Guam and thence to the Philippines and that is the traffic that we started escorting at about that time. Shortly before December 7 even that traffic, which included naval freight and freight and passenger vessels, was also sent south and around South New Guinea and thence up to the Philippines.

Mr. MITCHELL. Well, there is an area on the map, Admiral, that lies south of this ship lane, of those ship-lane lines from Puget Sound through to Japan and north of the Hawaiian Islands, that does not have any ship-lane lines drawn on that. Is that a part of the ocean that was not generally used?

ADMIRAL TURNER. Practically never do any ships go through that part of the ocean.

MR. MITCHELL. Is that term "vacant sea" a recognized maritime expression?

ADMIRAL TURNER. I never heard that term before but I think it is a good term.

MR. MITCHELL. So that after that diversion took place, according to the map there, there was practically little or no traffic in the areas followed by the Jap fleet which attacked Pearl Harbor, as shown in red on that map?

ADMIRAL TURNER. There was very little traffic there in any case. After the freezing of Japanese assets on July 26, within a short time there was no Japanese shipping between the United States and Japan and the American-flag shipping dropped off to practically nothing. Because those lines are there, it does not show a stream of ships even at any time. When shipping was going full blast even before the war there were very few ships in through there and going between Honolulu and Japan. I have gone that route and the chances are we didn't even see a ship there. That was much quicker than these [1944] northern routes. It is very easy to miss a ship if you do not want to be detected because there is only one ship along there every 2 or 3 days and sometimes by shifting your course a few miles every few hours, why, it is practically impossible for merchant shipping ever to detect a naval task force that wants to be undetected.

SENATOR BREWSTER. Mr. Mitchell, could I ask the witness a question?

MR. MITCHELL. Yes.

SENATOR BREWSTER. What happens to the Russian ships going to Vladivostok that were moving out of Seattle? Was there any change in those?

ADMIRAL TURNER. No, sir.

SENATOR BREWSTER. Those continued to move?

ADMIRAL TURNER. Yes, sir.

SENATOR BREWSTER. Those had been going from Japanese ports, had they not?

ADMIRAL TURNER. No, they did not.

SENATOR BREWSTER. Did the Japanese have surveillance of those ships?

ADMIRAL TURNER. Yes, sir, but they went through the Kurile Islands. I think they had no patrol, the Japs had no patrol. They had surveillance up there but they did not stop them and they would normally have gone through that area up here during the summer. Well, very few of them went into Vladivostok during the winter.

SENATOR BREWSTER. Now, could you give an approximate difference in distance, for instance, going from Seattle and San Francisco to the Philippines via the two alternate routes?

ADMIRAL TURNER. You mean via the maritime ports?

SENATOR BREWSTER. The great circle or the Hawaii-Torres Strait.

ADMIRAL TURNER. O, I would say roughly 4,000 miles farther.

SENATOR BREWSTER. So that this was a very important change when you rerouted these ships?

ADMIRAL TURNER. It was extremely important and was taken only because the shipping companies were very much opposed and we ourselves because it meant a longer time to get our production and our material in the Philippines, very much longer.

The Timing of the Japanese Attacks in the Pacific

JOHN FORD BAECHER, U.S.N.R.

Joint Congressional Investigation

DEPARTMENT OF THE NAVY,
OFFICE OF THE SECRETARY,
Washington, 4 April 1946.

[5315] Memorandum To: Mr. Seth W. Richardson.
Subject: Time Table of Japanese Attacks—source of material.
Reference:
    (a) My memorandum to Mr. William D. Mitchell, dated 29 Nov. 1945.
    (b) My memorandum to Mr. Seth W. Richardson, file 1083A (HLB) R#112, dated 22 Jan. 1946.
    (c) My memorandum to Mr. Seth W. Richardson, file 1083A (HLB), R#112, dated 24 Jan. 1946.

1. In response to the oral request of 28 March 1946 from Counsel for more specific data as to the information and sources of information which were heretofore forwarded in reference (a) at the request of Mr. William D. Mitchell, in reference (b) at the request of Senator Brewster (Record of Proceedings, page 7625) and in reference (c) at the request of Congressman Keefe, concerning the times of attacks by the Japanese on various places in the Pacific Ocean areas, the information, supplemented as requested, is restated and summarized for purposes of clarity as follows:

Place	Local time	Greenwich time	Washington time	Source of Information
Kaneohe, NAS	7:50 am, 7th	6:20 pm, 7th	1:20 pm, 7th	War Diary of Commandant 14th Naval District.
Pearl Harbor	7:55 am, 7th	6:25 pm, 7th	1:25 pm, 7th	Report by Admiral Nimitz dated 15 Feb. 1942 of the attack at Pearl Harbor and War Dairy of the Comdt. 14th Naval District, dated 3 Feb. 1942.

Source: Pearl Harbor Attack, *volume 11.*

Timing of the Attacks

Place	Local time	Greenwich time	Washington time	Source of Information
Singapore	3:00 am, 8th	8:00 pm, 7th	3:00 pm, 7th	Statement by Captain John M. Creighton, U.S.N., who was at Singapore.
Khota Baru	3:40 pm, 8th	8:40 pm, 7th	3:40 pm, 7th	This information obtained by oral inquiry of the War Department, Col. McNall, USA, G-2 MIS File.
Davso Gulf, P.I.	7:10 am, 8th	11:10 pm, 7th	6:10 pm, 7th	War Diary of U.S.S. *Wm. B. Preston*.
Guam	9:10 am, 8th	11:10 pm, 7th	6:10 pm, 7th	War Diary of Cmdt. U.S. Marine Corps, dated 31 March 1942.
Hong Kong	8:00 am, 8th	Midnight, 7–8th	7:00 pm, 7th	This information obtained by oral inquiry of the War Department, Major R.E. Guest, USA, G-3.
Wake	12:00 noon	1:00 am, 8th	8:00 pm, 7th	Report of Comdt. U.S. Marine Corps, dated 31 March 1942.
Clark Field, P.I.	9:27 am, 8th	1:27 am, 8th	8:25 pm, 7th	This information obtained by oral inquiry of the War Department.
Midway	9:30 pm, 7th	9:20 am, 8th	4:30 am, 8th	Log of the Coast Guard Cutter WALNUT.
Nichols Field (Manila)	3:00 am, 9th	7:00 pm, 8th	2:00 pm, 8th	Report of 16th Naval District Intelligence Officer, file 40207.

(sgd) John Ford Baecher
JOHN FORD BAECHER,
Lieutenant Commander, USNR.

The Effect of the Pearl Harbor Losses on the Course of the War

THEODORE S. WILKINSON, DIRECTOR OF NAVAL INTELLIGENCE

Joint Congressional Investigation

[1830] SENATOR BREWSTER. One other thing which I did not follow quite through is the matter of the fleet.

Speaking to you now as a naval officer of long experience, when you spoke of the fleet at Pearl Harbor, the American Fleet as being inferior to the Japanese, you meant in the relative strength of battleships, destroyers, carriers, the entire component of the fleet?

ADMIRAL WILKINSON. Including the Naval Air Force; yes sir. That is discounting any superiority of training and matériel, in which we hoped we were a little better off.

SENATOR BREWSTER. Yes. Is it not also true that the power of the fleet increased proportionately to its moving from its base?

ADMIRAL WILKINSON. Yes.

SENATOR BREWSTER. As I remember Admiral Leahy, his testimony before us in 1938, when we were considering expanding the Navy, he estimated we would need a superiority of approximately 2 to 1 in [1831] order to move into the Western Pacific, and take up the Japanese on equal terms.

That involved communication lines and everything else.

ADMIRAL WILKINSON. I think that is more than a fair statement, and when we did finally move into the Western Pacific in this war, we were more than 2 to 1.

SENATOR BREWSTER. So when you speak of the fleet as being inferior, our fleet being inferior, you compared the values side by side, rather than the fact that there was four or five thousand miles of water that we had to cover.

ADMIRAL WILKINSON. Yes, sir; a direct comparison.

SENATOR BREWSTER. It is probably useless to contemplate, except as it assists us in this lesson, but the price at Pearl Harbor was not only the price we paid at Pearl Harbor that day, but all the way on from Guadalcanal to Leyte, and even Okinawa, was it not, in the matter of the depletion of our naval strength?

Source: Pearl Harbor Attack, *volume 4.*

Perhaps I should confine it now to Guadalcanal, where we went to fight on a shoestring, to stop the Japs because we had to stop them right then.

ADMIRAL WILKINSON. I was thinking, Senator, that, of course, we could not say what the course of the war might have been. We might have gone out of Pearl Harbor with what we had in an attempt to relieve the Philippines, which might well have been disastrous in view of the Japanese islands and air fields, and the challenge we would have met from the Japanese Fleet.

The temporary losses at Pearl Harbor, and, of course, the actually complete losses of two battleships, undoubtedly reduced for a time the ratio and we had to wait until that ratio was restored and increased before we could successfully conduct the campaign in the Western Pacific. It is possible, if our losses had not been incurred in Pearl Harbor, other losses might have resulted subsequently, and that those losses might have been more permanent, not readily restored.

I cannot say what it may have been in the course of the war.

SENATOR BREWSTER. Well, after this initial upset, we did demonstrate a capacity to beat the Japanese on almost any terms from then on. We had no serious surprises, no serious upsets in our procedure, from then on.

ADMIRAL WILKINSON. No, sir. The first campaign in the South Pacific, in the vicinity of Guadalcanal, was pretty tough fighting. Our losses were heavy, and so were the Japs' losses, we hope, but thereafter we began to have disproportionate losses, comparing the Jap losses with ours.

SENATOR BREWSTER. I think it is proper to speak of it now. It is my understanding that in the Naval Affairs Committee I think Admiral Stark, or Admiral King—Admiral King, I think, testified that we had to go into Guadalcanal to stop it; we could not let the Japs go any further, so it was a calculated risk that we felt obliged to take.

ADMIRAL WILKINSON. Yes, sir.

SENATOR BREWSTER. Not because we felt it was necessarily easy or feasible, but it just had to be done with insufficient forces because of the losses at Pearl Harbor.

ADMIRAL WILKINSON. Yes, sir.

SENATOR BREWSTER. Is that right?

[1832] ADMIRAL WILKINSON. In part. The ships that were disabled at Pearl Harbor, the older battleships, would have been strong units in the South Pacific, but they would not have been particular well adapted to some of the fighting there which required faster vessels.

SENATOR BREWSTER. Yes.

ADMIRAL WILKINSON. Our greatest difficulty, as I recall, in the earlier days of the war, was the lack of carriers, and, of course, there were no carriers affected at Pearl Harbor.

SENATOR BREWSTER. The estimated losses—I recall getting this at that time from Admiral Stark—the losses incident at Pearl Harbor, it was estimated at that time had set us back a year. Did you hear such estimates at that time?

ADMIRAL WILKINSON. I defer to his judgment. I made no such estimate.

Senator Brewster. It would be true that if the fleet had remained in being, with the augmentations in the ensuing 12 months, our progress both in the South Pacific and in West Pacific could have been that much more rapid, because of the strength which we would have had if we did not encounter these losses, don't you think so?

Admiral Wilkinson. I should say so, unless we had undertaken an expedition for the relief of the Philippines in the crisis that was developing there before we were prepared for it, in which case, of course, we might have had heavy losses there, and then been worse off than we were to begin with.

Senator Brewster. I quite appreciate that. That is, if the Japs had not sunk these ships at Pearl Harbor, public opinion might have been for a relief expedition, although when I was at Pearl Harbor in 1940, the standing joke between the Army and Navy at that time was that the fellows in the Philippines were just out of luck, that we were not going to relieve them. There seemed to be a rather jovial aspect to it. The poor fellows were supposed to hold out for 6 months when they knew the fleet, very well, was not coming, because it did not have the strength to go into the western Pacific until it had the 2 to 1 superiority to the Japs, which it did not have. Did you ever hear such discussions?

Admiral Wilkinson. Yes. Not authoritatively, not in the sense that they were definitely doomed, but that it was difficult to relieve them.

Senator Brewster. I refer to the captains, not the top command. I refer to the boys down the line who felt they were up against it.

I think that is all that I have.

Rainbow 5: The Role of the Pacific Fleet

ADMIRAL RICHARD KELLY TURNER,
CHIEF, WAR PLANS DIVISION, U.S. NAVY

Hart Inquiry

[263] 1. Q. What is your name, rank, and present station?
A. Richmond Kelly Turner, Vice Admiral (Temporary Grade) United States Navy, in command of the Amphibious Forces of the Pacific Fleet.
2. Q. What were your duties during the calendar year 1941?
A. I was the War Plans Officer for the Chief of Naval Operations.
3. Q. How long previously had you been so detailed?
[264] A. I reported to that duty on October 25, 1940, having come from command of the U. S. S. ASTORIA, then a part of the Hawaiian Detachment of the Pacific Fleet.
4. Q. Were you, particularly during 1941, closely associated with the Chief of Naval Operations, Admiral Stark, even beyond the association which the preparation of formal war plans called for?
A. I was. I considered myself one of Admiral Stark's principal advisers. We were close personal friends, as well as closely associated officially.
5. Q. What was the official designation of the Department's basic war plan which was current during the latter half of 1941?
A. WPL-46; Rainbow 5, it was known as. That war plan was a joint plan between the Army and the Navy. It had its basis in an international agreement with the British Army, Navy, and Air Force. The conversations with the British leading up to preparation of that plan were held in February and March of 1941. It was a world-wide agreement, covering all areas, land, sea, and air, of the entire world in which it was conceived that the British Commonwealth and the United States might be jointly engaged in action against any enemy. On the conclusion of that agreement with the British, the WPL-46 was prepared after a great many talks with the Army and was approved by the Joint Board, the Secretaries of War and Navy, and by the President. The Navy issued their form of that war plan in May of 1941, and it is my recollection the Army form of it was issued about August.

Source: Pearl Harbor Attack, *volume 26.*

6. Q. Did WPL-46 contemplate any Allies, other than the British Empire?

A. It contemplated associated Powers, including the Netherlands East Indies, and such colonies of British Allies as were still in the war, for example, the Loyalist French Colonies.

7. Q. Against what prospective enemy nations was the plan intended?

A. It was intended against the Axis Powers: Germany, Italy, Japan, and the Powers that were allied with those principal Powers. It did not include any particular participation for the purpose of the plan by the Government of China. It did not include any association by Russia; as it was prepared and promulgated before the Russians were at war with Germany. After its promulgation, the War and Navy Departments made several tentative efforts to bring Russia within the scope of this or a modified plan. During the Fall of 1941, the Joint Board prepared some tentative bases for military conversations with Russia. The representatives of the Joint Board on two or three occasions discussed with the Russian military representative in Washington the question of making a common war plan, but nothing ever eventuated from those conversations during the time I remained in Washington.

8. Q. Did the plan, as put into effect, envisage alternative combinations of enemy nations?

A. It did. Without referring to the plan to aid memory, I believe it envisaged war in which either Germany and her European Allies were the sole enemies, or in which Japan was also engaged. The main basis of the plan, however, was a global war in which both Germany and her European Allies and Japan were at war with United States, the British Commonwealth, and the Netherlands East Indies. It was [265] agreed that if war was initiated by Japan, Germany would be brought in by offensive action against her by the United States.

9. Q. Then, during the period immediately preceding the issuing of WPL-46, I understand you to say that there was in the minds of your organization that the most likely combination of enemies would include Japan?

A. Yes, sir.

10. Q. In either or both of the alternative enemy combinations, what attitude, defensive or offensive, did the plan contemplate over the Pacific Ocean Areas?

A. The plan contemplated a major effort on the part of both the principal associated Powers against Germany, initially. It was felt in the Navy Department, that there might be a possibility of war with Japan without the involvement of Germany, but at some length and over a considerable period, this matter was discussed and it was determined that in such a case the United States would, if possible, initiate efforts to bring Germany into the war against us in order that we would be enabled to give strong support to the United Kingdom in Europe. We felt that it was encumbent on our side to defeat Germany, to launch our principal efforts against Germany first, and to conduct a limited offensive in the Central Pacific, and a strictly defensive effort in the Asiatic.

11. Q. At about what date was the Contributory Plan of the Commander, Pacific Fleet, approved by the Navy Department?

A. It was about September. Referring to the plan, it appears to have been distributed on July 21. As I recall it, there was some correspondence concerning some of the features, but I believe it was during September that it was finally approved by the Department.

12. Q. Was that interim correspondence cause by any particular disagreement on the part of your own organization with what had been advanced by Admiral Kimmel?

A. No essential disagreement whatsoever. The delay, as I recall it, was due, principally to technical reasons and time required for a careful review of the plan by various agencies in the Department.

13. Q. Do you recall Admiral Kimmel having in any way expressed disagreement with the defensive versus the offensive attitudes which were laid down in the basic plan, WPL-46?

A. So far as Admiral Kimmel was concerned, his part in the plan was not defensive. It required a limited offensive through the Central Pacific islands. It was realized that Admiral Kimmel did not have at hand all the material and men and organizations to proceed immediately with a strong offensive to the Gilberts or the Marshalls. The Navy Department was making every effort to try to set up base materiel and organizations that would permit Admiral Kimmel, in the course of a comparatively short time, to initiate such an offensive. Admiral Kimmel, whether in writing or orally, I don't recall, expressed the view that he did not have the forces suitable for conducting an offensive in the immediate future. There was no disagreement in the Department with such a view. We felt that the first part of the war in the Central Pacific would be largely naval and air, and that some time would elapse before we could seize and hold island territory. But it would be a grave error for anyone to get the idea that the war in the Central Pacific was to be purely defensive. Far from it. [266] While the Navy Department believed that our major military effort, considered as a whole, should initially be against Germany — that view, I may add, was also held by the War Department — we were all in agreement that the principal naval effort should be in the Pacific. The British Government did not hold such a view. They felt that our principal naval effort ought to be in the Atlantic and the Asiatic. [. . .]

14. Q. Other than as you have just testified, were there any other considerations lying behind the transfer of a considerable detachment of Admiral Kimmel's forces to the Atlantic, which step was somewhat concurrent with the date of issue of WPL-46?

A. In May of 1941, decision was reached jointly with the British Government to occupy the Azores. The force which was withdrawn from the Pacific at that time consisted of some Marine troops and transports, one or two carriers, I think a division of cruisers, some destroyers, and, as I recall, three battleships. Something like that was withdrawn from the Pacific for the purpose of supporting the occupation of the Azores. That project was abandoned and the occupation of Iceland by American troops was substituted. Some of the forces which were withdrawn for that purpose were then returned to the Pacific. The Department consistently made every possible effort to set up, in all of the theatres, the exact distribution of force which is set forth in WPL-46, and, at the time of the outbreak of war, substantially the forces established in that volume were present in all of the theatres.

15. Q. Did Admiral Kimmel make any particular protest against the transfer of that detachment from his command?

A. I recall no official protest. He did not approve it. As a matter of fact, he was not at once informed of the reasons for it. As I recall it, he asked to have those vessels returned as soon as they could be spared from the Atlantic. He felt that his strength here was none too great. That opinion was also held by the Department. There are two points that I would like to mention. In the first place, as you have said, I do not have at hand records of the correspondence which passed between the Department and Admiral Kimmel prior to December 7. As an assistant to Admiral Stark, I presented what Admiral Stark considered to be the principal papers in that case to the Roberts Commission and they can be found in the transcript of proceedings of that Commission. I remember most of those letters and dispatches, but am none too sure about the exact contents of each nor the dates. The second statement which I believe is pertinent is that the feeling by Admiral Stark and by all members of the Department with whom I ever talked was that of a very complete loyalty to the principal Commanders-in-Chief, who were Admiral hart in the Asiatic, Admiral Kimmel in the Pacific, and Admiral King in the Atlantic. I know Admiral Stark felt and I know I felt, that war was coming and we had, in those three officers, the best possible selection of officers in the Navy for the sea commands. The Department made every effort possible to hold their hands up, and such adjustments as had to be made between the three Fleets, due to many reasons, were considered at length and very carefully before they were made. But I believe that that feeling of essential loyalty ought to be recorded, as [267] well as Admiral Stark's policy of avoiding minor directives and interferences with the Commanders-in-Chief. He was especially careful, at all times, to give them as full a scope of action as it was possible to give.

16. Q. Both parts of that statement are considered to be entirely pertinent. There can well be added to the record the general belief throughout the forces in the field that such trust and confidence obtained throughout the period leading up to the war. There was the fact that we contemplated Allies, if we became engaged in the war. The examination returns to the incident of that transfer of forces from the Pacific to the Atlantic. As you recall the innermost opinions held by you and your associates, was that transfer in accord with your own conceptions of what the situation demanded or was it somewhat over-influenced by te British insistence?

A. The decision was made after a great deal of discussion. Of course, there were differences of opinion, but the Department was entirely loyal to that decision. The British did not insist too greatly. In fact, the expedition was cancelled at the request of the British when they became convinced that the Portuguese would resist the seizure of the Islands.

17. Q. It is in previous testimony that there was, some time during the Summer of 1941, a temporary detachment of surface vessels toward Australia. Did that have any particular part in the overall picture which was confronting the Navy Department?

A. That detachment went to Australia for the purpose of indicating to Japan solidarity between the United States and the British Commonwealth, and to indicate to Japan that if British interests were attacked that the United States would enter the war on the side of the British. Admiral Stark kept the Commanders-in-Chief informed, to the best of his ability, as to the international political situation and the probabilities of the future. While the Government could not guarantee that we would enter the war if Japan attacked Great Britain, they fully believed that we would do so. In our conversations with the British, we never could make a firm commitment that at any particular time the United States would enter the war for the reason that unless we were attacked first, the Executive Department did not have the power to put the Country into war. Conversations were held in the Far East with the Dutch and the British authorities, and joint plans, not too definite in nature, were drawn up, but we never could be sure that if the Netherlands East Indies or the British were attacked the United States would surely come into the war.

18. Q. During June and July, 1941, formal action was taken by our Federal Government to freeze Japanese credits. At that time or afterward, did your organization make a reestimate of the international situation in the light of the probability that the Japanese would be badly squeezed in obtaining strategic materials and so forth.

A. The possibility and consequences of action of that nature by the United States Government against Japan were thoroughly considered during our conversations with the British and during our preparation on WPL-46. We felt that that action was going to come sooner or later. We also felt, and I believe that the War Department felt the same way, that action of that nature would almost surely result in [268] war with Japan within a comparatively short period of time. While the subject of economic sanctions was discussed, we felt that there was no necessity for making any change in our planning.

19. Q. Then was it the case that such circumstances had really been included in the situation estimate which laid behind WPL-46 in the first place?

A. Yes.

20. Q. Did it occur to you, during 1941 or previously, that the Navy Department's general method of preparing, and of the administrative handling of its war plans, including keeping them in touch with events and developments, was in any way defective?

A. I shared the opinion with many others that the war plans which were in existence during 1940 were defective in the extreme. They were not realistic, they were highly theoretical, they set up forces to be ready for use at the outbreak of war, or shortly after, which could not possibly have been made available, and they were not kept up to date. When I went as War Plans Officer in October of 1940, I was shocked at the state of the war plans. There was the feeling then in Washington, which I did not share, that war with Japan might eventuate at any moment, and there was no plan for war with Japan. Immediately after my arrival and after a thorough discussion of the matter, we initiated the preparation and issue of WPL-43, Rainbow 3, which was a Navy Department War Plan not concurred in by the War Department. This called for a war with Japan alone, and with an entirely defensive attitude in the Atlantic. That plan was issued about January of 1941. We felt that it would be implemented by the War Department if war should eventuate. It must be understood that a war plan issued by the Navy Department, or by the Government, is principally a mobilization plan for placing in the hands of the Commanders-in-Chief the forces with which they are to initiate war and to give those Commanders-in-Chief general directives as to the strategic attitude which they should pursue. Rainbow 3 was, to all intents and purposes, and so far as the Pacific is concerned, approximately the same as Rainbow 5. Rainbow 3 did contemplate association with the British and the Netherlands East Indies on the Far East, but it did not go so far in that regard as Rainbow 5. Rainbow 3 was an interim plan. It was necessary, we all felt, to get out a war plan which the Government could carry out. Therefore, every effort was made to strip from the previous plans the unrealistic features, and to give to the new plan forces which could be provided and tasks which could probably be executed by Commanders-in-Chief. As soon as we issued Rainbow 3 and as soon as we issued Rainbow 5, the Navy Department immediately began moving forces to the different theatres in accord with the commitments made in those two plans.

21. Q. Then am I correct in understanding you to the effect that you did consider Rainbow 5 realistic, well described by the word "As-Is," not frozen, and sufficiently elastic insofar as developments could be seen?

A. Yes.

22. Q. Did you, during the Summer of 1941, make any special provision for keeping WPL-46 in step with changes in the general situation and with changes in availability of forces?

[269] A. Yes, I organized the War Plans Division into sections charged with maintaining close cognizance of the different war theatres of the world, and made every effort to keep Rainbow 5 up to date. Rather extensive amendments were practically ready for issue when war broke out. They were not issued in the form in which prepared.

23. Q. In pursuance of that objective, or for any other reasons, were any estimates of the situation, other than running estimates, made by the War Plans Division during the period of, say, August to December, 1941?

A. None other than running estimates. I believed then, and I still believe that those are the most valuable kind of estimates. The long, formalized estimates, as used in the War College, are useful for training, but I have not found them particularly useful during war or preparation for war.

24. Q. Was there, during that period from August on, any particular redistribution of the naval forces of our respective Allies actually made or promised?

A. The British promised to set up the Eastern Fleet as contemplated by our Joint Agreement which would consist of about six battleships, two or three aircraft carriers, and some additional cruisers and destroyers. This Fleet was to be based in the Indian Ocean. Its principal base was Trincomalee with an advance base at Singapore. They actually moved the PRINCE OF WALES and REPULSE and four destroyers to Singapore. En route there was, as I recall it, three battleships and one aircraft carrier additional to the HERMES at the time of the outbreak of war. Also a few destroyers and one or two cruisers. They were, so far as possible, making a loyal effort to carry out their commitments as to the distribution of forces for war. They also moved additional troops and additional aircraft to Malaya. We delivered, under lend-lease, some aircraft to them in the Far East and sent groups of experts and mechanics out to Malaya to show them how to use our airplanes.

25. Q. During the same period, did our own War Department plan and effect any increase in ground or air strength in the Pacific Ocean Area?

A. Yes, as soon as Rainbow 5 was agreed to, the War Department immediately initiated steps for reenforcing the Hawaiian Islands and the Philippines. They actually moved a considerable number of airplanes to the Philippines and considerable additional troops. They also initiated a very greatly accelerated training of Philippine soldiers and, during the Fall of 1941, undertook what was essentially a mobilization of the Philippine Army.

26. Q. Was your organization kept in touch and frequently consulted concerning other than the basic considerations leading to those steps?

A. We were consulted in detail every time the War Department contemplated a movement of that sort. We had prolonged discussions of ways and means. Our opinion was frequently asked as to the advisability of such and such a movement. At that time, the War Department did not dispose of many trained elements which could be moved overseas without a very bad interruption of their training program. The War Department, after June of 1941, was, I believe, as thoroughly convinced as the Navy Department that war with Germany and Japan was not far distant.

[270] 27. Q. Was your organization able to keep touch, during the latter half of 1941, with the actual ability of the Army forces, Hawaii, to meet their commitments?

A. Yes, sir, we had a very definite opinion on the subject. It was substantially the same as was held, I believe, by the War Department, that it would be highly desirable to have considerably greater strength in antiaircraft and airplanes and troops in Hawaii.

28. Q. Narrowing the examination down to the Hawaiian Area and forces

therein; did the War Plans Division, through the latter half of 1941, consider that the Pacific Fleet had sufficient forces to carry out its initial tasks?

A. We were not at all satisfied with the defensive cover that was being afforded Hawaii, and continued every effort to set up defenses in outlying islands, such as Midway, Wake, Palmyra, Johnston Island, and Samoa. These places were all strengthened, air fields were built or in process of building, and we were distributing forces to those positions. The principal reason for building the defenses there was to detect and ward off enemy attacks against Hawaii, and to afford defensive cover for the sea operations of our Fleet. It was not possible, of course, to provide such a cover to the northward, and that was always recognized as a weak spot in our defense. I may say that I, personally, was not in favor of setting up defenses in Wake. It was too far removed for proper support, and was certain to fall at an early date after the war broke out unless we could have an early successful engagement with the Japanese Fleet, which seemed unlikely. The other positions were considered of great value and work was pushed on all of them to the limit of our available resources. As regards the strength of the Pacific Fleet, we felt that it was adequate for the tasks assigned to it, although we would have been happy to have had greater strength.

29. Q. Did you consider the Fleet's logistics support to be adequate?

A. We believed it to be adequate for the initial Fleet operations, such as I have mentioned. We did not consider that it was adequate for an early offensive movement for setting up bases in the Marshalls. We did not have the units assembled for setting up such bases and we did not have the shipping to support the Fleet at an advance base, but we believed that we could obtain those forces within a reasonable time after the outbreak of war. That estimate, I believe, has been proved sound by events. We have provided far greater logistics support in the Pacific Ocean that I would have believed possible before the outbreak of war. I refer to our tremendous logistic effort in the South Pacific immediately following the outbreak of war.

30. Q. During the period of preparation of basic Rainbow 5, was it the opinion in your organization and among your associates that if war with Japan eventuated, it would be at our initiative or at that of the Japanese?

A. Always at the initiative of the Japanese. We did not believe it politically possible to initiate war against the Japanese. I, personally, did not believe it politically advisable.

31. Q. And did those opinions endure throughout 1941 up until 7 December?

A. Yes, sir.

SECTION SEVEN
The Index

The Index

A

aircraft carriers: reliance on for protection from enemy planes 252; speed of American 251

Aircraft Information Center, aka Combat Information Center: call-up of off-duty personnel, December 7, 1941 114; division of responsibilities within 111; inadequacies prior to attack 77–79; operation of on day of attack 80–81, 97–98, 100–01, 104, 110–17

Alaska 123; forces alert to war danger 12

Aleutian Islands 41, 372

Aliamanu Crater (Hawaii) 310

Allen, U.S.S. 338

Amagansett (Long Island, N.Y.) 137

Andrew, Adolphus 122, 352, 365

Antares, U.S.S. 335

anti-aircraft (Army/Pearl Harbor): few attacks aimed at 308; field exercises of mobile units 309; mobile units did not carry ammunition 310, 312; number of positions 310, 311; percentage of units on private land 313; relationship to Interceptor Command 309; Standard Operating Procedure 308–09; types of 315

anti-aircraft (Navy/Pearl Harbor) 59–60

Argonne, U.S.S. 268

Arkansas, U.S.S. 268

Asiatic Fleet 145, 146, 158, 230, 234, 236, 239, 240, 268, 270, 351, 352, 360; 1940 decision not to reinforce 361

Associated Press 188, 189

Astoria, U.S.S. 381

Atlantic: convoy losses in 8; Japanese hopes for diversion of U.S. forces into 58; strengthening outposts in 6; training of U.S. carriers in 75; transfer of U.S. forces to 383–84

Atlantic Charter 18

Atlantic Fleet 242, 351

Australia: attitude toward U.S.-Japanese negotiations 23; naval shipping pilots 373; U.S. naval vessels visit 385; Azores, proposed seizure of 383–84, 385

B

B-17 ("Flying Fortress") 81, 98, 113, 318, 322

Baecher, John Ford: testimony of 376–77

Bainbridge Island (Washington) 137, 138, 175

Baker Island 373

Bangkok 272

Barber's Point 336

Batavia (Dutch East Indies) 199, 200, 241; burning of codes by Japanese diplomats 300

battleships, speed of American 251

Bellinger, Patrick N. L. 249, 256

Bellows Field (Hawaii) 79, 318, 337

Berlin 127, 130, 131, 204, 221, 223, 224

Bethesda Naval Hospital 189

Bicknell, George W. xi–xii; duties of 53; on inevitability of war 58; intelligence reports of 59; "Mori conversation" transcript given to General Short 67; sources of G-2 information 54; testimony of 53–62

Bikar Island 244

Bishop's Point (Hawaii) 335, 336

"Black Chamber" 225

Bloch, Claude C. 141, 234, 256, 261, 288, 297, 298, 301, 305; commander-in-chief, U.S. Fleet 351

Borden, U.S.S. 254

Borneo 237, 238, 262, 265

Boulder (Colorado) 126

Bratton, Rufus S. 170, 171, 177, 179, 196, 269, 271, 372

Bremerton (Washington) 352

Britain 58, 59, 230, 235, 240, 243, 282; attack on her Far Eastern colonies likely to produce U.S. intervention 385; attitude toward negotiations between U.S. and Japan 23; exchange of information with U.S. concerning Japan 38; Far East contingency war planning with U.S. 381; Japanese embassy in destroys codes 159–160; radar developments in xii; *see also* England

Brown, Wilson 244, 245, 246

Bureau of Aeronautics (U.S.) 74, 75

Bureau of Navigation (U.S.) 355

Bureau of Ships (U.S.) 344, 346

Burgin, Henry T. xv; testimony of 307–16

Burma 58
Burma Road 10, 236
Burrows, William Ward 245

C

California, U.S.S. 82
Camranh Bay (Indochina) 240
Canada 229
Caribbean Sea 230
Cavite (Philippines) 122
Cheltenham (Maryland) 137, 147, 175, 180
China 40, 49, 270, 382; General Marshall and Admiral Stark oppose direct intervention in 241; intelligence information on Japan obtained from 38, 230, 241; rival governments in 27; shipping routes to 372, 373, 411; U.S. demand for Japanese withdrawal from 28–29, 31
"China net" 131
China Sea 239
Christmas Island 319
Clark Field (Philippines) 377
Clausen, Henry L. xii; testimony of own investigation aimed to resolve ambiguities in record and securing new data 68
Coast Guard 56, 336
code and ciphers (general): all nations involved in breaking 225; distinction between 224
codes and ciphers (Japanese): differing codes 121; difficulties imposed on interceptors by Japanese language 124–125; expected efforts to break their codes 224; German warning that some had been broken 220, 221, 223, 224; how often changed 224; importance of each related to difficulty 224; number in use at one time 224; significance of burning their codes 300–01; specific codes: J-19 161; LA 160, 166; PA-K2 160, 161, 166; "Purple" used for diplomatic communiques 138; transmitted by Morse code 121; U.S. Navy downplayed Japanese knowledge their codes compromised 221–22
codes and ciphers (United States) *see* Magic

Combat Information Center (Pearl Harbor) *see* Aircraft Information Center
Condor, U.S.S. 333, 334, 335
Co-Prosperity Sphere 30; meetings held to promote 58
Corregidor: radio intelligence unit at 272; *see also* Magic, Philippines
Craig, Melvin L. xvi; testimony of 328–32
Creight, John M. 377

D

Dale, U.S.S. 254
Davso Gulf (Philippines) 377
Department of Commerce 37
District Intelligence Office (U.S. Navy, Hawaii): tapping of phones at Honolulu consulate 62–68
Diamond Head (Hawaii) 55, 302, 315
Dusenbury, C. C. 177
Dutch East Indies 145, 201, 208, 209, 282, 372, 382, 385, 386; American response to an invasion 357; probability of an invasion 10, 17, 18, 146, 230, 356–57; *see also* Batavia, Netherlands

E

Eagle Squadron (R.A.F.) 73, 74
Elliott, George E. xii; testimony of 93–109
England 145, 146, 151, 160, 201, 208, 209; *see also* Britain
Enterprise, U.S.S. 76, 77, 79, 244, 246, 247
Espionage Act 144
Etorofu Jima (Japan) 51

F

Federal Bureau of Investigation (FBI) 53, 320, 321, 324, 327; wiretap on Japanese consulate, Honolulu xii, 62–68
Federal Communications Act 144
Federal Communications Commission (FCC) 168, 169, 171, 177, 201
Fiji 373

Fleming, Robert J. xii; testimony of 84–92
Florida 187
Forrestal, James V. 155, 195
Formosa: American consul in 40; Japanese military transports sighted near 9; see also Taiwan
Fort de Russy (Hawaii) 264
Fort Kamehameha 311, 329
Fort Leavenworth 71
Fort Shafter (Hawaii) 77, 97, 110, 111, 282, 287, 307, 310, 330, 331; geographic relationship to Pearl Harbor 111; guardhouse for Army drunk and disorderly 329; location of General Short's headquarters 106
Fort Weaver (Hawaii) 311
France 19
Furious, H.M.S. 73

G

Gamble, U.S.S. 254
Gardner's Island 283
Glorious, H.M.S. 73
Germany 58, 282; attitude toward Japanese expansionism 357; pre-war Germany first strategy 382
Gerow, Leonard T. 10, 11, 12
Gilbert Islands 383
Graves, A. B. C. 191
Great Britain *see* Britain, England
Grew, Joseph C. xi, 21, 44, 45; forwards Peruvian rumor of sneak attack 48–52; great value of his diplomatic reports for tracking changing Japanese attitudes 38, 39; Japanese economic goals in China 27; testimony of 26–32, 46–47, 48–52; U.S. policy goals in China 30, 31; U.S. proposals of November 26, 1941, not an ultimatum 28–32; warns State Department little information available locally on Japanese military moves 40, 49
Griswold, Benjamin H. 208
Guadalcanal 378, 379
Guam: danger of attack on 232, 236, 257, 258, 266; direction finding station for traffic analysis 240–41; radio traffic monitoring work 122, 137; shipping route near 372, 373; time of Japanese attack 377; to take precautions against sabotage 237; treaty obligation not to fortify 6
Guantanamo (Cuba) 343
Gues, R. E. 377

H

Haliena Field (Hawaii) 79
Halsey, William F. ("Bull") 76, 198, 261; carries planes to Wake Island 251; Admiral Kimmel's plans for in case war broke out 244, 245, 246; letter from Admiral Kimmel to 195–96
Hampton Roads (Virginia) 71
Harbin (Japan) 49
Harold, Ben 208
Hart, Thomas C. 360, 384; *see also* Asiatic Fleet
Harvard University 126
Hawaii 345, 352, 356, 357, 360, 361, 372, 373, 375, 387; Army coast artillery/lookout stations 290, 291; Army manpower limits in 290; damage caused by defective U.S. ammunition 315–16; governor encouraged to seek extra military protective measures 320–21; invasion scenario worked up by American planners in early 1930s 44; Japan uncertain of loyalty of Hawaiian Japanese 60–61; Japanese consulate: secret message of, December 5, 1941 161; Japanese culture and associations in 55; local Japanese fishing fleet 56, 327, 336–37; means of Japanese communication with suspected local spies 144, 327; military measures to avoid alarming civilian population 260, 297, 314–15; most U.S. economic and military-related information publicly available to tourists and spies 55, 57; radio stations 113, 116; sabotage operations feared 317–20, 323, 327; suspected Japanese spies in 301, 315, 324, 326–27; *see also* Pearl Harbor
Hawaiian Electric Company 327
Hawaiian National Guard 317
Heeia (Oahu, Hawaii) 137
Helena, U.S.S. 254, 269
Hepburn, A. J. 269

Hermes, H.M.S. 387
Hewitt, H. Kent 155, 156–57, 208
Hickam Field (Hawaii) 54, 114, 117, 291; construction difficulties at 318
Hicksville (New York) 72
Hirohito, proposed U.S. presidential message to 218
Hitler 24, 25, 220
Hong Kong 160, 240, 300, 377
Honolulu (Hawaii) 44, 79, 106, 113, 122, 161, 281, 315, 318, 332, 333, 335, 336, 337, 358, 372, 373; military authority in 321; new road from Pearl Harbor to 337; shipping from 374
Honolulu Gas Company 327
Honolulu Rapid Transit Company 327
Honshu Island (Japan) 47
Hopkins, Harry 213–14, 219; sees imminent outbreak of war 217–18; wishes U.S. could strike first blow 215
Hornbeck, Stanley K. 360
Howell Island 373
Hull, Cordell: anticipation of war x–xi; denied U.S. proposal of November 26, 1941, an ultimatum 28; high-level pre-war strategy meetings x–xi; Japan only respected military muscle 25; Japanese alliance with Germany 23–24; meetings with president 3, 4, 9; meetings with secretary of war 3 4, 7, 9, 13, 18; negotiations at a virtual impasse (September 1941) 231; on ongoing Japanese militarism 23–24; reasons for supporting permanent basing of fleet at Pearl Harbor 362–63; regarded Japanese proposal of November 20, 1941, as an ultimatum 26; testimony of 20–25;
Humber River (Britain) 74
Hurricane (R.A.F. fighter) 74

I

Iceland, seizure of 383–84
Imperial Beach (California) 137
India 58
Indian Ocean 387
Indiana, U.S.S. 212
Indochina 26, 27, 28, 29, 216; Japanese threat to 10, 230, 236; use of for further expansion 215, 218

Ingersoll, R. E. 165, 176, 177, 271, 343, 372
Interceptor Command 321
Italy 357, 382

J

Jacob Jones, U.S.S. 269
Jaluit (island) 43
Japan: areas closed to foreigners 47; battleships 47; build-up more than "saber-rattling" 48–49; carriers, strike distance to target 322; civilian/military cleavage in government 28; codes and ciphers *see* codes and ciphers (Japanese), Magic; danger of having contact with U.S. embassy 50; danger of voicing pro-foreign sentiments 46; desire for economic resources of South Pacific 58; diplomatic and military records destroyed August 1945 167; embargo as likely cause for war 385; few Americans remained in (November, 1941) 40; general military mobilization 40; impact of trade embargo on shipping 374; language based upon Chinese 125; merchant marine vessels ordered from Atlantic to Pacific 230; monetary cost of China war 27; navy cooperation with U.S. Navy (1920s) 268; newspapers 50; oil as limiting factor on any surprise attack 368; periodic "disappearance" of fleet 241; propaganda broadcasts 60; public opinion "easily molded" by government 27; reaction to U.S. Fleet remaining permanently at Hawaii 361; relative strength of U.S. fleet and its own 378; secret police 50; shipping routes nearby 372, 373; shipping routes to Hawaii 41; speculation as to initial target(s) 14; submarine activity around Hawaii suspected by Americans throughout 1941 253–54; surprise attack on Russia (1905) 52; surveillance down to block level described 56–57; torpedo modifications sought 343, 346–47; tourists to Hawaii as sources of pre-war intelligence 54, 57; trains 47; U.S. war plans against 381–88; wisdom of attack fleet routing xvi

The Index 395

JCD-42 (Joint Coastal Frontier Defense Plan/Hawaii) 288–89
Johnston Island 244, 247, 248, 388; reinforcements for 261
Joint Army and Navy Action [Plan] 1935 287–88
Joint Coastal Frontier Defense Plan 234
Joint Congressional Investigation and Report ix
Jupiter (Florida) 137

K

Kaala (Hawaii) 293
Kai-shek, Chiang 27, 29
Kanoehe Bay (Hawaii) 290
Kanoehe N.A.S. (Naval Air Station) 376
Kau Desert (Hawaii) 89
Khota Baru (Malaya) 240, 377
Kimmel, Husband E. 156, 157, 339, 343, 345, 383, 384; accusations against xiv; carrier search patterns in early December as providing de facto long distance reconnaissance 246–47, 261; court martial seemed probable 149, 150; defense of xiv–xv; discussions with General Short 266–67, 288, 302–03; incompatibility of simultaneous full training schedule and full war alert options 232–33; letter to Admiral Halsey 195–96; Magic intercepts not provided to 233–34; opinion of General Short 296; recommended for post by predecessor 368–69; testimony of 229–54, 294–306; unable to make own torpedo nets 346, 347; "war warning" of November 27 237–38, 239, 265; "war warning" type messages during first half of 1941 229–31; Washington "whispering campaign" against after attack 141
King, Ernest J. 155, 379, 384
Kirton Lindsey, Lincolnshire (England) 74
Knox, Frank 4, 7, 9, 10, 11, 17, 18, 21, 156, 195; discussions on keeping U.S. fleet at Pearl Harbor 360; explains why Admiral Richardson replaced 370; meeting with secretaries of state and war, December 7, 1941 13–14; White House meeting, November 25, 1941 22–23
Kobe (Japan) 40, 49
Kohtron (Indochina) 240
Kokee (Hawaii) 85, 90
Kolekole Peak (Hawaii) 87
Konoye, Fumimaro (Prince) 234
Koolau Mountains (Hawaii) 293
Korea, information from on Japanese military activities 38
Kra Peninsula 237, 238, 240, 272
Kramer, Alwin D. xiii, xiv; alleged by Safford to have seen "winds execute" 147, 148, 151; concedes only minimal change from earlier testimony 204–05; delivers Magic to White House in locked pouch 213, 214; hospitalizations of 188; relationship to Safford 190, 193; responsibilities of 134–35; service abroad 173; skill in Japanese 129; testimony of 129–39, 186–211
Kurile Islands 268, 274

L

Lahaina Roads (Hawaii) 353, 359; reconnaissance flights from 365
landowners (Hawaii) 314
law (Navy) 205–06
Layton, Edwin T. 302, 303; relays to General Short "war warning" message in November 257
Leahy, William E. 360–61, 371, 378
Lewis, Ted 189
Lexington, U.S.S. 71, 76, 245, 246, 247
Leyte (Philippines) 378
Lockard, Joseph A. 94, 95, 96, 97, 98, 101, 102, 104, 108, 109
London (England) 75, 230, 240, 300
Long Beach (California) 352

M

MacArthur, Douglas 167, 168, 284, 285; naval arm of 269; reorganization of Philippine army by 8; response to November 27 war warning from Washington 14; war danger warnings to 11–12
McCollum, Arthur H. xii–xiii, 139, 195,

199, 207, 209–10; career of 268–70; denies Safford's interpretation of why he sought to send another war warning message 273; prior work as Pacific Fleet intelligence officer 122; testimony of 121–28, 268–74

McIntire, Ross 192

Magic (Corregidor) 121, 122, 137

Magic (general overview): an Army-Navy co-operative endeavor 135, 136; cryptographic skills essential even for translators of messages 124–25; delay in translating due to place of interception 123; efforts to upgrade Japanese language background of cryptanalysts 131; impact of limited manpower 121, 122; Navy establishes Japanese language school 126; only handful of highly qualified translators available 124, 126, 131; origin of xii; psychological pressure of work 124; violation of Federal law xii, 143–44

Magic (handling of intercepts, Washington): all intercepts returned after officials read 136; change in delivery practices to recipients 143; denied to Ambassador Grew in Japan 51; number of copies of key intercepts distributed 136, 164–65; permanent file of all intercepts 175; State Department receipt of 20; system to determine if any messages missed by interceptors 128

Magic (intercept stations) 121; locations identified 137, 147; mail and airmail normal means of forwarding intercepts well into 1941 130; missing intercepts for December 1941 from East Coast posts 175; teletype used to speed up forwarding of intercepts 138

Magic (Pearl Harbor) 121; codes it could read 122; diplomatic codes could not be read 122–23; passed intercepts to Washington 127; quality of personnel 137; received information from own group of intercept stations 127

Magic (Washington, D.C.) 121, 123; Army component duty hours December 6, 1941 136; division of duties with Pearl Harbor and Corregidor 137–38; official versus longer actual hours of operation 129–30, 139; watch officers 130

Malacca Straits 230

Malaya 145, 230, 240

Manchuria 26, 28, 31; American consul in 40, 49: Japanese troops in 49

Mandated Islands (Japanese): airbases in 322; danger of offensive carrier operations being launched from 43, 44, 45; impossibility of penetrating with spies 43; minimal information on in U.S. hands 41–43; photo-reconnaissance of planned by U.S. 10; raids aimed at anticipated 294

Manila (Philippines) 141, 240, 377

Marianas (Islands) 41

Marshall, George C. xiii, xv, 8, 90, 172, 362; adage or urging nonmeddling in local commanders' decisions 19; letter to Republican presidential candidate Dewey 222; meetings with top civilian government official concerning pre-war strategy 7, 9, 17, 18, 22–23; testimony of 143–44, 282–86

Marshall Islands 42, 383; planned U.S. assault on 243–45; potential for U.S. bases in 388

Martin, Frederick L. 256

Martin-Bellinger Agreement 256, 296

Maui (Hawaii) 85

Mayfield, I. H. xv; role in taping of Japanese phones at consulate 62–68; testimony of 326–27

Mediterranean Sea 73

Miami (Florida) 193

Midway 6, 127, 234, 235, 244, 245, 246, 247, 248, 251, 252, 253, 319, 372, 377, 388; Army airplanes scheduled for 237, 298; Army reinforcements discussed 238–39; Marine airplanes provided 261

Miles, Sherman xi, 123, 143; length of service as G-2 (military intelligence) 36; number serving under his command 37–38; rewrote Hawaiian defense plans in 1929–1931 42; testimony of 35–45

Military Intelligence Division (G-2, U.S. Army): differences between pre-war and wartime structure 36; maintained constantly updated volumes on all countries 37; major role of naval intelligence in providing information 43; purposes of 36–37; rapid pre-war growth in personnel 37–38; severe

The Index   397

limits on information obtainable by military attaches 40; sources of information 37
Mitchell, William O. 376
Mitchell Field (New York) 78
"Mori conversation" 65, 66
Morse code: difference between English and Japanese forms 180–81; number of Americans who could intercept Japanese form 181
Morse Field (Hawaii) 85
Mount Haleakala (Hawaii) 85, 87, 88, 89, 92
Mount Kaala (Hawaii) 85, 88, 92
Munitions Building (Washington, D.C.) 5
Murray, Max 311, 312
Mutual Telephone Company (Hawaii) 280, 281

N

Nagasaki (Japan) 268
National Defense Law of 1920 4
National Guard 308
National Parks Service 89, 90
National Theater (Washington, D.C.) 216, 218
negotiations (U.S.–Japanese) Australian attitudes toward 23; British attitudes toward 23; considered effectively dead as of November 26, 1941, by Cordell Hull 16, 17; December 7, 1941, fourteen-part Japanese note ending negotiations 134–35, 138–41, 213–19, 267; Dutch attitudes toward 23; fleet basing at Pearl Harbor as increasing U.S. diplomatic strength 359, 361; Japanese proposal of November 20, 1941 23, 26; November 26, 1941, U.S. note to Japanese ambassador 16, 17, 26–27, 134; ongoing negotiations as diluting power of war-warning alerts to American commanders 13; stalemate in negotiations produces war-warning alerts to U.S. Pacific commands 12, 22; U.S. demand for Japanese withdrawal from China and Indochina 27; U.S. efforts to extend talks to allow time for further military build-up 23; U.S. Navy and Army convinced negotiations almost certain failure 257, 259
Netherlands: 58, 59, 243; provided limited military intelligence concerning Japanese activities 38–39; view of U.S.–Japanese negotiations 23; *see also* Dutch East Indies
Netherlands East Indies *see* Dutch East Indies
New Mexico, U.S.S. 133
New York Journal-American 187
New York Times 187
New Guinea 19, 373
Nichols Field (Philippines) 377
Nimitz, Chester W. 248, 368, 369, 376; discussions on permanent basing of Fleet at Pearl Harbor 360
Nomura, Kichisaburo 8
Norfolk (Virginia) 75
North Carolina, U.S. Army maneuvers in 10
Noyes, Leigh 144, 161, 162, 164, 180, 183, 200, 208, 209, 271

O

O-7 (U.S. submarine) 268
Oahu (Hawaii) 239, 245, 246, 247, 248, 249, 250, 261, 272, 270, 288, 290, 302, 323, 324
O'Donnell, Daniel L. 35
Office of Naval Intelligence (O.N.I.) 320, 324
Okinawa 378
Opana (radar site, Hawaii) 93, 96, 99; location and distance to Fort Shafter 110
Open Door Policy 26
Orlando (Florida) 110
Outerbridge, William M. xvi; testimony of 333–38

P

Pacific Fleet 233, 234, 270, 271, 351, 352
Pacific Ocean 6, 207, 231, 233
Pahoa (Hawaii) 85
Palau (Island) 43

Palmyra (Island) 234, 248, 319, 388
Panama: experimental weaponry in 315; Japanese legation in 221; pre-war upgrading of defenses 7; response to war danger alert of November 27, 1941 14; scrambler phone to 281, 284; sea routes westward from 372; warned of war danger 12
Panama Canal 230, 282
Panama Canal Zone 268
Panay, U.S.S. 58, 351
Paris (France) 283
PBY-3 247
PBY-5 247–48, 249
PBYs 308
Peace and War: United States Foreign Policy, 1931–1941 4, 40
Pearl Harbor: air attack viewed as possibility rather than probability xi, 21, 22, 42, 300; air combat December 7, 1941 82; aircraft not dispersed xv; aircraft shortages xv, 289, 295; alcohol and its alleged effect on readiness for attack xv–xvi, 328–32; Army-Navy cooperation agreement ("2 CL-41") 295–97; basing of U.S. Fleet at xvi, 25; best day for surprise attack 324; chief of U.S. Fleet opposed permanent stationing at 358; civilian location of much Army anti-aircraft weaponry 264, 298; concern over air defenses 256; ease of visual spying on American fleet 54–55; effects of successful assault on course of war xvi, 378–80; "emptiness" of sea routing chosen by Japanese 374; fleet unprepared for war (1940) 366–67; Japanese intelligence efforts concerning 20; Japanese war games to rehearse assault 51; lack of needed equipment xv, 247–48, 289, 295, 298; lack of torpedo nets, Washington explanation of 339–47; lack of "unity of command" 289, 295, 298; low water depth in harbor as protection against torpedo-plane attack 252, 359; Navy assistance to Army in housing anti-aircraft personnel 298; Navy role in defense of port 295, 296; November change in Army alert status classification 299; number of planes in attack 322; prompt Navy anti-aircraft response to attack 59–60; practical difficulties in long term stationing of fleet at 355; presence of fleet as discouraging attack 323; rationale for permanent basing of fleet at 356–57; relationship of Admiral Kimmel and General Short 288; relative losses to bombs and torpedoes 342–43; revisions in defense plans 42; sabotage: considered greatest danger, but did not materialize xv, 326–27; scrambler phone at 275–86; sneak attack rumors in January 1941, but none later 20–21, 48–52; suspected submarine contacts 253–54, 333–38; war alert (June 1940) 233; war danger warnings (1941) 12, 22, 275
Pensacola (Florida) 72
Pennsylvania, U.S.S. 352
Peruvian diplomatic rumor of Pearl Harbor attack, January 1941 48–52; Navy Intelligence rejected credibility of report 232; rumor forwarded to Pearl Harbor 231–32
Peiping (China) 272
Phillips, Walter C. 59; testimony of 276–79
Philippines 265, 284, 285, 286, 372, 377, 379; B17s shifted from Hawaii to 318–19; impossibility of quick military relief for 380; invasion danger (late November 1941) 17, 18, 232, 236, 237, 238, 257, 258, 262, 266; local militia called into U.S. service 231, 387; potential for use against Japanese expansionism 59; rearmament of 8, 387; shipping route to 373, 374; treaty obligation not to fortify 6; U.S. Army bombers to 237; war danger warning to 22
poison gas, reported use by Japanese in China 8
Port Arthur (Russia) 52, 273
Portland (Oregon) 170, 171
Powell, Carroll A. 191, 192, 198; testimony of 279–82
Preston, William B., U.S.S. 377
Prince of Wales, H.M.S. 387
Public Law 339 68
Puerto Rico 281, 360–61
Puget Sound (Washington) 368, 372, 373
purple machine 131, 138
Pye, W. S. 244, 252

Q

Quantico (Virginia) 72

R

radar (British) xii, 73–74; sharing of information with Americans 74–75, 87
radar (naval) 290; efficiency of shipboard radar in Pacific (October 1941) 76–77
radar (Pearl Harbor: Army system): abandoned sites then used for communication purposes 87–88; Admiral Kimmel's knowledge of the Army's system 304–05; choice of operating hours 261; duty routine of those assigned radar work 102–03; increase in operating hours after attack 105; increase in personnel after attack 103–04; protection of sites 95, 107–08; reduction in operating hours, November 1941 80, 95, 100, 107; secretary of war unaware of exactly how Pearl Harbor would utilize system 16; sighting of Japanese planes xii, 93–109, 112–15; sound detectors to be phased out after radar fully operational 292; training of Army operators 290
radar (Pearl Harbor: development problems): environmental objections to sites xii, 89–90; physical and intragovernmental obstacles to constructing 77–79, 85–92; problems reported to Admiral Kimmel, General Short, and others in November 1941 79, 82; shortages of related equipment 289–90
radar (technology problems): "dead" area near installations 78, 81, 94; difficulties imposed by novelty of technology 90–91; effective maximum distance 261, 289, 293; inability to distinguish between friend and foe aircraft 113; oil pump problems December 6–7, 1941, at site that spotted enemy planes 108–09; reliability of equipment 105
Rainbow 3 229, 386
Rainbow 5 xvi, 381–88; war alert of November 27 orders its implementation if hostilities erupt 16
Ramsay, Logan C. 249
Ranger, U.S.S. 75
RCA (Radio Corporation of America) 275, 276, 280
Reconnaissance (Pearl Harbor) 305–06, 322
Repulse, H.M.S. 387
Richardson, James O. xvi, 25, 297; did not expect air attack on Pearl Harbor 364; nickname 353; opposes basing fleet at Pearl Harbor 358–59; ordered to "request" permission for fleet to remain in Hawaii 356; orders June 1940 war alert in Hawaii 233; presidential ire over opposing Hawaii Fleet basing results in transfer 370–71; recommended Kimmel as possible replacement 368–69; testimony of 351–71
Richardson, Seth W. 376
Rochefort, Joseph J.: service at Pearl Harbor 127; service in Japan 127; skills of 122, 126, 127
Roosevelt, Franklin D.: believed war imminent 23, 213–19; conversations with policymakers on Far East situation 4, 5, 8, 9, 10, 17–18, 22–23, 24; insisted U.S. Fleet in Hawaii restrained Japanese expansionism 361; reaction to final pre-war diplomatic intercept xiv, 213–19; rejects firing first shot of war 215–16; relieves Admiral Richardson of command over policy disagreement 370–71; responsibility for Pearl Harbor? xiv; scrambled phone conversations with Winston Churchill 283
Royal Air Force (Britain) 73–74
Russia 151, 152, 154, 201, 209, 234, 284; Admiral Stark rejects likelihood of Japanese attack on 236; China expects summer 1941 Japanese attack on 230; discussion concerning joint war plans with 382; Japanese surprise attack on (1905) 52, 273

S

S-11 (U.S. submarine) 268
sabotage danger at Pearl Harbor: did

not materialize 326-27; primary danger in General Short's mind 15, 317-20

Safford, Laurence F. xiii; alleged efforts to force a change in his claim that he had seen a "winds" execute 155-57; concedes differences between anticipated form of "winds" execute and the version he saw 182-83; established first U.S. naval radio intelligence system 134; likely prosecution witness in any Kimmel court martial 150; ordered to destroy notes concerning how Magic functioned prior to Pearl Harbor 141-42, 146, 148; post-attack war work 148-49; prepared statement on how 14-point final Japanese diplomatic note handled 140-41; testimony of 133-42, 145-85; varied military service background 133

Saipan 43

Samoa 237, 238, 388

San Diego (California) 75, 252, 352

San Francisco (California) 98, 114, 138, 280, 352, 372, 373, 374

San Pedro (California) 269, 352

Santa Cruz Islands 373

Saratoga, U.S.S. 76, 245, 252, 360

Scapa Flow 73

Schulz, Lester Robert xiv; testimony of 212-19

Schuirmann, R. E. 209, 210, 235-36

scrambler phone controversy 275-86

Seattle (Washington) 374

Seventh Fleet 269

Shanghai (China) 122, 272; New Japanese divisions passing through 9

Shimoneski (Japan) 47

shipping (western), southward division of 372-75

Short, Walter C. 65, 66, 67, 106, 234; accusations against xiv; asserted long-range reconnaissance not his concern 260-61; assumed Navy doing extensive reconnaissance flights around Hawaii 307; believed Navy expected war in Washington-Pearl Harbor communications more than Army 262; believed Navy not expecting an attack on Hawaii 257-58; civilian reaction as inhibiting higher alert status 314-15; convinced War Department knew attack coming at least four hours before assault 258; defense of xiv-xv; did not inform Navy of limited nature of Army's alert 297; discussion with Admiral Kimmel concerning replacing Marines with Army units at Wake and Midway 238-39; equipment shortages 289-90; exchange of information with Admiral Kimmel xv, 266-67, 288, 302-03; inadequacies in developing coordinated fighter interception system reported to him 79, 82; intelligence reports provided to 59; intervention to speed up acquisition of radar sites 90; meetings with Admiral Kimmel 263, 265, 323; not informed the Japanese had burned their codes 267; orders reduction in operating hours of radar to extend life of equipment 80; photo-reconnaissance ordered November 27, 1941 14, 15; recognized need for build-up in reconnaissance aircraft 256; refused to order ammunition issued to mobile anti-aircraft units 311-12, 314; sabotage danger the most highly ranked 317-20; staff officers 84; testimony of 255-67, 275-76, 287-93, 317-25

Siam 230

Siberia 40, 49, 282

Singapore 160, 240, 377; British naval units at 387; threatening Japanese moves 10, 18

Solomon Islands 373

Sonnett, John S. 155, 156, 205-06, 208

South America 52

Soviet Union *see* Russia

Spitfire (British fighter plane) 74

Stark, Harold R. 4, 7, 9, 10, 11, 12, 17, 141, 156, 165, 199, 252-53, 352, 368, 369, 379, 381, 384; attendance at National Theater, December 6, 1941 216; correspondence with Admiral Richardson on permanent stationing of Fleet at Pearl Harbor 353-58, 365-66; knew Pearl Harbor putting war training above war danger 232-33; meeting with Kramer before Congressional investigation 209-10; meeting with top Navy personnel on war danger (December 1, 1941) 271; nickname "Betty" 216, 218, 353; November 1941: war unlikely 236; October 1941: minimizes war danger 235–36; opposition to permanent Fleet basing in Hawaii 363; Admiral Richardson, meeting with (October 1940) 360; testimony of 339–47; on uncertainty of Japanese military strength 47; view of torpedo net need at Pearl Harbor 339–47; White House conference (November 25, 1941) 22–23, 236

Stimson, Henry L. 21; closes post–World War I "Black Chamber" 225; December 7, 1941 (10:30 A.M.) meeting with secretary of state 13–14, 18; high level meetings discussing foreign situation/war danger ix, 5, 7; meetings with president 5, 9, 10, 17, 18, 22–23; phone calls from 12; phone calls to 11; testimony of 3–19

Stone, E. E. 175

submarine sightings (December 7, 1941) 333–38

Supreme Court 144

Suva (Island) 373

T

Taikohu (Japan) 49

Taiwan, Japanese troop build-up in 49; see also Formosa

Taongi Atoll (Marshall Islands) 244, 245

Taranto, British torpedo attack at 341, 346

Taylor, William E. G. xii, 305; testimony of 71–83

Territorial Department of Forestry (Hawaii) 90

Thailand 58, 230, 240; possible Japanese invasion plans for 10, 17, 145, 236, 237, 238, 262, 300, 301

Thames (River) 74

Tokyo 40, 49, 51, 59, 127, 130, 131, 144, 153, 161, 176, 181, 204, 221, 223, 224, 268, 272, 281

torpedo nets controversy (Pearl Harbor) 339–47; American modification of British net designs 342; British attitude on need of nets 339, 340; British design of torpedo nets 342, 344; Kimmel's lack of ability to construct 346; low water depth as protection against torpedo assault 252, 359; revision of earlier attack feasibility estimates 340–41

Torres Straits 372, 373, 375

Townsville (Australia) 319

"traffic analysis" 240–41; key locations 272; limitations on effectiveness 270; see also Magic

Trincomalee 387

Tripartite Pact 26, 27, 131

Truk (Island) 43

Trussel, C. P. 187

Turner, Richmond Kelly xvi, 165, 271, 272; testimony of 372–75, 381–88

Tyler, Kermit xii, 104; conversation with as recalled at the radar reporting site spotting unidentified planes 97–98, 104; duties vaguely defined 115; lack of training at Aircraft Information Center 113, 114; testimony of 110–17

U

United Air Lines 72

United Press 189

United States: economic sanctions against Japan 27, 232; lack of armaments in pre-war period 6; lack of shipping in Japanese waters 40, 41; war production potential of 28; see also related topics such as Magic, negotiations

University of California (Berkeley) 126

V

"vacant sea" 41, 44, 374

Vladivostok (Russia) 372, 374

W

Wake (Island) 6, 234, 244, 245, 247, 248, 251, 252, 253, 319; almost certain to be lost 388; Marine planes provided to 246, 261; proposed sending of Army aircraft 237, 298; proposed substitution of Army for Marine forces 238–39; time of Japanese attack 377; use as "bait" to trap Japanese naval units proposed 294

Walnut (Coast Guard cutter) 377
"War Cabinet" 4–5, 17
"War College" 23
"War Council" 3, 4, 5, 23, 24, 39
"war warning" message of November 27, 1941 302–03; General Short's reaction 262, 264–65
Ward, U.S.S. xvi, 254, 333–38
Warm Springs (Georgia) 212
Washington (D.C.) 75, 121, 131, 153, 187, 212, 223, 240, 270, 281, 360, 364, 368, 369, 371, 382, 386; burning of codes by Japanese embassy 300
Washington Chess Divan 191, 192
Washington Post 188
Washington Times Herald 188
Wasp, U.S.S. 75
Webster, Noah 31
Welles, Sumner 7, 18, 362
West, Charles W. 35
West Indies 358
West Virginia, U.S.S. 268
Wheeler Field (Hawaii) 76, 77, 79, 117, 318
White House 212, 213, 357; wartime development of "situation room" 217
Wilkinson, Theodore S. xiv, 207, 270, 271, 272, 273; testimony of 220–26, 378–80
"winds" (war warning) message and intercept controversy xiii–xiv, 131, 145–85; Japanese denied sending execute 167–68; meaning of "war" 158–59, 163, 165–66; Navy anxious not to miss the execute 166–67, 178; winds execute concerning war with Britain intercepted 177
Winter Harbor (Maine) 137, 147
Woodrum, Donald, Jr. 62
WPL-43 386
WPL-46 242, 243–44, 245, 250, 262, 294, 381–88

Y

Yamamoto, Isoroku 51, 52
Yokohama (Japan) 40, 49; naval port at 40
Yorktown, U.S.S. 75, 76

www.ingramcontent.com/pod-product-compliance
Lightning Source LLC
Chambersburg PA
CBHW051203300426
44116CB00006B/423